Social Welfare
for a Global Era

To the memory of Kwong-leung Tang, valued student, colleague, and friend
1954–2014

Social Welfare for a Global Era

*International Perspectives
on Policy and Practice*

James Midgley

Los Angeles | London | New Delhi
Singapore | Washington DC | Melbourne

FOR INFORMATION

SAGE Publications, Inc.
2455 Teller Road
Thousand Oaks, California 91320
E-mail: order@sagepub.com

SAGE Publications Ltd.
1 Oliver's Yard
55 City Road
London, EC1Y 1SP
United Kingdom

SAGE Publications India Pvt. Ltd.
B 1/I 1 Mohan Cooperative Industrial Area
Mathura Road, New Delhi 110 044
India

SAGE Publications Asia-Pacific Pte. Ltd.
3 Church Street
#10-04 Samsung Hub
Singapore 049483

Printed in the United States of America.

ISBN 978-1-4129-1802-2

This book is printed on acid-free paper.

Acquisitions Editor: Kassie Graves
Editorial Assistant: Carrie Montoya
Production Editor: Olivia Weber-Stenis
Copy Editor: Janet Ford
Typesetter: Hurix Systems Pvt. Ltd
Proofreader: Susan Schon
Indexer: Scott Smiley
Cover Designer: Anupama Krishnan
Marketing Manager: Shari Countryman

SFI Certified Sourcing
www.sfiprogram.org
SFI-00453

16 17 18 19 20 10 9 8 7 6 5 4 3 2 1

Contents

Acknowledgments   viii

Introduction—Welfare and the Global Era   x

    Key Concepts and Definitions   xi
    The Scope of This Book   xvi

PART I: The Global Context

Chapter 1: The Field of International Social Welfare   3

    Practical Aspects of International Social Welfare   4
    Academic Aspects of International Social Welfare   8
    International Social Welfare: Benefits and Challenges   13

Chapter 2: Understanding the Modern World: From Nation State to Global Era   19

    Nation States and the Emergence of the Global Era   20
    Nation States and the Modern World   24
    Social Conditions in the Modern World   28

Chapter 3: Globalization and the Global Era   37

    Globalization: Historical and Academic Perspectives   38
    Unraveling Globalization: Definition and Dimensions   41
    The Impact of Globalization   46
    Responding to Globalization   49

PART II: Promoting Social Welfare in the Global Era

Chapter 4: Families, Communities, and Nonformal Welfare   57

    The Nature of Nonformal Welfare   58
    Challenges to Nonformal Welfare   63
    Formalization, Integration, and Opportunities   67

Chapter 5: Nonprofits and Faith-Based Services: International Dimensions   **73**

    Defining Nonprofits and Faith-Based Organizations   74
    Nonprofits and Faith-Based Organizations in an International Context   80
    The Role of the Voluntary Sector   85

Chapter 6: Professional Social Work in the International Context   **91**

    The Nature of Social Work   92
    Social Work Around the World   98
    International Social Work: Challenges and Issues   102

Chapter 7: Welfare, Markets, and Commercial Provision   **109**

    Understanding Markets and Commercial Providers   110
    Varieties of Market-Based Welfare   114
    The Limitations of Markets and Commercial Provision   120

Chapter 8: Government Welfare in the Modern World   **127**

    Defining the State and State Welfare   128
    The Historical Evolution of State Welfare   132
    State Welfare Around the World   135

Chapter 9: Governments, Welfare, and Social Change   **145**

    Analyzing Social Change   146
    Changing State Welfare: From Golden Age to Crisis and Beyond   148
    The Future of State Welfare: Shaping the New Pluralism   156

Chapter 10: Social Welfare and International Social Development   **161**

    Features of Social Development   162
    Social Development: Theory and Practice   167
    Social Development: Limitations and Prospects   172

PART III: Social Welfare for a Global Era

Chapter 11: International Collaboration in Social Welfare   **179**

    History of International Social Welfare Collaboration   180
    Promoting International Social Welfare Cooperation   184
    Issues and Challenges of International Social Welfare Cooperation   190

Chapter 12: Epilogue: Toward a One World Perspective in Social Welfare   **197**

Roots of the One World Perspective   198
Elements of a One World Perspective   201
Challenges to a One World Perspective: Values and Power   204

References   **209**

Index   **229**

About the Author   **243**

Acknowledgments

I have been extraordinarily fortunate and privileged to have worked with many colleagues around the world who share my interest in international social development and social welfare. I have learned from their knowledge and experiences which have informed my own thinking in the field. Growing up in South Africa and my practice experience as a social worker in the informal settlements around Cape Town left an indelible legacy, and helped me to understand that there are no simple solutions to the problems of poverty and deprivation, inequality and oppression that continue to plague the world. My own teachers, including Richard Titmuss, Brian Abel-Smith, and Bob Pinker at the London School of Economics had a formative influence on my intellectual development, and I am fortunate to maintain close links with colleagues at the School, including David Piachaud and Tony Hall with whom I have collaborated on numerous occasions and to whom I owe a great debt.

I am grateful to many colleagues here in the United States who encouraged and supported my work. I profited greatly from the time I spent at Louisiana State University where friends, including Joachim Singleman and Michelle Livermore, helped me to understand that the social problems that characterize many developing countries are also to be found in the world's richest nations. I am deeply indebted to other colleagues in the United States, including Richard Estes, Fred Ahearn, Chuck Cowger, Michael and Margaret Sherraden, Howard Karger, Terry Hokenstad, Julian Chow, Doreen Elliot, and Nazneen Mayadas (who sadly passed away last year). They engaged me in many informative and pleasant discussions over the years. I also learned so much from the members of the International Consortium of Social Development (ICSD), and it has been a joy to collaborate with them.

I have also benefited from international collaborations with Leila Patel, Antoinette Lombard, and Eddie Kaseke in South Africa; Roddie Mupedsizwa in Botswana; Hye Kung Lee, Young Hwa Kim, Huk Ju Kwon, Joon Yong Jo, and other colleagues in Korea; Mitsuhiko Hosaka, Toshohiro Yogo, Takayoshi Amenomori, Shinichi Shigetomi, Miyuki Inaba, and others in Japan; Manohar Pawar, Richard Hugman, Mel Gray, and Paul Smyth in Australia; Adolfo Carzola and his colleagues in Spain; Lutz Leisering and his colleagues at Bielefeld; Ulrich Becker, Franz and Keebet von Benda-Beckmann, Bernd Schulte, Barbara Darimont, and others associated with the Max Planck Institute in Germany; Ngiam Tee Liang and Tan Ngoh Tiong in Singapore; Yapeng Zhu, Yuebin Xu, Xuilan Zhang, Fang Wei, Han Keging, and other colleagues in China; Espen Dahl and his colleagues in Norway; and James Lee, Raymond Ngan as well as Ceci Chan, Joe Leung, and Nelson Chow in Hong Kong. I am also grateful to other friends and colleagues who are too numerous to mention yet who influenced my ideas and writing in so many positive ways.

In particular, I want to pay tribute to the life and work of Kwong-leung Tang who was my student, colleague, and friend. He made an enormous contribution to international social welfare and will be sorely missed. Although I first met Tang and his wife Jackie when he was a student at the London School of Economics in the early 1980s, I benefited from his insights, wisdom, and critical perspective. My relationship with Tang (as well as other former students from Hong Kong, such as James and Angela Lee and Raymond Ngan) confirms yet again how much we academics learn from our students. In this regard I would like to thank the many student colleagues I have been privileged to work with over the years. They played an important role in shaping my ideas. It was a group of former students at LSU in the 1990s, including Michelle Livermore, Lolita Perkins, and Allison Nuestrom (who sadly passed away in 2015) who first encouraged me to write *Social Welfare in Global Context* published by Sage in 1997. Although this book is not a revised edition of the original publication, it draws on many of the ideas first articulated there. I am indebted to former Berkeley doctoral students, including Will Rainford, Amy Conley Wright, Dave Androff, Joon Yong Jo, Sirojudin, Sam Vo, and Mary Caplan who inspired me on many occasions.

I am also grateful to those who helped with the production of this book. It has been a pleasure to work with colleagues at Sage, and I am particularly grateful to Kassie Graves for commissioning this book and providing ongoing support. It has been a pleasure to work with her over the years. Thanks to Carrie Montoya for her assistance, Olivia Weber-Stenis for managing the book's production, Janet Ford for copyediting, Anupama Krishnan for designing a lovely cover, and Shari Countryman for marketing. No author could be more fortunate in working with such a dedicated and efficient team.

James Midgley
University of California, Berkeley

Introduction

Welfare and the Global Era

This book discusses the ways that families, communities, societies, and international organizations enhance social welfare (or wellbeing, as it is often called) in the evolving global era. It draws on a variety of theoretical perspectives that inform social welfare thinking and discusses the policies and practices that have evolved in different countries over the years to promote people's wellbeing. These practices, known as interventions in this book, are implemented by different agents and are shaped by culturally embedded institutions. Agents include administrators, social workers, and volunteers as well as organizations, such as nonprofits and government agencies. The major social welfare institutions include the family, community support networks, philanthropy, the market, and the state. The family and community networks are often referred to as nonformal institutions while philanthropy, the market, and the state are regarded as formal institutions. Together, agents, interventions, and institutions comprise a complex nexus of welfare provision that functions at the local, national, and international levels.

To analyze this complex system, the book focuses on the world's nation states, which are the building blocks of the modern world system. Today, nation states and their governments make a major contribution to social welfare, but as noted earlier they are not the only agents involved in this task: families, communities, nonprofit and faith-based organizations, and commercial firms also contribute. While social welfare agents and interventions operate at the local and national levels, international efforts to promote social wellbeing have expanded rapidly since the end of the Second World War, and today a variety of international organizations, nonprofits, foundations, and other donors also contribute. In addition, people's lives are increasingly shaped by international events and the process of globalization.

While this book focuses on the way that agents intentionally use interventions to enhance people's wellbeing, those activities that diminish social welfare should also be kept in mind. Unfortunately, what Titmuss (1974) called *social illfare* remains a depressing reality for hundreds of millions of people today, finding expression in widespread poverty, ill-health, hunger, and social deprivation. It is also the result of oppressive social structures, discrimination, and entrenched inequalities, and in the frequent conflicts that continue to plague many communities and societies. Ethnic, religious, and communal violence remains common and discrimination against women, migrants, minorities, and indigenous people is pervasive. Sadly, many governments also use violence to oppress their citizens and deny their civil and political rights.

Nevertheless, this book is cautiously optimistic arguing that it is possible through concerted effort to enhance the wellbeing of the world's peoples. However, this optimism should be qualified by a realistic understanding of the challenges ahead. Improvements in social welfare do not occur automatically, but involve a process of struggle that engages with the realities of politics and power. It also requires that the way power is exercised at the local, national, and global levels is understood. These issues are raised again in the final chapter of this book, but first some of the basic concepts and terms used in the field of international social welfare should be defined.

Key Concepts and Definitions

Many different terms have been used by scholars working in the fields of international social welfare. They include international (or comparative) social welfare, international (or comparative) social policy, cross-national welfare, cross-cultural welfare, and global social policy. While these terms allude to more or less the same thing, they have different connotations. The concept of international social welfare has the broadest meaning and encompasses nonformal welfare, the activities of faith-based and nonprofit organizations as well as the programs of governments and international agencies. International (or comparative) social policy (which is also sometimes known as comparative welfare state studies) is concerned with the policies and programs of different governments while global social policy focuses on the work of the international organizations. Cross-national is used in a narrower sense to refer to comparisons between a finite number of countries while cross-cultural connotes comparisons of culturally different societies. The term international social work refers to the professional activities undertaken by social workers in different parts of the world.

Although attempts have been made to standardize these terms, notably by Healy (1995), they are often used interchangeably. She helpfully suggests that the term international social welfare should be used as a broad umbrella concept to cover the many different policies and practices that enhance people's wellbeing around the world. She also suggests that the work of international organizations be included. This is a useful approach and accordingly, the term *international social welfare* is defined in this book as *policies and practices designed to promote social wellbeing in the international context.* However, it should be noted that the term is also used to refer to the academic study of these activities so that scholarly inquiry into social welfare in different countries is often referred to as international social welfare.

Three key ideas in this definition should be highlighted. First, attention is given to those practices known as interventions that are implemented by different agents in the context of established welfare institutions. Interventions include a large variety of policies, programs, services, and projects that are designed to improve social wellbeing. These interventions have the purposeful intention of enhancing social wellbeing, and are accepted in different societies as having this function. Although social wellbeing may result from unplanned and even haphazard activities, this book emphasizes those interventions that are intentionally used by welfare agents to promote social wellbeing. As mentioned earlier, interventions are shaped by institutions that are culturally accepted ways of doing things. The role of agents and institutions is discussed in more depth in the next chapter.

Second, the term social welfare is defined as a condition of wellbeing that exists when people's needs are met, problems are managed, and opportunities are maximized. As will be discussed again later in this chapter, most scholars define social welfare in unidimensional terms, for example stressing the way that social problems are solved or how people's needs are met. Some scholars are primarily concerned with human needs, contending that people's welfare is enhanced when policies and programs that meet needs are implemented. Others argue that wellbeing depends on people having opportunities to realize their potential. Recognizing the multidimensional nature of social welfare, this book amalgamates these three approaches and contends that meeting needs, managing problems, and realizing opportunities are equally relevant to understanding social wellbeing around the world.

Third, the notion of international is used in this book to refer to activities that cross national boundaries and operate at the international level. Mazower (2012) points out that the philosopher Immanuel Kant first used the term with reference to proposals to achieve peace between the European powers. However, the term was popularized in the early nineteenth century by the English utilitarian thinker Jeremy Bentham following the publication of his book dealing with international law. Adam Smith and David Ricardo's commentaries on international trade also fostered a greater awareness of commerce in other nations and later Marx and Engels augmented these developments by arguing that global prosperity could be achieved if the world's industrial workers unite against capitalist exploitation. Although the word international can be interpreted narrowly as *inter-nation state* in that it only involves interactions between people in different countries, activities that promote wellbeing also operate at the global level. As noted earlier, international organizations and nonprofits are actively involved in social welfare at the global level, and some scholars, such as Deacon (2007) and Yeates (2001, 2008) argue that more attention should be paid to their activities. Their argument is compatible with the way international social welfare is defined in this book.

The concepts global and globalization are widely used by scholars in the field of international social welfare. Today, the term global connotes a sense of universalism or holism that transcends the more specific meaning of the term international, which as noted earlier refers to interactions among a finite number of nation states. On the other hand, global connotes the totality of international exchanges, including those that transcend the activities of national governments. The term globalization refers to the process that fosters increased interactions and greater interdependence between nation states. As is shown later in this book, the concept of globalization is related to the idea of a world system (or world society and world culture) and has been employed by scholars, such as Wallerstein (1980) and Lechner and Boli (2005) who study the way current events are shaping the global era.

Social Welfare and Social Wellbeing

The concept of social welfare has been used for many centuries, but it is still poorly defined. It comes from the English word *farewell* which originally meant to go or travel well, but in its broadest sense, it now connotes a condition of *wellbeing*. This condition may characterize individuals when they have a sense of subjective contentment or it may characterize families that are close knit and caring. It also refers to communities and societies that are peaceful, cohesive, and enjoy high standards of living. These dimensions are reflected in the writings of social thinkers, religious teachers, and scholars who have debated the meaning of social welfare for centuries and have focused both on its subjective and objective aspects.

In many of the world's religions, the idea of wellbeing usually connotes a state of spiritual contentment achieved through worship and contemplation. Welfare has also been the focus of secular inquiry. For example, ancient Greek philosophers like Socrates and Aristotle believed that living a virtuous life is a primary requirement for individual wellbeing. Aristotle is credited with developing the concept of *eudaimonia*, which exemplifies virtuous conduct and the achievement of personal fulfillment. Similar ideas emerged in other cultures like China where Laozi emphasized the need for personal reflection and a willingness to be "at one" with the natural world and with changing events. Subsequently, many writers and social thinkers elaborated on this approach by stressing the importance of personal fulfillment and other subjective elements in order to achieve wellbeing. However, in the eighteenth century, the term acquired an economistic connotation referring to the satisfaction of material needs through the market. Bentham developed this idea to argue that wellbeing or "happiness" depends on the extent to which individuals are able to maximize their "utility." The notion of individual happiness has recently been resurrected by economists like Layard (2005) who used questionnaires and social surveys to measure people's subjective feelings of happiness.

Other thinkers are less concerned with subjective wellbeing than with the welfare of society as a whole. For example, in ancient China, Kung Fu Tzu (or Confucius as he is known in the West) argued that society's wellbeing depends on maintaining cherished traditions, respecting elders, and promoting social order that not only produces a harmonious society, but increases individual contentment. Many centuries later, following the English civil war, the concept of welfare was linked to the notion of the *Commonwealth*, which exemplifies the civic republican ideal of citizens working together through democratic institutions to promote their collective wellbeing. This idea was incorporated into the Preamble of the Constitution of the United States that charges the government with promoting the "general welfare" of the people. At about the same time, utopian writers in Europe argued that social wellbeing is best achieved if society is reorganized into cooperative communities. Democratic socialists developed this argument claiming that the state is a giant cooperative that promotes social wellbeing by regulating the market and providing extensive social welfare programs. It was largely through their efforts that many Western countries became known as "welfare states."

On the other hand, Marxists claim that social wellbeing can only be achieved when capitalism is overthrown and a worker's state is established. Market liberals also disagree with the democratic socialist view, and drawing on Bentham's argument, they believe that wellbeing is the result of individuals pursuing their own interests or "utility." In the 1980s, British Prime Minister Margaret Thatcher popularized this idea insisting that there is no such thing as society and that welfare depends on individual effort. Accordingly, she argued that governments should create an environment that maximizes individual utility and limits welfare programs to those who are unable to function independently. It is in this context that the term social welfare is often used to refer to social programs for poor people, and unfortunately it has lost its earlier, noble meaning. It has even become a term of abuse. For example, politicians on the political right in some countries frequently castigate the so-called "welfare state" and denounce welfare recipients for being work-shy and irresponsible.

These very different perspectives have all contributed to a rich body of academic literature on social welfare, however as noted earlier, the term is still poorly defined and different writers, including social policy scholars, social workers, psychologists, sociologists, and philosophers define social welfare in different ways. Bradshaw (1972) points out that social policy writers often link the concept of welfare to the satisfaction of *social needs*, but the idea of need is also used in other social sciences like psychology. In 1943, the psychologist Maslow constructed a hierarchy of human needs that included requirements for biological survival, such as nutrition, safe drinking water, shelter, and personal safety as well as psychological needs for affection, self-esteem, achievement, and creativity. His hierarchy of needs is still widely cited today. In an analysis of the way the concept is used in social policy, Dean (2010, 2015) confirms its historic link with the subject's social democratic values observing that the term social needs also refers to the notion of social rights, which implies that governments have an obligation to ensure that all citizens enjoy a socially acceptable standard of living. In the 1970s, this idea found expression in the Basic Needs approach adopted by the International Labour Organisation (ILO) and in the writings of development economists, such as Streeten and his colleagues (1981) who argued that meeting people's needs for nutrition, health, shelter, and education should be the main goal of development. It also finds expression in the programs of the United Nations, such as the Millennium Development Goals and the new Sustainable Development Goals, which both seek to reduce the incidence of poverty, improve nutrition and health, promote gender equality, and meet other targets.

Social workers take a different approach arguing that social welfare depends on solving *social problems*, such as poverty, crime, drug addiction, homelessness, mental illness, and divorce. When the profession emerged in the late nineteenth century, most social workers were concerned with helping families facing problems and although social work is also engaged in community work, policymaking, and advocacy, it is primarily a problem-solving profession. However, social work's definition of social problems has become much more flexible than its original approach that focused narrowly on "social pathologies," such as poverty, crime, and mental illness. Today, social workers recognize that violence, poverty, hunger, and discrimination are social problems that also need to be addressed. However, many social scientists believe that social problems are socially constructed and that social problems are defined differently in different societies. This difference is especially true when considering moral behavior. For example, divorce is viewed as a social problem in some societies while this is not the case in many others. Similarly, gay and lesbian relationships are not tolerated in some societies while in others, same-sex couples have the right to marry. Individuals, families, communities, and societies also differ in the extent to which they manage problems. For example, conflict is managed quite well by some families, but in others it damages relationships and may even result in the disintegration of the family. Crime is more effectively prevented and controlled in some communities than in others, and similarly, some societies have lower unemployment than others.

Another approach to defining social wellbeing focuses on *opportunities*. Although neglected in mainstream social policy, it is clear that achieving wellbeing is dependent on people's ability to realize their goals. This idea is not new, but it has recently been popularized by Sen's (1985, 1999) capabilities approach. It is also widely recognized that opportunities can be enhanced by education and most governments now invest extensively in schools, universities, and vocational training. However, there are many impediments to using opportunities effectively. In some societies, rigid social barriers, discrimination, and oppression prevent people from realizing their potential, and in other societies widespread violence is a major barrier to progress. Also, as mentioned earlier, some governments trample on human rights and deny their citizens the opportunity to enjoy a good standard of living. Since achieving opportunities is directly affected by wider social conditions, policies that enhance human rights, peace, and social justice should be adopted.

This book contends that these three dimensions—meeting needs, managing problems, and maximizing opportunities combine to comprise the basic requirement for attaining social wellbeing, and accordingly it defines social welfare as *a condition of social wellbeing which exists when social needs are met, social problems are managed, and social opportunities are maximized*. To achieve a condition of wellbeing, welfare agents purposefully implement interventions in the context of the major welfare institutions. The opposite of social welfare is *social illfare,* and similar to social wellbeing, social illfare may characterize individuals, families, communities, and societies. At the societal level, social illfare is manifested in deprivation and unmet needs, pervasive social problems, and a lack of opportunities for people to maximize their potential.

Using these three dimensions, social science research methods can be employed to assess the extent to which individuals, families, groups, organizations, communities, and even whole societies experience social wellbeing. Data collected routinely by government agencies or censuses are widely used to measure welfare conditions around the world, and often discrete statistical measures are combined to create composite or aggregate indicators that give an "indication" of social conditions in different countries. Examples are the Index of Social Progress or ISP (Estes, 1984), the Physical Quality of Life Index or PQLI (Morris, 1979), and the Human Development Index or HDI developed by the United Nations Development Programme (UNDP) (1990). This latter index has been augmented with measures that focus on gender and other aspects of social progress (UNDP, 2013). Other techniques for measuring social wellbeing include surveys, ethnographic studies, and documentary analyses. Using these techniques, social scientists have shown that there are significant differences in the degree of social wellbeing in different societies.

The Scope of This Book

This book is concerned with policies and practices implemented by agents within the context of cultural institutions at the international level. Although it has a decidedly practical focus, it draws on theoretical ideas that provide an intellectual basis for the field. Originally, research in international social welfare was largely descriptive, but a body of theoretical knowledge that uses the insights of different disciplines as well as interdisciplinary fields has evolved to provide useful interpretations of welfare institutions around the world. Although dominated by social policy scholars who are primarily concerned with the role of governments, the field has been augmented by many more studies of nonformal institutions, faith-based organizations, and the nonprofit sector, markets, and social development. Although a complex body of academic literature has emerged, it provides analyses that have direct relevance for practitioners and policymakers.

The book is divided into three parts. Part I provides a contextual background and framework for the rest of the book while Part II is concerned with the major agents, interventions, and welfare institutions mentioned earlier. Part III focuses on international collaboration in social welfare and speculates on whether a one world perspective that views social welfare holistically at the global level is likely to emerge. Advocating for this approach, it argues that the many policies and practices discussed in this book should be integrated at the international level to maximize the wellbeing of people, families, and communities everywhere.

In Part I, the first chapter defines the field of international social welfare by distinguishing between its practical and academic aspects. Its practical aspects are concerned with the agents, interventions, and institutions that promote social welfare while the field's academic aspects refer to the work of scholars in different disciplines, interdisciplinary subjects, and professions that have studied international social welfare. Chapter 2 examines the modern world and focuses on the way sovereign nation states emerged to comprise the building blocks of the global system. Although nation states are increasingly subject to global forces, they continue to frame people's experiences. The chapter reviews different classifications of the world's nation states and points out that they are not equal in terms of political and economic power. It concludes with a brief overview of current conditions in the modern world. Next, Chapter 3 discusses the concept of globalization and offers an overview of the history of globalization and the way it has been defined. The effects of globalization are then examined showing that while some scholars emphasize its positive impact, others stress its negative consequences. Other scholars take a more nuanced position contending that globalization has both a positive and negative impact on people's lives. Finally, proposals for addressing the negative impacts of globalization are reviewed.

Part II of the book has seven chapters that deal with the major welfare institutions and the way they function at the family, community, national, and international levels. It also discusses the involvement of multiple agents that implement a variety of interventions within the framework of these institutions. Chapter 4 discusses nonformal welfare institutions, such as the family and local community support networks. It draws on the limited literature on this subject, but shows that nonformal institutions play a critical role in meeting social needs around the world today. It notes that efforts to integrate the nonformal and formal sector through innovative social policymaking are having positive effects. Chapter 5 discusses the role of faith-based and nonprofit organizations in social welfare. Although the nonprofit sector has historically been viewed as separate from government welfare, the situation is changing as a result of government contracting for services, subsidies, and other innovations. Similarly, it shows that market-based activities are increasingly incorporated into the nonprofit sector. Chapter 6 illustrates the role of the professions in international social welfare by discussing the contribution of social work. It shows that social workers are employed by governments, nonprofits, and faith-based organizations in many countries where they deal primarily with social problems in fields of practice, such as child welfare, mental health, and medical social work. Chapter 7 examines the growing importance of the commercial social welfare sector. Until recently, welfare programs were believed to be the responsibility of governments and nonprofits, but today commercial firms are playing a more significant role in the field. The chapter discusses the way that privatization and outsourcing has fostered the involvement of commercial providers in social welfare, and reviews some of the criticisms of the market approach. Chapter 8 deals with government social welfare. It defines the public sector, traces the history of government involvement, and provides an overview of statutory provisions around the world. Drawing attention to the role of social services, subsidies, tax incentives, and statutory regulation, the chapter identifies the key features of state welfare in different groups of countries and regions. Chapter 9 continues the discussion on state welfare by considering the way government welfare provisions have changed since the end of the Second World War. It notes that many social policy scholars characterize recent events as a crisis that has undermined the welfare state. It discusses alternative explanations, paying particular attention to recent debates on social investment, which some scholars believe is positively shaping the pluralist welfare systems of many countries. Chapter 10 provides an account of the social development approach and the way that social development has been adopted by governments as well as faith-based and nonprofit organizations in the developing countries—and also to some extent in the Western countries. It reviews the practice strategies that are used to promote social development and shows how these emphasize the role of community-based social investments and participatory programs.

Part III of the book focuses on the way social welfare has become internationalized. Chapter 11 discusses international collaboration in social welfare by tracing the history of cooperation between governments and nonprofit agencies as well as the work of international organizations, such as the United Nations and the World Bank. The chapter also reviews some of the challenges and controversies attending international social welfare collaboration. Chapter 12, the book's Epilogue, concludes by arguing for a one world perspective that may provide a holistic framework for policy and practice as well as scholarly analysis in international social welfare. Drawing on cosmopolitan ideas based on social democratic thinking, it proposes steps that should be taken to end the fragmentation of the field. It articulates the values underpinning a one world perspective and notes that issues of power need to be addressed if the struggle to enhance social welfare for the world's people in the global era is to bring positive change.

Part I

The Global Context

The Field of International Social Welfare

This book defines *international social welfare* broadly to include a great variety of practical activities that promote social wellbeing around the world. The term is also used to refer to the academic study of these activities. As mentioned in the book's introduction, practical activities, which are known as interventions, include policies, programs, services, and projects. These interventions are implemented by different agents in the context of culturally embedded institutions. The field's second aspect, namely the academic study of international social welfare, is concerned with documenting, classifying, analyzing, and evaluating these activities. Scholars have also developed theories that explain how welfare institutions evolve and function in different societies, and in addition to studying welfare institutions, they have undertaken research into policies and programs that operate at the international level. Academic inquiry into international social welfare has expanded rapidly in recent years. Today, scholars in sociology, political science, and economics, and in interdisciplinary fields, such as social policy, development studies, and social work all contribute to understanding the complex ways that social welfare is promoted in the global era.

The chapter begins with an account of the practical aspects of international social welfare by describing the different types of interventions that are used to enhance social wellbeing. These include social policies, social plans, social services, programs, and projects. It then discusses the major welfare institutions that provide a cultural context for the implementation of interventions. These institutions also shape the way different agents implement interventions. Next, the academic study of international social welfare is examined by tracing the historical evolution of the field and discussing the multiple contributions of scholars working in different disciplines and interdisciplinary subjects over the years. Different academic approaches are reviewed and some of the methodological issues arising from international social welfare scholarship are discussed. Finally, the benefits as well as the challenges of engaging in international social welfare are considered, revealing that today there is a greater awareness of the challenges facing international social welfare practice and scholarship and that many of these challenges are being addressed. This augurs well for the future and suggests that the field is rich with opportunities to contribute to social wellbeing around the world.

Practical Aspects of International Social Welfare

The practical dimensions of international social welfare are concerned with interventions that are purposefully designed to promote people's wellbeing. Although some commonplace activities like showing kindness to others are not usually regarded as interventions, they contribute to social wellbeing and should be kept in mind, especially when considering the role of nonformal welfare institutions. Also, those activities that diminish social wellbeing by fostering illfare should also be kept in mind. Nevertheless, this book focuses on those interventions, including policies, plans, services, programs, and projects that are purposefully intended to enhance social wellbeing.

Policies are prescriptive statements that define goals and govern the implementation of services and programs. Policies are formulated by many different organizations, including nonprofits and commercial firms, but many social welfare scholars focus on the policies and programs of governments, which may be contrasted with other types of government policy, for example dealing with national defense, the environment, or international relations. Government social policies are based on legislation and implemented by public agencies responsible for the major social services. As discussed in Chapter 8, governments also use incentives, regulations, the tax system, and mandates to implement their policies. Although formulated primarily by politicians and their professional staff, interest groups, lobbyists, the media and public opinion can also affect the formulation of social policies. The implementation of government social policies is usually the responsibility of the civil service, which is also responsible for evaluating outcomes; however, it is now quite common to contract out or outsource services to nonprofits and commercial providers.

Plans direct and facilitate the implementation of policies by setting quantifiable goals that are implemented according to a predetermined time scale. Plans concerned with social policies are known as social plans and are focused on improving health, education, employment, standards of living, and enhancing social service coordination and delivery. In Western countries, social planning is usually undertaken through the regular budgetary process, whereas in many developing countries, separate governmental planning agencies are created at the national level to formulate long-term plans that define social and economic development goals. Planning is also undertaken, although on a lesser scale, by nonprofit and faith-based organizations and commercial firms.

Services are well-established provisions designed to benefit particular groups of people (known as clients or sometimes as consumers) on a regular basis, and are the primary means governments use to implement social policies. Generally, social policy writers focus on the "big five" social services that include social protection (including social insurance and social assistance), health and medical services, educational programs, housing, and the social work services. This latter group is also known as the personal social services, human services, or family welfare services. They include mental health, child welfare, and family services as well as services provided to elders and people with disabilities. Although some writers believe that transportation services, nutritional programs, and the correctional system should be regarded as social services, they are seldom included in the social policy literature. Although the social services have historically been administered by government agencies, it was mentioned earlier that they are often contracted out or outsourced to nonprofits and commercial providers.

Services are very similar to programs and the two terms are often used interchangeably, although programs are usually of shorter duration than services. Projects are small-scale and time-limited interventions usually implemented at the local level by nonprofit and community associations, but of course, government can also implement these types of projects. Projects are widely used in developing countries to serve low-income communities and they are often funded by international donors through aid programs. Generally, projects are concerned with achieving short-term goals, such as constructing maternal and child health clinics, or establishing youth centers or cooperatives. Unlike projects, programs may comprise a number of projects, but they are not usually located in particular communities. Like services, programs are often funded by governments, but contracted out to nonprofits and commercial providers.

People, groups, and organizations that implement interventions are known as agents. Welfare administrators, managers, policymakers, planners, and professionals, such as social workers, teachers, and nurses are readily identified as welfare agents, but the contribution of paraprofessionals and volunteers should also be recognized. Families, grassroots community associations, and clubs are also welfare agents as are formal organizations, such as nonprofit and faith-based organizations, commercial firms, and government agencies, including social service departments or ministries. Welfare agents also include foundations and international organizations, for example the United Nations, International Labour Organisation (ILO), and the World Bank. As will be apparent, many different individuals, groups, and organizations function as welfare agents to promote social welfare in the global era.

The Role of Welfare Institutions

Welfare agents do not operate in isolation, but channel their activities through culturally embedded institutions. These include nonformal institutions, such as the family and community as well as formal institutions, including philanthropy, the market, and state. These institutions have evolved over the centuries and shape the activities of agents who promote social wellbeing at the individual, family, community, and societal levels—as well as the international level. Although the major welfare institutions are briefly described in this chapter, they are examined in more detail in Part II of this book. The role of different agents operating within the context of these institutions is also considered.

Some welfare institutions are more prominent in some societies than others. Nonformal institutions are especially important in traditional communities in the Global South while statutory institutions play a more prominent role in the Western nations. Nevertheless, both formal and nonformal institutions operate throughout the world today. As in the Western countries, the governments of developing countries have assumed greater responsibility for social welfare, especially after the Millennium Development Goals were adopted in 2000 by the member states of the United Nations. Government involvement is set to continue with the recent adoption of the UN Sustainable Development Goals. Also, the number of nonprofit organizations has increased rapidly in the developing world where they previously played a minor role. Another development is the greater prominence given to the market in social welfare and the emergence of new institutional approaches like social development.

The oldest and most pervasive nonformal welfare institutions are composed of family and community welfare practices. The family is arguably the most important nonformal welfare institution since it is the locus of care, nurturing of children, and support of needy family members. Throughout history, women assumed primary responsibility for caring, but this situation is changing, particularly in Western countries, where men are much more involved than before. Traditionally, the family has also been the site of economic activities. For centuries, family members worked together in agriculture, herding, trade, and similar activities to meet their material needs. With industrialization and the expansion of wage employment, the family has been distanced from these livelihood activities, but even today family members share resources and many assist in running family businesses. Families also seek to solve social problems, often with the help of kin, friends, neighbors, and other community members.

Welfare practices also operate at the community level through social supports and reciprocal obligations. Throughout the world, many local people use community support networks and participate in projects that promote community wellbeing; many also belong to member-owned mutual aid associations and cooperatives. These activities are particularly strong in the Global South where village people collaborate to build wells, bridges, and roads, and where farmers help each other with planting and harvesting crops. However, similar cooperative activities are also found in Western rural communities. Community support networks also function in the cities of Western countries where neighbors often provide care for elders, small children, and needy families.

Nonformal welfare practices give expression to institutionalized cooperative values and expectations rooted in reciprocal exchanges. Cultural expectations of this kind are particularly strong in traditional communities in the Global South and among migrants in Western countries where familial, kin, and clan networks link people together. Unlike many Western countries where family obligations have been eroded by a decline in the extended family and by the rise of individualism, families in traditional communities are major providers of social welfare. Nonformal welfare is also enshrined in religious mandates to give alms, care for the needy, and support those who provide religious charity. These ideals continue to motivate many people who give generously to charities and support the work of faith-based organizations around the world.

Nonformal welfare practices may be contrasted with *formal social welfare institutions* that include faith-based and secular philanthropy, the state, the professions, the market, and new institutional practices like social development. They are known as formal institutions because they use organizations, policies and procedures, and often employ staff to achieve welfare goals. *Faith-based philanthropy* is arguably the oldest formal institution since hospitals, asylums, and orphanages under religious sponsorship catered to those in need for many centuries. However, many faith-based organizations no longer restrict their work to charitable activities, but provide educational and medical services and engage in social development projects. Many have also adopted managerial procedures to enhance their efficiency. In addition, their services are usually not limited to their own congregants, but cater to other groups as well.

Religious philanthropy is augmented by *secular philanthropy*, which grew rapidly in Western countries in the nineteenth century. Although many nonprofits were founded by pious social reformers, they were not linked to any particular denomination and instead based their activities on what was regarded as a scientific approach that would be efficient and effective. Since then, the *nonprofit, voluntary,* or *third sector* has grown exponentially and now functions as a distinctive welfare institution around the world. Although nonprofit organizations were previously not very prominent in the Global South, they are now extensively involved in social welfare, often with the assistance of international donors and foundations.

During this century, the government or *the state* assumed a major responsibility for social welfare. Although previously limited in scope, government welfare programs expanded rapidly in the years following the Second World War and now consume sizable revenues in the Western nations. They also grew rapidly in the Global South. Governments are the primary provider of education, health care, and social services today and they also address a range of social problems, including poverty, crime, homelessness, and ill-health. In addition to providing social services, governments promote welfare through mandates, regulations, subsidies, and incentives and often the tax system is used for this purpose. Through legislative and executive power, they have the authority and resources to promote social wellbeing on a major scale and it is for this reason that many welfare scholars focus on their activities.

The *professions* comprise another institutional approach to promoting social wellbeing. Professionals, such as social workers, nurses, teachers, lawyers, and physicians staff the social services both in the governmental and nonprofit sectors and many also work as independent providers. Although different professionals are involved, this book focuses on the role of *professional social work* to illustrate the way professions contribute to social welfare. Best known for their casework and counseling, social workers bring their skills, values, and knowledge to bear on welfare issues, and in addition they are involved in community organization, residential care, and social service administration. Social workers are also employed by government social service agencies and especially in fields such as child welfare, mental health, and family services; they also work in nonprofit organizations and some are finding employment with commercial providers.

Although the *market* is an economic institution, it also contributes to social welfare. To meet their needs, families have traded and purchased commodities on markets for centuries and used financial firms to obtain insurance and save for retirement. However, markets have not been as important as the family, philanthropy, or the state, and it is only recently that commercial enterprises have become extensively involved in social welfare, particularly in Western countries. Unlike voluntary organizations, commercial firms are motivated by profits rather than altruism and many have secured lucrative social service contracts from governments. Accordingly, their involvement is controversial. Although many believe that social welfare should not be driven by commercial considerations, others contend that efficiency is increased when competition and the profit motive governs welfare policies and practices.

Another institutionalized approach for promoting social wellbeing, particularly in the Global South is *social development*. Social development differs from other welfare institutions in that it links social programs directly with economic development. Social development advocates argue that social wellbeing can best be enhanced by harnessing economic growth to create employment, generate incomes, and raise standards of living. Social development projects and programs are implemented largely by grassroots community organizations and nonprofits with the support of governments and international organizations and they make extensive use of social investments to enhance the wellbeing of families, communities, and societies. Although social development emerged in the Global South, it is being adopted in Western countries, even though it has not attracted much attention from social welfare scholars in these countries.

Academic Aspects of International Social Welfare

In addition to comprising a practical field, the term international social welfare refers to academic inquiry into social welfare undertaken by scholars working in different disciplines and interdisciplinary fields, and also by practitioners who have documented welfare projects and programs in many countries. Political scientists and sociologists are arguably the most prominent disciplinary scholars in the field, but economists and anthropologists have also contributed. In addition, scholars in interdisciplinary fields, such as social policy and development studies have undertaken extensive research into international social welfare. Social policy scholars are primarily concerned with statutory programs and their work is often known as comparative welfare state studies. The international organizations also contribute by hosting conferences and producing reports, statistical compendia, and studies of international social welfare. Today, an extensive amount of information about international social welfare is available, providing a solid foundation for practitioners committed to improving social welfare around the world.

Although writers, such as Bentham and Kant laid the foundations for the study of international social welfare, its origins are usually traced to the reports and other documents produced by the leaders of nonprofit organizations and social reformers in the nineteenth century who also collaborated internationally to share information, document new approaches, and replicate innovations. This was the case in the United

States where several European innovations were adopted. For example, Hokenstad and Midgley (2004b) point out that the first settlement houses in the United States were established after American reformers visited Britain and learned about their activities. Similarly, Rodgers (1998) reveals that many American social reformers went on "sociological tours" to Europe in the early decades of the twentieth century to study welfare innovations in the region. These developments contributed to the first academic studies of international social welfare, for example the work of Armstrong (1932), a Berkeley law professor who was one of the first to document social insurance and related social protection programs in Europe and other Western countries. Her work is important because it was used to inform the American government's own social insurance retirement system, which was introduced in 1935. A very different example is a study of the social service programs established in the British colonies before the Second World War by Mair (1944), a British anthropologist who wrote one of the first academic accounts of social welfare in the Global South.

However, these are early and isolated examples of international social welfare research and it was only in the 1960s that comparative studies began to appear regularly. Scholars at the London School of Economics, under the leadership of Richard Titmuss, led the way by comparing developments in countries, such as France, Sweden, and the United States with Britain's social policies. In addition, Titmuss and his colleague Abel-Smith (1961) undertook advisory missions to developing countries like Mauritius and Tanzania to assist their governments to formulate social policies. Their work was accompanied by the work of Jenkins (1969) and Rodgers, Greve, and Morgan (1968), who documented and compared the statutory social welfare programs of several Western countries. Other scholars produced case studies of a single country, and particularly countries about which little was known. One example is Madison's (1968) pioneering account of social welfare in the Soviet Union, which exposed Western readers to a welfare system that had been ignored by Western scholars. Some writers like Friedlander (1955, 1975) documented the activities of international organizations, such as the Red Cross and the United Nations High Commission for Refugees (UNHCR), anticipating the subsequent emergence of the field of global social policy. In fact, Friedlander (1975) defined international social welfare as the study of these organizations and their services.

Some social welfare scholars were less interested in documenting social welfare interventions and sought to test theoretical propositions. For example, Rimlinger's (1971) pioneering analysis of the evolution of government welfare in Europe, America, and Russia built on Wilensky and Lebeaux's (1965) earlier research which claimed that statutory welfare programs invariably expand in societies that are undergoing industrialization. Numerous other studies designed to test their welfare industrialization hypothesis were also undertaken at this time. Subsequently, theoretical inquiry increased rapidly and involved scholars in a variety of social science disciplines. In addition, some scholars like Titmuss (1971) focused on normative questions. His study of blood donation in different countries provided support for his view that social welfare should be motivated by altruism rather than markets. Since then, different normative positions in social welfare have been identified and debated.

Historically, international social welfare scholarship focused on Europe and North America and it was only in the 1980s that academics began systematically to document social welfare in the Global South. Some early studies, such as Dixon's (1981) account of social welfare in China, and Onokerhoraye's (1984) survey of the Nigerian welfare system were descriptive country case studies, but a number of books that focused on policy and theoretical issues also emerged. One of the first was by MacPherson (1982) who drew on international structural or "dependency" theory to offer a critical interpretation of social policy in the Third World, as it was then known. Another example is Midgley's (1984) account of social security and inequality in the Global South. Subsequently, MacPherson and Midgley (1987) collaborated on a metatheoretical examination of various issues relating to the study of social policy in the developing world.

Academic inquiry into international social welfare has increased significantly since the 1980s. Although the field has historically been dominated by Western academics, scholars from all over the world now contribute. Universities outside Europe and North America have established courses in social policy and social work and engaged in international social welfare research. Some have formulated unique academic approaches. One example is the emergence of "welfare science" in Japan, which Furukawa (2008) reveals is based mostly on sociological research. Similar developments are taking place in China where social welfare is growing rapidly as an academic subject. However, despite many achievements, scholarly inquiry into international social welfare still faces a number of methodological and other challenges. Some of these challenges are discussed later in this chapter, but first reference should be made to the different approaches and methodologies used by international social welfare scholars. As mentioned in this book, Deacon (2007) and his colleagues associated with the journal *Global Social Policy* made a major contribution to the methodology of international social welfare. Focusing on the work of the international organizations, they promoted a more incisive understanding of the way social wellbeing is enhanced at the global level.

Approaches and Methodologies

Today, scholars from different disciplines and interdisciplinary and professional fields bring very different perspectives to the study of international social welfare. Using a macroperspective that focuses on the nation state, social policy scholars are primarily concerned with government programs, while anthropologists focus on families, local support networks, and traditional welfare practices. Political scientists and sociologists are primarily interested in theoretical questions relating to government provisions, while social workers are largely concerned with practical matters. However, because very different perspectives are used to study international social welfare, scholarship in the field remains fragmented and no coherent approach that integrates these diverse insights has emerged. Nevertheless, theoretical and practical knowledge about international social welfare has benefited from the different approaches of academics in these different fields.

The academic study of international social welfare has several distinctive features. First, it is *descriptive* because it seeks to document and compare social conditions and social welfare programs in different societies. Using the *case study* approach, this research focuses on statutory provisions in social security, health care, housing, education, and the social work or personal social services. A great deal of international research using the case study approach has now been published. This ranges from comparative studies of one social service like social security to the whole social service systems of different countries. Although single country case studies are not technically international in scope, they also contribute to international social welfare knowledge. Studies of the welfare systems of different countries have been accompanied by studies of social spending, which have been used by social policy scholars to determine what is known as the *welfare effort* of different countries. One early example is Aaron's (1967) analysis of the statistical correlates of government social spending in twenty-two Western countries. He found that a large number of economic and political factors contribute to government spending and that it is difficult to identify a single determinant of the expansion of statutory programs. On the other hand, Wilensky (1975, 2002) used extensive statistical data to confirm his earlier conclusion that welfare effort is primarily attributable to industrialization.

Although many international social welfare scholars favor the use of case studies, others use whatever comparative information they can find to either validate or refute generalizations. This approach is known as the method of *selective comparisons* and may be contrasted with the more rigorous *systematic comparisons* approach that is based on case studies. Although Titmuss (1971, 1974) persuasively used selective comparisons to support his views about the desirability of state welfare, his technique was heavily criticized for being biased and unscientific. Jones (1985) pointed out that moral crusading is not the same as a rigorous analysis based on a careful assessment of comparative data, and Pinker (1979) claimed that Titmuss unfairly presented his arguments in ways that favored his own normative preferences. Nevertheless, selective comparisons are frequently used in international social welfare research today, and despite criticism, they have permitted broad and interesting analyses of social welfare institutions in the global era.

Descriptive studies of social welfare interventions have been accompanied by studies of *social conditions* around the world. Because governments and international organizations routinely collect data on health, life expectancy, education, income, housing, and other social conditions, scholars have access to a vast store of statistical information. These data are produced by many international organizations as well as governments and nonprofits, and are also used to develop aggregate *indicators* that permit researchers to create profiles of social conditions in different countries. In addition, social surveys and other techniques are employed to study social conditions. Often, research into social conditions has facilitated the formulation of social policies that enhance social wellbeing.

The case study approach is augmented by *typologies* that seek to classify government welfare provisions around the world. They offer conceptual models and classifications of government welfare provisions. As we discuss again in Chapter 8, many typologies have been constructed and they are very popular. One of the first was Wilensky and Lebeaux's (1965) "institutional" versus "residual" typology, which was originally used to characterize different approaches to social welfare in the United States, but it was subsequently employed to classify the welfare systems of different countries. Using this approach, the European countries are said to be committed to an institutional model whereas the United States favors a residual approach. Titmuss (1974) augmented this typology by adding the "work performance model," which he believed characterizes some European and communist countries, and where he argued participation in the labor force is generally a prerequisite for receiving social welfare benefits. Subsequently, Esping-Andersen's (1990) typology of welfare regimes was widely adopted to classify Western countries, but his approach has also been used by Gough and his colleagues (2004) to create a typology of the welfare systems of developing countries.

Secondly, international social welfare scholarship seeks to *analyze* and *explain* the causal factors that shape welfare provision around the world. This research has focused on the factors that prompted the expansion of government welfare in the twentieth century. As noted earlier, Wilensky and Lebeaux (1965) argue that this came about because of industrialization and some studies have confirmed this finding. Since then, the role of interest groups and political parties in advocating for state welfare expansion in these countries has been examined and today numerous theoretical explanations of the determinants of government welfare have been formulated. In addition, theoretical work has drawn attention to the role of gender, racial and ethnic diversity, the environment, and globalization in social welfare. The insights of Marxism, corporatism, feminism, interest group theory, and other theoretical perspectives have also been used to analyze social welfare around the world.

Thirdly, international social welfare scholarship is concerned with *evaluating* the impact of welfare interventions. Evaluations are much more widely used today than in the past when social programs were funded without requiring assessments of their effectiveness. In addition, evaluation research was often poorly designed and badly implemented. Today, demonstration projects are widely used and many sponsors now require that outcome studies are undertaken as a condition for funding. This is particularly true of social development projects financed by international donors. Furthermore, evaluation studies are now more carefully designed and randomized trials are more frequently used. One example of this approach is Banerjee and Duflo's (2011) evaluations of poverty alleviation programs in developing countries. In addition, there is a far greater emphasis on evidence-based policymaking and program implementation. Nevertheless, greater effort is needed to ensure that welfare interventions do, in fact, achieve their goals.

Evaluating the effectiveness of welfare programs requires that the values and ideological beliefs that shape social welfare interventions are understood. For this reason, international social welfare scholarship is also *normative* in that it seeks to identify and assess the ideological preferences that motivate different social welfare policies and practices. As noted earlier, Titmuss pioneered normative analysis in social policy contending that social policy decisions are invariably political and reflect deeper social values. Since then, many other scholars have excavated the ideological basis of social welfare; George and Wilding's (1976, 1994) formative analysis has been particularly influential.

Finally, building on its normative commitments, international social welfare is an *applied* field because it is concerned with formulating social policies and implementing interventions that promote social wellbeing. Drawing on evaluative research as well as normative analyses, the writings of social welfare scholars have influenced policymakers and administrators in governments and nonprofit organizations as well as the international organizations. In addition, social science inquiry has been used to develop curricula to prepare practitioners in a variety of fields, but particularly in social work and social administration. Although practitioners do not always recognize the relevance of academic research, practice is shaped by the theoretical ideas and findings of international social welfare scholars.

International Social Welfare: Benefits and Challenges

Apart from being personally rewarding, engaging in international social welfare has many benefits. It facilitates the sharing of knowledge and experiences and promotes the acquisition of appropriate skills. Fortunately, information about social conditions around the world, the cultural diversity of the world's peoples, and the ways that welfare institutions function in different societies is now readily available. As shown earlier, international social welfare scholarship has generated a good deal of knowledge about welfare interventions and institutions in many different countries. In addition, practice innovations have been documented and many more evaluations of the outcomes of social programs have been undertaken. This has enhanced the effectiveness of international social welfare practice.

An important benefit of international social welfare research is that people's awareness of neglected or poorly understood social conditions is heightened, thus facilitating effective responses. For example, the World Health Organization's (WHO) role in increasing awareness of HIV/AIDS and dispelling popular myths about the pandemic was critically important in identifying its cause and developing an effective treatment. The organization also informed the work of activists who challenged popular prejudices and mobilized support for effectual remedies. Another example of how international social welfare draws attention to neglected problems comes from the field of family studies. The worldwide dissemination of research undertaken in the United States about family violence and the incidence of child abuse helped create awareness of these problems in societies where they would not have been openly discussed. More recently, as information about the genital mutilation of girls in some cultures has become available, efforts to eradicate this harmful practice have intensified.

Another benefit is that international social welfare promotes policy learning. There are many examples of how knowledge of social welfare programs and policies in some countries has fostered the introduction of similar programs elsewhere. It was noted earlier that Armstrong's (1932) comparative study of social insurance informed social security policy in the United States. However, as will be discussed later, it is important that policy learning does not result in the crass replication of programs, but that they are culturally appropriate and carefully adapted to fit local conditions. Although it was widely assumed in the years following the Second World War that the developing countries would benefit from copying the social welfare policies and programs of Western countries, the need for appropriate policy learning as well as reciprocal exchanges is now recognized. Indeed, some Western countries are emulating innovations from the Global South. A good example is the conditional cash transfer demonstration program established in New York in 2007 after the city's mayor Michael Bloomberg visited Mexico and learned about the country's *Oportunidades* program (now known as *Prospera*). Another example is the dissemination of information about the work of microenterprise programs in developing countries which has fostered the creation of small businesses among poor people in other parts of the world.

International information exchanges are also beneficial because they foster the evaluation of social programs. Projects and programs benefit from studies of their impact in other countries and provide useful information about which interventions are efficient and effective. Knowledge about the impact of social welfare in other countries is also relevant when persuading policymakers about the need for new programs. If programs have been demonstrated to be effective in other countries, politicians and civil servants may be more inclined to consider emulating them when seeking to address local problems. International comparisons may also have wider political implications. For example, American politicians on the political right often claim that the country's allegedly high social spending is having a negative impact on economic development. However, comparative analysis shows that social spending in the United States is not exceptionally high by international standards and that many Western countries with a solid record of economic growth spend considerable sums on social programs.

Engagement in international social welfare also promotes professional development. The expertise of practitioners increases by sharing information, attending international conferences, and undertaking study visits abroad. Although these exchanges are sometimes dismissed as amounting to little more than "welfare tourism," international contacts between government policymakers, administrators, social workers, and the staff of nonprofit organizations help improve welfare interventions. Professional associations also benefit by sharing knowledge with their counterparts in other countries, and today exchanges of this kind are commonplace. Many governments, international organizations, and foundations also use the professional expertise of these associations as well as the contribution of knowledgeable consultants to advise on policy, and increasingly, teams of international experts are assembled by international organizations and foundations for this purpose. Professional associations also advocate for the adoption of policies that enhance people's social wellbeing around the world.

Challenges to International Social Welfare

As in other fields, those who engage in international social welfare face challenges ranging from mundane practical difficulties, such as obtaining visas to work in other countries to more profound concerns, such as understanding cultural differences and forging collaborative relationships with colleagues abroad. The nuances of understanding other cultures and being culturally competent present a particular challenge. Visitors to other countries often do not realize that their words, behaviors, and even gestures can be misunderstood and may even be offensive. Fortunately, there is a greater awareness of these challenges today, and many sponsoring organizations offer orientation courses before sending their staff, interns, and volunteers abroad. In addition, many nonprofit organizations that facilitate international exchanges and volunteer opportunities have introduced language courses and usually provide information on the politics and cultures of different societies so that visitors have at least a basic preparation in cultural competence.

In addition to the difficulties facing those who work and travel abroad, issues that challenge the field as a whole should be appreciated. These involve understanding how innovations can be usefully transferred from one country to another and how colleagues in different societies can collaborate. While increased collaboration and policy learning brings positive benefits, it was noted earlier that this process has often been accompanied by unilateral transfers involving the uncritical replication of programs. As Midgley (2011a) argues, the tendency to emulate Western social policies is attributable to the legacy of European colonialism, but as MacPherson and Midgley (1987) summarized many years ago, this approach is wasteful and ineffective. Fortunately, there is a greater awareness today of the need for policies and programs that are appropriate to local economic, social, and cultural conditions. Nevertheless, influenced by political pressures and the allure of international aid, many governments continue to rely on Western expertise and inappropriate unilateral transfers still take place. On the other hand, it was noted earlier that some Western countries are now adopting innovations from the Global South. This augers well for promoting reciprocal and mutually beneficial exchanges.

Academic inquiry into international social welfare also faces challenges. The very different methodological approaches and disciplinary perspectives used in the field provide only partial glimpses into the complexities of international social welfare. For example, by focusing narrowly on the social policies and programs of governments, social policy scholars imply that welfare is the exclusive prerogative of the state and fail to recognize the contribution of families and communities or the role of faith-based and nonprofit organizations. To properly understand how welfare institutions operate, a broader approach is needed. Another problem is the tendency to ignore the work of scholars in other disciplinary fields. For example, few welfare scholars appreciate the significant contribution made by anthropologists who have undertaken extensive research into nonformal welfare institutions in the developing world. One attempt to address this problem is Furuto's (2013) collection of case studies of social welfare in East Asia countries, which draws on the insights of different disciplines and covers the contribution of multiple welfare institutions. More studies of this kind are needed as are attempts to formulate a conceptual approach that integrates the disparate perspectives of different social scientists studying international social welfare.

Ignorance of the contribution of colleagues in other fields results in duplication and inefficiency. One example is the growing interest in social investment among European social policy scholars (Hemerijck, 2013; Morel, Pallier, & Palme, 2012; van Kersbergen & Hemerijck, 2012) who appear to be unaware of the way the concept has evolved in development studies and social development. Their own scholarship could be enriched by understanding social development's contributions to the field. At the same time, scholars in development studies remain largely unaware of the work of Western social policy writers. The recent increase in research into cash transfers (known generically as "social protection" in development studies), is a welcome development, but as Midgley (2013a) observes it is unfortunate that those who write on the subject remain largely oblivious of the work undertaken in social security by Western scholars.

A related problem is that many social policy scholars are ignorant of the contribution of academics who pioneered the study of social welfare in the Global South and this has perpetuated the erroneous belief that the developing countries have limited and poorly developed welfare provisions. This attitude reflects wider prejudices about the developing countries that can be readily dispelled by perusing the literature. One example of the ignorance of prior work in the field is the claim by Haggard and Kaufman (2008, p. 1) that the study of social welfare in the Global South is of "recent vintage." As was shown earlier, academic inquiry in the field goes back many decades; indeed, Surender's (2013) comprehensive overview reveals that it has a long and rich history.

Another challenge is the lack of standardization of terminologies. Many concepts are poorly defined, fostering ambiguities and hampering effective policy formulation. One example concerns the use of the term "welfare state," which is widely used, but poorly defined. As Clark (2004a) points out, confusion about the meaning of the term has hindered rather than helped comparative research. Another example is the use of the terms "social security" and "social protection." In the United States, social security refers to the federal government's old age retirement, survivors', and disability social insurance program, while in Britain it includes social assistance, unemployment benefits, and other income maintenance programs. In Latin America, the term includes health care and other provisions. The recent popularization of the term "social protection" in development studies further confuses matters. Obviously, the lack of a standard definition presents a challenge to researchers who want to compare social security programs around the world. As Midgley (2013a) observes, it also presents a challenge to policymakers who need to use standardized terminologies when formulating policies and enacting legislation.

These challenges are compounded by concerns about the accuracy of statistical data about social conditions and social programs. Although data are widely used in international social welfare today, they are often unreliable. Statistics collected routinely by government agencies leave much to be desired, and in many cases, estimates and even guesstimates are used. However, their limitations are seldom mentioned. This problem is particularly pertinent to the statistics that measure progress in meeting the United Nation's Millennium Development Goals. Despite the confidence with which these data are cited, Pogge (2010) points out that accurate information about the living standards of small farmers, informal sector workers, and other low-income people is seldom available. Unless this problem is resolved, it is difficult to reach accurate conclusions about the effectiveness of poverty alleviation programs.

Another problem is that culturally specific perspectives are often used to study social welfare in other countries. Although Esping-Andersen's (1990) three world's typology was intended to classify government programs in Western countries, it has been used in other regions of the world, which artificially distorts reality and limits understanding of the way welfare institutions function in different societies. The widespread use of the term "welfare state" is another example of the imposition of inappropriate theoretical constructs on other cultures. It can foster a Eurocentric, and even as Walker and Wong (2013) suggest an ethnocentric analysis of international social welfare. Instead of imposing Western concepts and typologies *etically* to analyze welfare in other world regions, an *emic* analysis based on a culturally grounded, "bottom-up" perspective would yield more meaningful results.

Despite these challenges, much progress has been made. A good deal of information about social conditions and social programs around the world is now available. Research into the work of nonprofit and faith-based organizations has also expanded and much more is known about family and community support networks. Scholars like Furuto (2013) combine studies of these different welfare institutions to present a more comprehensive picture, and as Deacon and Stubbs (2013) observe, there is a greater awareness among Western social policy scholars of the need to integrate disparate methodological perspectives to formulate a unified conceptual approach that can grasp the complexities of international social welfare. Fortunately, practitioners and scholars are more mindful of the need for cultural appropriateness, and it is encouraging that mutually beneficial reciprocal exchanges are now taking place. There is also a greater awareness among academics of the need to learn from each other. These developments suggest that the challenge of formulating a one world perspective in international social welfare can be met.

❖

Suggested Additional Reading

Although more work needs to be done to define basic terminologies and provide a sound conceptual basis for the field of international social welfare, some of the issues arising from the study of social welfare around the world are addressed by the following authors. In order to provide a better understanding of the many complex factors that promote peoples' wellbeing around the world, they provide an overview of the field, discuss methodological problems, and contribute to the integration of different academic and theoretical approaches.

- Deacon, B., & Stubbs, P. (2013). Global social policy studies: Conceptual and analytical reflections. *Global Social Policy, 13*(1), 5–23. This article by two leading scholars of "global social policy" focuses on methodological issues with reference to different theoretical perspectives.
- Fitzpatrick, T., Kwong, H. J., Manning, N., Midgley, J., & Pascall, G. (Eds.). (2005). *International encyclopedia of social policy.* London & New York: Routledge.

Although primarily concerned with government social policy, this important reference source covers diverse aspects of social welfare around the world. It also addresses methodological and other issues related to the study of international social policy.

- Jones, C. (1985). *Patterns of social policy*. London, UK: Tavistock. Although this book was published many years ago, its extensive discussion of the methodology of international social welfare and the challenges facing the field is still relevant today.

- Kennett, P. (Ed.). (2013). *Handbook of comparative social policy* (2nd ed.). Northampton, MA: Edward Elgar. Originally published in 2004, this edited collection contains many useful contributions from leading scholars working in the field of international social welfare. It ranges over a number of important topics and covers events in many different countries.

- MacPherson, S., & Midgley, J. (1987). *Comparative social policy and the Third World*. Brighton, England: Wheatsheaf. This was the first book to examine the study of social policy in developing countries systematically with reference to practical as well as theoretical issues. The book makes a plea for the formulation of culturally rooted approaches that foster a better understanding of social welfare in the Global South.

2

Understanding the Modern World: From Nation State to Global Era

To understand the way welfare agents and institutions promote social wellbeing today, it is important to understand and appreciate the modern world, its architecture, and the way it evolved over the centuries. The modern world is the result of the profound social, demographic, economic, cultural, and political changes that have taken place over the last three centuries. Of these, political events have played a particularly important role in shaping its features. Political forces resulted in the emergence of nation states and in geopolitical arrangements that persist up to the present day. There are now approximately 190 sovereign member states of the United Nations as well as other political and juridical entities that exercise authority over their citizens. Despite the emergence of the global era and the importance of global forces, nation states still comprise the building blocks of the modern world.

Nation states are a recent invention emerging out of the religious wars that followed the Protestant Reformation in Europe in the sixteenth century when the principle of sovereignty over citizens within a demarcated territory was institutionalized. Although this principle originally required that national populations adopt the religion of their rulers, religious affiliation was in time replaced by a new allegiance to the nation state and a growing identity around nationality. Whereas people previously located their identity in the clan or village, or in their religion, language, and culture, most now identify with their country and many do so with great conviction. Indeed, nationalism is a powerful ideology that not only prompts pride, but a willingness to serve and even die for the nation.

However, interactions between national states and their people have increased rapidly in recent times leading to greater independence and even in a degree of economic, political, and social integration that few scholars would have anticipated. The process driving these events is known as *globalization*. The term has enjoyed considerable popularity in academic, political, media, and business circles since the 1980s when significant changes in geopolitical arrangements and in the world economy fostered a greater awareness of the role of global forces in international events. Because of globalization, some scholars believe nation states are in decline and some even argue that they are being replaced with a "borderless world." However, although significantly affected by globalization, the institutions that shape social welfare today operate primarily at the national level and it is premature to declare the end of the nation state. The agents and interventions that foster social wellbeing can also be understood in the context of the nation state.

This chapter discusses the role of nation states and the way they are being affected by the global era. It begins with a brief historical overview of the rise of nation states showing how social, political, and economic events, including imperialism, increased trade, and political domination formed the modern world. Although it is unlikely that this history can be reduced to a few pages of text, the chapter hopes to provide a brief overview that serves as a backdrop to the book. Next, the way nation states are classified is discussed, specifically how the member states of the United Nations have been grouped in many different ways that reflect historic, political, and cultural alliances. This is followed by an overview of current social conditions, which reveals that despite significant social progress, there are huge disparities in welfare among different nations. It is the goal of international social welfare to address these disparities and foster continued improvements in wellbeing for the world's people.

Nation States and the Emergence of the Global Era

For most of human history, people lived in small communities and pursued their livelihoods mostly as farmers, but also as herders, fishers, and hunter gatherers. Comprising interconnected families, these communities also framed life experiences and shaped identities. Cooperation was an essential means of survival at a time when life expectancy was low and poverty and deprivation were widespread. It was also through collective action that communities dealt with adversities, resisted invaders, and even mobilized for war. Although self-contained and bound by common linguistic, religious, and clan loyalties, most communities were absorbed, usually through military subjugation into empires that emerged thousands of years ago in Mesopotamia, Egypt, and China. However, this did not undermine the role of the community in shaping lives and identities. Generally, life was experienced within the local community, which also determined people's identities and their view of the world.

In addition to identifying with their community, most people were bound by a common language, religion, and culture. These affiliations were more important than the empires that governed them. Although ruled and taxed by the empires and conscripted into their armies, imperial power did not influence people's daily lives to a great extent and most people regarded the imperial authorities and their political centers as remote. Many of the ancient empires had people of very different cultures and although absolute loyalty to imperial rule was enforced, religious and linguistic diversity was often tolerated. It was in this context that the familial and community roots of identity were transcended by a wider cultural affiliation that the Greeks called *ethnos* and the Romans called *natio*. Both terms have survived up to the present day, but the latter *natio* or nationality has acquired a political connotation and now refers to membership of a nation state through citizenship. Today, nationality is defined by governments in legal terms and citizenship is acquired either through birth or naturalization. Although the idea of citizenship emerged in the ancient world, particularly among the Romans, it only applied to those who were born into the empire's ruling ethnic and political group. Nevertheless, members of subjugated groups were sometimes rewarded with citizenship status. Today, citizenship is a ubiquitous reality and being a citizen of a nation state often forms the basis for identity and loyalty. On the other hand, *ethnos* or ethnicity is a cultural concept and membership of an ethnic group is determined primarily by birth. Both ethnicity and nationality remain a powerful source of identity in the modern world.

Although people with the same language and religion shared a common identity, Gellner (1983) believed that few envisaged or even desired political autonomy within a distinctive geographic territory that they could call their own. This changed as a result of the religious wars that devastated vast areas of continental Europe in the wake of the Protestant Reformation. Wilson (2009) reveals in a graphic history of this period that the conflict was eventually resolved by the Treaty of Westphalia in 1648, which not only divided territories and populations on the basis of the religion of their rulers, but granted sovereignty to these rulers and legitimated their right to govern those who lived within their territories. This event undermined the authority of the Holy Roman Emperor and the Catholic Church and laid the foundations of modern nation states. It is the legitimation of sovereignty over territory and populations that characterize nation states today.

These developments were augmented by increasing trade, a growing and literate middle class, and urbanization and industrialization, which all contributed to the emergence of modern nation states. The appealing ideology of nationalism further reinforced these trends fostering new emotional ties among national populations. During the French revolution, the Jacobins successfully used the threat of foreign invasion to galvanize people around the idea of a common national identity and subsequently Napoleon exploited this idea to mobilize massive armies to pursue his continental ambitions. Nationalist writers, such as Herder, Mazzini, and Kossuth fueled nationalist sentiment, claiming that nationality was not merely a political idea, but an organic expression of belonging and identity. National solidarity based on territory, a common language, religion, and culture became a popular and emotionally powerful ideal.

Spencer and Wollman (2002) point out that many political elites actively encouraged nationalist sentiments among the population in order to exercise social and political control. Earlier notions of citizenship were redefined in nationalist terms to become a basis for electoral politics. As a result of these developments, many small previously independent states amalgamated, and in the nineteenth century, large new countries like Germany and Italy emerged. Although many were actually composed of people of different cultures and even languages and religions, identification with the nation state, its leaders and homeland became a preeminent value. In existing multicultural states, such as Britain, France, and the United States, nationhood was prioritized to assert the primacy of nation states rather than communities, ethnicity, or religion. However, loyalty to the nation state has not replaced ethnic or religious identity, and indeed both continue to be powerful forces today. Recently, with the rise of *jihadi* militancy, religious and national identity has been conflated, and for many the idea of the *caliphate* is appealing.

When nationalism was shaping the modern world, the seeds of internationalism were also being sown. Mazower (2012) believes that the precursor of today's international organizations was the Concert of Europe, which was formed by the "Great Powers" of Austria, Britain, Prussia, and Russia after the defeat of Napoleon's armies. Cosmopolitan ideals were also being disseminated at this time. In 1795, the great philosopher Immanuel Kant advocated the creation of a European government which could end conflict between the continent's nations, and in the mid-nineteenth century, Marx and Engels campaigned to promote solidarity among the world's industrial workers. At the same time, anarchists struggled to replace the governments of nation states with new forms of political and economic organization. Paradoxically, the rise of nationalism in Europe also contributed to internationalist ideas, particularly through the writings of Mazzini who believed that strong independent nations were best equipped to forge international agreements. Cosmopolitan ideals were also fostered by the nationalist uprisings of the 1840s that challenged the ubiquitous institution of monarchy and promoted liberal democratic and republican principles. These principles were compatible with Kant's belief that peace could best be achieved through international cooperation among republican governments.

Although the European nation state emerged out of the decline of the old imperial order, these same sovereign nation states now embarked on the largest imperial project in history. Originally motivated by the lure of foreign riches, Iberian and other European traders mounted expeditions around the world that resulted in violent conflicts with native people. As wealth was repatriated, European rulers supported these mercantile adventurers by providing military and administrative resources to subjugate and colonize native lands. The imperial project was augmented by missionaries who sought to Christianize and "civilize" supposedly primitive people, and by settlers who established plantations and businesses that often cruelly exploited local labor. By way of clarification, it should be pointed out that the settlement of colonists in territories occupied by indigenous people is known as *colonialism*, while the exercise of political power over other nationalities is known as *imperialism*. Both colonialism and imperialism continued right up to the late twentieth century.

The creation of nation states and the sweeping influence of nationalism also inspired some nationalists in the colonial territories to struggle for sovereignty. In the early decades of the nineteenth century, nationalist movements ended Spanish rule in Central and South America resulting in the creation of new, independent states. However, at the same time, Britain and France followed by Germany and Belgium scrambled to acquire control over new lands and peoples in Asia and Africa. Although local people resisted, they were brutally suppressed. Nevertheless, nationalist fervor was aroused laying the foundations for the freedom struggles that characterized the twentieth century. Already, in the late nineteenth century, Filipinos fought against American colonization, and in India the nationalist movement began to mobilize and garner support, particularly among the educated middle class. Both India and the Philippines became independent countries after the Second World War as did Indonesia, which had been under Dutch rule since the seventeenth century. In Africa, the independence struggle resulted in the emergence of new nation states in the latter half of the twentieth century; although some European powers, notably France, resisted decolonization with bloody consequences, the European imperial era was effectively over. Hong Kong's reversion to Chinese rule in 1997 symbolically marked the end of the European imperial epoch. These events were augmented by the collapse of the Soviet Union at the end of the 1980s, when many of Russia's old imperial territories secured sovereignty. Although some European nations still retain colonial possessions and superpower influences still impact international events, these developments fulfilled the ideals of nationalism and produced the current architecture of the modern world.

Today, the nation state is the world's primary geopolitical unit. National sovereignty is enshrined in international law, and imperial adventures like the invasion of Iraq by the government of the United States and its allies in 2003 are widely condemned. National governments, their policies, and laws impinge on many aspects of daily living and nationalism inspires many people who are emotionally attached to their country. In some parts of the world, it drives secessionist movements. Nationalism resulted in the breakup of Yugoslavia, and drives Palestinians and Tibetans who want independence. In Western countries, such as Canada, Spain, and the United Kingdom linguistic and ethnic minorities are also campaigning to secede. A special and unusual case is the Kurdish people who are citizens of several countries, but aspire to have their own nation state. These nationalist campaigns have not always succeeded, but continue to mobilize considerable political support.

Although the modern world consists of sovereign nation states, they do not have equal status or equal influence, and the reality of power in the world limits the extent to which they are able to determine their own affairs. As is discussed later, the modern world may be conceptualized as a structured pattern of power relationships organized around a number of political power centers. These relationships reflect the differential influence of some nation states over others, and the ability of the governments of some nation states to exercise diplomatic, military, and economic power to serve their own interests. In some cases, military power is employed, but a more subtle means of influence, known as soft power is also used. Although the imagery presented in this chapter may suggest that the modern world is comprised of equal sovereign nation states, massive global inequalities persist.

However, nation states are not isolated entities. They interact more frequently with each other and some are even seeking political and economic integration; many more nation states are entering into economic, political, and cultural agreements. Also, some scholars even believe that the nation state is in decline. Already in the early 1990s, Omhae (1991, 1996) declared the end of the nation state, and more recently Jessop (2013) repeated his earlier claim that nation states have become "hollowed out" by globalization. However, it has already been argued that it is premature to talk about globalization as a transcendent force that is obliterating the nation state. The continued power of nationalism to motivate secessionism clearly challenges this idea.

On the other hand, there is no doubt that globalization is shaping the modern world and that a new global era is emerging. Cooperation among nation states has increased in many fields of activity, including social welfare, and their growing interdependence is widely recognized. Efforts to promote economic and political interdependence and even integration continue. Today, international organizations engaged in global governance, such as the United Nations and its affiliate agencies, the World Bank, and the International Monetary Fund (IMF) play a major role in global affairs. While nation states remain the building blocks of the modern world, they and their people will be increasingly affected by global forces.

Nation States and the Modern World

The United Nations has approximately 190 member nation states that account for the vast majority of the world's population of about seven billion people. Only a small minority live in territories that are not members of the organization. Nations are distinctive political and juridical entities with governments that exercise sovereignty over a demarcated territory and its population. Although most people who live within nation states are citizens, they also contain immigrants and other residents who are subject to their sovereignty. Citizens have rights as well as duties and obligations, such as obeying laws, paying taxes, and serving in the military. Through legislative or executive action, the governments of nation states formulate and implement policies and their laws and regulations are binding on citizens and noncitizens alike. Governments also manage relationships with other nation states and have the right under international law to use military power to defend their territories. Nation states also have judicial authorities that interpret laws and uphold constitutional provisions; in addition, they have administrative bureaucracies that implement laws and policies.

Some territories do not belong to the United Nations even though they are in many respects similar to nation states. These include Hong Kong, a special administrative region of the Peoples' Republic of China, which has authority over its internal affairs. Several small territories remain under the jurisdiction of former imperial powers, such as the British Falkland (or Malvinas) Islands off the coast of Argentina, and the Caribbean territory of Martinique, which is an overseas department of France. Some territories are seeking independence, such as the Serbian Province of Kosovo and the Palestinian territories and may be admitted to the United Nations in the future. Taiwan (the Republic of China) is a special case, and although it is for all intents and purposes a sovereign nation state, its UN membership was terminated when the Peoples' Republic of China was admitted to the United Nations. The organization's newest member is the Republic of South Sudan, which seceded from the Republic of Sudan in 2011.

Nation states vary enormously in population size, geographic features, natural resources, and level of economic and social development. Some countries contain people of many different languages, religions, and cultures while others have homogenous populations. Generally, they are geographically and demographically small. Diversity is more common in large nation states, such as China, India, Indonesia, Nigeria, and Russia, but it is also found in very small countries like Singapore whose citizens have different religious and cultural affiliations. In many of these countries, political elites have sought to transcend ethnic and religious differences by promoting national loyalty. As noted earlier, the world's nation states also differ as to the extent that they can exercise diplomatic, political, and economic power to influence international affairs.

To better understand this modern world, and simplify what is a complex international system, it is helpful to understand how the world's nation states are classified. These classifications group countries into manageable categories that reflect differences as well as similarities based on geographic, cultural, economic, and political criteria. Although widely used, these classifications are artificial and subject to change. They often serve political or economic purposes, such as promoting regional cooperation and economic development; the way these classifications help promote international collaboration will be discussed later.

The most common basis for classifying the world's nation states is *geographic contiguousness*. Classifications of this kind follow natural geographic boundaries based on coastlines, mountain ranges, and other natural divisions. This criterion has been used since ancient times to categorize the world's nations, and clearly the continents of Africa, Asia, Europe, and the Americas reflect this type of classification. However, this approach has obvious limitations. Some regions like the Pacific islands do not fit the continental model, while some continents like Australia comprise just one country. In addition, some continents like the Americas consist of distinctive regions, such as the Caribbean and Central America that arguably merit separate classification. Another problem is that geographic regions often contain people of very different cultural affiliations so that classifying them on the basis of geographic location alone creates an artificial grouping that fails to capture cultural realities. One way of dealing with this issue is to create subcontinental or subregional groupings that recognize cultural, social, and economic characteristics.

Cultural features, such as linguistic and religious affiliation are also used to classify the world's nation states. For example, the countries of South America, which are largely Spanish speaking and mainly Catholic, are often grouped together. This is also the case with the states of the Middle East and North Africa, which are predominantly Muslim and Arab speaking. Cultural similarities are often linked to geographic regions. For example, the nations of Africa are often divided into the Arab-speaking states of the north and the sub-Saharan countries, which are believed to share many common features. However, classifying Africa's nation states in this way is dubious since both the north and sub-Saharan regions contain people of different languages, religions, and ethnicities. This is also true of the East Asian nations that are believed to share a common Confucian heritage, but in fact have very different cultural affiliations. Nevertheless, this approach has been widely used in the media, and it also has academic supporters like Huntington (1996) who believe that the world's nation states can be divided into separate "civilizational spheres" consisting of African, Islamic, Sinic, Hindu, and Western (or European) groupings. He also argued that nation states are becoming less important than cultural identity, and that cultural rather than national affiliation will be the basis for future conflict. Huntington bleakly concluded that the "clash of civilizations" will eventually dominate international relations.

The world's nation states are also classified in terms of *political* groupings or "power blocks" as they are sometimes called. Following the Napoleonic wars in the nineteenth century, European countries formed political alliances based on membership of the Concert of Europe, but in time, allegiances shifted and different blocks emerged. In the nineteenth century, the extension of Western imperial rule over most of the globe reflected the power of different metropolitan nations, especially Britain and France, but also Russia, Germany, and the United States. Established political groupings were significantly modified in the early twentieth century and alliances shifted again. During the First World War, Germany and Austria were aligned against Britain, France, Italy, and Russia, but during the Second World War, the Allied Nations fought against the Axis powers of Germany, Japan, and Italy. With the ascendancy of the Soviet Union and the United States after the War, older imperial groupings were replaced with new Cold War spheres of influence. These spheres were often referred to as East versus West: the United States and its allies formed the West and the Soviets and their allies comprised the East.

Many scholars working in the field of international relations analyze these power blocks in structural terms stressing the way they comprise relatively stable relationships between powerful nations and their allies, which create durable international structures. The centers of world power are often referred to as "poles" so that prior to the Second World War, the world was seen as a multipolar system with Britain, France, Germany, Japan, the Soviet Union, and the United States comprising major poles around which their allies and imperial possessions clustered. During the Cold War, the world was viewed as comprising two major poles, namely the Soviet Union and the United States. Following the collapse of the Soviet Union, the United States was regarded as the preeminent center of a unipolar world. With the rise of China and other developing countries, the growing influence of the European Union, the world is again viewed in multipolar terms.

The world's nation states are also classified in terms of their membership in *international political, military, and economic organizations*, which often reflect their membership in power blocs and political alliances. Some nation states are part of economic alliances, such as the Organisation for Economic Co-operation and Development (OECD) and the North American Free Trade Agreement (NAFTA). Other groupings like the North Atlantic Treaty Organization (NATO) are military alliances while others, such as the Commonwealth are based on historical linkages forged by the British imperial legacy. Some groupings that reflect cultural commonalities like the Arab League also promote economic and political cooperation. The European Union is arguably one of the largest and most significant alliances. Although it was originally composed of a small number of European countries that sought to promote trade and economic collaboration, it now includes 28 member states with a combined population of about 500 million people. In addition to its original economic mission, it also created a common currency, removed border controls between most of its member states, and fostered political, educational, and judicial cooperation.

Nation states are also grouped in terms of *economic and social development* criteria. The World Bank's annual *World Development Report* classifies countries on the basis of gross national product (GNP) as low-income economies, middle-income economies, upper-middle income economies, and high-income economies. High-income economies include the Western nations as well as oil rich countries, such as Kuwait and the United Arab Emirates, while low-income economies include predominantly agrarian nations, such as Malawi and Nepal. The United Nations Development Programme (UNDP) places less emphasis on GNP and instead uses the Human Development Index (or HDI) to classify countries in terms of their level of social development. The HDI is believed to be a more useful indicator of social conditions than GNP because it shows that some countries with high GNP levels lag behind on indicators of social wellbeing.

The classification of countries in terms of these economic and social development criteria reflects an earlier classification of the world's nations into the "developed" and the "underdeveloped" countries. The underdeveloped countries were located mostly in Africa, Asia, and Central and South America while the developed countries were mostly in Europe and North America. This approach was widely used by economists and aid officials in the years following the Second World War and also reflected earlier colonial linkages. However, economic development classifications overlap with political alignments. For example, the concept of the Third World (usually believed to comprise a development category) was originally a geopolitical concept associated with the Non-aligned Movement. The movement was established in Bandung, Indonesia, in 1955 when the governments of a number of developing countries created a political grouping that would be independent of superpower influence and serve as a 'third force' in global political affairs. This idea drew on the writings of Mao Zedong whose theory of the three worlds differentiated between a First World consisting of the Western capitalist countries, a Second World made up of the Soviet Union and its allies, and a Third World representing the previously colonized nations of Africa, Asia, and Central and South America. Although China was originally a part of the Soviet sphere of influence, its government increasingly resented Soviet control and decided to align with nations, such as India, Indonesia, Egypt, and Yugoslavia that were equally disenchanted with superpower dictates.

Nevertheless, the Third World was widely regarded as a development rather than political category and was extensively used as a synonym for the earlier term "underdeveloped" country. However, its use was increasingly criticized for implying that the people of Africa, Asia, and Central and South America were economically and socially backward, and therefore, "third rate." This concern was reflected in the decision of the Brandt Commission (Brandt, 1980) to divide the world's nations into the "North" and the "South." The industrial countries of both the capitalist and communist worlds were designated as the Global North while the Global South comprised the low-income developing countries, including communist countries, such as China, Vietnam, and North Korea. Although this classification is still widely used today, its validity has been questioned as the countries of the South have become increasingly differentiated in economic and social terms. For example, some previously low-income countries, such as Korea, Singapore, and Taiwan have recorded high rates of economic growth and major improvements in standards of living, and are no longer included in the South category. Although this calls into question the usefulness of dividing the world's nations in terms of development criteria, the term "developing countries" is still widely used. Newer terms that are also used for classification include "two-thirds world," "majority world," "emerging economies," and "newly industrializing countries."

Although it may be argued that attempts to classify the world's nation states are futile and that each country should be given equal prominence, these classifications have obvious value in reducing a complex global system to manageable categories that not only facilitate comprehension, but have policy relevance. Efforts to promote collaboration between governments can be fostered when nation states with similar interests and needs are grouped together. However, it is difficult to choose between these various categories, which in any case are subject to change. Although these different classifications continue to enjoy popularity, this book uses the well-established practice of dividing nations on a geographic and regional basis. Those regions mentioned most frequently are East Asia, Australasia (and the Pacific), South Asia, the Middle East and North Africa (MENA), sub-Saharan Africa, Europe (including Eastern Europe and Russia), North America and Central and South America (including the Caribbean).

Social Conditions in the Modern World

The term "social conditions" has been defined in different ways. As Hall and Midgley (2004) point out, some social scientists equate the concept with poverty while others broaden it to refer to standards of living or to nutrition, health, and educational status. In this book, the term is linked to the concept of social wellbeing discussed in the introduction: A condition of social wellbeing exists when people's needs are met, problems are managed, and opportunities are maximized. The term is applied at different levels ranging from the individual experience of wellbeing to the wellbeing of families, communities, and societies. However, social conditions not only reflect levels of social wellbeing, but also allude to conditions of *social illfare* as revealed in a high incidence of poverty and deprivation, pervasive violence, and limited opportunities. Although these two notions are expressions of the same phenomenon, both should be kept in mind when discussing social conditions around the world.

Generally, accounts of social conditions focus on social wellbeing at the societal level and usually statistical data collected by governments are used for this purpose. Today, a good deal of information relating to human needs, the management of problems, and opportunities is available. These data are employed by academics, international organizations, and governments. In addition to censuses and adminis- trative data routinely collected by government agencies, information is also collected through social surveys and other sources. Data are often aggregated to construct social indicators that allude to social conditions. Perhaps the most widely used indicator is the Human Development Index or HDI developed by the United Nations Develop- ment Programme (UNDP) in 1990. The HDI features prominently in the UNDP's annual *Human Development Report*. The World Bank's annual *World Development Report* also contains extensive statistical data relating to social conditions in different countries. Other detailed statistical reports are published by the United Nations, the OECD, and regional organizations. However the limitations of these data should be recognized since statistical information collected by governments is often unreliable and of dubious validity.

Although the data reveal a very complex pattern, it is possible to reach some general conclusions about social conditions today. First, people all over the world experience levels of wellbeing that are historically unprecedented. Never before in human history have standards of living, as reflected in income, health, and education been so high for so many. However, and this is a major caveat, there are huge disparities between world regions and between countries in these regions. Also, within different countries, some people enjoy very high standards of living, others have adequate incomes and reason- ably good standards of living while others live in poverty and deprivation. Generally, levels of wellbeing are higher in the countries of the Global North than the South. A second generalization is that social conditions in the modern world have improved steadily over the last century and that significant gains in life expectancy, health, edu- cation, income, and nutrition have been recorded. A third conclusion is that progress in this measure has been uneven; reports on the implementation of the Millennium Development Goals (United Nations, 2010) reveal that less progress has been made in some areas, such as housing, employment, and maternal and child health. There have also been some setbacks. In some countries, natural disasters, political upheaval, and violence have impeded and even reversed progress.

Current Social Conditions: An Overview

With regard to current social conditions in the modern world, the point has been made that levels of social wellbeing are highest in the Western countries while the lowest are found in the agrarian developing countries of the Global South. However, as suggested earlier, social conditions vary enormously between the Western and developing countries, and these two broad categories are increasingly viewed as being of limited value when classifying the world's nation states and analyzing their social conditions. Better insights can be gained into current social conditions by referencing the regional groupings referred to earlier in this chapter.

When reviewing the data on these regional groupings, the world regions with the highest levels of wellbeing are Europe, North America, and Australasia. Although there are significant variations between the nations of these regions, they have a very low incidence of absolute poverty coupled with high standards of health, nutrition, literacy, educational opportunity, and housing. On the other hand, they are not devoid of social problems. Although crime rates in Europe are low, immigration and a failure to accommodate religious and ethnic diversity has created tensions. Furthermore, secessionist movements are active. In addition, the recent global financial crisis resulted in high rates of unemployment in many European countries. Crime and gun violence in the United States is high and is regarded as a major problem; on the other hand, the country has coped better with ethnic diversity than most. Inequality is another problem. Although many Americans enjoy high standards of living, social conditions among many African-American and Latino communities are poor. There are disparities also in access to health care, education, and other social services among different ethnic groups, and generally income inequality is higher than in other Western nations, even though it is increasing in these other Western countries as well. The world regions with the lowest levels of social wellbeing are sub-Saharan Africa, South Asia, and Central America. These regions have sizable rural populations and many people are engaged in subsistence agriculture. Many countries have a high incidence of absolute poverty, low nutritional status, and poor health conditions that are often related to communicable diseases and malnutrition. These countries also have comparatively low levels of literacy and limited educational opportunities. Within sub-Saharan Africa, standards of living are highest in South Africa and its neighboring states, such as mineral rich Botswana and Namibia. However, South Africa has high rates of crime and unemployment and marked inequalities in income and wealth. Some countries in the region have experienced high levels of violence. Because of political, religious, and ethnic tensions, people in a number of African countries have suffered terribly because of conflict. This is also the case in some South Asian nations, particularly Afghanistan and Pakistan where the problem is exacerbated by foreign intervention and the increase in *jihadi* violence. Generally, Central American countries have higher standards of living, but poverty is widespread and inequality remains a major problem.

Other regions, such as South America, the Middle East and North Africa, and Central Asia fall between these two groups. Many of the countries in these regions are relatively urbanized, and as a result of economic growth have a sizable middle class that enjoys a comparatively good standard of living. However, unemployment among young people is high and is regarded as a serious problem, particularly in North African countries. On the other hand, the oil-rich Gulf States have a shortage of workers and rely on migrant labor from South Asia and elsewhere, which fosters ethnic tensions. The Gulf states also have high standards of living. Many countries in the Middle East, North Africa, and Central Asia have authoritarian governments, but have been challenged by secularist democratic movements as well as Islamic traditionalists. Gender inequality in these regions is among the highest in the world. Political conflict in parts of the Middle East and North African region has caused great suffering, particularly to women and children. However, many South American countries have democratized in recent years and some now have women heads of state. Although the nations in this region have achieved comparatively high levels of wellbeing, good health conditions, and educational opportunities, income inequality remains very high and shelter is a major problem as evidenced in sizable informal settlements. Although the region has a low incidence of absolute poverty, many rural families and those living in informal settlements struggle to make ends meet.

East and South East Asia comprise a world region with countries, such as Japan, Korea, and Singapore that have high standards of living, but the region also contains lower-income countries, such as the Philippines, Thailand, and Vietnam that are experiencing significant rates of economic growth and social improvements. The region has attracted attention because of the rapid economic growth in a number of countries in recent times, but many countries in this region still have sizable agrarian populations and rural-urban inequalities are marked. These are accompanied by income and wealth inequalities. Rates of crime and violence are not considered to be a major problem, but ethnic minorities complain of discrimination and limited opportunities. In some cases like China, violence occasionally erupts in regions populated predominantly by minority groups. These problems are augmented by censorship and human rights concerns in several of the region's countries. Environmental pollution resulting from rapid industrialization and urbanization is also a significant problem, especially in China. Gender equality has improved, but discrimination against women remains a problem.

Social Change and Progress

Another generalization about social conditions asserts that there has been unprecedented social progress in all the world regions since the end of the Second World War. With independence from European imperial rule, many nationalist governments adopted policies that they believed would generate mass employment and eliminate poverty. They also introduced modern health services, expanded educational opportunities, and embarked on community-based social development initiatives. In Europe, where many countries had been devastated by the War, reconstruction became a high priority. This was also the case in East Asia where reconstruction involved the adoption of export-led industrialization policies that generated wage employment and improved living standards. In Latin America, industrialization policies adopted before the War were maintained, contributing to further modernization and urbanization.

With the demise of imperialism, steady economic growth, and the emergence of a new educated middle class in the years following the Second World War, many people identified with socialist and populist movements that promised a better future. Social democratic ideas exerted considerable influence in many parts of the world and Marxist movements that deviated significantly from Soviet-style communism also proliferated. Communist governments assumed office in several Asian countries and in Africa. Elsewhere, developments in public health and modern medicine fostered rapid increases in life expectancy, and literacy rates rose as many more children enrolled in school. All over the world, state-sponsored social services expanded. With economic growth, many rural people moved to the cities in search of employment and higher incomes. High levels of employment were achieved in the Western countries and the participation of women in the labor force increased rapidly. New international organizations like the United Nations facilitated the adoption of international human and social rights treaties, which promoted social progress around the world.

However, social progress has been uneven, and there have even been reversals. The Cold War and regional conflict undermined the progressive momentum of the postwar era. As the Superpowers vied for control, wars and insurgencies broke out: first in Korea and Vietnam, but subsequently in Africa, Asia, and Latin America. In the 1960s and 1970s, global economic growth slowed, and as fewer employment opportunities became available, the informal economy accompanied by sprawling informal urban settlements proliferated throughout the Global South. Many developing countries also became seriously indebted due to imprudent lending, and because of the Oil Shocks of the 1970s their economies were affected, seriously impeding further social progress. The Western countries were also affected by escalating energy costs and inflation accompanied by high unemployment that resulted in stagnating incomes and retrenchments in the social services. Conversely, the export-led industrialization policies adopted in Japan, Korea, Taiwan, and China resulted in sustained growth, transforming traditional agrarian economies and raising standards of living. The creation of the European Common Market and subsequently the European Union mitigated most of the negative effects of economic stagnation, but even here, high unemployment retarded progress.

The popularization of market liberal ideas in the 1970s and 1980s undermined the welfare statism that propelled social service expansion. It also contributed to a reversal in social progress. The imposition of structural adjustment by international organizations, such as the IMF and World Bank exacerbated social problems in the Global South. With the collapse of the Soviet Union, it appeared that market liberalism had triumphed and renewed economic growth in the world economy in the 1990s appeared to confirm this conclusion. However, restructuring in the Soviet Union and Eastern Europe was accompanied by widespread social deprivation. In many developing countries, poverty rates increased following the imposition of structural adjustment, and life expectancy even declined. The HIV pandemic also contributed to the situation. In addition, major financial crises in Central and South America and East Asia had a negative impact on living standards. With the global financial crisis that began in the autumn of 2007 (which is also known as the Great Recession), the belief that prosperity is the inevitable result of free market capitalism was undermined.

Since the beginning of the twenty-first century, there have been significant setbacks in social progress, resulting primarily from civil conflict, foreign invasion, and terrorism, although it is fair to say that in some parts of the world natural disasters have also retarded progress. Terrorism has become a global phenomenon as *jihadis* have launched devastating attacks on civilian targets not only in the Western nations, but in Afghanistan, Iraq, and elsewhere. The invasion of two sovereign nation states, Afghanistan and Iraq by the United States and its allies caused massive suffering and economic destruction. The region has also been destabilized as religious conflict has escalated, particularly in Syria, but also in Pakistan and elsewhere. Although Pinker (2011) points out that military conflict in the world as a whole has declined, violence continues to devastate the lives of millions of people.

Nevertheless, despite setbacks the overall trend toward progress has been maintained. Since the 1990s, just two decades ago, social conditions have continued to improve in all world regions, although progress between the regions remains uneven. The World Summit on Social Development and the adoption of the Millennium Development Goals (United Nations, 1996, 2000) have contributed to improved social conditions as governments around the world as well as international donors have made a concerted effort to reduce poverty and address other forms of social deprivation. The adoption of the Sustainable Development Goals in 2015 will reinforce these efforts. The most significant improvements in social conditions have taken place in East Asia, and particularly in China where the dramatic decline in poverty accounts for the greater part of global poverty reductions. Indeed, the country has been transformed from a predominantly agrarian society with relatively low standards of living to a global power. Although Japan, Korea, and Taiwan had already achieved high levels of living by the 1990s, other countries in the region, such as Malaysia, Thailand, and Vietnam have also recorded major social improvements.

The poorest world regions, mainly sub-Saharan Africa and South Asia have also experienced steady social improvements. Standards of living have risen in India and Indonesia, two of the world's largest countries, as a result of economic growth and sound social development policies, despite having a high proportion of the world's poor. Conditions have also improved in the sub-Saharan African countries, such as Ghana, Kenya, and Namibia among others. Even some of the poorest countries in these regions, such as Bangladesh, Ethiopia, and Uganda have recorded social gains. Although social conditions in sub-Saharan Africa have been viewed negatively for many years, there is widespread consensus that the region is making social and economic progress. On the other hand, both regions have been marred by violence. The Rwandan genocide, a disastrous civil war in Sri Lanka, and ongoing violence in the Congo and other sub-Saharan African countries have seriously affected social wellbeing. The setback in South Sudan is particularly disappointing since the country's historic peace agreement and independence from Sudan has been shattered by ethnically based political struggles. The people of Afghanistan have suffered terribly as a result of the Soviet invasion, the brutal rule of the Taliban government, and the subsequent invasion of the country by the United States and its allies. Another major setback has occurred in Somalia where warring clans and Islamic militants have caused massive social disruption. Violence is also endemic in Libya and in parts of Nigeria where *Boko Haram* has wreaked havoc. These and other conflicts have produced a huge global refugee population which remains unresolved as millions of displaced people now struggle to survive in other countries. The collapse of the Soviet Union and communist rule in Eastern Europe and Central Asia caused widespread deprivation as unemployment soared because of economic restructuring. With serious cuts in social services, living standards among those who depended for their livelihoods on state-owned enterprises declined and pensioners were also seriously affected. However, with the accession of East European countries, such as Poland,

Hungary, and East Germany to the European Union, economic and social conditions have improved. Standards of living have also improved in Russia, the Ukraine, and other East European countries despite the negative impact of economic restructuring. On the other hand, the genocidal violence that accompanied the breakup of Yugoslavia was a major setback, which was exacerbated by the failure of Western countries to intervene promptly. The failure to mitigate linguistic conflict in Ukraine has also precipitated a tragic outbreak of violence which risks escalation because of superpower involvement.

Despite these problems, the gains recorded in Europe and North America in the immediate postwar decades have been consolidated, and people in both regions now enjoy high standards of living. However, the Great Recession generated high rates of unemployment in both regions, particularly in highly indebted Southern European countries where social conditions have stagnated. Youth unemployment is a serious problem in these countries and is exacerbated by the sizable numbers of refugees and migrants from Africa and the Middle East in search of work. This development has also intensified ethnic tensions resulting in occasional, but serious outbreaks of violence. Although unemployment soared in the United States, the adoption of stimulus policies mitigated its impact and steady growth has returned. Other Western countries, such as Australia, Canada, Japan, and New Zealand were also affected, but they have nevertheless been able to maintain high levels of social wellbeing.

Uneven progress also characterizes the Middle East and North Africa. Until recently, the region enjoyed steady yet unremarkable improvement as a result of economic and social development, but the invasion of Iraq by the United States and its allies, the devastating civil war in Syria, and violence in several other countries has marred progress. Struggles between secularists opposed to authoritarian governments and traditionalist Islamic factions have aggravated the problem as has the persecution of Shia, and other minorities in a number of countries. The bombing of Yemen by the Saudi government and its allies has exacerbated these tensions and because of the wider geopolitical conflict between Saudi Arabia and Iran, many have been killed and many families have suffered great hardship. A number of countries in the region have been completely destabilized, and in addition the Palestinian people continue to suffer under a brutal military occupation and colonial settlement. Obviously, these events have negatively affected social conditions and retarded social progress. On the other hand, the region also has several oil-rich countries where governments have used oil revenues to promote economic and social development.

In South America, the widespread violence that accompanied military dictatorships, civil wars, and insurgencies in the 1970s and 1980s has abated and with democratization a number of governments assumed office that are committed to interventionist economic and social policies. In countries like Brazil and Chile, economic development accompanied by sound social policies have contributed to significant social improvements, and the adoption of social protection and especially conditional transfers in Brazil, Mexico, and other countries is having a significant impact on poverty. Pension privatization that began in Chile and extended to other Latin American countries has been modified by progressive governments and some countries like Bolivia have introduced one of the few universal retirement pension programs in the world. Although the region still has high levels of income inequality, several governments have adopted policies designed to foster greater social inclusion.

Despite unevenness and setbacks, it is likely that the quest for continued progress will be sustained. However, this should not foster complacency. Indeed, there are many who will take a far more dismal view of the world social situation than the one adopted in this chapter. They will interpret the data differently and stress the negative rather than positive aspects of social change in recent decades. In addition, many will emphasize the continued threats that face humankind, such as violence, oppression, consumerism, and militarism. Because more countries today possess nuclear weapons, the threat of a worldwide conflagration is high, even though it is seldom given attention. Similarly, environmental degradation and climate change pose a serious threat to social wellbeing around the world. The consumerist obsession of the Western countries is pervading other societies, and although consumption is an important ingredient in economic development, its impact on the environment as well as people's attitudes needs to be addressed. Oppression remains a way of life in many societies where authoritarian governments deny human rights and participation in the political process. In addition, traditional cultures often sustain hierarchical social arrangements as well as gender inequalities. Debt bondage, human trafficking, and even slavery are still to be found in many parts of the world. The arms trade fuels militarism and corruption in many countries. Nevertheless, it is encouraging that these and other problems are being addressed not only by progressive governments, international organizations, and social movements, but by many individuals who are committed to change. Because of these efforts, it is possible to adopt an optimistic attitude and agree with Kenny's (2011) conclusion that things are indeed getting better. Academics and practitioners engaged in international social welfare can help to ensure that this trend continues.

Suggested Additional Reading

The following books and reports elaborate on the issues raised in this chapter and will be of interest to readers who wish to go beyond a narrow focus on social welfare policies and programs to examine the way the modern world evolved and is evolving. Useful information about the current world situation is provided in the reports produced by the international agencies listed below. Additional literature sources dealing with globalization are provided at the end of the next chapter.

- Ferguson, N. (2003). *Empire: The rise and demise of the British world order and the lessons for global power.* New York, NY: Basic Books. Although a large number of academic books on European imperialism have been published, the author's account attracted a large readership and resulted in a popular television program. The author argues that while European imperialism was brutal, it also had positive effects. Although many will disagree with his perspective, he offers a readable and comprehensive account of British imperialism and its role in creating the modern world.

- Midgley, J., & Piachaud, D. (Eds.). (2011). *Colonialism and welfare: Social policy and the British imperial legacy.* Cheltenham, UK: Edward Elgar. The role of colonialism in shaping the welfare systems of countries that were previously under European imperial rule has received relatively little attention in mainstream social policy circles. Focusing on the British experience, the book shows that a complex pattern of welfare provision emerged in different colonial territories and that these have since evolved in interesting ways.

- Spencer, P., & Wollman, H. (2002). *Nationalism: A critical introduction.* Thousand Oaks, CA: SAGE. Surveying scholarship into nationalism over many years, this book offers a helpful introduction to the field. It also traces the history of nationalist thought and examines current expressions of nationalism, including the effects of globalization on nationalism and the persistence of national sentiment among immigrant communities.

- United Nations Development Programme (annual), *Human Development Report.* New York, NY; World Bank (annual), *World Development Report.* Washington, DC; United Nations (intermittent), *Report on the World Social Situation.* New York, NY. These publications by the international agencies provide extensive information about the world social situation. Different issues focus on different topical themes. Although the UNDP and World Bank reports are published annually, the United Nations *Report on the World Social Situation* is released every few years or so. All are indispensable sources of information about the modern world today.

Globalization and the Global Era

The scale and intensity of international activities has increased exponentially in recent times, and today the world's nation states and their citizens are affected by global forces to a greater extent than ever before. Today, people easily use the Internet to communicate with friends, colleagues, and relatives abroad, travel to other countries, and are better informed about international events. Although people in the cities of Western countries experience these effects to a greater degree than those living in rural communities in the developing nations, globalization is affecting people's lives everywhere as they are exposed to the global media and subject to international economic trends. In addition, the world's nations are becoming more interdependent as financial transactions and trade accelerate. Governments also collaborate more extensively, particularly through international organizations that promote exchanges and cooperative ventures. Although nation states are still the building blocks of the global era, their actions are increasingly shaped by international forces.

These changes have come about as a result of a process that social scientists call *globalization*. The term is also used in media, political, and business circles and in everyday speech, but it means very different things to different people. It is usually defined narrowly in unidimensional economic terms to refer to increased international trade, the spread of global finance capitalism, the outsourcing of production, and similar economic activities. Generally, this approach elicits the criticism that globalization amounts to little more than international predatory capitalism. Conversely, many economists, politicians, and business people view economic globalization as a positive force that promotes international trade, generates employment, and raises standards of living.

Other social scientists define globalization as a multidimensional process composed of social, technological, demographic, and cultural aspects. They point out that the global forces affecting people all over the world today not only involve economic activities, but bring about improvements in communication technologies, greater cultural diffusion, and increased migration and population movements. Generally, those who define globalization as a multidimensional process take a positive view of its effects stressing its potential to transcend national loyalties and foster new cosmopolitan ideals. Some even contend that globalization will eventually have a positive psychological impact creating "global citizens" who embrace international values. On the other hand, many are appalled by the idea that loyalty to the nation state might be supplanted by a new global identity and an allegiance to a vaguely defined world government.

These different definitions of globalization have created a complex body of theory that will be clarified in this chapter. It begins by situating debates on globalization in an historic context and notes that while the term globalization has only recently been popularized, many examples can be given to show how trade, migration, and diplomacy extended over vast territories since ancient times. Nevertheless, many social scientists believe that recent events, including economic liberalization, rapid developments in communications, and increased migration and cultural diffusion have fostered the emergence of a new global era. Drawing on scholarly debates on these issues, the chapter defines globalization, examines its different dimensions, and then discusses its economic and social impact. It concludes by reviewing proposals for addressing globalization's negative effects.

Globalization: Historical and Academic Perspectives

It was mentioned in a previous chapter that for most of human history people lived and experienced their lives in small rural communities with little or no contact with the outside world. Nevertheless, they were affected by international events. Many communities were a part of larger empires and paid taxes to the imperial authorities. Local produce was sold or bartered in nearby market towns, which were integrated into trade networks that extended internationally. Some people went to study in distant centers of learning and some went abroad on pilgrimage. This exposure to international events sometimes had negative consequences. Epidemics originating in other parts of the world often devastated local people, and they were also subjected to appalling violence when foreign invaders rampaged through their communities looting and killing.

The historical record reveals that the process known today as globalization is hardly new. For example, the Phoenicians, Persians, and Greeks developed extensive commercial, military, and diplomatic linkages that extended over large territories. By 1,200 BCE, the Phoenicians had established a far-flung maritime trading network that reached across the Mediterranean; later, the Greek city states also traded and established colonies throughout the region. Alexander's military conquests extended Greek influence as far as India; and with the rise of the Roman Empire, trade and diplomacy expanded across the Mediterranean into Northern Europe and Asia. By the second century, the Silk Road stretched from Constantinople to China's ancient capital of Chang'an. Because the world's nations were extensively engaged in international trade and diplomatic exchanges at this time, the term *ancient globalization* is sometimes used to characterize this era.

Imperial power and religious conversion also fostered greater international linkages. In the first millennium of the Common Era, the Catholic and Orthodox faiths extended over most of Europe and the Middle East claiming adherents among people of different cultures. In the Far East, Chinese imperial rule encompassed a large territory with diverse nationalities; and with the expansion of Islam, a common religious-based identity as well as the Arabic language was widely adopted. However, none of these empires had a truly global reach, and over the centuries, international economic, social, political, and cultural exchanges waxed and waned. It was only with the advent of the European imperial epoch that international exchanges extended on a worldwide scale. As a result of European imperialism, the world became significantly globalized and by the beginning of the twentieth century, trade and related economic activities among the different empires and their possessions flourished. In addition, many local people adopted the languages, religious beliefs, and cultural attitudes of their rulers. International cooperation among social reformers, nonprofit organizations, and governments also accelerated. Because trade and other exchanges flourished at this time, the late nineteenth century is sometimes characterized as the *first globalization.*

With the collapse of European imperial rule after the Second World War, a new world order consisting of sovereign nation states emerged to create the architecture of the current global era. Motivated by nationalist fervor, political elites in the new nation states adopted an inward-looking attitude intended to promote the interests of their own countries; at the same time, many nation states sought to grow their domestic economies by adopting import substitution policies. For this reason, the period from the end of the War to the 1970s is believed to have reversed the first globalization and is sometimes referred to as the period of *endogenous development.* However, despite the triumph of nationalism, new international forces were already at work. Although the old European empires were swept away, Cold War rivalries between the superpowers established new imperial structures. The creation of international organizations, such as the United Nations and its affiliate agencies in 1945, and the IMF, and the World Bank (which were established at the mountain resort of Bretton Woods in New Hampshire in the United States in 1944) also contributed to the resurgence of global economic, political, and cultural relationships. With the collapse of the Soviet Union and the international adoption of market liberal economic policies in the 1980s and 1990s, globalization again became a major force in world affairs. The *second globalization,* as it is sometimes called, had arrived.

Academic Perspectives on Globalization

Although academic inquiry into globalization is often believed to have originated in the 1980s, social thinkers and historians have analyzed relationships among the world's nations since ancient times. In the fourth century BCE, the Greek historian Herodotus wrote about Persian society, and over the centuries, many other publications about diverse people and nations were published. Accounts of the travels of Marco Polo and other adventurers attracted great public interest in Europe, and although crude and incomplete, the first maps of the world were produced at this time fueling the imagination of thinkers who speculated about worlds beyond their own. With the expansion of European mercantilism, cartographers developed the first modern maps and globes that were not only used for navigation, but decorated the homes of aristocrats and wealthy merchants. Despite the efforts of religious traditionalists to maintain a Ptolemaic view of the planet, consciousness of the world as a whole increased. Commentaries on international economic affairs proliferated during the Enlightenment when Adam Smith and David Ricardo analyzed the role of international trade concluding that trade contributed hugely to national prosperity. In 1848, Marx and Engels's *Communist Manifesto* offered an astonishingly prescient analysis of global capitalism that could easily be mistaken for a commentary on today's world economy.

In addition, some scholars began to advocate for increased international cooperation. Kant's ideas about how peace could be forged between the European nations and Bentham's advocacy of international law were particularly influential. Inspired by their writings and a widely shared revulsion against the carnage of the Napoleonic wars, campaigners mobilized international support for peaceful cooperation, and following the first international peace conference in Brussels in 1848, academic interest in international cooperation increased. Marx's writings had a particularly powerful impact, influencing scholars, working class movements, and activists in many different countries. As a result of his writings and personal involvement, the International Workingmen's Association (the First International) was founded in 1864. As is discussed in more depth in Chapter 11, these activities sparked a great deal of interest in international affairs, and during the early decades of the twentieth century, many more publications on international cooperation emerged.

However, academic interest in the field declined after the Second World War when the social sciences became largely concerned with domestic affairs. Reflecting the growing preoccupation with domestic economic growth, economists in many countries focused on managing the national economy while many sociologists and political scientists based their work on endogenous models derived largely from an analysis of American society. The new interdisciplinary field of development studies also focused on the nation state and offered recommendations on how governments could promote economic growth. At the time, the field was informed by modernization theory, which stressed the need for national policies that would foster urbanization and industrialization (Hagen, 1962; Hozelitz, 1960; Lerner, 1958). Originating in the United States, this theory not too subtly proposed the cultural westernization of the Global South. In response, a group of social scientists, known as the dependency school, including Frank (1967, 1975), Rodney (1972) and Amin (1974), rejected modernization theory's endogenous emphasis and instead attributed economic conditions in the developing world to international forces, such as neo-colonialism, capitalism, and exploitation. Although many developing countries had secured independence from imperial rule, they claimed that international exploitative relationships that expropriated the wealth of these countries were being perpetuated. Their work attracted a good deal of academic attention and placed international exchanges at the center of development thinking.

Dependency theory's formative contribution paved the way for the more encompassing analysis of world systems theory. Its leading exponent, Wallerstein (1980), argued that the capitalist world economy should be conceptualized as a holistic system characterized by ever-changing volatile forces. Instead of viewing the international order as composed of autonomous nation states, he contended that the world system itself should be treated as the unit of analysis. His account had a profound effect altering prevailing social science perceptions of international affairs and contributing to the formulation of the concept of globalization. Another important theoretical development came from scholars associated with the world cultures, world society, and world polity approaches. As Lechner and Boli (2005) explain, they focused on the way institutions originating in some societies have been adopted and institutionalized at the global level. These institutions are not merely the sum of national experiences, but assume a truly global reality. A similar approach is found in the work of Lash and Urry (1987), and Offe and Keane (1985) who argued that the international economy is best understood at the global level where a new phenomenon they call "disorganized capitalism" had emerged to replace the relatively stable state-managed capitalism that characterized national economic activities after the Second World War.

Similar ideas were expressed by postmodern theorists who claimed that the era of modernity based on the nation state had come to an end. Lyotard (1984) argued that the "grand narratives" of Enlightenment thought had collapsed, resulting in widespread fragmentation, uncertainty, insecurity, and instability, all of which, he believed, now characterized international affairs. Mass consumerism is a feature of modern life and contributes to what Bauman (1992) contends is a condition of "world disorder." McLuhan (1962) and McLuhan and Powers (1989) drew attention to the role of the media in creating a "global village" in which information flows encompass people all over the world. These formative ideas were further developed by Castells's (1996) notion of the network society, and by Giddens (1999) who coined the phrase "time and space compression" to suggest that people's perceptions of the world had changed so that it was increasingly perceived as a "single place." The emerging imagery of globalization was aided by satellite photographs from space, which for the first time showed the earth as a radiant blue sphere marked by the contours of the continents and draped with swathes of white clouds. As these photographs were widely disseminated, people became conscious of the planet as a whole and also of the unity of the modern world.

Unraveling Globalization: Definition and Dimensions

The academic conceptualization of the global economy as a unitary system reflected the economic changes that profoundly affected the world's nation states in the 1970s and 1980s: These involve currency deregulation following President Nixon's 1971 decision to delink the dollar from the gold standard; increased international investment and financial speculation; the adoption of export-led industrialization policies, particularly by East Asian countries; and the outsourcing of production from the Western nations to countries with lower labor costs. Another factor was the oil shocks of the 1970s, which had a detrimental impact on domestic economies around the world. Of decisive importance was the advocacy of market liberalism (or "neoliberalism," as it is known) by the IMF, the World Bank, and the governments of Britain and the United States. Together with the popularization of market liberal ideas in academic and policy circles, market liberal ideas were diffused through international aid and especially structural adjustment programs. What Williamson (1990) famously called the Washington Consensus sought to replace the interventionist policies of the developing countries with liberalized markets, which involved greater international economic integration. The collapse of the Soviet Union accelerated these trends. As a result of these developments, it could justifiably be claimed that a global capitalist economy—the *third globalization*—had arrived.

Originally, the concept of globalization was defined narrowly in economic terms to connote the liberalization of economic markets. This definition of the term was adopted by many academics, politicians, and members of the business community and popularized by journalists, such as Thomas Friedman of the *New York Times* and George Monbiot and Larry Elliott of *The Guardian* newspaper in Britain. From this perspective, globalization is viewed as an economic affair in which investment, trade, and flexible production will eventually displace domestic economies by creating what Omhae (1991, 2005) describes as a borderless global market. Market liberal economists argue that this development is highly desirable since it is only through an open global economy that prosperity will be achieved.

Other social scientists have challenged the unidimensional economistic view as well as the assumption that capitalist globalization has positive effects. They view globalization as a multifaceted process comprising economic as well as cultural, political, demographic, and technological dimensions. The multidimensional approach has been promoted by Giddens (1999), Scholte (2000), Held (2000, 2005), and Held and McGrew (2002) among others who believe that globalization is not only concerned with economic exchanges, but reflects innovations in communications, greater exposure to the world's diverse cultures, enhanced political cooperation, increased migration, and a growing awareness of the world as a single place. However, most scholars recognize that economic factors are of critical importance in understanding globalization, and most take a benign view of globalization, stressing its positive effects and potential to promote cosmopolitan values.

In addition to the unidimensional economistic and multidimensional approaches to understanding globalization, some social scientists highlight only one noneconomic dimension. For example, Castells (1996, 2001, 2004) emphasizes the way communications networks have created a global "information society," and this theme has since been echoed by many writers—particularly with the rapid and exponential increase in Internet communications. On the other hand, Iriye (2002) stresses the role of international organizations and civil society institutions in promoting the emergence of what he calls a "global community." Iriye's perspective is echoed by Keane (2003) who believes that the era of "global civil society" has arrived. Social policy writers like Deacon (2007) focus on the role of international organizations and point out that international collaboration in social welfare has expanded with positive consequences for people's wellbeing around the world.

Other writers stress globalization's cultural aspects observing that enhanced inter-action between the world's people involves a greater appreciation of cultural diversity as well as the diffusion of cultural traits. As a result of globalization, many more people are exposed to the music, art, food, literature, and customs of other countries. These trends are augmented by international migration and population movements. Some scholars believe that cultural diffusion has profound implications for attitudes and perceptions about the world. World culture scholars, such as Lechner and Boli (2005) contend that institutionalized practices, such as the Olympic Games, research univer-sities, and air travel are no longer rooted in national experiences, but have assumed a truly global character.

Robertson (1992) develops this theme to stress globalization's psychological dimensions and the way that people, particularly younger people are adopting a new mindset that transcends the strictures of localism and nationalism. He believes that earlier experiential frames that linked personal identity to village life or the nation state are being transcended by the emergence of a global identity and a sense of global rather than national citizenship. However, because nationalism remains a powerful force in the modern world and ethnic and religious identity continues to influence people's lives, global citizenship is unlikely to be achieved in the foreseeable future. In addition, as was mentioned earlier, global forces affect people in different ways. While urban dwellers and citizens of high-income nations are exposed to these forces to a greater extent than ever before, they do not influence the lives of people in rural communities in the Global South to the same degree.

Toward a Definition

This book adopts the multidimensional definition of globalization. It recognizes the centrality of global capitalism in world affairs, but seeks to replace the narrow economistic preoccupation of many writers with a broader perspective that incor-porates the different dimensions mentioned earlier. It argues that globalization tran-scends exchanges between nation states by fostering a dynamic system of relationships at the global level. Also, the term has a broader connotation than "international," which, as was mentioned in the book's introduction, refers to interactions between discrete nation states. Drawing on Wallerstein's conceptualization of the world sys-tem, globalization is viewed as having an independent reality that is more than the sum of its constituent parts. Although nation states remain the building blocks of the global era, their actions are increasingly subsumed within a global system of exchanges and interdependence. This idea is expressed in terms such as "shrinking world," "global village," "borderless world," and the cosmopolitan one world idea. Nevertheless, it must be stressed that globalization is still largely dependent on the exchanges that take place between nation states.

These exchanges can be encapsulated in terms of the three "I's" of globalization—namely increased *interaction* between nation states and their people; second, greater *interdependence* between the nation states; third the ultimate *integration* of their economic, political, and social institutions. When defining globalization, a distinction should be made between the idea of globalization as an ongoing process and related terms like *global* or *globality*, which refer to a condition brought about by the process of globalization. It should also be recognized that the term *globalism* refers to the normative advocacy of globalization and in this sense shares many similarities with the concept of cosmopolitanism referred to earlier.

Regarding the first of the "I's," *interactions* between nation states, changes in the global economy since the 1970s have fostered many more economic exchanges among the world's nation states that have been accompanied by increased contacts between their citizens through e-mail and the Internet, international travel, and increased commodities trade, to give just a few examples. Increased interactions between nation states are also due to international organizations, such as the United Nations, the World Bank, and the International Labour Organisation (ILO) all of which have fostered more frequent exchanges among their member states. In addition, people from different countries now move readily across borders as tourists, workers, and students and many migrate permanently. Although it was shown previously that people living in nation states have always interacted with each other, the extent of these exchanges is historically unprecedented. This is especially true of migration. Although only a small proportion of the world's population consists of migrants, many millions of people now leave their countries to seek work abroad or to flee violence and oppression.

Increased interaction between nation states has promoted greater *interdependence*. Local economies now rely more than ever before on trade and many are dependent on consumers in other countries purchasing their products. Similarly, financial investments in other countries generate rates of return essential for the livelihood of many savers and pensioners. Interdependence is also revealed in the income from tourism that contributes to economic prosperity in many countries. Interdependence has also increased as a result of improvements in communication technologies affecting millions of people around the world. International collaboration in eradicating polio and other communicable diseases is also leading to greater interdependence as resources and expertise are more widely shared. Other forms of scientific, educational, and cultural exchanges have also enhanced interdependence among the world's people.

As a result of increased interactions and growing interdependence, the economies and other institutions of some nation states are gradually *integrating*. The best example is the European Union, which is arguably a paragon of economic, social, and political integration. Although its member states retain sovereignty, they benefit from economic integration, increased cooperation, and even a common currency. Anderson (2009) points out that these developments have not only fostered integration, but promoted the emergence of a common European identity. Nation states in other parts of the world are also cooperating far more extensively than before through regional and other organizations that may eventually foster greater integration. Although controversial, international trading treaties are also accelerating this process. However, it should be recognized that the quest for integration is not new. Although often overlooked, the colonies of North America, which had their own currencies and political institutions, united in the late eighteenth century. However, the pursuit of integration is controversial even in Europe where nationalist sentiments continue to simmer.

While many nationalists reject integration, it is the goal of cosmopolitans to achieve the fourth "I" in the globalization process, namely the complete *internationalization* of human affairs.

Many social scientists will contest this definition of globalization. Indeed, the very idea of globalization is controversial since some scholars claim that it is vague, contradictory, and even meaningless. Krugman (1996) was one of the first to argue that much of the literature on the subject amounts to "globaloney." He points out that the concept is used to attribute economic problems in different parts of the world to globalization when this is not the case. For example, he challenges the widely accepted belief that deindustrialization and job losses in the United States are due to unfavorable trade and the outsourcing of production; he contends that falling investment and productivity are to blame. Reich (1991) also questions the view that international exchanges invariably benefit Western countries by pointing out that multinational corporations based in the Global South play an important role in the global economy. They also sell their products and invest in the Western countries. Cohen (2006) argues the claim that globalization is impoverishing the developing nations is belied by rising living standards in East Asia and elsewhere where export-led industrial policies have been adopted. Careful historical research by Hirst and Thompson (1996) contests the view that globalization is a twentieth-century phenomenon by pointing out that the volume of world trade in the nineteenth century exceeded that of recent times. Similarly, Ghemawat (2011) challenges the claim that a borderless globalized world has emerged and argues that the current situation amounts to little more than "semi-globalization." A somewhat different criticism comes from Petras and Veltmeyer (2001) who dismiss much social science writing on globalization arguing that it reifies what amounts to little more than imperialism. The term globalization, they claim, masks the continued domination of the world by the United States and its allies and should be recognized for what it is. Another criticism is that the concept does not actually explain current international events since it is so infused with the preferences and attitudes of academics in the West that it has little explanatory meaning.

These criticisms reveal the extent to which the discourse on globalization simplifies what is an exceedingly complex phenomenon. It has been shown already that globalization cannot be defined as a unidimensional process rooted in capitalist economic relations, but that it encompasses many facets. The problem of definition is compounded by the tendency to reify globalization as if it were an objective "thing" with its own almost anthropomorphic volition rather than a social process subject to human forces. Another issue is that nation states continue to comprise the modern world system and that some, such as China, Brazil, and India now play an important role in international affairs. Their growing economic and political influence also questions the view that globalization is propelled by the economic power of the Western nations. Equally dubious is the view of some scholars that national identity is being replaced with a cosmopolitan commitment to create a truly global community. However desirable this ideal may be, it is far from being realized. But, these and other criticisms do not invalidate the concept of globalization, which despite its limitations, captures many aspects of the modern world and reveals the way international forces shape people's lives today.

The Impact of Globalization

Controversies about the definition of globalization pale in comparison to the strong views expressed about its impact. Many critics contend that globalization has a harmful effect on people's livelihoods while others argue that globalization has raised living standards, particularly in the developing countries. Yet others take a more cautious view, noting that globalization has had both positive and negative effects. However, these criticisms focus narrowly on the economic impact of globalization, and the situation becomes more complicated when its effects on culture, population movements, communications, and international cooperation are examined. To clarify what is a convoluted debate, it is useful to separate discussions about the impact of economic globalization from its other dimensions. It is also useful to contrast opposing points of view, including the conclusions of those who recognize that globalization has both positive and negative consequences. Accounts of the impact of globalization are certainly affected by the way globalization is defined. The economistic definition is based on a particular discourse that is ideologically shaped by the proponents and opponents of market liberalism. On the other hand, the multidimensional view is concerned with the effects of many processes that are not as dependent on ideological proclivities.

With regard to the impact of economic globalization, neoliberal economists, such as Bhagwati (2004), Lal (2000, 2006), Omhae (2005), and Wolf (2004) praise the internationalization of capitalism. They believe that globalization stimulates economic growth by fostering investment, creating employment, and raising standards of living. They insist that it is only by integrating domestic markets into the world economy that prosperity can be assured. The record, they claim is clear. Reviewing the statistical evidence, Lal (2006) argues that poverty has fallen significantly in countries that have liberalized markets and linked them to the global economy. Similarly, Bhagwati and Panagariya (2013) point out that standards of living have risen in those parts of India that have been integrated into global markets while poverty remains widespread elsewhere. Obviously, international trade is a vital factor, and as Bernstein (2008) notes, there is a good deal of historical evidence to show that it has promoted growth and prosperity. Many advocates of economic globalization point to the experience of East Asian countries that adopted export-led industrialization policies and created wage employment on a significant scale. They also claim that multinational corporations have played a major role in promoting trade and creating jobs. Omhae (2005) points out that they are adaptive and innovative, and Wolf (2004) agrees, contending that these corporations have contributed hugely to economic development around the world. By promoting trade, competition, efficiency, and market liberalization, neoliberal writers challenge what Lal (2000) calls the *dirigisme* dogma of state management, which many countries adopted after the Second World War. Economic globalization, they believe, is fostering the emergence of a dynamic and prosperous world. Globalization also has benefits that reach beyond economic activities. For example, Norberg (2003) contends that it has promoted peace and democracy.

Supporters of economic globalization also challenge the popular view that globalization has been especially harmful to people in the Western countries. They point out that many pensioners in these countries profit from mutual funds that invest their savings in global financial markets. The importation of competitively priced goods has also benefited many ordinary families in these countries who purchase inexpensive goods and now have higher disposable incomes. Although it is recognized that global competition and the outsourcing of jobs has created challenges, Bhagwati, Binder, and Friedman (2009) contend that these challenges can be managed by adopting policies that promote entrepreneurship and innovation. Also, by responding to international competition, new economic activities such as sophisticated high-tech innovations transcend the limitations of conventional industrial wage employment. Some globalization advocates invoke Schumpeter's (1939) argument that the process of creative destruction is an essential ingredient in economic growth. Despite its costs, globalization has many positive benefits.

Opponents of economic globalization reject these arguments, pointing out that far from producing prosperity, globalization has wreaked destruction. Echoing Lash and Urry's (1987) earlier analysis of the disorganized nature of contemporary capitalism, Bauman (1998) believes that globalization has disrupted traditional economic activities and caused havoc. Gray (1998) challenges claims about the benefits of globalization as being little more than "delusions." Hertz (2001) argues that globalization involves a "silent takeover" as international capitalism exploits workers, undermines democracy, and impoverishes many societies. Criticizing the role of large corporations, Korten (1995) argues that they engage in numerous harmful activities, and in fact now "rule the world." Although globalization has created employment in many poor countries, wages are low and working conditions are usually appalling. In addition, Calbezas, Reese, and Waller (2007) point out that many children and women working in factories are exploited and mistreated. In recent years, suicides among workers in the electronic industry in China and devastating fires resulting in the deaths of garment workers in Bangladesh caused an international outcry. The violation of working standards is exacerbated by environmental pollution as factories dump harmful waste into the environment. Speth (2009a, 2009b) contends that these negative environmental impacts invalidate claims about globalization's benefits.

These writers challenge neoliberals who believe that globalization has produced positive effects all over the world by arguing that workers in the Western countries have suffered greatly. Many are harmed by the outsourcing of jobs and the importation of cheap goods that have flooded domestic markets, undercut local producers and distributors, and caused layoffs and unemployment. Many communities in these countries have been devastated as traditional industries have closed, high-paying skilled jobs have disappeared, and many young people are compelled to accept low-wage jobs with few opportunities. Aronowitz (2005) argues that structural unemployment in Western countries is likely to remain high in the face of global competition, and Uchitelle (2006) even believes that American workers have become "disposable." Many other scholars, including Cowen (2011), Noah (2007), and Hytrek and Zentgraf (2007) believe that globalization is responsible for economic stagnation, low wages, and high inequality in the United States. Because of globalization, the unions have been enfeebled and progressive governments are unable to maintain their social services. Another negative impact of globalization concerns social welfare. Many writers claim that globalization undermines government welfare programs. Jessop (2013) argues that the state has been "hollowed out" and that welfare provisions have been retrenched. Mishra (1999) agrees, and in an extensive review of the evidence takes a pessimistic view of the ability of governments to address social problems and meet the needs of their citizens.

Critics also argue that the benefits of globalization have flowed to multinational corporations, businesses, and political elites rather than to hardworking people and their families. Despite the recent Great Recession that began in the autumn of 2007 and continued for several years, Western financial institutions continue to engage in high risk, but profitable investments. Several writers argue (Crouch, 2011; Grupp, 2008; Korten, 1995) that large multinational firms also derive huge benefits from taxation policies that protect their profits, and they increasingly use their economic and political power to control the global economy. Free trade, Chang (2008) contends, is a myth that Western governments and corporations manipulate to their own advantage. Woods (2006) shows how international organizations such as the IMF and the World Bank promote global capitalism by insisting on the adoption of neoliberal policies in countries that receive financial aid. The World Trade Organization (WTO) is equally committed to the spread of global capitalism. As Stiglitz (2002) points out in a widely cited critique, many Western governments condone these activities. Of course, these arguments are countered by the advocates of globalization.

Debates about the impact of globalization's other dimensions are less polarized, but disagreements have also been expressed about the negative effects of communication technologies, population movements, and the diffusion of cultures. In many cases, these aspects of globalization affect different groups of people in different ways. For example, tourists flying into London stimulate the local economy and create jobs, but aircraft noise and air pollution has a harmful effect on the wellbeing of hundreds of thousands of people living under the flight path to Heathrow Airport. By increasing communications between the world's people, the Internet has brought huge benefits, but it is also used by traffickers and sexual predators to exploit vulnerable women and children. In addition, Internet scams have trapped millions of unsuspecting people, particularly the elderly. Another contention is that government welfare services have been harmed by globalization. However, scholars like Swank (2002) have questioned this conclusion for exaggerating globalization's impact, and others like Kwon (2001) have argued that the Korean government actually expanded its welfare services when challenged by global economic forces. Paradoxical consequences also arise from population movements as different groups of migrants respond differently to the challenges of living in a new society. While some adapt easily, others struggle to find work and acceptance. These problems are exacerbated when host communities are hostile to newcomers.

The complex effects of globalization are perhaps most dramatically illustrated with reference to the issue of cultural diffusion where many competing claims about its benefits versus harmful effects have been made. Traditionalists believe that the diffusion of Western culture undermines cherished values, and as cultural identities are weakened, many people become insecure, frustrated, and angry. Ruthven (2004) believes that people often turn to religious fundamentalism in search of meaning and some even resort to violence and terrorism. Chua (2003) argues that increasing violence in the Philippines is the result of globalization where inequality has increased and where local customs and values have been undermined. On the other hand, some scholars welcome cultural diffusion claiming that it enhances the cultural awareness of people in the Western countries whose lives are enriched by travel, enhanced communications, and migration. Cultural diffusion has also fostered a greater acceptance of diversity and tolerance. Cowen (2002) predicts optimistically that cultural diffusion will eventually result in a new hybrid, syncretic world culture constructed from the most valued features of many different societies.

It should also be noted that some scholars adopt a nuanced view of globalization's impact recognizing that globalization is an extremely complex process, which has a different impact on different people and societies. Probing globalization's many dimensions, Rodrik (2011) argues that it is unhelpful to treat globalization as if it was a single phenomenon that can be evaluated in terms of simple criteria. To understand its complex effects, it is necessary to unravel the way the different dimensions of globalization affect people's lives around the world. Even forceful critics of economic globalization, such as Gray (1998) and Hertz (2001) have adopted a balanced view. In principle, they are not opposed to markets, but rather to the predatory way they operate. Although Chang (2008) criticizes free trade, he does not reject the importance of trade, and argues instead for trade regulations that protect newly industrializing countries and their workers. Summarizing the findings of a major study of the effects of globalization on poverty, Harrison (2007) reports that trade and export-led development have indeed reduced poverty in the developing world, but he finds that poor people have been seriously harmed by international financial speculation and other forms of economic exploitation. Although it is clear that there are winners and losers, many scholars believe that it is possible to minimize globalization's negative impact and harness its power for the good of all.

Responding to Globalization

Many scholars have offered proposals for responding to globalization's negative effects. Most focus on globalization's economic impact and some have made helpful suggestions for ameliorating its harmful consequences. These range from advocating for import and currency controls in order to protect the domestic economies of low-income countries to large-scale proposals for reforming the global economy and establishing new governance institutions that promote equitable growth, democracy, and global social justice. Some proposals are pragmatic and some have already been implemented while others are less practical and have gained little support in policy circles. However, this should not preclude a full discussion of the potential of these different recommendations to bring about significant change.

One approach, which was advocated by the dependency writers in the 1970s, proposes that the development countries be "delinked" from the global economy and that this can best be achieved by adopting trade barriers and other measures that protect the developing countries from global capitalism. Of course, protectionism has been practiced by many countries, including the Western nations for many years. Despite rhetorical claims about the benefits of "free trade," restrictions on trade and on the free flow of currencies remain widespread. Even countries that are champions of free trade like the United States continue to use tariffs as well as subsidies to protect domestic production, primarily agriculture. With the creation of the WTO in 1995, attempts to liberalize trade have increased, but as the current Doha Round of negotiations have stalled, further liberalization seems unlikely. In addition, political support for new trade compacts like the Transpacific Partnership agreement appears to be waning. Nevertheless, most economists believe that trade plays a major role in economic development, although some scholars like Chang (2008) recommend that newly industrializing economies judiciously adopt tariff and other measures to protect their nascent industries. Echoing these ideas, Saul (2005) argued for a new "positive nationalism" that strengthens the ability of the developing countries to participate in the global economy on equal terms with Western nations.

Another response to globalization recommends the localization of economic activities. Hines (2000) outlines a number of policy approaches that foster this goal both at the national and community levels. For example, he believes governments should protect domestic industries; communities should purchase domestically produced commodities; and consumers should shop locally. Imhoff (1996) observes that an increasingly appealing version of the localization strategy, particularly in the Western countries, is community-supported agriculture, which involves the creation of community or "farmers" markets where locally produced vegetables and fruits and other products are sold. In fact, farmers markets have spread rapidly in many Western countries in recent times. Local currencies designed to stimulate community-based consumption have also been introduced. Instead of using a country's national currency, Mecker-Lowry (1996) explains that people exchange time and other vouchers that are honored by local businesses.

Activism and protests against global capitalism and particularly international organizations, such as the IMF, WTO, and World Bank comprise another response to the challenges of globalization. Among the best publicized protests took place in Seattle in the United States in 1999 during an international meeting of the WTO that resulted in the cancellation of the opening ceremony. Although the meeting continued until its scheduled conclusion, many delegates from developing countries did not agree to the final protocol, which supported claims that the protests were successful; however, the protests were accompanied by widespread property damage, injuries, and arrests. The "battle in Seattle" as it is known has since been emulated in many other cities. Although it cannot be claimed that these protests have reformed the existing world order, public consciousness has been raised resulting in tangible action. Consciousness-raising has facilitated boycotts of corporations that exploit women and employ child labor, and firms that avoid paying taxes have also been targeted. In some cases, reform-minded shareholders have insisted that the firms in which they have a stake adopt humane employment policies and practice social responsibility. Pressure has also been brought to bear on large pension funds in both the public and private sectors to embrace socially responsible investments. As a result of these efforts, there is greater public support for initiatives that address globalization's negative effects.

In addition, activists have formed coalitions with more traditional nonprofits and human rights organizations to campaign for positive change. Prokosch and Raymond

(2002) observe that these organizations have linked with protesters from the Occupy, Environmental, and Women's movements as well as the members of the World Social Forum, which was created as an alternative to the World Economic Forum—the club of multinational executives and politicians that meets annually in the resort town of Davos in Switzerland. In a study of the role of nonprofits, Elliott, Kar, and Richardson (2004) found that hundreds of activist organizations are involved in antiglobalization activities. Similarly, Appleby (2005) reports that the number of Catholic and other faith-based nonprofits that participate in antiglobalization campaigns has increased in recent times. Many are also involved in international activism. Brecher, Costello, and Smith (2000) suggest that these developments are contributing to the emergence of an alternative "globalization from below" strategy.

Support for fair trade is another response to the challenges of economic globalization. Recognizing that small farmers growing commodities, such as coffee, tea, cotton, and fruits and vegetables as well as producers of handicrafts and textiles are severely disadvantaged in the international economy, nonprofit organizations have been created to market their goods in Western countries. Building on the pioneering efforts of some Western churches that first marketed imported commodities from developing countries among their own congregations in the 1950s, fair trade organizations now rely on supermarkets and retail chains to sell their products. They also publicize their activities seeking to attract more consumers, especially among sympathetic middle-class people in the Western countries. Their efforts have been quite successful and there is a growing demand for products labeled with a fair trade logo. Fair Trade shops selling crafts and textiles have also proliferated. Nicholls and Opal (2005) report that a number of fair trade licensing organizations that negotiate favorable terms for small producers with import distributors have been established, and they also certify the authenticity of fair trade products. In addition, fair trade organizations actively support farmers and cooperatives in the Global South by providing technical assistance, increasing access to credit, and fostering the diversification of their activities. Ransom (2001) points out that the goal of these activities is to bypass intermediaries who siphon off significant amounts in the supply chain and to avoid commodity exchange markets. In this way, producers receive higher incomes, which benefits their own families as well as the local community.

Another way of ameliorating globalization's negative impact is to advocate for increased international aid to developing countries. Both Soros (2002) and Stiglitz (2007) urge the IMF and the World Bank to increase the flow of financial aid to these countries without imposing strict conditionalities. An important commission appointed by the ILO (2004) to address the challenge of globalization made various recommendations to reform trade and the global financial system, and in this way promote a "fairer globalization." It also recommended that supranational organizations respond positively to the needs of people who are negatively affected by globalization. In addition, the imposition of a Tobin tax that would levy a charge on international financial exchanges and create a fund that can be used to promote development in the Global South is widely favored among activists and reformers. These and other reforms respond positively to the challenges of globalization and could significantly improve international efforts to address world poverty.

However, many remain skeptical about the possibility of reforming the global economy and argue instead for its complete transformation; they believe that new global governance institutions are badly needed. They contend an equitable global economy will not emerge by reforming the WTO or IMF, but by creating a completely new world order based on democratic and social justice principles. A large number of proposals for achieving this goal have been formulated. Monbiot (2003) urges the creation of a new World Fair Trade Organization that would direct trade for social purposes, and he also advocates the resurrection of Keynes's proposals for an international currency. Bello (2002) suggests establishing a new Economic Security Council that would direct the global economy. Held (2004) argues for a number of initiatives based on social democratic ideas that he believes could form the basis for a new "Global Covenant," and the Fabian Society (2005) in Britain has produced a set of similar proposals based on social democratic ideals. However, these ideas are not only dependent on greater cooperation among the world's nation states, faith-based, and nonprofit organizations, but on a commitment to cosmopolitan values. These ideas are discussed in more depth in the final chapter of this book.

---❖---

Suggested Additional Reading

The literature on globalization is now very extensive and the number of books, journal articles, and reports by international agencies on the subject has proliferated in recent years. As explained in the chapter, the issues are complex. Globalization has been defined in different ways by different writers and very different views on globalization's impact on peoples' wellbeing have been expressed. In addition there are very different proposals for addressing its negative impact. The following is only a sampling of some of the most important books on the subject.

- Bhagwati, J. N. (2004). *In defense of globalization.* New York, NY: Oxford University Press. Written by a leading market liberal scholar, this book vigorously supports the internationalization of economic activities and contends that increased trade, financial flows, outsourcing, investments, and the activities of multinational firms stimulates national economies, creates employment, and raises incomes. The author uses extensive data to support his case.
- Giddens, A. (1999). *Runaway world: How globalization is reshaping our lives.* London, UK: Profile Books. This brief and readable book adopts a multidimensional view of globalization stressing the way increased economic exchanges, improvements in communications and travel, the diffusion of culture and increased cooperation among the world's nation states is reshaping people's lives everywhere. Although the author recognizes that globalization has negative effects, he points out that it has also brought many benefits.
- Held, D., & McGrew, A. (2002). *Globalization/Anti-globalization.* Cambridge, UK: Policy Press. Discussing the many different changes that have contributed to globalization in recent years, the authors pay particular attention to the different

normative approaches that the supporters as well as opponents of globalization have adopted. Addressing what are a complex set of arguments, they tease out major perspectives in the field.

- Monbiot, G. (2003). *Manifesto for a new world order.* New York, NY: New Press. The author who is a respected British journalist has written extensively on globalization's negative effects, but in this book he offers a set of proposals for addressing its harmful consequences, and for promoting a new world order in which the global economy will be managed to improve people's lives. His review of a range of policy options for dealing with globalization's negative impact is particularly helpful.

- Scholte, J. A. (2000). *Globalization: A critical introduction.* New York, NY: Palgrave. This book is widely used as a standard textbook on globalization at universities around the world. It adopts a multidimensional view and comprehensively examines the many different facets of the globalization process. It also contains useful insights into how the modern world is changing as a result of globalization.

- Stiglitz, J. E. (2002). *Globalization and its discontents.* New York, NY: Norton and Stiglitz, J. E. (2007). *Making globalization work.* New York, NY: Norton. This Nobel prizewinning author is well known for his criticism of the IMF and World Bank where he served as chief economist and gained insights into the way these organizations promote market liberalism, particularly in the developing countries. In his second book, he discusses different policy options for addressing globalization's negative effects and for using global economic resources to raise standards of living everywhere.

Part II

Promoting Social Welfare in the Global Era

4

Families, Communities, and Nonformal Welfare

Although not always recognized by social welfare scholars who tend to focus on the role of nonprofits and governments in promoting people's wellbeing, families and communities have not only cared for their members for millennia, but continue to do so today. In addition, almsgiving and religious mandates to provide for those in need have augmented traditional family and community support networks since ancient times. Also, in many countries and especially in the Global South, people have formed mutual aid associations, such as burial associations, savings clubs, benevolent societies, and rotating savings and credit associations, known as ROSCAs. These mutual aid associations also help each other with harvesting crops or storing grain communally. These and other "nonformal" or "traditional" institutions (as they are loosely known) have been studied by anthropologists for many years, but it is only recently that social welfare scholars began to examine their contribution. Much of this research has focused on the developing world, but interest in family and community support networks, and particularly in the way women provide care has grown among Western academics.

A better understanding of the role and functioning of nonformal welfare institutions has direct policy implications. As government social services have come under budgetary pressure in many Western countries, it has been argued that families should assume greater responsibility for the wellbeing of their members and that people in need should turn to their friends and neighbors as well as local faith-based and nonprofit organizations for assistance. It has also been proposed that the governments of developing countries should integrate grassroots mutual aid activities with statutory social protection programs. In some Islamic countries, governments have formalized the collection and payment of *zakat*, which was previously an individual matter while others have actively promoted the creation of faith-based organizations that receive *zakat* payments to fund their operations.

This chapter begins by tracing the historical role of nonformal welfare and discussing how its ability to provide care has been affected by social change. There is a good deal of research to show that traditional helping practices have been undermined by urbanization and industrialization. The way that scholars define nonformal welfare is then examined. As will be shown, they try to conceptualize the complex systems of provision that comprise nonformal welfare and define their scope. However, this task is complicated because nonformal welfare often overlaps with the services of nonprofits and statutory agencies. For example, as many faith-based organizations have emerged over the years to give expression to culturally institutionalized charitable practices, the line between voluntary giving and formally organized social services has become blurred.

In addition, nonformal welfare institutions are experiencing formalization. One example is the imposition of statutory mandates on families to care for their members, even though most do so already. Another example is the tendency for grassroots mutual aid associations to adopt bureaucratic rules and operating procedures, and comply with government regulations. Although formalization has advantages, some believe that government intervention dampens people's participation and inhibits spontaneity. Nevertheless, strengthening the nonformal sector presents an opportunity to respond to the needs of many millions of people who do not benefit from the services of nonprofit organizations and government agencies. Recognizing the challenges facing the nonformal sector, the chapter concludes by discussing the positive contribution nonformal welfare makes to enhancing social wellbeing around the world.

The Nature of Nonformal Welfare

The nonformal welfare sector is rooted in patterns of culturally embedded reciprocal obligation and mutual aid that can be traced back to prehistoric times. Cooperation was essential for survival as bands of hunter gatherers comprising primarily family members sought to meet their needs for food and shelter, deal with adversity, and care for those in need. With the advent of pastoralism and settled agriculture, social support networks became more complex and began to encompass the wider kin and clan as well as people who were not related to each other, but lived in close proximity and shared a common language and religion. These community support networks augmented family obligations and strengthened wider bonds of social solidarity. Nonformal welfare practices also acquired a cultural dimension as traditional care was institutionalized through community sanctions, ceremonies, legends, and religious teaching. The latter played a particularly important role, and in time all the major faiths extolled the virtues of almsgiving. In addition, monastic institutions that cared for the sick, destitute, and disabled proliferated. The endowment of orphanages, convents, and hospitals by wealthy families also became common. Assisting those in need became an obligation in all the major world religions even though giving was based on different principles. For example, in Judaism *tzedakah* is viewed as a righteous duty, while in Islam the payment of *zakat* and *sadaqah* is believed to purify the giver. The idea that helping the poor blesses the giver and reaps future awards is common among many religions. In Catholicism, Franciscan teaching not only made a virtue out of giving, but of identifying with the poor by living a life of modest simplicity.

Cooperation and social support were also driven by pragmatic considerations. Communal grain storage and harvesting and the construction of shared facilities, including wells, drains, and irrigation systems emerged as a logical way of serving common interests. Many communities forged agreements on managing commonly owned assets to assure the preservation of the Commons. Self-interest also prompted the emergence of early cooperatives, such as artisan guilds and mutual aid associations. The first guilds emerged among stone masons in the ancient civilizations to represent the interests of their members, train apprentices, and ensure that those who were injured or too infirm to work were cared for. The widows and other dependents of deceased craftsmen were also helped. Later, in Roman times, guilds were established among lawyers and physicians as well. The guilds are the precursors of today's trade unions and professional associations, and their communal funds established to meet social needs presaged the emergence of social insurance.

In the Western nations, the process of industrialization that began in the eighteenth century had a major impact on nonformal welfare. New employment opportunities in industry attracted many people to the cities where they could earn cash wages and raise their living standards beyond what was possible through agrarian employment. With urbanization, the traditional extended family with its elaborate system of expectations and obligations declined in size and influence, and with increased geographic mobility, family members no longer lived in close proximity to each other in small cohesive communities. Both factors limited the family's ability to provide care, and as Wilensky and Lebeaux (1965) famously argued, these changes created pressures on governments to expand statutory programs. In addition, urban overcrowding, unsanitary conditions, crime, and widespread poverty prompted reform movements that eventually resulted in government intervention and the creation of statutory welfare services. The nonprofit sector also grew rapidly at this time. With the expansion of statutory welfare services, mutual aid associations that previously catered to large numbers of people declined in importance. Kidd (1999) points out that the friendly societies, which had about eight million members at the beginning of the twentieth century in Britain, all but disappeared following the introduction of statutory social security later in the century. Although these developments had a major impact on traditional welfare, family and community social support networks still play a significant role today and mutual aid associations thrive in many parts of the world. Also, needy people around the world continue to receive charity from temples, mosques, and churches as well as services from faith-based organizations. Although these activities suggest that the nonformal sector remains vibrant, many believe that policies that promote traditional welfare are needed to ensure its continued functioning.

Analyzing Nonformal Welfare

As noted in the introduction to this chapter, academic interest in nonformal welfare has increased significantly in recent years. Although a good deal of anthropological research into family and community social networks had previously been published, little consideration was given to how these networks enhanced people's wellbeing or how governments could promote nonformal welfare. With the rise of the political right in the 1980s, it became apparent that state welfare would not continue to expand as had previously been the case, and attention focused on the role of the family and local community as an alternative source of aid. New opportunities for commercial providers to participate in social welfare were also created and nonprofit and faith organizations were encouraged to assume greater responsibility for those in need. In the Global South, growing populist sentiment questioned the state's dominant role in social welfare and many activists campaigned for greater community involvement.

It was in this context that social welfare scholars began to pay attention to nonformal welfare. In the late 1980s, a group associated with the Max Planck Institute in Munich (Benda-Beckmann et al., 1988) published a major collection of studies showing that nonformal welfare contributes significantly to social wellbeing in the Global South. A study of social security in developing countries by Midgley (1984) also found that nonformal welfare helps to meet the needs of poor people in the developing world who have little access to statutory social security programs. He also urged governments to integrate the nonformal system with statutory provisions. Gilbert (1976) made a similar point in his study of communal grain storage and other cooperative practices in the developing world. Subsequently, van Ginneken (1999, 2007) of the International Labour Organisation (ILO) reiterated these proposals pointing out that the integration of traditional welfare with modern statutory social protection could extend coverage to the excluded majority who had very limited access to the formal social security system. Previously, the ILO played a major role in identifying the needs of urban informal sector workers who were and still are engaged in the great variety of economic activities, but who lack the advantages enjoyed by workers in regular wage employment. Since the discovery of the informal sector in the 1970s (Bromley & Gerry, 1979; Hart, 1973), the organization has urged its member states to abandon policies that seek to suppress informal employment and instead provide protection and supports. Recently, these proposals have been augmented by a growing interest in microinsurance, which focuses on the capacity of mutual aid associations to provide social protection. Numerous proposals for linking mutual aid with statutory social protection have been made, and again the ILO has played a leading role in promoting this approach (Churchill, 2006). Another development is the introduction of micropensions by mutual aid associations and microfinance organizations that have established long-term savings and insurance products designed to provide modest pensions in old age (Midgley, 2012).

A number of pioneering studies of social support networks in Western countries by scholars such as Wenger (1984) and Whittaker and Garbarino (1983) complemented these developments and showed that despite the existence of modern social services, many people in need turn to relatives, friends, and neighbors for help. At the time, Grannovetter (1973) examined the way people use social networks to find employment. Studies also recognized that informal networks are particularly important in providing child and elder care, and support for people with disabilities. Attention also focused on the role of women as caregivers showing that they carry a disproportionate and often onerous responsibility for informal care. Although some politicians extolled the virtue of family support, which they claimed is more effective than government provision, this usually means that women assume responsibility for caring for needy relatives. In a detailed study of informal caregiving in Europe, Daly and Rake (2003) found that women are twice as likely to provide care as men. In the United States, Hooyman and Kiyak (2008) report that women comprise about 75% of elder caregivers and that daughters are twice as likely as sons to care for their elderly parents. A recent study by Levitsky (2014) found that family care continues to place huge demands on women in the United States, and that few benefit from government services when caring for elders.

When analyzing nonformal welfare, scholars have speculated on the factors that gave rise to the nonformal welfare system and legitimated its functioning. While some regard nonformal welfare as a natural expression of the deep desire among human beings to cooperate and help each other, others take a more instrumental view and see the nonformal welfare as a response to social needs and a way of achieving welfare goals. Kropotkin's (1902) work is often cited as an example of the former approach. Vigorously rejecting the popularity of Social Darwinism at the end of the nineteenth century, he drew on a sizable body of biological and anthropological research to argue that despite conflict and competition, cooperation is a natural proclivity among humans and indeed all animals. More recently, de Waal (2009) drew on scientific research to conclude that cooperation and altruism are natural mammalian traits and that greed and the pursuit of self-interest is contrary to human nature. The idea that modern social welfare programs are a natural expression of people's inborn altruism has also been expressed in many introductory social policy textbooks that highlight the role of caring sentiments in the expansion of both voluntary and statutory services. Titmuss (1971, 1974) is probably the most eloquent exponent of this idea, claiming that modern social services may be likened to a gift given freely to an anonymous stranger solely on the basis of need.

In addition to claiming that nonformal welfare emerges to respond to social needs and risks, some scholars contend that traditional welfare practices facilitate the adaption of traditional communities to modernity and are a precursor to modern welfare systems. Geertz (1962) was one of the earliest exponents of this interpretation, arguing on the basis of his research into ROSCAs in Indonesia that these organizations function as middle-rung institutions that bridge the gap between the traditional and modern economy and promote participation in modern finance and production. Several studies of women's participation in these organizations (Ardener & Burman, 1995; Bortie-Doku & Aryeetey, 1995) also highlight their role in creating small enterprises, accessing capital, and acquiring business acumen. Little's (1965) research into voluntary associations in West African cities found that these associations facilitate migrants' adaption to urban life. As has been mentioned already, mutual aid associations paved the way for the emergence of the friendly societies and statutory social insurance in Western countries, and this has led some to conclude that they are a precursor of modern forms of social protection. Scholars like Townsend (1994) have even argued on the basis of an extensive study of households in South India that mutual aid activities in the region can be likened to modern commercial insurance. Although these findings have been questioned, these studies have relevance for policy; however, they have not featured prominently in policy debates about the role of nonformal welfare in social policy.

Defining Nonformal Welfare

Welfare scholars have struggled to define nonformal welfare and identify the different forms it has taken around the world. Even nomenclature has proved to be problematic as the limitations of terms, such as "informal," "nonformal," "traditional," and even "unorganized" have been recognized. In a thoughtful analysis, the Benda-Beckmanns (1994) show that what are regarded as informal activities are often based on highly prescribed and institutionalized practices. For example, far from being informal, the Islamic injunction of *zakat* is governed by a highly formalized body of *sharia* law. The term "traditional" is also problematic since many religious people believe that the teachings of their faiths are perfectly suited to the modern age. As mentioned earlier, another issue is that many nonformal welfare institutions are undergoing formalization. This is especially true of grassroots mutual aid associations that are adopting bureaucratic operating procedures, opening bank accounts, and even hiring staff. Since they are transforming into nonprofit organizations, it is misleading to describe them as informal.

It has also been difficult to identify different types of nonformal welfare and delimit their scope. It was mentioned at the beginning of this chapter that the family, community support networks, grassroots mutual aid associations, and religious charity are usually associated with nonformal welfare and it makes sense to group traditional welfare practices in terms of these four categories. For example, a study of nonformal social protection in Botswana by Mupedzisa and Ntseane (2014) used a similar approach to categorize different types of provision showing how family and community networks operate and how mutual aid associations function. They note that family obligations are deeply institutionalized and linked to wider community support networks and cooperative practices. Many case studies of nonformal welfare focus on one of these types of provision. For example, an interesting collection of case studies by Shigetomi and Okamoto (2014) of self-organizing activities in local communities in Asian countries focuses exclusively on the way they mobilize local networks to raise standards of living through a variety of agricultural and other productive activities. Another example is the way religious practices enhance social welfare in Russia's Tartarstan region. In addition to giving *zakat* and *sadaqah* to those in need, Kuznetsova and Round (2014) report that people participate in a variety of charitable societies and also use local mosques as a locus of nonformal care.

However, it should be recognized that these different types of nonformal welfare overlap. For example, in many developing countries, family and kin obligations to care for their members often extend into the community where many local people are in fact related to each other. Another problem is that the gradual transformation of mutual aid associations into nonprofits makes it difficult to distinguish between the two. Nevertheless, this classification of nonformal institutions does facilitate the comprehension of what are complex patterns of provision. Also, despite their limitations, terms such as "informal," "nonformal," and "traditional" are useful for connoting those culturally institutionalized welfare practices that can be distinguished from statutory, nonprofit, and commercial welfare services, which have a formal, organizational basis and rely on regularized operating procedures rather than spontaneous or discretionary practices.

Challenges to Nonformal Welfare

Many of the studies cited earlier take an optimistic view of nonformal welfare showing that it plays a major role in promoting social wellbeing around the world. As noted earlier, many emphasize the way traditional institutions strengthen families, foster social solidarity, and meet social needs. However, as Midgley (2011b) observes, these interpretations should be tempered by studies that show that nonformal welfare faces numerous challenges, especially because of rapid social change. The tendency to view the nonformal sector in a positive light and even to romanticize traditional institutions has also inhibited a careful assessment of their contributions. These challenges need to be taken into account when formulating proposals for strengthening traditional welfare practices and integrating them with modern social services.

While recognizing that nonformal welfare is ubiquitous and that it contributes to peoples' wellbeing, many scholars have drawn attention to the way traditional practices are being undermined by economic, social, and political change. This problem has been raised many times in the past. Industrialization, urbanization, and the spread of modern attitudes and beliefs over the last two centuries had a profound effect on traditional welfare in Western countries. In the developing world, the problem was already recognized in colonial times when administrators became aware of the growing numbers of beggars, abandoned street children, and destitute elderly on the streets of the cities who were not being cared for by their families. As Midgley (2011a) reports, it was in the context of rapid social change and the declining effectiveness of traditional welfare institutions that the first statutory welfare services were introduced by the colonial authorities in many developing countries.

Many studies focus on the way the traditional extended family with its elaborate system of expectations and obligations has declined in size impeding the functioning of the nonformal welfare system. In one of the first studies of family change in the Global South, Goode (1963) demonstrated that traditional consanguine family relationships were being transformed by industrialization and urbanization. He pointed out that families have become much smaller and many younger family members readily move to the cities to work. Fewer live with their parents and other relatives after they marry.

Focusing on the implications of the inexorable trend toward consanguinity, many welfare scholars have shown that these changes have undermined the family's role in providing care. For example, Apt (2002) reported that many families in Ghana are motivated to assist their older relatives in need, but that declining numbers of children and geographic distance make it difficult for them to provide help. This trend has serious implications for elder care in African countries. In Asian countries, where family care obligations are highly institutionalized, the numbers of elderly people living alone has increased, and many feel isolated and even abandoned. For example, the rate of suicide among elders in Korea is reported to be the highest in the world (*The Economist,* 2013). Social support networks in many rural communities in the Global South have also been weakened as more young people move to the cities.

It has also been argued that modernization has fostered secularism, individualism, and similar values associated with the spread of market liberalism and that this undermines traditional welfare practices. With the ascendancy of these values, family obligations have weakened and religious mandates to give to those in need are no longer as strong as before. Although many people continue to provide for their elders, fewer accept that they are also responsible for other needy relatives. In an interesting study, Azaiza (2007) attributes the decline of family support among the Arab community in Israel to the rise of individualism that has fostered a growing indifference to the needs of relatives. Similar trends have affected traditional mutual aid associations which rely on trust and cooperation, but Loewe (2006) observes these associations are sometimes harmed by the self-interest of some members who use these organizations for their own benefit. A study of burial societies in Botswana by Ngwenya (2003) found that families often engage in bitter disputes about how payout funds should be distributed. Van Leeuwen (2005) notes that male family members often expropriate the funds accumulated by women who participate in savings clubs and mutual aid associations. These and other studies belie the image of traditional families as harmonious and well integrated.

This raises the wider issue of whether traditional values, beliefs, and practices are always benevolent and invariably enhance social wellbeing. Traditional culture has often been portrayed in a very positive way by scholars who emphasize its role in providing care and promoting social solidarity. However, there are aspects of traditionalism that many find objectionable. Some claim that traditional cultures require an unquestioning obedience to parental authority and deny young people an opportunity to critically assess the beliefs they were taught as children. Strong community pressures reinforce what some claim is a stifling culture of conformity. Observance of traditional dress codes, ceremonies, and practices, such as arranged marriages inhibit choice and freedom of expression. In particular, the harmful effects of traditional patriarchal practices on women's rights have long been recognized and challenged. These issues have become increasingly apposite as traditional communities actively resist the influence of modernity and assert their traditional customs and values. In some African countries, the notion of gay rights is regarded as a decadent Western import, while in Pakistan some traditionalists oppose the education of girls and modern medical services, such as immunization. With the rise of Islamic fundamentalism in many parts of the world, traditional beliefs have been vigorously enforced. These developments raise complex issues, and while different views on traditionalism should be respected, this should not preclude a frank discussion about its merits and limitations.

Some scholars are less concerned with the negative impact of modernity on traditional culture and have instead shown that nonformal welfare institutions are under pressure because of economic and political changes. In particular, they highlight the role of poverty in impeding traditional responses to social need. In a poignant study, de Bruijn (1994) found that the loss of livestock and widespread poverty caused by desertification and drought had undermined a deeply institutionalized culture of social support among Fulbe pastoralists in Africa's Sahel region. Although mutual obligations are still observed, families are now too poor to assist their needy kin. Her findings show that even the most culturally embedded traditional welfare practices are rendered ineffective by economic adversity. More recently, Shang (2008) reported that many extended families in rural China would like to care for orphans and the needy children of relatives, but that many struggle to cope because they lack the resources to assume the additional costs required to house, feed, and educate these children. Poverty also impedes the effectiveness of mutual aid associations. A study in Uganda (Kasente, Asingwire, Banugire, & Kyomuhenda, 2002) found that many members of these associations have difficulty making regular contributions because their incomes are below subsistence poverty levels preventing them from participating effectively. Although families in Western countries like the United States are better able to cope, the costs of caring for elders is considerable, yet as Levitsky (2014) points out, there is little political demand for government involvement.

In addition, traditional family and community support systems have been undermined by disasters, violence, and other events. The poorest countries in the world are often most disadvantaged by natural disasters that devastate local communities and impede their ability to support their members. Storms and floods as well as droughts and famines are commonplace in these countries and are expected to become more frequent as the effects of climate change are more widely felt. Endemic diseases like HIV/AIDS also debilitate traditional welfare institutions. As is well known, AIDS has devastated whole communities in many parts of the world and especially in sub-Saharan Africa, where Mokomane (2012) reports that many families are facing unprecedented demands to care for relatives and especially children affected by the crisis. The recent Ebola crisis in West Africa has had similar consequences.

Violence has an extremely deleterious effect on the traditional welfare system. Apart from causing widespread injury and death, many communities have been devastated by civil wars and religious and ethnic conflicts that have shattered their social support networks. Violence disrupts the livelihoods of many families, and as they flee and become dependent on relief provided by refugee agencies, their traditional welfare function becomes ineffectual. It is paradoxical that violence today is often associated with traditionalism. Various religious and ethnic minorities, and perhaps most obviously *Salafist jihadis* have taken up arms to enforce their "traditional" values and beliefs on others. But, by killing and maiming those whose values they deprecate, these groups devastate communities with centuries-old welfare practices rooted in religious beliefs. The brutal attack by Islamic State extremists on Christian and Yazidi communities in Syria and Iraq, which have historically provided care and support for those in need is one tragic example of the vicious use of violence against minorities. Another comes from the forcible abduction and rape of girls and young women by *Boko Haram* in Nigeria. Ongoing political and civil conflicts in many parts of the world have had a similar effect on families and communities undermining their ability to provide care.

The traditional welfare system has also been harmed by the actions of governments. Indifference, corruption, state sponsored violence, and questionable policy decisions have all contributed to the problem. Despite best intentions, inappropriate policy decisions also undermine or place additional strains on nonformal welfare institutions. For example, many governments have vigorously promoted family planning to reduce population growth, but this has resulted in smaller families contributing to a decline in traditional support. Arguably, the most dramatic example is the Chinese government's one-child policy, which has major implications for future elder care. Another example comes from the Western nations where a greater emphasis on home-based services has placed greater strains on families and particularly women caregivers. There have been similar developments in African countries where governments are now promoting home-based instead of residential care. Mokomane (2012) reports that this trend has negatively affected women who are compelled to give up regular employment to care for sick and needy relatives. Many girls who leave school to provide care are also denied opportunities to realize their potential through formal education. Another problem is that indigenous communities with strong traditional welfare institutions have been affected by government policies that allow encroachment on traditional lands. In some cases, these policies have even required the resettlement of indigenous people. Traditional caring is also undermined by rigid immigration policies that often result in the separation of family members. One particularly distressing example comes from the United States where deported immigrants are separated from their children who were born in the United States. Because these children are viewed by the authorities as citizens, they are not deported with their parents and most are placed in foster care or given up for adoption. The *New Internationalist* magazine (2013) reports that hundreds of thousands of deported families have been harmed by this policy.

The promotion of market liberalism by many governments is also having a negative impact. In addition to promoting individualism, marketization is undermining traditional economic activities. For example, Okamoto (2011) reports that herders in Mongolia face serious challenges as a result of the country's transition to a market economy where cooperative practices previously supported by the government have been abandoned. Another problem is the retrenchment of statutory programs in many Western countries. The adoption of welfare-to-work programs has reduced the time mothers can spend with their children, and in some countries like the United States, many states have adopted a particularly coercive approach which has seriously affected family care. Indeed, some scholars believe that these developments, as Chappell (2010) put it, amount to a war against the family. It is clear that traditional welfare institutions need to be strengthened within a wider policy framework that integrates nonprofit, statutory, and commercial provisions.

Formalization, Integration, and Opportunities

It was mentioned earlier that traditional welfare practices in many parts of the world are experiencing formalization as many mutual aid associations are adopting modern governance and budgetary procedures and evolving into nonprofits. Religious charity given privately by individuals is also being increasingly redirected to fund the activities of faith-based organizations. These developments have been augmented by government policies that regulate nonformal practices, or formalize family and religious responsibilities through statutory mandates. However, the trend toward formalization has been haphazard and few governments have adopted policies based on a careful assessment of the role nonformal practices can play. Also, few have sought to harmonize traditional and modern welfare institutions or integrate them within a coherent welfare system that incorporates nonprofit and commercial provision.

Historically, there have been few attempts by governments to formalize traditional welfare and it is only relatively recently that this practice has become widespread. One of the oldest examples is the creation by the Caliph Omar in the seventh century of a state-managed fund known as a *Beit-ul-mal,* which collected *zakat* contributions and distributed them to those in need. However, the practice was subsequently abandoned so that paying *zakat* again became an individual responsibility. In medieval Europe, the payment of tithes was regulated by both Canon and secular law, and as de Schweinitz (1943) reveals, the early English statutes paved the way for the Poor Laws that specifically required that a portion of the tithe be allocated to meet the needs of poor people.

More recently, some governments have fostered formalization through statutory regulation. For example, some now require mutual aid associations to register and comply with regulations. Ngwenya (2003) reports that in Botswana, traditional burial associations must register with a government agency and provide annual reports and statements of accounts, but few comply. Similar legislation was enacted in South Africa to regulate the activities of local ROSCAs known as *stokvels,* but it appears that noncompliance is widespread. Legislation has also been introduced to require families to care for their members and to impose penalties for those who fail to do so. Mandates to care for children are now very common in the child welfare legislation of many countries. Although the vast majority of families raise their children in a loving and nurturing environment, the problem of child abuse and neglect has become more widespread prompting state intervention. Mandates to care for elders are also enshrined in the statutes of some countries, including Canada, the United Kingdom, and some American states, but Ting and Woo (2009) observe that they are seldom enforced. Perhaps the best-known is Singapore's *Maintenance of Parents Act* of 1995 that allows elders to apply for a judicial maintenance order to require their children to provide for their needs. Although this legislation was intended to deter neglect, a number of older parents have successfully secured maintenance orders against their children, suggesting that even societies like Singapore that value traditional culture require the legal enforcement of filial piety. However, as Rozario and Kay (2014) point out, the numbers are small, and in many cases relatively small sums of money are involved. Also, the courts and social workers usually seek resolution through mediation rather than mandatory orders.

In addition to government regulation, it was mentioned earlier that formalization has occurred as mutual aid associations have evolved into nonprofits. In some cases, this has resulted in the creation of quite large and sophisticated organizations. One example is the Self-Employed Women's Association (SEWA) which emerged out of collaborative efforts of women *bidi* or cigarette rollers in the city of Ahmedebad in India when they realized that by collaborating they could bypass exploitative middle men and obtain better prices for their products. As Chen (2008) reports SEWA provides various services, including education, childcare, insurance, and micropensions to more than a million members. It also engages in lobbying and advocacy for its members. Another example comes from the Philippines where a group of women coconut harvesters formed a savings club which has grown into a large nonprofit with about 700,000 members. Known as the Center for Agriculture and Rural Development (CARD), it is registered as an insurance company and a bank and has branch offices all over the country. Alip and Amenomori (2011) reveal that its traditional savings scheme has been augmented by services and insurance products for its mostly poor members.

Many local mutual aid associations that have formalized continue to serve their communities, and in some cases they have joined with others to form national organizations to represent their interests. Lewis and Kanji (2009) report that local burial societies in Ethiopia, known as *iddirs,* have formed a national federation to coordinate their services and to lobby for support. A similar national association of *stokvels* has been in existence in South Africa for many years (Lukhele, 1990). Many other grassroots associations are also formalizing. One example is the Jansenville Development Forum in South Africa, which Wilkinson-Maposa (2008) reports is a community nonprofit that emerged out of the efforts of local people and grassroots associations that collaborated on social development projects. Like SEWA, the Forum engages actively in lobbying and advocacy.

Some traditional communities have also lobbied to protect their traditional way of life. Activism has been particularly strong among the First Nations in Canada, Native Americans in the United States, and indigenous people in Australasia, but highly vulnerable groups in other parts of the world are also mobilizing. Mander and Tauli-Corpuz (2006) provide case examples from many countries of how indigenous communities are resisting exploitation by large corporations of the natural sources they have historically stewarded. While some have been more successful than others, the plight of these communities has been widely reported in the media and with growing support, local and international resources have been mobilized to protect their habitat and traditional institutions. In many cases, political pressure has been brought to bear on governments to address the problems these communities face.

Formalization has also involved a degree of commercialization as some mutual aid associations have launched for-profit services or otherwise collaborated with commercial firms. Midgley (2012) points out that marketization is quite common among associations that offer savings opportunities and insurance products, such as micropensions and other term life policies. In addition, well-established insurance firms have recognized that mutual aid associations are a way of reaching many more consumers and increasing their profits. Accordingly, many commercial insurance firms have contracted with mutual aid associations to recruit customers. Amenomori (2010) reports that the Delta Life Insurance Company in Bangladesh enrolled almost a million poor families in its low-cost life insurance program in this way. Commercial providers are also making headway selling funeral policies to low income families. Collins, Morduch, Rutherford, and Ruthven (2009) observe that some funeral parlors in South Africa have successfully marketed commercial burial insurance to poor families who simultaneously contribute to traditional burial associations.

Opportunities for Integration

It has already been mentioned that governments have been urged to adopt policies that integrate nonformal welfare with the modern statutory system in order to extend protection to those who are excluded. It is believed that this will foster a coherent system of provision that harmonizes the contribution of traditional welfare practices as well as the services of nonprofits and commercial providers. International organizations like the ILO have made a significant contribution to fostering closer association between statutory and nonformal provisions. However, progress has been limited, and generally the integration of nonformal welfare and statutory provision has proceeded on an incremental basis. Nevertheless, some progress has been made paving the way for the adoption of a more comprehensive approach that will integrate nonformal and formal welfare in the future. Positive steps have been taken in some countries to incorporate informal sector workers into modern social insurance programs that cater primarily to those in formal wage employment. Although some of these programs usually allow for the enrollment of self-employed workers and their employees, casual workers, agricultural laborers, and domestics are usually excluded. Extending social protection to these workers or establishing special programs to meet their needs should be a priority, but as van Ginneken (2010) notes very few governments in the Global South have introduced policies of this kind. Exceptions include some higher-income countries in Latin America, Asia, and North Africa, which have extended coverage to informal sector workers, and in some cases like Peru and South Africa, domestic workers have recently been included as well. Special programs for informal sector workers have been created in several countries. One of the best-known is India's "welfare funds," which Sadhak (2013) reports provide access to medical, education, and other social services to designated occupational groups in what is known as the "unorganized" sector. Another example comes from Indonesia where Sirojudin and Midgley (2012) report that the government has established a special agency that contracts with nonprofits to enroll informal sector workers in its social security program. Micropensions are also being established in some countries. The rapid expansion of social assistance in many developing countries is also playing a positive role. Although not targeted specifically at informal sector workers, Barrientos (2013) notes that conditional cash transfer programs, such as Brazil's *Bolsa Família* and India's National Rural Employment Guarantee scheme are reducing the incidence of poverty in many developing countries.

Some governments have promoted integration by supporting families and community groups that provide care. Historically, governments have expected families to care for needy relatives, and as noted earlier some have enacted legislation to enforce this requirement. Also, social assistance payments were seldom made to families who had relatives able to care for their needy members. In addition to abolishing the relatives' responsibility requirement, payments to caregivers are being introduced in many more countries; in some Western nations, this approach is now well established. In addition, these payments often extend to non-family members like neighbors. With the popularization of consumer-directed care, people with special needs are able to employ caregivers of their choice, including relatives. However, much more needs to be done to reinforce traditional familial obligations through payments of this kind. Whitworth and Wilkinson (2014) observe that cash transfers in South Africa could be more effectively linked to the country's cultural tradition of *ubuntu* that embeds individuals within a wider system of community networks. They argue that ways should be found to ensure that payments to individuals are integrated with traditional community activities and support these activities.

An inclusive approach that promotes the integration of nonformal and statutory welfare together with the activities of nonprofit and commercial providers into a comprehensive pluralistic system of provision is badly needed. However, some scholars, such as Benda-Beckmann and Kirsch (1999) believe that government direction of this kind stifles traditional welfare practices. Similarly, some Islamic scholars are critical of the way *zakat* payments have been formalized by some Muslim majority countries, such as Pakistan and Saudi Arabia, contending that this is a private matter for individuals to decide. On the other hand, it has already been noted that many scholars and international organizations like the ILO favor integration believing that this approach will extend social protection to many more people and promote the achievement of a social security floor that guarantees an adequate standard of living for all (ILO, 2011). However, integration must also involve a wider commitment to social welfare by governments. Examples have already been given that show how government indifference and bad policy harm nonformal institutions. These must not only be corrected, but a proactive and comprehensive approach that enhances the wellbeing of all its citizens should be adopted.

❖

Suggested Additional Reading

Nonformal welfare institutions have not received much attention from international social welfare scholars, but the literature on the subject is growing as the importance of understanding the contribution of the family, community support networks, and similar practices is being recognized. The following are some sources that help provide additional information about the way nonformal welfare institutions function in the global era.

- Apt, N. A. (2002). Aging and the changing role of the family and the community: An African perspective. *International Social Security Review, 55*(1), 39–47. In this interesting article, the author examines traditional forms of family care for elders in African countries showing that the family and community support systems are being affected by declining family size, increased migration of young people to urban areas, and changing attitudes about family responsibility.

- Benda-Beckmann, F. von, Benda-Beckmann, K. von, Casino, E., Hirtz, F., Woodman, G. R., & Zacher, H. F. (Eds.). (1988). *Between kinship and the state: Social security and law in developing countries.* Dordrecht, Netherlands: Foris. This collection of studies of nonformal welfare institutions in a number of developing countries was one of the first of its kind. Although now rather out of date, many of the case studies included in the book are still relevant and the discussion by the editors of methodological issues remains highly topical.

- Gray, M., Coates, J., & Yellow Bird, M. (Eds.). (2008). *Indigenous social work around the world: Towards culturally relevant practice.* Burlington, VT: Ashgate. Although this book is designed for professional social workers who work in different countries and cross-cultural settings, it provides helpful insights into the way nonformal institutions operate in different countries. It raises interesting questions about how social workers should address social needs in different cultural contexts.

- Levitsky, S. (2014). *Caring for our own: Why there is no political demand for new American social welfare rights.* New York, NY: Oxford University Press. This interesting book focuses on the way families in the United States are increasingly assuming responsibility for the care of their elders. It shows that nonformal welfare institutions are not confined to the developing countries, but play a major role in the Western nations as well. The book draws attention to the lack of political support among many families for increased government intervention in the field.

- Midgley, J., & Hosaka, M. (Eds.). (2011). *Grassroots social security in Asia: Mutual aid, microinsurance, and social welfare.* New York, NY: Routledge. Although anthropologists have documented the activities of savings and credit clubs in developing countries for many years, it is only recently that social welfare scholars have become interested in the way these nonformal practices are evolving into microinsurance organizations that receive regular contributions from their members and help them to meet the risks that endanger their wellbeing. Focusing on Asia, it contains several country case studies that show how these organizations cater to their members and their needs.

5

Nonprofits and Faith-Based Services: International Dimensions

Throughout the world, hundreds of millions of people engage with nonprofit and faith-based organizations on a daily basis. While many of these organizations provide conventional social services, a variety cater to their own members, and others advocate for social change. Some are motivated by religious beliefs while others are based on cooperative principles. Several cater to particular groups of people while others have a wider remit. Some operate at the community level while others are very large and serve people in many different countries. Together, they comprise a large and complex system of provision that can be distinguished from the services of governments and commercial firms as well as the traditional welfare obligations of families and communities. It is for this reason that nonprofits and faith-based organizations are often viewed as comprising a separate domain, which is known as the voluntary or third sector.

As noted in Chapter 3, today's nonprofits are descended from the grassroots mutual aid associations and faith-based organizations that have existed around the world for many centuries. However, as mentioned it is difficult to draw a clear line between nonformal welfare and modern nonprofit and faith-based organizations. It is also difficult to distinguish between nonprofits, government agencies, and commercial firms. For example, many nonprofits are adopting managerial and budgetary procedures similar to those of for-profit enterprises with the result that the line between nonprofits and for-profits has become blurred. Similarly, many are subsidized by governments and subject to statutory regulations casting doubt on their independence from government control. Nevertheless, nonprofit and faith-based organizations have proliferated in recent years and become very important contributors to social welfare. Academic inquiry in the field has also increased rapidly. Previously, few scholars paid much attention to these organizations assuming that government social welfare would be the primary means of meeting social needs. With cutbacks in government spending in many Western nations and the increasingly important role of nonprofit organizations in the developing countries, this assumption is no longer widely held.

This chapter discusses the role of nonprofits and faith-based organizations in social welfare. It focuses primarily on social service organizations that seek to improve people's wellbeing, but the activities of cooperatives, volunteer organizations, social enterprises, and advocacy organizations are also discussed. The chapter begins by reviewing the way scholars have conceptualized, defined, and classified nonprofits and faith-based organizations. It then traces their history showing that they expanded rapidly in the nineteenth century, and that after being sidelined by the state in the twentieth century, are again playing an important role in social welfare. The services of nonprofits and faith-based organizations around the world are briefly examined and the chapter concludes by discussing their role in social welfare.

Defining Nonprofits and Faith-Based Organizations

Nonprofit and faith-based organizations are just two of many terms that are used to connote the great variety of nongovernmental and noncommercial organizations that comprise the voluntary sector today. Others include charities, religious organizations, philanthropies, voluntary organizations, nongovernmental organizations (NGOs), membership organizations, social enterprises, tax-exempt organizations, foundations, and community-based organizations (CBOs). Generally, the term nonprofit is preferred in the United States while the term voluntary organization is used in other Western countries. The terms NGO and CBO are popular in development and particularly in the field of international aid where large international nonprofits make an important contribution. More recently, the terms social enterprise and social business have also been popularized. Sometimes, these terms are used synonymously, but in many cases they have a different connotation.

Not all nonprofits or faith-based organizations are concerned with social welfare in the sense that the term is used in this book. Sports and cultural organizations, professional associations, educational institutions, such as private universities and religious bodies, operate on a nonprofit basis, but are not primarily involved in social welfare. Nevertheless, there is an overlap—for example, when hospitals managed by religious orders provide services to poor people. In addition, some organizations like cooperatives are not always classified as nonprofits, but they cater to the social needs of their members and clearly have a welfare as well as economic function. Although volunteer organizations are nonprofits, they differ substantively from other nonprofits. This is also the case with social enterprises and advocacy and lobbying organizations.

Groups campaigning to bring about progressive social change are usually regarded as nonprofits, but the situation is complicated because different advocacy organizations with different political affiliations have different ideas about what progressive social change involves. As a recent controversy in the United States reveals, advocacy groups on the political right that campaign against immigration, gay rights, and abortion have been granted tax exemptions even though many believe that their activities are contrary to the spirit of progressive advocacy. Another complication is the ambiguous link between advocacy organizations and popular social movements. While social movements often reflect the activities of activist organizations, they are based on wider sentiments and broad popular support for social causes.

Social welfare scholars have struggled to come to grips with these issues for many years. Nevertheless, progress has been made as academic research in the field has grown rapidly, and as a number of specialized academic institutions concerned with the study of nonprofits have emerged. One of the best known is the Comparative Nonprofit Sector Project at the Center for Civil Society Studies at Johns Hopkins University in the United States, which pioneered the international study of nonprofit organizations. Scholars, such as Salamon and Anheier (1997) who have played a leading role in the Project have reviewed a plethora of definitions by experts, governments, and international organizations and concluded that nonprofits are distinctive because they are formal organizations which operate outside the government bureaucracy; do not generate profits; are self-governing; and promote people's participation. Despite identifying these general features of nonprofits, they believe that it is extremely difficult to formulate a precise definition of nonprofits and that it is sufficient to have a general understanding of their services. They suggest that it is also useful to understand the many different types of nonprofits that have been established over the years, including the nonprofits mentioned earlier, such as traditional social service agencies, faith-based organizations, membership societies, social enterprises, volunteer organizations, and advocacy organizations. They believe that faith-based organizations are a special type of nonprofit which are inspired by religious ideals and focus largely on the provision of social services.

The problem of definition is further complicated because nonprofits and faith-based organizations form a part of a larger nexus of activities, which comprise a distinctive third or voluntary sector. Other terms for the voluntary sector include independent sector, or more generally philanthropy and civil society. This latter term has become popular in recent years to differentiate between the state and market. The concept of social capital has also been used in the field to connote the durable social networks that emerge among people and foster social solidarity and civic engagement. However, both civil society and social capital have a far broader connotation than voluntary sector, which refers primarily to the activities of nonprofit organizations. Another term which is popular in Europe is social economy, which is sometimes used as a synonym for the voluntary sector and sometimes in a more nuanced way to refer to the activities of social enterprises. All are part of a separate domain of welfare activities that can be distinguished from the state, market, and nonformal welfare system.

Historical Perspectives

It was noted earlier that modern day nonprofits and faith-based organizations are rooted in centuries-old religious philanthropy and cooperative mutual aid activities. The cooperative movement and trade unions originated in the guilds of the ancient civilizations while faith-based organizations evolved out of the monasteries, temples, and mosques. Religious conviction also motivated wealthy families to provide endowments to construct places of worship, schools, hospitals, almshouses, and orphanages. With the growth of the merchant class in Europe in the middle ages, these endowments became more common prompting the enactment of the first European legislation designed to regulate charity. This was the Elizabethan statute of Charitable Uses of 1601 that provided a legal basis for charitable giving and was widely copied in the American states and in other British colonies. However, Islamic law regulated charity long before this statute was enacted. As Dallal (2004) points out the *sharia* provides a legal basis for Islamic giving prescribing how endowments or *waqf* should be made, and how Muslims should pay *zakat* and *sadaqah,* both of which are forms of charitable giving.

The work of the religious orders was augmented by the lay societies. Among the earliest are the *confraternia* that emerged in medieval Europe and spread to Latin America and other Catholic countries. Composed of leading citizens as well as artisans and merchants, they raised funds for charitable causes and also held processions and ceremonial meetings. Some lay societies like the Ladies of Charity, which was established by St. Vincent DePaul in Paris in 1617 to mobilize wealthy women for charitable work, not only engaged in fundraising, but ministered directly to those in need. A similar practice emerged in Protestant churches where deacons assisted by volunteers visited poor people's homes and provided pastoral counseling and advice. Some churches sent charity visitors to needy families to determine the reasons for their distress and to propose remedies. One of the best known is St. John's in Glasgow where the minister Thomas Chalmers insisted that poor relief should be accompanied by a thorough investigation of the applicant's circumstances.

Despite the dominance of religious philanthropy, secular charities also emerged. One early example is the Foundling Hospital which was founded in London in 1741 by the wealthy shipowner and merchant Captain Coram. Catering to abandoned and orphaned children, it still operates as a child welfare agency. Coram also engaged in fund-raising activities similar to those used by nonprofits today. Building on his relationship with wealthy families and the famous composer Handel, he hosted fashionable musical events to finance the hospital's programs. Another example comes from China during the late Ming period when, as Smith (2009) reveals, some high ranking officials who had retired from the imperial court to their rural estates joined with local landowners and merchants to create benevolent societies that undertook charitable acts, such as food distribution, the burial of beggars and paupers, and the creation of dispensaries and soup kitchens. Anticipating the animal rights movement of the twentieth century, they purchased animals awaiting slaughter and arranged for them to be set free. Their work spread throughout China and augmented the charitable activities of the temples and monasteries.

At this time, membership associations like the friendly societies proliferated throughout Europe and this was accompanied by the growth of the cooperative movement. Although neither was directly associated with the church, many of their members were deeply religious. Religious charity dominated welfare provision in Catholic countries and especially in Latin America and, following the Reformation, the philanthropic activities of the Protestant churches expanded, and some also engaged in advocacy. For example, in the eighteenth century, the Quakers began to challenge the ancient institution of slavery, and by building coalitions with other evangelicals and middle-class sympathizers they helped forge an international movement that campaigned for abolition. However, nonprofits were not always tolerated, and in some countries like France during the revolution, the Jacobin government suppressed their activities. There were similar developments in Prussia in the early nineteenth century. Later in the century, when Pope Leo XIII issued the Encyclical *Rerum Novarum*, nonprofits and faith-based organizations secured widespread recognition. The Encyclical introduced the concept of subsidiarity by which governments are urged to devolve responsibility for the social services to local communities and nonprofit organizations and to restrict their involvement to issues that required national intervention. A related development was the theory of sphere sovereignty formulated by Abraham Kuyper and other Calvinist theologians in the Netherlands, which Daly (2006) points out influenced the emergence of state funded church education and social services in the early twentieth century. These developments subsequently shaped the corporatist welfare systems that emerged in some European countries.

European imperialism also prompted the expansion of nonprofits and faith-based organizations. In Latin America, the evangelical activities of missionaries were accompanied by the construction of schools, hospitals, and orphanages and some of the orders like the Jesuits advocated for the human rights of indigenous people. Protestant missionaries were equally active, and in the British Imperial territories their schools and hospitals were well regarded. Midgley (2011a) notes that the settlers often established charities to help needy Europeans, but did not serve native people until relatively late in the colonial era. Of course, indigenous people who were subjected to imperial rule already had strong family and community social support networks as well as mutual aid associations. In addition, indigenous charitable organizations had already been established in countries such as China, India, and Japan. Amenomori (1997) reports that in Japan in the nineteenth century the philanthropic activities of the temples and monasteries were augmented by charitable organizations founded by merchants and retired government officials.

As industrialization and urbanization contributed to an increase in poverty and deprivation in the Western countries in the nineteenth century, the numbers of nonprofits and faith-based organizations grew rapidly. With the concentration of poor families in urban slums, and a growing incidence of alcohol abuse, crime, and family disintegration, church missions were established in many poor communities to provide relief and promote Christian values. Many churches also established Sunday schools and other educational programs. With the growth of the middle class, support for the charities increased, and in addition there was growing support for their reform campaigns. Middle-class women were particularly active in these campaigns. Believing that alcohol abuse was a major cause of poverty, many joined the temperance movement, and there was growing support for abolishing child labor and improving working conditions. The campaign for universal schooling also attracted widespread support. These efforts inspired wider international reform movements. As discussed in Chapter 11, international movements campaigning for peace and women's rights also emerged at this time.

These efforts were accompanied by the growth of membership associations among working people. In addition to the friendly societies, working men's clubs were established in the industrial cities of Europe and North America in the late nineteenth century to provide a congenial opportunity for people to gather and socialize. With the growth of the trade unions, employment conditions improved and many more families were covered by union-sponsored health and social insurance programs. In addition, the unions and cooperatives campaigned vigorously to improve social conditions, and as progressive political parties were elected to office many of these campaigns resulted in tangible social reforms. Religion played a major role in these efforts as European Christian Socialists and supporters of the Social Gospel movement in the United States advocated for greater government involvement in social welfare.

A major development in the history of nonprofits was the creation of the Charity Organization Society and the Settlement Houses, both of which Leighninger (1987) reports significantly contributed to the development of professional social work. The Charity Organization Society, which was founded in London in 1869, formalized the practice of recruiting women volunteers to investigate and address the circumstances of applicants for poor relief. In addition, the Society sought to coordinate the activities of local charities and to prevent duplication. These efforts were a precursor of community social service planning organizations like the United Way, which serves communities throughout the United States today. The settlements, which also emerged at the end of the nineteenth century, encouraged young people with a university education to live and work in community centers in deprived areas where they introduced a variety of educational and recreational activities designed to expose poor people to the benefits of a "better life." Settlements leaders were also active in advocacy and in campaigns for greater government involvement in social welfare.

These campaigns contributed to the rapid expansion of statutory welfare programs during the twentieth century. Governments' involvement in education, health care, and housing increased rapidly at this time, and by the mid-twentieth century, most people in the Western countries were covered by these programs. Although nonprofits continued to play a significant role, their contribution was increasingly viewed as peripheral to state welfare, and some even believed that the nonprofit sector would eventually wither away. This is ironic since nonprofit organizations advocated for the expansion of government welfare. In addition, many leading proponents of government welfare, such as Prime Minister Clement Attlee in Britain and Harry Hopkins in the United States originally worked in the settlements as did William Beveridge who is widely regarded as the founder of the British welfare state. In addition, he was the author of an important book about nonprofits published at the height of government social services expansion in 1948. In the United States, Harry Hopkins was one of the first federal officials to formulate proposals for coordinating government and voluntary services, but Morris (2010) observes that for several decades, political parties, reformers, and academics prioritized government intervention. This was also the case in the developing countries where it was generally believed that economic and social progress would come about through government economic planning and social service provision. In the communist countries, nonprofits practically ceased to exist and the activities of faith-based organizations were closely monitored.

This situation changed at the end of the twentieth century as nonprofits again assumed a major role in social welfare. As governments inspired by market liberal ideology were elected to office in Britain, the United States, and elsewhere, a far more pluralist welfare system emerged. This was facilitated by the practice of contracting with nonprofits, which Sanger (2003) observes became common in the United States in the 1980s and has since been emulated elsewhere. The imposition of structural adjustment programs in the Global South, which reduced government spending also increased the involvement of nonprofits. In addition, there was widespread disillusionment about government inefficiency and corruption, and increasingly international donors redirected aid originally intended for government programs to nonprofit organizations instead. As nonprofits became active, a new emphasis on gender, the environment, and human rights emerged and terms such as "empowerment" and "participation" were frequently used. Sometimes referred to as popular or alternative development, prevailing ideas about development were challenged by the increasingly robust nonprofit sector. Another factor was the collapse of the Soviet Union, which was accompanied by an influx of funds from wealthy Western foundations which supported the creation of nonprofits in the former communist countries. By the beginning of the twenty-first century, many scholars commented on the remarkable resurgence of nonprofits and their growing importance in social affairs. Coupled with the widespread use of the Internet and social media, many believe that a vibrant civil society comprising nonprofits, faith-based organizations, and popular movements has now emerged to balance the role of the state, market, and family in social welfare.

A parallel development at this time was the expansion of commercial providers in the welfare field. Their role is discussed at more length in Chapter 7, but it should be noted that market ideas have exerted considerable influence on the nonprofit sector in recent years as notions of social entrepreneurship, social enterprise, and "philanthrocapitalism" have enjoyed growing popularity. In addition, Sen's (1985, 1999) theoretical work that emphasized the importance of individual choice and capability enhancement inspired many scholars who were critical of government involvement in social welfare and believed that nonprofits and commercial providers should play a much more extensive role in the field.

Nonprofits and Faith-Based Organizations in an International Context

No one knows how many nonprofits and faith-based organizations there are in the world today. Although estimates have been made, they are based on limited and inaccurate data. In Western countries like the United States, most of these organizations apply for tax-exempt status so that a good deal of information about their activities is available. This is also the case in countries where they are required by law to register with the government. However, many small organizations do not register and sometimes the official data do not distinguish between nonprofits and other types of organizations, such as religious congregations or professional associations. Nevertheless, it is likely that millions if not tens of millions of nonprofits are active around the world today. Anheier (2005) estimates that in the United States alone, there are approximately 1.6 million organizations with tax exempt status, and about a fifth of these provide welfare services. He points out that these data give some indication of the country's vibrant nonprofit sector that attracts sizeable donations every year, employs large numbers of staff, including professionals, and makes a significant contribution to social wellbeing. He also observes that nonprofit organizations are extensively subsidized by the government of the United States.

In most Western countries, nonprofit and faith-based organizations are associated with conventional welfare services, and indeed these services comprise a major part of the voluntary sector. Both secular and faith-based organizations are engaged in social service activities. Contracting with governments to provide services (or "outsourcing" as it is more commonly known), has become a major source of revenue for nonprofits and faith-based organizations, and as Sanger (2003) observes contracting has contributed significantly to their involvement in the welfare field. However, nonprofits are required to lobby and compete for these contracts and many are only able to secure short-term awards. On the other hand, Patel (2005) reports that in South Africa nonprofits have benefited from direct, long-term government subsidies rather than short-term contracts with the result that welfare services for children, needy families, elders, and people with disabilities are provided largely by the voluntary sector. However, Anheier (2005) notes that in the Scandinavian countries, it is accepted that social welfare services are the responsibility of government agencies while nonprofits are largely concerned with cultural, advocacy, and cooperative activities.

In Europe, where the principle of subsidiarity has been widely adopted, faith-based organizations are particularly prominent in the welfare sector. In addition, many European countries collect what are known as "Church taxes" to fund religious congregations and their social services. Anheier (2005) reports that these revenues are augmented by donations, support from large foundations, and government subsidies so that in some European countries, such as the Netherlands and Belgium, nonprofits and especially faith-based organizations are the largest employers of welfare personnel. Similarly, in Ireland, Peillon (2001) observes that church sponsored organizations dominate the welfare field. Faith-based organizations are also extensively engaged in welfare activities in other parts of the world like Latin America, where Sanborn (2005) points out that many organizations catering to poor and disadvantaged families are affiliated with the Catholic Church. Organizations representing other religious traditions are also active in other nations. They play a significant role in Muslim majority countries, and Terao (2002) reports that new Buddhist and Taoist social service agencies have emerged in Taiwan to augment the traditional welfare activities of families, clan associations, and temples. In the United States, Bartkowski and Regis (2003) point out that the federal government expanded its support for faith-based organizations through a legislative innovation known as charitable choice enacted in 1996, which was subsequently augmented by President Bush's decision to create the first Office of Faith-Based Community Initiatives in the White House in 2001. These developments contributed significantly to the expansion of faith-based organizations in social welfare.

Nonprofit organizations that cater primarily to their members are active in many countries. As noted earlier, the friendly societies, trade unions, and cooperatives paved the way for the growth of organizations of this kind, and they now have millions of members. In addition to traditional agricultural and consumer cooperatives, which have a sizeable membership in the Global South, cooperatives attracting middle-class members have emerged in many Western countries. Kelly (2012) believes that this development is fostering an "ownership revolution" that will challenge the dominance of neoliberal economic ideas. There has also been a rapid growth of cooperatives providing childcare, home help, and similar services in these countries. In addition, new types of membership associations, such as self-help and peer support groups now play a major role in social welfare and provide an opportunity for people with similar problems to share experiences and address the challenges they face. These organizations are particularly active in the field of addictions; some, such as Alcoholics Anonymous (AA) are well known and serve members all over the world and some combine peer support and services with advocacy. One example is the Independent Living Movement which was founded in California in the 1950s by people with disabilities themselves. The organization has now spread to other countries and it provides a range of services to its members and also campaigns for disability rights. The mental health consumer movement has similar goals, but it has not achieved the same degree of international success.

Advocacy organizations play a major role in social welfare today. As mentioned previously, they campaigned for social reform in the Western countries in the nineteenth century, but until recently have not been very active in other parts of the world. During the colonial era, the imperial authorities suppressed advocacy movements, and in the Soviet Union and other communist countries, advocacy was practically unknown. Today, advocacy organizations committed to social causes operate in many countries and at the international level as well. Some focus on issues such as child labor and trafficking, while others represent the interests of particular groups such as indigenous people, elders, women, ethnic and minorities, immigrants, gay people, and many more. Some are very large and successful. In the United Sates, the AARP (previously known as the American Association of Retired Persons) has a membership of about 40 million elders, and as Lynch (2011) shows, it exerts considerable political influence. Similar organizations are becoming more common in the developing world. For example, in India, membership organizations composed of *Dalit* people have been established to campaign against caste oppression, and Williams (2007) reports that federations of these organizations have been formed in some states increasing their effectiveness. More recently, Gerbaudo (2012) observes that social media is increasingly involved in advocacy. In 2011, it played a major role in challenging dictatorships in North Africa and the Middle East.

A good deal of activism also takes place at the community level. As Dominelli (2006) suggests, women's groups have featured prominently in these activities reflecting growing resistance to entrenched patriarchal attitudes and the dominance of men in local affairs. Community activism has been inspired by the pioneering work of Saul Alinsky (1946) in the United States who formulated a set of guidelines that have since been adopted by many activist groups. The writings of Paulo Freire (1972) have been equally influential and his theory of conscientization, as well as the notion of empowerment, is widely used by community organizations. Often local activism is linked to national advocacy organizations, such as The Association of Community Organizations for Reform Now (ACORN) in the United States, which coordinated a sizeable number of community partners throughout the country until it suffered from negative media coverage following allegations of mismanagement and inappropriate staff decisions. Although ACORN has been disbanded, Atlas (2010) reports that its affiliated organizations continue to function at the local level.

Many governments are suspicious of nonprofits; Tanaka (2002) reports that the government of Singapore exercises careful control over nonprofits. In the Middle East and North Africa, Clark (2004b) points out that the authorities have been equally vigilant approving of nonprofits engaged in traditional welfare activities, but suppressing those that they perceive to be a threat. However, she notes that this has posed a challenge since Islamist organizations like the Muslim Brotherhood effectively combine their social service, education, and health care programs with political objectives. In addition, the region's educated youth and growing middle-class, which have become increasingly involved in philanthropy, generally oppose authoritarian rule fermenting the recent political upheavals that still reverberate throughout the region. Although the governments of Communist China and Vietnam have encouraged the expansion of nonprofits, they also regulate their activities to ensure that they do not campaign on what are regarded as "political issues." Nevertheless, the number of nonprofits registered with the government of China has grown exponentially, and in addition unregistered organizations have become more common (Huang, Deng, Wang, & Edwards, 2013). However, to avoid a negative public opinion backlash, the government has exercised a degree of caution in controlling their activities. On the other hand, the Cuban government continues forcefully to manage civil society activities.

Nonprofit organizations engaged in development comprise a major part of the voluntary sector in the Global South today. They have expanded rapidly in recent decades as international donors increasingly fund their activities. Some are small grassroots associations, others function at the national level, and yet others are large international nongovernmental organizations. (Their activities are discussed at more length in Chapter 11). As mentioned earlier, nonprofits in the development field are known as nongovernmental organizations (NGOs) reflecting the original use of the term in the United Nations Charter of 1945 (Lewis & Kanji, 2009). In addition, faith-based organizations have become increasingly involved in development projects in the Global South. Marshall and Van Saanen (2007) note that faith-based organizations representing many different denominations provide nutritional programs, water supply, and community development activities that augment the hospitals, schools, and traditional social service agencies established by missionaries.

Midgley (2014) observes that a primary characteristic of nonprofits in the development field is their commitment to both economic and social development programs and projects. As mentioned earlier, this is also a feature of cooperatives, which integrate economic activities with health, education, childcare, and other social services. It also characterizes many community development organizations with their roots in traditional communal village activities. Sooryamoorty and Gangrade (2001) point out that these activities formed the basis of the community development programs introduced by Gandhi and Tagore in India before independence, which inspired the British colonial authorities and subsequently the United Nations to promote community development around the world. Although community development was originally managed by government agencies, the involvement of countless independent nonprofit community development organizations has changed the field significantly.

This is also the case in Bangladesh where nonprofits play a very active role in the country's development. Bangladesh also has some of the best known development nonprofits in the Global South, including the Grameen Bank founded by Muhammad Yunus in 1983, and BRAC (originally known as the Bangladesh Rural Advancement Committee). Founded by Fazle Hassan Abed in 1972, BRAC is involved in a wide range of development activities targeted at the poorest rural families, especially landless laborers and poor women. Transcending an earlier commitment to provide disaster relief, it now promotes local economic activities as well as health, education, and nutritional services through a countrywide network of village organizations. Smillie (2009) reports that BRAC has expanded its activities to other developing countries, including Afghanistan, Sri Lanka, Tanzania, and Uganda. Serving more than 120 million people, it is believed to be the largest nonprofit engaged in development in the world.

With the resurgence of market liberalism in the 1980s, the view that nonprofits should embrace business methods became popular and laid the foundations for the social enterprise approach and for a new emphasis on entrepreneurship, managerial efficiency, and market participation in the voluntary sector. Thompson and Scott (2014) reveal that while there is no standard definition of a social enterprise, the term is widely used to characterize nonprofit organizations that compete in the market with other enterprises, have social goals, and reinvest their profits rather than distributing them to shareholders. They point out that many different types of organizations, including cooperatives, faith-based organizations, fair trade bodies, microfinance banks, credit unions, and community-based organizations are included. However, Nicholls (2008) observes that advocates of the social enterprise approach recognize that success is not only dependent on the adoption of business methods, but of entrepreneurial skills that foster innovation and competitiveness. These qualities are particularly important as many more nonprofits compete for contracts from governments and foundations, reflecting, as Anderson (2014) points out, a wider commitment to social innovation and the adoption of market principles in the nonprofit sector. Salamon (2014) agrees, noting that the marketization of nonprofit activities is fostering a revolution on the frontiers of philanthropy today.

There are many different types of market related nonprofit activities. Corporate social responsibility is the oldest. Based on long-standing paternalistic practices among business leaders, it refers to the allocation of resources to nonprofits. In Latin America, Aguero (2005) reports that corporate social responsibility plays a major role in the region's nonprofit sector noting that, in Brazil alone, 734 large firms reported that they had social responsibility programs. In addition, a number of philanthropic or social venture funds have been created to attract donors and commercial investors wishing to invest in social programs. However, unlike social enterprises, these funds pay dividends. As shown in Chapter 7, social venture funds and other market innovations, such as social impact bonds, link the interests of nonprofits and commercial providers in social welfare. An interesting version of this approach is Big Society Capital, an organization created by the British government in 2010 to allocate unclaimed funds in dormant bank accounts to enterprising nonprofit organizations (Nicholls, 2014). Large philanthropic foundations founded by wealthy people have a similar mission. Hammack and Anheier (2013) point out that many have sizeable resources, and through grant making exert considerable influence on the nonprofit sector. Although primarily based in the United States and other Western countries, these philanthropic foundations are appearing in other parts of the world as well. They place great emphasis on entrepreneurship and managerial efficiency further contributing to the way that nonprofits operate today. Although many in the voluntary field are dismayed by the new emphasis on managerialism and marketism, others like Bishop and Green (2008) claim that "philanthrocapitalism" as they call it, can save the world.

Finally, mention should be made of the contributions of millions of ordinary people who donate to nonprofits and faith-based organizations or volunteer their time to support their activities. Today, volunteering is extensive and contributes significantly to the work of nonprofits around the world. Anheier (2005) reports on a study of thirty-five countries which found that the contribution of volunteers was equivalent to almost 17 million full-time staff. The highest rates of volunteering were found in European countries, such as the Netherlands and Sweden. The Internet has also facilitated giving through various websites like *GiveDirectly* and through social media appeals that help people with urgent needs.

Nonprofit organizations that recruit and deploy volunteers have become much more common. Initially, volunteering was associated with governmental programs like the Peace Corps, established by President Kennedy in the United States in the 1960s to send volunteers to work in community projects in the developing world (Cobbs Hoffman, 2000). Since then, this approach has been emulated by many other governments as well as nonprofit organizations that not only recruit volunteers for international development, but for domestic social service as well. Today, these organizations sponsor a great variety of programs in the Western countries, and increasingly in developing countries as well where youth organizations associated with political parties or religious bodies often engage in community service projects. In the United States, Bass (2013) reports that multiple volunteer organizations sponsored by the government as well as other organizations now provide services to communities throughout the country.

The Role of the Voluntary Sector

As the preceding discussion reveals, a great variety of nonprofit and faith-based organizations are engaged in social welfare around the world today providing social services, serving their members, and advocating for social causes. Their contribution is recognized and their strengths are widely commended. In particular, they are admired for creating an alternative to both the state and market and for fostering people's democratic participation in social affairs. They are believed to generate social capital, promote social solidarity, and strengthen civil society. In addition to these goals, they are said to be highly innovative and able to identify and respond to problems that others have failed to address. Unlike governments bound by regulation and bureaucratic procedures, they are dynamic and able to adapt rapidly to new circumstances. They are responsive to their members and the people they serve. Unlike businesses which are driven by profit, they provide low-cost services and are motivated by an altruistic concern for those in need. Many nonprofits are also engaged in advocacy and mobilize popular support for social causes. They have often exposed corrupt government and business practices and brought about progressive reforms. For these and other reasons, it is argued that nonprofits and faith-based organizations play an indispensable role in social welfare—and in society in general.

However, these organizations face a number of challenges, including some that are well known. The duplication of services, a lack of funds, poor management, and the personal agendas of nonprofit leaders have been discussed in publications about nonprofits for decades. However, it is difficult to generalize and to identify challenges that apply equally to all nonprofits and faith-based organizations. In fact, many well-known critiques reflect a simplistic image of traditional nonprofit welfare agencies rather than the diverse and complex organizations that comprise the voluntary sector. While some problems are particularly challenging for one type of nonprofit, they may not affect others. Also, the situation is fluid so that a problem that is pressing today may not be so vexing in the future. Although these cautionary observations should be kept in mind when assessing the role of nonprofits and faith-based organizations in social welfare, some general issues affecting many if not most nonprofits should be examined.

One of these is funding and the availability of well-trained staff and other resources. Although many people believe that nonprofits are largely financed by private donors, few recognize that they rely extensively on government tax exemptions, direct subsidies, and contracts and that they would be unable to function effectively without this support. However, this does not mean that the voluntary sector is awash in government funds. In fact, many struggle to meet their objectives. Salamon (2001) believes that despite tax advantages, a sizeable donor base, and government contracting, funding is a major problem for the nonprofit sector in the United States. The Great Recession has exacerbated the problem as budgetary cuts have reduced the funds available for nonprofits in many countries. However, it is clear that budgetary constraints are not limited to periods of austerity, but present a perennial challenge. One potential solution, Salamon (2014) points out, is the infusion of more funds from private investors and corporations into the nonprofit sector. As mentioned earlier, social venture funds, social impact bonds, and other forms of investment in nonprofits are expanding rapidly.

Although contracting for services has greatly increased the resources flowing to nonprofits, outsourcing has not been a stable source of revenues. As mentioned previously, many nonprofits enter into short-term competitive contracts that require a great deal of time and effort to prepare. In addition, consulting with donor agencies and clarifying specifications is very time-consuming. The consequence of failing to secure contracts is not only viewed as a waste of time, but can be quite serious since these organizations may need to cut services and lay off staff. On the other hand, governments are not always able to evaluate outcomes effectively, and scholars like Scott and Russell (2001) point out that there is a tendency for civil servants to routinely renew existing contracts without closely evaluating their effectiveness. In some cases, they are pressured by politicians and other interest groups to renew these contracts without undertaking careful evaluations.

This raises the wider issue of the relationship between nonprofits and funders, which in addition to governments include foundations and international aid organizations. Reference has already been made to the way the governments of a number of countries exert control over nonprofits. Even in countries like India where nonprofits have flourished, local activists have been outraged by the government's decision to restrict the flow of international funds to organizations that engage in advocacy (*The Guardian*, 2013). Similar restrictions have been adopted in countries such as Egypt and the Russian Federation in recent years. However, many governments use more subtle means to control nonprofits like rewarding organizations they approve of with subsidies and contracts. Already in the 1990s, Hulme and Edwards (1997) warned of the dangers of nonprofits becoming too close to the state. This is equally true of relationships with foundations and business firms. Although these organizations obviously have the right to decide how to allocate their funds, excessive control stifles the vibrancy of nonprofits and limits their effectiveness. As mentioned earlier, large foundations exert considerable influence over nonprofits and, in a penetrating analysis, Eckl (2014) contends that some unhelpfully shape the way problems are defined and managed, crowding out alternative perspectives that may be more useful. Faith-based organizations face similar challenges. For example, Calderisi (2013) reports that Catholic social organizations often struggle to balance the Church's teachings with their own agendas.

The independence of nonprofit organizations is also challenged by the wider social and political environment in which they operate. Zimmer (2001) observes that the prevailing corporatist welfare system in Germany, which enshrines the principle of subsidiarity, is slow to respond to innovation so that existing practices tend to be perpetuated. Although the system was somewhat liberalized in the 1990s, the nonprofit sector is still shaped by this system. The frequent use of contracting for services under the so-called welfare "reform" legislation enacted in the United States in 1996 has also affected the voluntary sector. Hasenfeld and Garrow (2012) contend that the agendas of many nonprofits in the United States have been redefined by managerialism and the wider climate of neoliberalism, thus inhibiting their ability to advocate for social rights and social justice. Similar views have been expressed about the way nonprofits are shaped by the wider neoliberal climate. Choudry and Kapoor (2013) believe that a culture of managerialism is fostering the "NGOization" of nonprofit activism in the Global South. They believe that this reflects the continued capitalist colonization of the people and cultures of the developing world. Georgeou (2012) claims that even international volunteers are being indoctrinated by the global neoliberal agenda.

However, some critics like Lang (2013) claim that nonprofits themselves are not the passive victims of these wider forces, but have in fact enthusiastically embraced professionalism and managerialism. Many organizations claiming to represent the interests of their members and of the constituencies they serve are now dominated by careerist staff and highly paid managers who pay lip service to the ideals of democratic participation. In the developing world, Choudry and Kapoor (2013) assert that many nonprofits willingly collaborate with international donors to further the careers of their staff and managers. This has not necessarily reduced the effectiveness of these organizations that usually benefit from effective management, but it has undermined the ideals on which the nonprofit sector has historically been based. On the other hand, proponents of social enterprises believe that nonprofits should be run on business principles and that this means that their staff should receive competitive salaries and others perks. Pallotta (2008, 2012) is an enthusiastic advocate of the promotion of a business culture among nonprofits, which he argues should embrace capitalism instead of "charitable works."

It is clear that the role of the voluntary sector has changed dramatically in recent times and that its historic mission to serve those in need and to advocate for progressive social change has been attenuated by managerialism, professionalization, and marketization. Although opinion polls reveal that many people continue to trust nonprofits, many believe that this trust is being eroded. Reports of abuse, mismanagement, and the extravagant lifestyles of some senior nonprofit managers in the United States undermine support for nonprofit activities and harm their contribution to social welfare. Doubts about the impact of nonprofits in the Global South have also been raised by many scholars. Despite the sizeable resources they receive, Mwansa (2013) contends that nonprofits have not contributed significantly to poverty alleviation in Africa. Even thoughtful and sympathetic scholars like Bebbington, Hicky, and Mitlin (2008) conclude that nonprofits have failed to forge a viable alternative approach to development that transcends the limitations of statism and market liberalism.

Although nonprofits and faith-based organizations are faced with these and other challenges, it should be recognized that they have made a huge contribution to social welfare and that they continue to play a pivotal role in promoting people's wellbeing around the world. However, they could be more effective if incorporated into a coherent system of provision that balances the role of the state, family, market, and voluntary sector. Unfortunately, an uncoordinated and even haphazard system of provision prevails in many nations. This is the case in Eastern Europe, where Kuti (2001) contends that the rapid expansion of nonprofits has resulted in duplication, unhelpful competition, and confusion. Similar reports have come from many other countries. Clearly, governments and nonprofits should collaborate more closely to formulate policies that incorporate their respective contributions into a pluralist welfare model that enhances the wellbeing of all.

❖

Suggested Additional Reading

Although international social welfare scholarship has focused primarily on government provision, this situation has changed as the role of non-statutory providers such as nonprofits and faith-based organizations has been recognized. Their programs and projects have been widely documented and the literature on their role in international social welfare has increased substantially. The following books are illustrative of the literature on the subject and show how nonprofits and faith-based organizations contribute to social wellbeing around the world today.

- Anheier, H. K. (2005). *Nonprofit organizations: Theory, management, policy.* New York, NY: Routledge. Written as an introduction to the nonprofit sector by one of the world's leading authorities on the subject, this book provides a comprehensive, readable, and valuable introduction to the work of nonprofit organizations. Although written primarily for students in Western countries, its insights are relevant everywhere.
- Bebbington, A. J., Hicky, S., & Mitlin, D. C. (Eds.). (2008). *Can NGOs make a difference? The challenge of development alternatives.* New York, NY: Palgrave Macmillan. This collection examines the way nonprofit organizations have contributed to international development over the years. Although supportive of the work of nonprofits, the authors point out that there are many challenges facing nonprofits seeking to promote social wellbeing in the Global South.
- Clark, J. (2004). *Islam, charity, and activism.* Bloomington, IN: Indiana University Press. Islamic teaching provides the basis for social welfare in many countries, and in this book the author discusses the way middle-class Muslims in Egypt and other Middle Eastern countries provide support for Islamic faith-based organizations and strengthen social networks that link professionals, volunteers, and people in need.
- Lewis, D., & Kanji, N. (2009). *Non-governmental organizations and development.* New York, NY: Routledge. Focusing on the role of nonprofits in the Global South, this is a readable and comprehensive introduction to the different ways that nonprofit organizations contribute to development. In addition to the role of traditional nonprofit organizations, the authors discuss the contribution of grassroots associations as well as international donors in social welfare.

- Marshall, K., & Van Saanen, M. (2007). *Development and faith: Where mind, heart and soul work together.* Washington, DC: World Bank. Since the late 1990s, there has been growing interest in the contribution of faith-based organizations to social welfare in Western countries, and in this book the author shows how these organizations are playing an increasingly important role in development. Both authors work at the World Bank and have promoted a greater awareness of the role of faith-based organizations in development.

- Salamon, L. M. (Ed.). (2014). *New frontiers of philanthropy: A guide to the new tools and actors reshaping global philanthropy and social investment.* New York, NY: Oxford University Press. The editor of this hefty, but comprehensive tome is an acknowledged authority on the nonprofit sector having worked in the field for many years. In this collection, he examines the way traditional nonprofit approaches are being superseded by market-based interventions, such as corporate social responsibility, impact investment, cause marketing, and similar innovations. The book provides an up-to-date and insightful account of the changes that are taking place in the nonprofit sector.

Professional Social Work in the International Context

ocial work is an example of how the professions contribute to social welfare. Although other professions, such as nursing and teaching also promote people's wellbeing by addressing their health and educational needs, it was noted earlier in this book that social work has historically been dedicated to solving social problems and that it is a good illustration of how professional institutions enhance social welfare. For this reason, this chapter focuses exclusively on the social work profession and its international role. Although social work has not achieved the same status and recognition as older professions, such as medicine and law, it has created professional associations, expanded its membership, established professional training schools, and secured recognition from governments, nonprofit agencies, and the other professions all of which support its claim to be the prime profession engaged in social welfare.

Social work emerged in the Western nations at the end of the nineteenth century and spread to other countries. Today, it is well established internationally. Throughout the world, social workers are employed in nonprofit and government organizations that provide a variety of social services. They are trained at professional schools established at universities and other tertiary level institutions in many countries. Professional associations have also been created to represent social workers' interests, ensure compliance with ethical and professional standards, and lobby on social causes. International associations that promote professional social work have also been active for many years.

International exchanges between social workers have grown rapidly in recent years. Social work students learn about practice trends in other countries and many schools provide field placements abroad. However, few would claim that the profession has done enough to promote international awareness among its members. In most countries, social workers are employed in agencies that serve local communities and most are preoccupied with domestic problems. Although social workers are not disinterested in international activities, they are not always able to incorporate information from other countries into their daily practice, even though most recognize that they can benefit by learning from colleagues abroad. In fact, there are many advantages in promoting greater international awareness. Practice innovations can be more widely tested, and by being knowledgeable about different cultures, social workers are better able to serve clients who come from other societies. This is increasingly important as many countries become culturally more diverse. For these and other reasons, current efforts to promote international social work are to be welcomed.

This chapter provides an overview of social work in the international context. It begins by defining social work and tracing its historical development. It then describes the features of social work practice and characteristics of social work education around the world. Next, it discusses some of the issues and challenges facing the profession and the ways that social workers have responded to these challenges. There have been lively debates among social workers on many issues affecting professional education and practice over the years. By grappling with these challenges, social workers can enhance their effectiveness and ability to promote the wellbeing of their clients around the world.

The Nature of Social Work

It was suggested earlier in this book that social work is primarily concerned with problem solving and this is recognized in many formal definitions of the profession. For example, Barker (2003, 2013) defines social work as "the professional activity of helping individuals, groups, or communities to enhance or restore their capacity for social functioning and creating societal conditions favorable to this goal." Other definitions are more ambitious and emphasize the profession's social change, preventive, or developmental functions. For example, while recognizing that social work is concerned with "problem-solving in human relationships," the International Federation of Social Workers and the International Association of Schools of Social Work resolved at a meeting in Melbourne, Australia, in 2014 to adopt a formal definition that commits the profession to "promote social change and development, social cohesion, and the empowerment and liberation of people." As is shown later in this chapter, many other definitions can be given that reflect very different opinions about social work's proper scope and function.

Arguably, the profession can best be defined by examining the task social workers undertake and the settings in which they work. Historically, they have been associated with what are known as the *practice methods* and the *fields of practice*. Social work scholars usually identify three practice methods: namely, casework (or clinical or "direct" practice), group work, and community work. Community work is also known as community organization or community practice. In addition, some scholars regard administration, planning, and policy practice as practice methods and some also view research as a practice method. Increasingly, social development is also classed as a social work practice method. Generally, the practice methods are grouped into two categories: direct or micropractice, and indirect or macropractice. Casework or clinical social work that involves direct counseling forms the core of micropractice while community practice, administration, and policy practice are categorized as macropractice. Group work, which includes group psychotherapy is generally regarded as a form of micropractice. However, there are differences of opinion about which methods actually belong to social work. Some scholars believe that administration, planning, and research are not uniquely associated with social work and should not be regarded as practice methods. Instead, they stress social work's face-to-face interaction with clients, which they believe is a distinctive characteristic of all social work practice.

The practice methods are applied in a variety of *fields of practice*, including child welfare, mental health, medical social work, school social work, aging, substance abuse, disability, probation and correctional social work, income maintenance, community work, and youth social work to name a few. These fields have been associated with the profession for many years. In addition, the organizations or *agencies* that employ social workers are also associated with these fields. The majority of social workers are employed in child welfare, mental health, and medical social work and in most countries these services are provided by nonprofits, faith-based organizations, and government agencies. However, social workers are also finding employment in for-profit organizations providing substance abuse counseling, child guidance, and marriage therapy, and some practice independently as counselors and therapists. The people who are served by social workers are known as clients or sometimes as consumers or service users. The majority of social work's clients come from low-income families although, of course, social workers also serve middle-class and higher-income clients.

Although most social workers lay great stress on their professional status, the staff of philanthropic and faith-based organizations as well as government agencies who do not have professional credentials are often called social workers. The term is also used to designate government employees who administer statutory income maintenance programs. To promote social work's status, professional associations in many countries have campaigned to restrict the term to those who hold formal social work credentials, and some governments have enacted "title protection" legislation or introduced registration and licensing that restricts the use of the term to those with these credentials. The profession's status has also been bolstered by the expansion of university-level training, which is recognized by many governments and employers. Although social work attracts people from many different backgrounds, the majority of students and professionally qualified social workers are women. For example, Weismiller and Whitaker (2008) report that in the United States more than 80% of students are women. Also, many students come from middle-class families.

There have been long-standing debates about social work's role and functions in society, but generally scholars have identified four major functions. The first is the profession's *remedial* function, which is widely reflected in social work practice today. This function is also known as social work's *problem-solving* or *helping* function. Second, social workers are involved in programs that seek to *prevent* social problems from occurring. Third, social work has an *integrative* function by which it seeks to foster harmony and social solidarity. Finally, social workers are engaged in activities that *promote* social welfare by bringing about positive social change. As is discussed later, there are disagreements among social workers about which of these functions should be given priority.

These functions are realized through the different practice methods. Casework is primarily concerned with the remedial function while youth and community programs give expression to social work's preventive function. Community-based services as well as family social work are concerned with promoting social integration. Community practice also seeks to promote change by raising the consciousness of local people and organizing them to campaign for improved services and programs. Advocacy and lobbying are also regarded as important ways of promoting change. In many developing countries and increasingly in Western countries, social work's promotive function finds expression in social development projects that seek to improve people's welfare through raising their standards of living. However, it should be recognized that a particular practice method can have multiple functions. For example, direct practice is not only concerned with remediation, but with promoting personal growth and change, and it may also involve prevention; for example, when clients are counseled to adopt healthier lifestyles and engage in recreational and other social activities that contribute to their wellbeing. Direct practice with families experiencing serious interpersonal problems can also prevent their breakup and promote their integration.

The Historical Evolution of Social Work

Social work emerged in the late nineteenth century out of the activities of charities that sought to help poor people in the rapidly industrializing cities of Europe and North America. The most important were the poor relief charities and settlement houses. Although a large number of charities gave financial aid to poor families, the Charity Organization Society, which was founded in London in 1869, is best known for transcending the poor relief approach by recruiting middle-class women volunteers to visit needy families, diagnose their problems, and formulate treatment plans. In addition to helping family members find employment or engage in self-employment, they provided counseling and referrals for medical care, job training, and other services. This approach was believed to foster a scientific solution to the problem of poverty. In time, charity visiting became known as casework and although most caseworkers dealt with the material needs of poor people, they also sought to resolve their personal problems. Casework was also applied in new fields of practice, such as child welfare, hospital social work, and probation, which emerged as new government and nonprofit agencies specializing in these fields were established. By dealing with the problems of their clients, caseworkers hoped to restore them to self-sufficiency and independent functioning.

The settlements were not concerned with treatment, but with improving local social conditions. The first settlement house, known as Toynbee Hall, was established in a poor community in London in 1884. It relied on student volunteers to run adult education classes, youth clubs, and recreational activities in order to promote participation and social cohesion. The settlements also engaged in community organizing by mobilizing people to work on neighborhood improvement projects, and bring pressure to bear on local politicians for increased resources. Many settlement house leaders also lobbied for social reform. For example, Jane Addams and her colleagues at Hull House in Chicago, which was founded in 1889, established close links with national political leaders encouraging them to address social problems, such as child labor, infant mortality, and poverty. She and other settlement leaders also established good relationships with African-American civil rights leaders and supported their campaigns. As these social reform efforts gathered support, many students who had worked in the settlement houses found employment in the government social service agencies that were established at the time to manage the government's new welfare programs.

Lubove (1965) points out that many young educated women were attracted to volunteer in the charities and settlement houses because they were denied entry to the established professions, such as law, medicine, and engineering. Employment opportunities for women in business firms and government agencies were also limited. In time, the volunteers campaigned for full-time, paid positions, and inspired by the emerging women's professions of nursing and teaching, they sought to professionalize their activities. The volunteers recognized that this required the acquisition of professional credentials through formal training programs, and soon the first social work schools owned by the charities and settlements were created. It is widely believed that the first of these proprietary schools, as they were known, was established in 1904 in New York by Mary Richmond of the Charity Organization Society, but Kendall (2000) pointed out that a nonprofit organization in Amsterdam actually established the world's first social work training program in 1899. In 1903, the London Charity Organization Society collaborated with the Fabian Society to create Britain's first social work program. The settlement houses in Chicago established the city's first proprietary training school in 1908.

With the expansion of social work education, many social workers acquired credentials that improved their employment prospects and professional status. Many also supported the efforts of social work leaders like Richmond to establish the first professional associations that would represent their interests and enhance their status. The first of these associations emerged in the United States at the end of the First World War. Another important development was the affiliation of several proprietary schools with prestigious universities, such as Columbia University, the University of Chicago, and the London School of Economics. By creating professional associations and promoting university level professional education, the founders of social work facilitated the growth of the profession as well as new employment opportunities for social workers.

Academic affiliation also fostered the publication of the first social work books and journals and the emergence of a more theoretically grounded approach to practice. Arguably, the most important social work book at the time was Richmond's *Social Diagnosis* (1917) that drew on medicine to define the social worker as a "social physician" capable of dealing with people's social problems. This approach offered an appealing conceptual exposition of practice that emphasized the need for a scientific and professional response to social problems. Her contribution was subsequently augmented by the adoption of Freudian psychoanalytic theory by Mary Jarrett and her colleagues at Smith College. Psychoanalysis became very influential in the United States and reinforced social work's dominant remedial approach. Although conceptual models of community practice based on settlement work also evolved, they did not exert the same influence as clinical practice. An important development was the adoption of the common or "generic principles" that were believed to govern all forms of social work practice. This resulted after the Second World War in the greater integration of the different practice methods into a coherent unitary model that was adopted in many American schools of social work. However, while many students were now trained in all practice methods, casework remained the preeminent practice approach, and this is still the case today.

Women also pioneered social work's development in Europe where Healy (2008) reports that proprietary schools were established on the initiative of Alice Salomon in Germany and Helene Radlinska in Poland. While some schools were affiliated with universities, others were tertiary level vocational institutions under government sponsorship. Known as *fachochschule* in Germany, the vocational training model was adopted in several other countries as well. Social work also assumed different features in different European countries. In France, it was closely related to public health and social assistance, while in Germany, the Netherlands, and Belgium it was linked to faith-based organizations that were subsidized by the government. In Sweden, the first training program was established in 1921 by Stockholm municipality and a local association of social workers. Here, the primary emphasis was on preparing students to practice in statutory settings. In Germany, Denmark, and the Netherlands, social work's historical evolution was also influenced by the ideas of Adolph Diesterweg who advocated for the training of social pedagogues to engage in community-based social education and social action programs. Although similar to community work, social pedagogy has a stronger educational component. Today, social pedagogy is practiced in youth work, residential care, and other settings in several European nations. In Britain, social work was originally more vocational than in the United States and closely linked to the different fields of practice. It was only after the 1960s and the adoption of American social work theory that greater conceptual sophistication and standardization was achieved.

Social work emerged in several African, Asian, and South American countries in the early decades of the twentieth century. The oldest school of social work in Latin

America, and indeed in the developing world as a whole was established in Santiago, Chile, in 1925. However, in some countries, social work emerged earlier as a specialized curriculum within the department of sociology—this was the case at the University of Cape Town in South Africa where a social program was established in 1924. Similarly, social work courses were established at the University of Peking with the support of an American foundation in the same year. In Argentina, the first proprietary school was established in 1930 and this was followed by the creation of a social work program at the University of Buenos Aires in 1933. These developments were augmented by the introduction of diploma level social work training programs at several Australian universities in the 1930s. Other important developments at the time were the creation of the Tata Institute of Social Sciences in Mumbai and the founding of a social work training program in Cairo in 1936.

Although social work schools were founded in several Eastern European countries before the Second World War, many were disbanded after the advent of communism. In Poland, on the other hand, social work continued to grow and by the mid-1980s, the country had 16 schools of social work whose graduates staffed the government's social services. In Yugoslavia, five professional training schools were also created to train social workers to provide staff for the public social services. These schools were similar to the German vocational schools, but in 1972 the University of Zagreb established the country's first university training program. Since the collapse of communism, social work has expanded steadily in Eastern Europe, and in Russia; Tan (2012) reports that social work has grown very rapidly in China over the last two decades. As the problems associated with industrialization and marketization became apparent, the government supported the expansion of training programs believing that the social work profession would contribute to the creation of a harmonious society. Hugman (2010) reports that in recent years social work has also grown rapidly in other former communist Asian countries, such as Cambodia and Vietnam.

The historical evolution of social work in the Global South in the years following the end of the Second World War was facilitated by different organizations. Among these were Christian missionaries who created professional schools in countries as diverse as India, Uruguay, and Zimbabwe. The Catholic Church played a particularly important role establishing a number of schools of social work in Latin American countries. International organizations, such as the United Nations and UNICEF contributed by providing consultants and technical assistance, and in countries such as Jordan and the Sudan, the first training programs emerged out of these efforts. The governments of Western countries such as Britain, France, and the United States also supported the spread of social work through their aid programs providing scholarships for students and academics from developing countries to study in the West. Scholarships to study in the Western countries were also made available to practitioners who it was hoped would assume leadership positions in the rapidly expanding public social services. This often resulted in the replication of Western social work theories and practice methods that has fostered vigorous debates about what Midgley (1981) calls "professional imperialism." Many social work educators in Latin American countries have taken a particularly strong position on this issue. Queiro-Tajali (2012) reports that in the 1960s, educators drew on the writings of Paolo Freire, liberation theology, and Marxism to challenge the remedial approach imported from the West, and offered an alternative *reconceptualization* of social work as an activist and liberating profession.

Social Work Around the World

Nobody knows how many professionally qualified social workers there are in the world today. Accounts of social work in different countries seldom provide estimates of the number of social workers, the agencies where they work, or even the number of professional training schools and their student enrollments. Estimates are available for some Western countries, such as the United States where Weismiller and Whitaker (2008) report that more than 600,000 people are employed in occupations designated as social work. However, not all of them hold professional qualifications, and of those that do, only 130,000 belong to the National Association of Social Workers (NASW), the country's leading professional association, which also has the largest membership in the world. In most other countries, the number of social workers is much smaller. For example, Noble and Nash (2012) estimate that Australia only has about 16,000 professional social workers. Further indication of the size of the profession is provided by Hall (2012) who reports that the International Federation of Social Workers (IFSW) has 80 national member organizations with a total international membership of about 500,000. Since many countries do not have professional associations, this is an undercount but it seems that compared to other professions, such as nursing and teaching, the number of social workers in the world today is quite small.

Despite the lack of statistical data, descriptive studies of social work provide some indication of the tasks social workers undertake and the settings in which they work. For example, Bettman, Jacques, and Frost (2013) confirm the point made earlier that most social workers engage in direct casework practice and deal with the problems of their clients. In many countries, the largest proportion of social workers practice in the fields of child and family welfare, mental health, medical social work, aging, probation, and statutory income maintenance. Similarly, Saracostti, Reininger, and Parada (2012) observe that in Latin American countries, most social workers are employed in statutory or faith-based agencies serving needy families with children. This is also the case in Europe where Campanini (2012) notes that government and faith-based agencies that serve needy families are the major employers of social workers. Similarly, case studies of social work in the Middle East by Soliman (2013) and East Asian and Pacific nations by Furuto (2013) confirm that most social workers are employed in social service agencies providing casework services. In China, many social workers are employed by the Ministry of Civil Affairs and the provincial and municipal governments to staff the country's urban social services (Ku, Yueng, & Sung-Chan, 2005). Hall and Midgley (2004) report that in many low-income developing countries, social workers are primarily responsible for urban-based welfare services directed at poor families, neglected and abandoned children, destitute elders, and people with disabilities; often residential services are used to cater to their needs.

As mentioned earlier, social workers in European countries are involved in social pedagogy and youth work, and in many Western countries they also find employment in schools where they provide career guidance and counseling. Social workers also practice psychotherapy, and particularly marital and child counseling. Clinical social work is well established in the United States and in some other Western countries. However, psychotherapy services are not usually provided by social workers in the Global South and they are also limited in Europe where counseling and family therapy are regarded as the proper domain of psychologists. Indeed, Campanini (2012) reports that these services are legally restricted to psychologists in Italy. Nevertheless, many social workers who are employed in conventional social agencies do provide counseling to help clients with emotional problems. However, very few are independent providers. Private practice is probably best developed in the United States where many states have enacted legislation that recognizes licensed social workers as qualified mental health providers, which entitles them to be reimbursed by commercial insurance carriers. In addition, some clients are willing to pay fees for psychotherapy out of their own resources.

In many developing countries, social workers are employed by community and social development agencies. An edited collection by Spitzer, Twikirize, and Wairire (2014) reveals that social workers in East African countries are very active in these fields; Mwansa and Kreitzer (2012) observe that this involvement has helped the profession to transcend its colonial preoccupation with remedial services. South African social workers have made a particularly important contribution by promoting developmental social work since the Mandela government adopted a White Paper that reorganized the country's social services in the late 1990s (Lombard & Twikirize, 2014; Patel, 2005). Nevertheless, Patel and Hochfelt (2012) report that remedial and residential services and the use of direct practice methods continues to feature prominently in South Africa's welfare system. Cox and Pawar (2006) observe that developmental social work has also been more widely adopted in Asian countries. For example, in India many social workers are employed in the country's Integrated Child Development Scheme (ICDS) which provides preschool education and nutrition to millions of poor children (Conley, 2010). The adoption of the Millennium Development Goals and the new Sustainable Development Goals also has implications for the social work profession. Indeed, Elliott (2012) suggests that social workers will be more extensively involved in social development in the future. Midgley (2010) agrees, believing that developmental social work will become more common in the Western countries as well. The adoption of the *Global Agenda for Social Work and Social Development* by the IFSW and IASSW in 2014 (Bailey, 2014) suggests that this prediction may be realized.

Government ministries and local authority social welfare agencies have been the primary employers of professional social workers around the world for many years, but the situation is changing as services are increasingly contracted out or outsourced to nonprofits and commercial providers. Although well established in the Western countries, outsourcing is becoming common in the Global South as well. Nevertheless, governments still employ a significant proportion of social workers particularly in the field of child welfare. In the United States, for example, child welfare services continue to be delivered primarily by the states and local government agencies. Also, social workers in some countries are involved in the provision of statutory income maintenance programs. This is the case in several European nations where these programs are often administered by local government agencies. However, Midgley (2004) reports that income maintenance is no longer a social work responsibility in Britain and in the United States.

Although governments are major employers of social workers, nonprofit and faith-based organizations also rely extensively on social workers, particularly in Western countries with a well-developed voluntary sector. As mentioned earlier, many faith-based organizations in Latin America also employ social workers. Employment opportunities in nonprofits have expanded rapidly in many low-income developing countries where international aid programs now fund many nongovernmental organizations. Although social workers in these countries have been affected by the retrenchment of statutory services following the imposition of structural adjustment programs, contracting or outsourcing has somewhat eased the situation. For example, Kreitzer (2012) points out that new employment opportunities have been created through outsourcing in many African countries, particularly in social development programs funded by international donors. On the other hand, she points out that outsourcing has created new challenges for the profession as social workers are increasingly involved in preparing proposals, bidding, and other managerial tasks.

Social workers have also become involved in activities not conventionally associated with the profession. Mapp (2008) points out that they work with street children, families affected by civil wars, trafficked women and children, former child soldiers, refugees, and victims of the HIV/AIDS pandemic. In India, social workers have been employed in factories as labor welfare officers for many years where they provide counseling and other services to workers and their families. In addition to working in conventional social agencies, Queiro-Tajali (2012) reports that some social workers in Latin American countries are employed by cooperatives or by community-based organizations serving poor families in the urban informal settlements. Some social workers are engaged in political advocacy and collaborate with progressive politicians who champion social causes, and some have also been elected to political office. For example, in the United States a number of social workers currently serve in the Congress, and in state and local governments. However, very few social workers are involved in these activities in other countries.

The extent to which social work has been recognized as a profession varies. In many countries, social work is relatively unknown and few members of the public are well-informed about social work's role. This is especially true in the developing world. Despite government support for social work in China and Vietnam, Hugman (2010) observes that few people are familiar with the profession. Unfortunately, in some countries where social workers are responsible for child protective services or for determining eligibility for income support, they are not viewed positively and in some cases they have been criticized and even caricatured in the media. On the other hand, concerted efforts have been made to promote a positive image of social work. In some countries, such as Israel, the United States, and Taiwan, professional associations have taken steps to promote the profession's image by celebrating an annual social work day, and by establishing close links with political leaders. Mwansa (2012) reports that some political leaders in South Africa have actively supported the profession by highlighting its role in helping orphan survivors of the HIV/AIDS pandemic. On the other hand, Kreitzer (2012) observes with reference to Ghana that more needs to be done to promote the social work profession. This is true of many other countries as well.

An indication of the profession's limited recognition is the relatively low salaries that social workers receive and their generally uncongenial working conditions. Although this is also true of other professions like teaching, studies have shown that social workers have not fared well in terms of salaries or promotion opportunities. As noted earlier, social workers in government service have been badly affected by retrenchment and many have been laid-off. Queiro-Tajali (2012) points out that in Latin American countries, well-paid government social service jobs are less available than before and salaries have declined. She cites a workforce study undertaken by the University of Buenos Aires in 2007 which showed a steep decline in social work salaries in recent years. Another relevant factor is gender discrimination. Similar to teaching and nursing, most social workers are women and in addition to being underappreciated, they are often subjected to discriminatory practices.

However, the social work profession has historically been committed to improving salaries and working conditions, and securing recognition for its members from governments, nonprofits, international organizations, and the public at large. Professional associations in some countries like the United States have successfully campaigned for title protection, registration, and licensing and they continue to foster improved standards in professional education. Indeed, professional education is well developed around the world today. Barretta-Herman (2012) reports that the International Association of School of Social Work (IASSW) has 410 member schools, but not all of them have joined the association so data about student enrollments around the world are limited. More recently, the association's President reported that the organization had 406 member schools in 62 countries (Nadkarni, 2014). Most of these schools are located at universities, but professional training also takes place at specialized tertiary institutions. This is the case in Germany and several other European countries; also in Indonesia where social work was originally offered at vocational schools reflecting the influence of the Dutch educational model introduced during colonial times. However, social work programs have been created at several Indonesian universities in recent years, and it is likely that university-level training in the country will continue to grow.

In India, social work is well established at universities where master's degrees are widely offered. In China, Tan (2012) notes that there are more than 200 university-based programs offering undergraduate education, and training at the master's level is also becoming available. Recently, new social work schools have been established in former Communist countries, such as Cambodia, Mongolia, and Vietnam. Hugman (2010) reports that the first degree in social work in Vietnam was introduced in 2000, but thirty universities have established programs since then. In Korea and Japan, social work education has historically been offered at universities and many social workers are employed in government agencies. Despite the growth of social work in Asia, Pawar and Tsui (2012) point out that professional education in the region is poorly standardized and except for a few countries, such as Japan, Korea, and Taiwan, strong professional associations have not emerged. On the other hand, Queiro-Tajali (2012) reports that professional associations are well established in Latin American countries where they collaborate and share experiences. Africa has fewer university-level schools of social work, but here some governments have created paraprofessional training programs for community workers who provide extensive services in the rural areas. However, to strengthen the profession's contribution to social development, greater effort is needed to integrate their activities with professional social work.

To promote standardization and enhance the status of social work education, the IASSW and the IFSW adopted the Global Standards for Education and Training in Social Work in 2004. The standards are not, as the drafting Committee (Sewpaul & Jones, 2004) points out, intended to rigidly prescribe requirements for social work schools similar to the accreditation standards used in some countries, but rather to provide guidelines and assist them to enhance quality. The Standards cover nine topics, including curriculum, field work, admission requirements, goals, ethics, and faculty resources among others. Although some scholars like Healy (2008) hail the standards as an important step toward achieving international recognition for social work, there are others who have taken a more critical position.

International Social Work: Challenges and Issues

Over the years, social workers have engaged in lively debates on the challenges facing the profession. These have fostered a greater awareness of key issues and enhanced social work's ability to respond to challenges. One of these concerns professionalism. Although most social workers are committed to professionalism, some have argued that the quest for professional status has diverted social workers from their mission to address poverty and oppression and that their preoccupation with professional recognition, career opportunities, and improved salaries has impaired their ability to solve the serious problems facing the world's people. This argument has been made by radical social workers for many years who believe that social work will be more effective if it abandons its self-interested pursuit of professionalism and joins with community activists, volunteers, and progressive political leaders to promote social justice. Recently, this issue has surfaced in debates on the Global Standards with some critics arguing that the promotion of standardized professional education undermines collaboration with those who do not have professional credentials. Others are skeptical of social work's claim to be a profession arguing that it lacks the high training standards, specialized skills, and public recognition of the established professions, such as law, medicine, and engineering. This criticism was first levied at social workers more than a century ago and although the professional associations have sought to address these concerns, social work's professional standing is still questioned. Even in the United States, where social work is highly professionalized, Stoesz, Karger, and Carrillio (2010) have castigated the low standards which they believe characterize social work education. This has impaired social work's professional standing. Nevertheless, despite these and other criticisms, most social workers remain committed to professionalism.

A related issue is the adoption of managerialism by nonprofits and statutory social welfare agencies, which emphasizes efficiency and the use of evidence-based practice to produce positive outcomes at optimal cost. Many social workers believe that this approach has undermined social workers' historical use of insight, intuition, and empathy when dealing with the problems of their clients. Social work, they believe, should not be viewed as a science, but an art in which relationships between practitioners and clients are fundamentally important. There has also been a lengthy debate among social workers about evidence-based practice and the extent to which scientific research should guide decision making. As Opych and Yu (2014) point out, very different points of view on this issue have been expressed and it remains unresolved. Others like Ferguson (2008) deplore the spread of managerialism since it diverts social work from its commitment to bring about progressive social change. Instead, he contends, a return to radical practice is needed. Dominelli (2002) agrees, urging social workers to be much more actively engaged in anti-oppressive practice.

There have also been disagreements about social work's functions and the proper roles social workers should play in society. There is little agreement about which of social work's functions should be given priority. While some believe that the profession's historic commitment to remedial practice should be maintained, others want more emphasis on prevention, social integration, or social change. Strong views have been expressed about social work's remedial function and use of direct practice, which some contend diverts the profession from its historic mission to promote progressive change. In the 1990s, Specht and Courtney (1994) provoked a lively debate by claiming that by embracing clinical practice, social workers had abandoned their historic mission to serve poor people. Others argue that social work should be more actively involved in prevention. Although neglected by the profession, they claim that preventive social work is much more effective than the crisis-driven, problem-solving approach characteristic of most social work practice. To complicate matters further, critics like Margolin (1997) take a jaundiced view of these debates claiming that they obscure the profession's role in exercising social control and perpetuating the existing power relationships.

These differences of opinion reflect the different definitions of social work which have been formulated by scholars and professional associations over the years. As noted earlier, many definitions focus on social work's problem-solving function, but others are more expansive emphasizing its role in achieving social justice by empowering and liberating people, thus challenging the view that social work is primarily concerned with social control. Unfortunately, these different interpretations foster a one-sided view that maintains long-standing divisions within the profession and undermines its multifaceted contribution. Although social work has been primarily engaged in remedial practice, it has already been shown that innovative forms of social work practice have evolved in many parts of the world. To resolve the issue, Hugman (2010) urges that a "pluralist and inclusive" view that recognizes and celebrates these different forms of practice should be embraced. His argument will resonate with many social workers who are committed to a generic approach that draws on core knowledge, skills, and values, and finds expression in roles that simultaneously foster remedial, preventive, and promotive functions.

Another major debate concerns international exchanges between social workers and the best way of sharing of knowledge and practice experiences. Social work emerged in the Western countries and spread throughout the world as missionary organizations, charities, and governments promoted the adoption of Western social work. At the time, this was thought to be highly desirable since innovations in the West were believed to be "superior" and worthy of emulation. It was only in the 1960s that scholars such as Almanzor (1967), Khinduka (1971), and Shawky (1972) drew attention to the cultural inappropriateness of Western social work and its limited relevance to economic and social conditions in the Global South. As awareness of the problem intensified, some scholars proposed new forms of engagement that they believed properly reflected the needs and circumstances of different societies. Midgley (1981) argued for greater *pragmatism* and *indigenization*, while Walton and El-Nassr (1988) urged the *authentization* of social work so that it would reflect the social, cultural, economic, and political characteristics of the societies in which it evolved. Since then, Hugman (2010) observes that the issue of appropriate transfers has been widely debated in the literature, and, as a collection by Gray, Coates, and Yellow Bird (2008) reveals, the search for indigenous forms of practice remains an important concern.

However, not everyone is persuaded that social workers should be wary of adopting innovations from other countries. In a spirited debate, Huang and Zhang (2008, 2011) take issue with Gray, Midgley, and other proponents of indigenization, pointing out that social workers benefit from international transfers and that they are quite capable of adapting innovations to fit their own needs. They also contend that cultures are dynamic and readily absorb and adapt new ideas and practices. However, Gray and Coates (2010) challenge some of these arguments noting that the uncritical replication of Western social work has been widespread in the past and continues today. For example, George and Krishnakumar (2014) observe that many schools of social work in India continue to perpetuate a Western model. Clearly, greater discretion in adapting cross-cultural innovations and promoting reciprocity and mutually beneficial learning is needed. However, significant efforts have been made to promote appropriate training and practice in many parts of the world. Osei-Hwedie, Ntseane, and Jacques (2006) at the University of Botswana have forged an indigenous training approach that is well suited to the country's needs. Similarly, vigorous criticism of the Global Standards by scholars, such as Yip (2004) and Gray and Fook (2004) on the grounds that the standards limit the ability of social work schools to develop indigenous training programs; these criticisms reflect an ongoing concern with the challenge of promoting useful and constructive international social work exchanges.

The issue of social work's proper role and functions mentioned earlier is related to debates about the profession's involvement in social justice. The view that social workers should challenge injustice by promoting progressive change goes back to the profession's inception when reformist founders, such as Jane Addams and Florence

Kelley in the United States, and Beatrice Webb in Britain, engaged in activism and political lobbying. This idea has been prominent in academic circles and among the professional associations that make frequent references to social work's progressive mission. Terms such as social change, empowerment, and social justice now pervade the academic literature and feature prominently in social work curricula, especially in Western countries. However, despite the rhetoric, there is little evidence that the profession has been extensively involved in activities that promote change. Most social workers are employed by conventional agencies that expect them to deliver services to needy clients and their families rather than to lobby on social causes. Very few professional associations engage in activism and fewer have openly challenged governments that violate human rights. In the United States, Harding (2004) points out that the profession remained silent when sanctions and embargoes imposed by Western countries in the 1990s caused great suffering and the deaths of many children in Iraq. In the Philippines, Yu (2006) reports that the profession failed to challenge the human rights violations of the Marcos regime. Writing about India, George and Krishnakumar (2014) castigate the profession for failing to take a stand against the deeply institutionalized practice of dowry, which they argue has been responsible for the deaths of many women. The profession has also been largely silent on issues such as the invasion of Iraq, the continued occupation of Palestine, the oppression of gays in several African countries, and the denial of national rights in Tibet and elsewhere. Instead, the rhetoric of social justice is used in the abstract and the indelicacy of mentioning specific abuses is avoided.

However, it should be recognized that some social workers have responded to the challenge and their contribution to promoting social justice should be recognized. Some South African social workers actively opposed the government's racist *apartheid* policies; this was also the case in Chile where radical social workers were brutally oppressed by the Pinochet regime. Less dramatically, it was mentioned previously that some social workers in the United States have been elected to office and play a vital role in progressive politics. In addition, some schools of social work have prioritized human rights content to educate students about social justice, and a great deal of progress has been made in sensitizing them to racism, gender discrimination, and other forms of oppression. The academic literature on diversity has increased very rapidly over the years and many issues that would previously have been avoided are now openly discussed. Educating students about these matters is important not only because it fosters tolerance, but helps them deal with inflammatory issues.

Although these and other issues pose difficult challenges to social work, they have been widely debated and are being addressed. However, much more needs to be done to enhance social work's status and effectiveness internationally. The profession has grown enormously over the years, but many countries still lack professional associations and social workers do not exert much influence or enjoy the recognition they deserve. Despite the rhetoric, social workers and their professional associations are not adequately involved in the political process. In addition, the problem of cultural difference needs further discussion and the search for universal ethics to which all social workers can subscribe should be pursued through a process of dialogue that may foster a greater commitment to progressive change. Serious efforts should be made to unify the profession and ensure that different perspectives on social work's functions and practice methods are accommodated. By enhancing unity within the profession, social work's ability to enhance people's wellbeing around the world will also be enhanced.

Suggested Additional Reading

Until fairly recently, very few books on social work in the international context were available and most were highly specialized. Therefore, it is encouraging that many more books on the subject are now available to meet the growing interest of students in the field. The following books should be helpful. The article by Sewpaul and Jones listed below should also be consulted since it provides useful insights into the role of international organizations in promoting social work education around the world.

- Bettman, J. E., Jacques, G., & Frost, C. J. (Eds.). (2013). *International social work practice: Case studies from a global context.* New York, NY: Routledge. This edited book comprises a useful collection of case studies of social work practice in different countries. The collection shows that social workers play an important role in child welfare, family and couples counseling, care of elders, substance abuse, and other fields. The editors also discuss key issues of interest to social work practitioners around the world.
- Cox, D., & Pawar, M. (2006). *International social work: Issues, strategies, and programs.* Thousand Oaks, CA: SAGE. This comprehensive overview of professional social work practice around the world is an extremely helpful introduction to students wishing to learn more about the field. It is not only concerned with professional social work, but with related topics, such as social development, globalization, and human rights.
- Healy, L. M. (2008). *International social work: Professional action in an interdependent world.* New York, NY: Oxford University Press. This very readable text is designed to introduce students to the field of international social work. It provides a particularly helpful historical perspective on the evolution of social work in different countries and covers related issues, such as social work education, the activities of the international social work organizations, and social work ethics.
- Hugman, R. (2010). *Understanding international social work: A critical analysis.* New York, NY: Palgrave Macmillan. This sophisticated analysis of important issues in international social work will stimulate debates on the meaning of the term, the profession's relevance to economic, social, and cultural diversity, and the role of ethics in professional practice. It offers a particularly insightful account of the impact of international exchanges among professional social workers.
- Spitzer, H., Twikirize, J. M., & Wairire, G. G. (Eds.). (2014). *Professional social work in East Africa: Towards social development, poverty reduction and gender equality.* Kampala, Uganda: Fountain. This is only one of several books that have emerged in recent years to provide detailed information about professional social work in different parts of the world. Focusing on East Africa, the editors have assembled a sizeable collection of contributions from social work scholars and

practitioners in the region, which provides helpful insights into their educational and practice roles.

- Sewpaul, V., & Jones, D. (2004). Global standards for social work education and training. *Social Work Education, 23*(5), 493–513. This article provides useful insights into how social work education is evolving around the world to set professional standards that students should meet to become effective practitioners.

7

Welfare, Markets, and Commercial Provision ❖

It is only recently that commercial firms providing social services on a for-profit basis have begun to play a significant role in social welfare. Although people have for centuries purchased services of various kinds to enhance their wellbeing, these transactions took place within the traditional culture where reciprocal obligations rather than the profit motive characterized economic exchanges. They were accompanied by family and community social supports, and in time, by the services of nonprofits and government agencies. During the twentieth century, government welfare services expanded rapidly, and because it was widely accepted that the state should be responsible for the wellbeing of its citizens, the role of markets in social welfare declined. However, as criticisms of government welfare intensified in the 1980s, some governments reduced social spending, privatized statutory services, and contracted with nonprofits and business firms to provide services on their behalf.

It was in this context that commercial providers became more extensively involved in social welfare. While some writers approve of this development, others are highly critical, arguing that it has negatively affected people's wellbeing. These critics believe that there is a fundamental contradiction between welfare and the market. The former is by definition concerned with altruism, care, and collective provision, while the latter is concerned with maximizing profits. Strong feelings have been expressed on this issue, and indeed many social welfare scholars not only reject the market, but refuse to discuss its role in social welfare. However, as will be shown, commercial providers are playing an increasingly important role and their contribution should be carefully assessed so that appropriate policies for regulating and integrating market provisions into a comprehensive welfare system can be formulated.

This chapter discusses the role of markets and commercial providers in social welfare. It clarifies terminologies, defines the scope of for-profit services, and discusses the different ways that markets and commercial firms have been incorporated into social welfare. Attention is focused on the role of privatization policies and the use of contracting or outsourcing, which has increased the number of commercial firms in the field. These policies accompany wider efforts by governments to create social, political, and economic conditions in which markets flourish. Advocates of the market approach believe that deregulation, privatization, lower taxes, and incentives will promote a vibrant market society in which people will be able to meet their own social needs. Of course, supporters of state welfare disagree, believing that social wellbeing is best enhanced by governments. These views are discussed later in this book. In the meantime, this chapter clarifies terms and concepts and traces the history of market welfare. It also discusses the different ways that commercial providers contribute to social welfare today, and then considers the policies governments have adopted to facilitate their involvement. In particular, it examines policies that encourage people to use for-profit services and to become "welfare consumers." It concludes by reviewing the limitations of the market approach and arguments against its involvement in social welfare.

Understanding Markets and Commercial Providers

Commercial firms that sell welfare services for profit include small and medium-size businesses as well as large corporations. Known as "for-profits" or commercial providers, they have been involved in social welfare in the United States for some time and are now playing a larger role in other Western countries and in the developing world as well. It is likely that their role in social welfare will continue to expand. Commercial providers are legal entities that enter into contracts with their customers and are required by law to fulfill their obligations. On the other hand, they enjoy legal protections which indemnify their owners against insolvency provided that they do not illegally or recklessly mismanage their enterprises. In most countries, governments also ensure that commercial firms operate within a wider legal framework of property rights and the enforcement of contracts. This, it is claimed, ensures fair and open competition, promotes trust, and fosters efficiency. Since commercial providers compete against each other, it is said that they are highly effective in providing goods and services at optimal cost, and that they innovate to produce new products that respond to market demand.

Markets have existed since ancient times facilitating the exchange of agricultural products, crafts, and artisanal services. In addition, families paid traditional healers when they became ill, or contributed to the costs of educating their children at religious schools. However, these transactions were embedded in social relationships and were shaped by the cultural norms of obligation and reciprocity that characterized traditional societies. Often, providers were well-known members of the community and payments were made in kind. These practices differ greatly from the way people use markets today. Markets are now largely disassociated from social networks and usually involve impersonal transactions based on price rather than relationships. Also, consumers today have access to many more providers and markets are much more complex than before. In the past, financial, commodity, and property markets were relatively distinctive and operated on a limited scale. Today, they have become very intricate systems of exchange that overlap so that it is difficult to distinguish between the multiple transactions that take place in these different markets.

The aggregation of these markets comprises what is often referred to as "the market." The term "market economy" is widely used to connote those countries where market transactions rather than traditional forms of exchange or government control characterize economic life. The goods and services traded on markets are known as commodities, and although the term originally connoted agricultural products, it now refers to any entity that is bought and sold on markets. Those who believe that markets are the best way of organizing economic affairs are known as market liberals, and as Haring and Douglas (2012) observe, they dominate economics today. Drawing on the work of their nineteenth century neoclassical predecessors, they claim that markets are self-regulating and highly efficient. They have formulated very complicated mathematical models to demonstrate that markets are the best way of producing and trading goods and services. Some economists, who are known as "market fundamentalists" or more usually as "neoliberals" go further arguing that market exchanges should be applied to all social relationships and indeed that society as a whole should be shaped by market behavior. Harvey (2005) points out that the term "neoliberalism" refers to an ideology advocating the marketization of economic and social relations and that it has largely replaced the earlier term "capitalism" popularized in the nineteenth century by Karl Marx and Friedrich Engels. Neoliberals are enthusiastic advocates of marketization, which is a process by which human activities not previously in the market are commodified and subjected to market transactions.

Because markets have been in existence for centuries, neoliberal economists believe that they are naturally rooted in human relationships and arise spontaneously to satisfy people's wants and needs. Hayek (1948, 1960) is arguably the best-known proponent of this view, but he nuanced his interpretation by recognizing that government rules and regulations are required to ensure that markets function properly and that they are not manipulated or distorted by greedy business people. However, he argued that state involvement should be restricted to providing a legal framework for market exchanges. In this way, self-interest is channeled in acceptable ways by entrepreneurs who promote economic growth for everyone's benefit. Also, Slater and Tonkiss (2001) point out that Hayek believed that markets are central for the functioning of modern democratic societies and the best way of promoting individual liberty. His approach is compatible with the views of Friedman (1962; Friedman & Friedman, 1980) who is also internationally known as a leading neoliberal.

Although neoliberals desire the complete marketization of social life, markets have historically been viewed more narrowly as a forum for economic transactions and as a separate domain distinguishable from the activities of governments, families, and communities. Adam Smith, the eighteenth-century founder of modern economics was an enthusiastic advocate of markets, but he believed that they should function in tandem with the state. While markets facilitate economic exchanges, the state is responsible for law and order, the construction of roads, and other forms of infrastructure. It should also provide education and care for those who are unable to work. Many years later, this idea was formalized by Samuelson (1954) in his theory of public versus private goods. Using sophisticated econometric techniques, he demonstrated the respective advantages of government versus commercial provision. In social welfare, the idea that private and public services are separate domains was most eloquently articulated by Titmuss (1974) who insisted that social needs differ substantively from economic wants. While markets are effective mechanisms for trading commodities, social services provided by the state are the best means of enhancing social wellbeing. Titmuss's argument was widely accepted in the 1950s and 1960s, and coupled with the idea that citizens have social rights, he provided a persuasive rationale for the rapid expansion of state welfare. Of course, many market liberals disagree with both Samuelson and Titmuss, arguing that there are no differences between human needs and economic wants and that both should be satisfied through markets.

Despite the popularity of Titmuss's interpretation, the welfare statism of the post-Second World War years was challenged by a plethora of studies published in the 1970s and 1980s that purportedly demonstrated the harm that government welfare intervention had caused. (These are discussed in more detail in Chapter 9 of this book). In addition to attacking state welfare, market liberals offered numerous proposals for increasing the role of commercial firms in social welfare. By the 1980s, some governments had already begun to outsource the social services, and many neoliberals urged that this practice be extended. Some like Friedman (Friedman & Friedman, 1980) argued for the complete privatization of government welfare programs claiming that markets are the best way of providing health care, education, housing, and even social protection. Although it is widely accepted that social protection should be a state responsibility, numerous proposals for privatizing retirement pensions and even unemployment insurance have been made. For example, scholars associated with the Institute of Economic Affairs in London like Seldon (1996) argue that commercial providers operating in the marketplace are well-equipped to provide these services.

As is well known, these ideas exerted considerable influence and provided an intellectual basis for the popularization of market liberalism in the 1980s, especially by the Reagan and Thatcher governments which embarked on a systematic program of deregulation and denationalization, tax reductions, privatization, and the outsourcing of public services. They augmented the advocacy of markets by emphasizing the importance of restoring traditional values, and were often referred to as the "radical right" (Midgley, 1991). The marketization trend also affected countries that had historically been regarded as paragons of welfare statism like Sweden, where Gilbert (2002) points out that the electoral defeat of the Social Democratic party by a pro-market

Conservative coalition in 1991 resulted in the introduction of educational vouchers, commercially managed retirement accounts, and other pro-market innovations. Since then the Swedish and other Nordic welfare states have experienced a significant growth of market provision.

In Britain and the United States, the Blair and Clinton governments did not reverse the changes introduced by their neoliberal predecessors with the result that the role of commercial providers continued to expand. In addition, they promoted the incorporation of business practices into government administration. Motivated by Osborne and Gaebler's (1992) theory of reinventing government, they prioritized notions of efficiency, targeting, evidence-based practice, and managed care in the social services. Le Grand (2007) points out that a related development was the creation of internal markets, which require government agencies to compete with each other for resources. In addition, he notes that quasi-markets that facilitate consumer choice in accessing services through vouchers have been widely adopted in many Western countries, particularly in education and health care. However, many governments meet the costs of these vouchers, and in this way continue to fund the social services.

During the 1980s, the International Monetary Fund (IMF) and the World Bank, which had previously promoted government programs in the Global South changed their lending practices to promote what the World Bank (1991) called "market friendly" development policies. Since many developing countries had become heavily indebted and sought credit from these agencies, structural adjustment programs that required market reforms were widely imposed as a condition for aid. National planning that had been adopted in many of these countries was largely abandoned and austerity measures that drastically reduced budgets and the civil service were imposed. Nationalized industries were sold at a fraction of their actual cost, or otherwise simply shut down. Government social services and community development programs were severely affected and the imposition of user charges further limited people's access to health and education. Some governments like the Pinochet military regime in Chile enthusiastically embraced the market approach by privatizing the country's social insurance program. As Borzutzky (2008) reveals, the military government's actions were informed by the ideas of Friedman and his colleagues at the University of Chicago. The collapse of the Soviet Union as well as increased globalization and economic liberalization in the 1990s, facilitated the worldwide spread of market liberal policies and the expansion of what Sanger (2003) calls the "welfare marketplace."

As noted later in this book, the expansion of the welfare market since the 1980s has also been influenced by Sen's (1985, 1999) writings, which advocate greater individual responsibility, choice, and the exercise of capabilities in social welfare. Although Sen (1985, 1999) and Nussbaum (2011) are not neoliberals, their ideas reflect a strong commitment to individualism and rational choice that Dean (2009) points out is highly compatible with the view that the recipients of welfare services should be weaned from their supposed dependency on the state and encouraged to exercise choice and access the services they need and want. Their ideas have exerted a growing influence on social welfare scholars who have historically been opposed to the market liberal approach.

Varieties of Market-Based Welfare

Various proposals for increasing the role of markets and commercial providers in social welfare have been made in recent years. They include privatization, contracting, and other innovations. Although the term privatization is used loosely to describe any type of market intervention, in this book it connotes the sale of the government's social services to commercial owners. Contracting is the outsourcing of social services through purchase of service contracts with business firms (and of course nonprofits) which then provide these services on a government's behalf. These innovations are accompanied by policies that increase the demand for commercial services, particularly among those low-income families who do not have sufficient resources to purchase services on the market. These policies, which are intended to stimulate the demand side of the market by promoting "welfare consumerism," will be discussed in more detail later. On the other hand, privatization and contracting are intended to stimulate the supply side of the welfare market. However, it should be recognized that supply and demand side policies overlap and are mutually reinforcing.

Market liberals believe that both supply and demand side marketization policies are most effective when they operate within a wider culture of individual responsibility, choice, and competition. Accordingly, they urge governments to promote a culture of this kind. As noted earlier, this does not preclude government involvement, but requires that the state's role is redefined. Instead of planning and managing the market, owning enterprises, and providing extensive social services, governments should inculcate market values and behaviors among their citizens. Recapitulating the ideas of both Hayek and Friedman, Taylor (2012) argues that governments should enforce property rights and contracts, and prevent the emergence of monopolies and other market distortions; they should also reduce taxes and ease regulations that inhibit innovation. In addition, government should promote self-reliance, hard work, and a desire to succeed. Provided these principles are adopted, markets will function efficiently and promote economic growth, create employment, and raise incomes. Similarly, Newt Gingrich (1995), the former speaker of the House of Representatives in the United States believes that by fostering competition and entrepreneurship, the welfare state will be replaced by a vibrant "opportunity society" in which people will work hard, strive for success, and meet their own social needs.

Although market liberals agree on these general principles, they disagree about the extent of government involvement. Taking a radical neoliberal position, Friedman and Friedman (1980) believed that all public goods and services, including parks, roads, water supplies, and welfare services should be transferred to private ownership. Other market liberal scholars are more sympathetic to Samuelson's notion of public versus private goods and believe that governments have a role to play in economic and social affairs. Many also recognize that there are major impediments to privatizing all collectively owned amenities; however, they generally support the marketization of the social services through privatization and outsourcing. They point out that people have historically purchased housing, food, medical care, and education through the market and that even at the heights of welfare statism in the mid-twentieth century, market exchanges were hardly extinguished. There is no compelling reason, they contend, that social services should be provided by the state.

Promoting the Supply Side

Privatization is arguably the best known method of increasing the supply side of the welfare market. By transferring the ownership of the social services to commercial firms, market liberals believe that competition will increase, prices will fall, and the quality of services will improve. Although privatization is usually associated with the sale of the nationalized state-owned enterprises that began in the 1980s and continues today, social service privatization has not been as dramatic and generally governments have preferred to retain ownership and outsource the social services. Nevertheless, public ownership of drinking water and sanitation has been widely transferred to private enterprises, and in some cases, government hospitals, and educational facilities have also been sold. Sometimes, governments have retained some control over these privatized services either through co-ownership or regulation and oversight.

This is the case with the Chilean social insurance retirement system that was privatized in the 1980s by General Pinochet's military government. Although the government retained control over the system, investment firms were allowed to receive members' contributions, manage their accounts, and pay benefits. Borzutzky (2002) points out that the privatization of the system did not abrogate the involvement of the state, but in fact required regulation as well as substantial subsidies. The Chilean innovations were widely emulated in Latin American countries and in Eastern Europe, often at the behest of the World Bank (1994), which vigorously promoted pension privatization in the 1990s. However, it should be noted that some governments have since re-nationalized their pension programs or otherwise significantly modified the way they function. Hujo and Rulli (2014) observe that this is the case in both Chile and Argentina. Also, in some cases like Hong Kong, where a social insurance retirement program had not been established, the government rejected proposals from several leading academics to introduce social insurance and instead in 1995 created a commercially managed savings program known as the Mandatory Provident Fund Scheme. Chung (2014) reports that it now caters to about 70% of the working population, but as will be shown a significant number of its members are dissatisfied with the way the program operates.

The supply of commercial providers can also be increased through purchase of service contracting, which is also known as outsourcing. As noted earlier, this involves governments entering into legally binding agreements with both commercial and nonprofit providers to deliver services on their behalf. The contract may be limited to some part of the service, such as cleaning or delivering meals in a residential facility, but it may also involve managing the service as a whole. Various funding methods are used to promote contracting, including fixed fee payments, reimbursements for approved services, capitation payments, and user charges. Contracts may be relatively short-term covering only a few years or less, or they may involve commitments for longer periods of time. Generally, contracts are put out to competitive bidding with the successful bid based on price and the prospective quality of the service. As these different arrangements suggest, contracting is a complex, multifaceted, and time-consuming activity. It is also subject to lobbying by commercial providers, which often puts undesirable political pressure on government agencies.

Contracting for services has become popular in recent years, but it is not new. Over the centuries, armies have been provisioned by private providers and the construction of roads, bridges, and other projects was often contracted out. In the social welfare field, Gibelman (1998) notes that contracting became fairly common in the eighteenth century as local municipalities in Britain and the United States paid host families to care for orphans and elders without relatives who were receiving benefits under the Poor Law. This practice was known as "boarding" or "farming out," and it was augmented by a procedure known as "auctioning" by which bidders competed with each other to take charge of needy people at the lowest cost. Outsourcing accelerated as private almshouses or workhouses that contracted with municipalities to house the poor proliferated in the nineteenth century. Today, contracting is widespread, and as Sanger (2003) reveals, many different types of social services are now outsourced. They include domiciliary services for elders and people with disabilities, employment training programs, prisons, substance abuse and mental health clinics, various types of residential facilities, child welfare programs, and child and family counseling services, among others. Commercial firms also provide support services, such as data processing, supplying equipment, and maintaining and cleaning social service facilities.

Although nonprofits still dominate the field, the growing involvement of business firms in social welfare is having a profound effect, particularly in the United States where the government's welfare to work program, which was introduced in the mid-1990s, greatly expanded the role of commercial firms in the field. A parallel development at the time was the more frequent contracting of correctional services to business firms. Contracting soon extended to many other social services, and today some very large and profitable corporations are engaged in social welfare. Some implement large-scale child welfare, employment training, correctional, and other services. There have been parallel developments in Britain, and in some other Western countries, and although not used as extensively in Europe, contracting is expanding rapidly. For example, Gilbert (2002) reports that when the German government's child care services were outsourced to nonprofits, commercial providers also secured contracts to deliver these services. In addition, business firms are now significantly involved in health care in many European and other Western nations, including Britain where the country's venerable National Health Service contracts extensively with commercial providers. This is also the case in the Nordic welfare states like Sweden where the government has extensively outsourced its health services. Its educational voucher program is also one of the largest in the region. In the developing countries, contracting with businesses to deliver government services is not as widespread, but even here the role of commercial providers is expanding.

A novel version of contracting involves the funding of social service programs by commercial investment firms. As mentioned in Chapter 5 of this book, there has been a significant growth in social venture funds, which, when coupled with corporate social responsibility programs, inject resources into the nonprofit sector, and in this way release state funds for other programs. Nicholls (2014) reports that a major innovation is the social impact bond that mobilizes commercial investments for social projects subject to the state repaying the investment plus a profit if the project has measurable positive outcomes. This approach originated in Britain in 2010, but has since been replicated on a limited basis in Australia, the United States, and elsewhere—primarily in the fields of corrections and delinquency prevention. It is likely that these bonds will be used more widely in the future.

The supply side of the welfare market is also boosted when governments create new opportunities for business firms to expand their services in parallel with government programs, or otherwise to fill gaps in existing services. This is facilitated by easing regulations that impede business involvement and introducing incentives and subsidies to providers. The governments of several Western countries have used this approach to expand commercial provision in fields such as long-term residential care, domiciliary services, and childcare. As will be shown, their involvement is greatly facilitated when governments stimulate the demand side of the welfare market by providing vouchers that permit low-income families to access commercial providers. In the United States, the multibillion dollar nursing home industry, which is controlled by a few large corporations, is primarily funded in this way.

Promoting the Demand Side

On the demand side, various policies have been adopted to promote the utilization of markets by needy people. Although many families already use the market, others rely on governments for health care, education, housing, and other social services. Rather than being passive beneficiaries of state welfare, market liberals believe they should become consumers able to exercise choice, act independently, and enhance their own wellbeing. This approach is sometimes referred to as welfare consumerism. It is not only targeted at people with low incomes, but at all citizens who, it is argued, should meet their social needs in the same way that they meet their consumption wants.

However, the success of the welfare consumerist approach depends on two factors: first that welfare recipients are properly integrated into the market and internalize market values and behaviors; and second, that they have the resources to purchase the services they need. As will be shown, various proposals for enhancing market integration have been made and these are accompanied by policies and programs that increase the purchasing power of needy people. This goal is achieved by providing vouchers, subsidies, direct payments, savings accounts, and similar innovations that give welfare clients the resources they require to become welfare consumers. Both factors promote the demand side of the welfare market.

Market liberals claim that many low-income people are poorly integrated into the market and instead rely on state benefits and social services. Accordingly, they lack the personal motivation and attitudes required to function effectively in a market society.

If low-income people are properly integrated into the market, they will adopt market values and be able to use markets effectively. For this reason, market liberals place great store on welfare to work programs that move people from "passive" dependency to "active" employment; they commend the adoption of programs of this kind, which Moreira and Lødemel (2014) report have been established in many Western countries since the 1990s. Market liberals also support job training and placement services that facilitate access to remunerative and satisfying employment.

These initiatives are augmented by microenterprise programs, which are believed to be an effective way of promoting market integration, particularly in the developing world. In addition, market liberals believe that poor people should be provided with access to credit and be educated in financial matters. As is well known, the Grameen Bank and its founder, Muhammad Yunus achieved international fame, as well as the 2006 Nobel Peace Prize, for the Bank's microfinance and microenterprise programs. Of course, social banks and credit unions that serve low-income communities have been in existence for many years, and as Weber (2014) notes, they generally have a good record of extending credit as well as banking facilities to people who are unable or do not wish to use commercial lenders. Drawing on Sen's work, Stoesz (2013) believes that community-based banks and credit unions are an effective way of promoting self-reliance and integrating poor people into the welfare marketplace.

Another proposal for promoting market integration comes from Prahalad (2005) who claims that poor people will learn market behavior when business firms sell commercial products to people living in informal urban settlements and deprived rural communities in the Global South. In addition, he argues that large corporations that have largely ignored these markets will increase their sales and prosper. His "bottom of the pyramid" (BoP) approach has been augmented by proposals to expand microfranchises operated by women in poor communities, which Fairbourne, Gibson, and Dyer (2007) believe will diffuse market values and foster market integration. As mentioned in Chapter 4 of this book, traditional welfare institutions, such as burial societies and mutual aid associations are being exposed to commercialization as rival business firms sell new products that compete with their activities.

The demand side of the welfare market depends on poor people having the purchasing power to access the services of commercial providers, and a number of recommendations have been made for providing them with the resources they need to purchase these services. One of the earliest was Friedman's (1962) proposal that income should be subsidized through a negative income tax. Although his proposal was widely debated in the 1970s, it was not implemented. However, it paved the way for the introduction of tax credits in the United States and some other Western countries by which governments subsidize the wages of low-income workers. In this way, their incomes increase and they are better able to use the market. Minimum wage mandates that have been widely adopted around the world have a similar function. In some countries, the tax system also provides credits that subsidize the costs of child care, education, and medical services that increases the disposable incomes of many families.

Purchasing power can also be increased through the use of vouchers. Like shopping coupons, they reduce the costs of goods and services. Today, vouchers usually take the form of direct bank transfers or electronic cards. By subsidizing the cost of services, Steurle (2000) points out that they not only meet social needs, but allow people to exercise choice. This is especially true of educational vouchers which Le Grand (2007) reports have been used in many countries to allow parents to choose between different schools, and in this way to increase competition between schools and improve educational quality. Educational vouchers are usually available to all citizens, but other types of vouchers are targeted at low-income families to subsidize the costs of child care, housing, and food. In the case of child care and housing, vouchers are primarily intended to meet needs rather than promote market competition, but they do increase the supply of commercial providers. This is also the case with nutritional vouchers, such as the Supplemental Nutrition Assistance Program (SNAP) in the United States, which allows recipients to use their vouchers at commercial supermarkets and grocery shops. Hoefer and Curry (2012) point out that it is one of the largest voucher programs in the world.

Vouchers are also an important way of subsidizing the costs of home-based care for elders and people with disabilities. In several countries, they are used to pay relatives or neighbors to care for elders and people with disabilities who live in their own homes. This limits the use of residential services and augments the services of commercial home help providers. Some countries also provide kinship care payments to relatives who care for neglected or orphaned children. There has also been a rapid growth in what is known as consumer directed care in a number of Western countries. Leece and Bornat (2006) explain that government agencies using this approach allocate a fixed annual sum of money to elders and people with disabilities who use these funds to purchase the domiciliary and other services they require. Also known as direct payments or personal care budgets, this approach is similar to issuing vouchers that allow clients to exercise choice and make decisions that enhance their own wellbeing. A different, but quite radical idea comes from Murray (2006) who proposes that the total per capita cost of welfare spending in the United States, which amounts to approximately $10,000 per annum, be paid to each citizen through a voucher that can be used to purchase social services of their choice. Of course, his proposal also requires that the government's existing welfare programs be terminated.

Another way of increasing the demand for commercial services is to create subsidized and tax advantaged savings accounts that promote the accumulation of funds for retirement, health care, schooling, and home purchase. As mentioned earlier, tax advantaged retirement savings accounts managed by commercial providers have been established in many Western countries. Although these programs are available to all citizens, others are targeted at low-income families. An important example is the Individual Development Account (IDA) developed by Sherraden (1991), which matches the savings of poor people enabling them to accumulate funds for education, homeownership, and small business start-ups. Midgley (2014) observes that IDAs have been created in a number of countries, but are still limited in scope. Cheung and Delavega (2011) report that some countries have also established tax advantaged child savings accounts which help low-income families with children save for educational and other purposes. One of the best-known is the Child Trust Fund that was established in Britain in 2005, but was subsequently abolished by the Conservative coalition government.

Finally, several Western governments have introduced tax incentives that encourage people to purchase commercial insurance and savings products that provide income protection in old age. These products coexist with the government's statutory retirement system, and in some countries like the United States, they are extensively used. Although it was previously believed that social insurance pensions would provide an adequate income for retirement, many claim that tax advantaged savings accounts are needed to supplement statutory social insurance programs. Some governments have also introduced mandatory supplementary pensions managed by commercial providers, which augment the statutory social insurance program. However, in most cases, the decision to open a commercially managed retirement savings account is entirely voluntary.

The Limitations of Markets and Commercial Provision

Despite the enthusiasm with which neoliberals extoll the virtues of markets, their limitations are widely recognized, not only by left-wing critics, but by some market liberals themselves. Markets, they concede, are subject to distortions, manipulation, and other imperfections, and they also experience periodic cycles of rapid growth followed by slumps that have serious economic as well as social consequences. As the Great Recession tragically demonstrated, market vicissitudes create mass unemployment, poverty, homelessness, and other social problems. For this reason, there is growing support for government policies based on Keynesian principles that not only remedy these effects, but create long-term stability. Although market liberals recognize that recessions have serious consequences, they reject Keynesian remedies and believe that recessions will be automatically corrected by the market. Also, Taylor (2009) argues that government interference only exacerbates matters.

Despite driving economic growth, markets have a destructive effect on traditional culture. In the *Communist Manifesto* of 1848, Marx and Engels argued that while rampant capitalism massively increases production, it also destroys the traditional economy. Although they thought this was a good thing, heralding the transition from feudalism to the capitalist mode of production, and ultimately to socialism, other writers lament the passing of traditional society. Some like Gandhi sought to preserve the traditional culture believing that India's centuries-old way of life could be maintained by improving the village economy rather than adopting the Western industrialization policies favored by Nehru and the Congress leadership. In the United States, neoconservatives and communitarians, such as Kristol (1978) and Etzioni (1993) also worry that rampant capitalism undermines traditional values. They contend that individualism, the relentless pursuit of profits, and a culture of mass consumerism are weakening community bonds contributing to a decline in stability and increased social problems, such as delinquency and the breakdown of the family. Although they do not wish to abolish markets, they believe that commercial activities should be confined to economic exchanges and subjugated to social and cultural norms.

A related problem is that markets amplify inequalities that foster divisions between people of different occupational, income, ethnic, and religious backgrounds. Their polarizing effect was emphasized by Marx who argued that the owners of capital were becoming wealthier while the living standards of workers were deteriorating. This view has been restated by numerous scholars over the years, and most recently by Piketty (2014) in his analysis of income and wealth inequality in Western countries over the last three centuries. Inequality accompanying rapid economic growth in the Global South has also created a pattern of distorted development in which the benefits of growth accrue disproportionately to political and military elites, the business community, and the urban middle class (Midgley, 2014). In many countries, markets have exacerbated tensions between different ethnic and religious groups, and in many cases, ethnic and indigenous minorities have been left behind. Although these effects have often been tempered by redistributive policies as well as economic and social interventions that improve the standards of living of low-income families, these policies have been weakened by the ascendancy of market liberalism, exacerbating wealth and income inequalities. Even market liberals like Murray (2012) are concerned that inequality in the United States has become so entrenched that the country is in danger of coming apart.

Critics of market liberalism urge governments to address this problem by reinstating redistributive policies and intervening vigorously in the economy to promote decent employment with good living standards for all. In addition, they argue that the statutory social services and government social protection programs should be strengthened. As mentioned earlier, advocates of this approach, such as Samuelson and Titmuss draw a clear distinction between economic and social goods believing that market exchanges are appropriate for the sale and purchase of commodities, but not for social welfare. Some critics argue that it is morally repugnant to subject social welfare to market exchanges; they contend that altruism, care, compassion, and even love are not commodities that should be bought and sold. In an extensive critique, Kuttner (1997) argues that there are limits on what can and should be subjected to market transactions. Not everything, he contends, is for sale. More recently, Sandel (2012) reiterated these views by deploring the penetration of market transactions into all spheres of life, which he claims undermines the very basis of morality and sociability.

Titmuss (1971) was a vociferous critic of the marketization of social welfare. He famously castigated the buying and selling of blood claiming that donations by anonymous strangers exemplify the collective gift-giving that underpins the social welfare system. Like other social goods, blood is not a commodity, but a need which is not amenable to consumer choice. Unlike normal market transactions in which consumers exercise choice based on price and quality, they cannot choose whether or not to consume blood, and in addition they do not have adequate information about its costs and quality. Asymmetrical information, which is a technical term referring to imperfect consumer knowledge, is a major reason for frequent market failures in social welfare. A related problem is the emergence of private sector social service monopolies. Pawar (2014a) points out that the outsourcing of water management has resulted in the emergence of large monopolies that raise prices to increase their profits. Like many other scholars, he believes that water is a social good that should be supplied on the basis of need.

Another problem is the manipulation of markets by business firms. There is a good deal of evidence to show that social service privatization has been accompanied by unscrupulous practices and even corruption. Unfortunately, outsourcing often involves dubious relationships between commercial providers and politicians who direct contracts to those businesses with which they have favorable relationships. In some cases, this involves bribes or other subtle rewards that distort markets and challenge the popular belief that businesses compete fairly for contracts. In addition, business firms often collaborate with political elites who use public funds to serve their own interests rather than the needs of those they purportedly serve. The privatization of the Chilean social insurance retirement system is a good example of this practice. Borzutzky (2008) shows that the costs of the so-called "reform" of the system enriched commercial investment firms at taxpayer's expense, but did not serve low-income workers and particularly women who were unable to accumulate sufficient funds in their accounts to meet their retirement needs. In addition to influencing the political process, some businesses have engaged in outright fraud and deception. Drakeford (2000) reports that the creation of "personal pensions" by the British Conservative government in the late 1980s involved the deployment of thousands of hard-selling salespeople who persuaded unsuspecting buyers to establish commercial retirement accounts that subsequently proved to be of little value. These examples lend credence to Chang's (2008) claim that the rapid growth of outsourcing has been a major cause of corruption around the world.

In fact, business firms have historically relied on politicians for their success. Although Hayek and other neoliberals claim that markets emerge spontaneously, Polanyi's (1944) magisterial account of the spread of capitalism in Europe in the nineteenth century showed that political and business elites used their influence and authority to engineer the so-called free market to their own advantage. Although this undermined the power of aristocratic landowners, it benefited the rapidly growing merchant and industrial class. Similar practices are used all over the world today as business elites collaborate with politicians to manipulate markets for their own ends. The rescue of large banks and financial institutions by governments during the Great Recession is a dramatic example of how the resources and power of the state are used to protect markets. This is not a new development, since as Prins (2014) points out banks in the United States have historically relied on governments to safeguard their interests. Many other examples can be given of how elites in the United States are able to enjoy what Johnston (2007) calls a "free lunch" at taxpayer's expense.

Lobbyists play a major role in promoting commercial interests in the Western countries. In the United States, literally tens of thousands of lobbyists swarm around the centers of political power to secure advantages for their commercial clients. These rent-seeking practices are so successful that they are being widely emulated around the world. Political influence also ensures that tax loopholes are maintained. Although governments are deprived of billions of dollars that could be used to fund the social services, commercial interests have successfully resisted attempts to remedy the problem. A related development is the use of privatization and outsourcing to limit the collective power of the trade unions. These techniques have been used in the United States, Britain, and elsewhere to curtail their ability to secure higher wages and decent working conditions for their members.

Although market liberals believe incompetence and waste are an inherent characteristic of government administration, many examples of the failures of privatization and outsourcing can be given. In some cases, such as the privatization of the railways in Britain, inefficiency and ineptitude resulted in widespread consumer dissatisfaction as well as serious and even fatal accidents. There have been numerous scandals in the privatized correctional industry, and in commercially managed services for young offenders that are reminiscent of the accounts in Charles Dickens's novels of how the owners of private orphanages in nineteenth-century Britain maximized profits by depriving inmates of food and decent living conditions. Less dramatically, Chung's (2014) study of the attitudes of members of Hong Kong's commercially managed Mandatory Provident Fund Scheme reported widespread dissatisfaction with the system and its management.

There is evidence to show that outsourcing reduces costs, but this is often due to lower wages and poorer working conditions in contracting firms. Unfortunately, Sanger (2003) points out that there is a lack of sound empirical data on which to base conclusions about the impact of outsourcing, and anecdotal examples are widely used to challenge or justify the claim that commercial firms are much more efficient than public providers. Certainly, many examples of how contracting has improved services in transportation, construction, and other fields can be given. On the other hand, many examples of the inefficiencies of commercial providers can also be given. However, Chang (2008) points out that many highly efficient state-owned enterprises have been privatized or partially privatized for ideological rather than efficiency reasons. The key to success may not lie in ownership as such, but in leadership, staff morale, resources, and similar factors.

Although social welfare scholars have historically viewed the social services as public goods to be provided through collective means, the expansion of commercial firms in the field is a reality that should be recognized. It should also prompt an appropriate policy response that transcends the rhetorical denunciation of commercial activity. Few social welfare scholars have seriously examined the role of markets in social welfare and many have simply denounced their growing influence in the welfare field. However, a more pragmatic and engaged response is needed to formulate policies that can effectively regulate markets and use them in positive ways. As is shown in Chapter 9, some proposals for accommodating markets and commercial providers within a pluralistic welfare system have been made. These need to be more systematically debated.

---❖---

Suggested Additional Reading

Because they are generally critical of the involvement of commercial firms in the welfare field, few social welfare scholars have written about the role of markets in enhancing social wellbeing. On the other hand, there is a very sizeable literature about markets and their benefits and limitations. The following books examine different aspects of markets and also discuss the role of commercial social services in social welfare. They will be helpful to readers wishing to have a better understanding of the issues.

- Bartholomew, J. (2015). *The welfare of nations.* London, UK: Biteback. This book is a good example of the now substantial literature arguing for a reduced role for government in social welfare and the greater use of markets to meet people's needs. Ranging over developments in a number of countries, the author musters evidence to show that state welfare has harmed the economy, undermined family and community supports, and fostered dependency. These countries, he contends, would have been better off if they had not created welfare states.
- Cassidy, J. (2009). *How markets fail: The logic of economic calamities.* New York, NY: Farrar, Straus and Giroux. In this book, the author provides an engaging account of the history of neoliberal thought and its limitations. Ranging over the work of leading theorists in the field, he critically assesses their contribution showing that their ideas bear little relevance to the real world where economic activities do not comply with their abstract theoretical models. The book was published at the height of the Great Recession and is a particularly helpful account of the weaknesses of market liberal ideas.
- Friedman, M., & Friedman, R. (1980). *Free to choose.* London, UK: Secker & Warburg. This landmark book by the famous Nobel prize-winning economist and his wife makes a vigorous argument against government regulation of the economy and involvement in social welfare contending that markets are the best way of meeting people's needs and ensuring prosperity.
- Haring, N., & Douglas, N. (2012). *Economists and the powerful, convenient theories, distorted facts, ample rewards.* New York, NY: Anthem Press. The authors of this provocative book take a very critical view of the trend toward marketization in Western countries arguing that much of the academic research that supports the expansion of markets is flawed, and in fact reflects the influence that business and political elites exert on modern day economics, which has become increasingly dependent on obscure mathematical models that bear little relevance to real life. They claim that few economists are willing to challenge these models because of the recognition and funding they receive from powerful interest groups.
- Le Grand, J. (2007). *The other invisible hand: Delivering public services through choice and competition.* Princeton, NJ: Princeton University Press. The author of this very readable book contends that economic liberalization and marketization have positively affected social wellbeing in Western countries, and that by stimulating greater competition and allowing ordinary people to exercise choice when using the social services, the welfare systems of several Western countries have improved. While he does not propose that governments disengage from social welfare, the further liberalization of the welfare state will, he contends, bring positive benefits.

- Sanger, M. B. (2003). *The welfare marketplace: Privatization and welfare reform.* Washington, DC: Brookings Institution Press. This book focuses on the way government agencies in the United States are contracting or outsourcing the social services to nonprofit and commercial providers. The author provides an interesting analysis of outsourcing primarily at the local level, and concludes that current practices leave much to be desired, particularly since careful evaluations of the outcomes of outsourced services are seldom undertaken. To address this problem, she believes that more—rather than less—government oversight is needed.

Government Welfare in the Modern World

Governments (which are referred to as "states" in this book) are arguably the most important providers of social welfare today. Previously, they were primarily concerned with law and order and defense, but during the twentieth century, state intervention extended into many spheres of everyday life, including social welfare so that it is now widely accepted that governments should educate children, prevent disease and malnutrition, protect the environment, and provide a range of social services. Following the rapid expansion of government involvement, the principle of state responsibility for social welfare has been enshrined in the constitutions of many countries and in international treaties and declarations. State involvement has been most extensive in the Western countries where government spending on health, education, social protection, and social services has reached record levels. Before the collapse of the Soviet Union, social spending in the communist countries was also substantial, and in the developing countries of the Global South, it increased steadily in the years following the Second World War. Despite retrenchments and restructuring in recent years, governments continue to be extensively involved in social welfare.

The expansion of state welfare has attracted a good deal of scholarly interest. Over the last fifty years, many historians, political scientists, and sociologists have studied the way governments have intervened to promote social wellbeing, and as noted earlier in this book, the specialized interdisciplinary field of social policy emerged to investigate different aspects of government welfare. Originally, social policy was largely descriptive and focused on the social services, but over the years it has become much more conceptual, and today a substantial body of theory about state welfare has emerged. Typologies of different types of government provision have been constructed and theoretical explanations of the evolution of state welfare have been formulated. As a result of this scholarship, much more is known about state welfare around the world.

In addition, normative theories that take different positions on the role of the state in social welfare have been articulated.

Drawing on this scholarship, this chapter offers an overview of state welfare in the global era. It begins by examining the way the state has been defined, paying particular attention to the concept of the "welfare state," which is widely used in social policy circles today. Next, it traces the historical evolution of state welfare showing that while some governments previously intervened to promote the wellbeing of their citizens, state involvement in social welfare grew very rapidly to reach unprecedented levels of social spending and service provision in the twentieth century. Around the world, governments created systems of welfare provision comprising the statutory social services, subsidies, tax incentives, judicial rulings, and statutory regulation. Although this has produced a very complex system, the chapter attempts to summarize some of the key features of state welfare in different parts of the world. In the next chapter, the way state welfare has changed in recent years is examined with reference to different beliefs about government and its proper role in social welfare.

Defining the State and State Welfare

Although the term "government" is widely used as a synonym for the state, it is generally accepted that the state is a more encompassing concept involving not only the legislative and executive branches, but the judiciary, military, and many other agencies that have legislative and administrative authority within a sovereign territory. This authority includes the power to make decisions, enact laws and regulations, implement policies, and compel compliance with these policies. Although most definitions recognize that the state is distinctive in its exercise of power, different views about the nature and functions of the state have been expressed. Some scholars focus on its organizational features, such as those mentioned previously while others emphasize its institutional characteristics highlighting the way states embody culturally accepted practices that have evolved over the years to shape political activities. Yet others regard the state as an arena in which the interests of different groups are represented, or in which different groups struggle to control state power.

Despite these different interpretations, most scholars accept the formative definition of the state by the German sociologist Max Weber who, as Knuttila and Kubik (2000) point out, stressed its exclusive ability to use coercion to ensure compliance with its laws. Weber claimed that no other organization or group has a monopoly over the use of power, which most citizens recognize as legitimate. In his magisterial account of the evolution of government since ancient times, Fukuyama (2011) takes a similar approach pointing out that all societies have institutions for the exercise of power that depend to varying degrees on popular legitimacy. In traditional societies, governance rested with local leaders and elders, but was legitimated by community meetings and extensive participation usually by men in decision making. In the ancient civilizations, power rested with a monarchical executive with absolute authority, but even so the support of aristocrats, religious elites, and free citizens was required to legitimate monarchical power. These societies also had sizable bureaucracies and systems of codified law that were in many ways similar to those of modern states. Nevertheless, they differed significantly from modern states, which as discussed earlier in this book, emerged after the Westphalian system was adopted in Europe in the seventeenth century and subsequently in other parts of the world. These states formalized the decision-making process and adopted procedures for implementing policies and programs. The branches of government became distinct, and constitutional provisions were gradually introduced. These events laid the foundations for modern states that emerged in their current form when formalized procedures for ensuring popular representation through the electoral process were adopted, and civil, political, and social rights were institutionalized. However, there are significant differences in the extent to which states today uphold rights, are efficient, accountable, and committed to enhancing the wellbeing of their citizens.

Diverse opinions have been expressed about the functions of the state and about what its functions should be. While Western liberals and social democrats regard the state as benign, acting in the best interests of its citizens, Marxists and critical theorists believe that it is little more than a willing agent of the capitalist class that submissively serves its interests. Radical populists and market liberals also view the state in negative terms as oppressive of individual liberty. Many also believe that the state undermines the ability of communities to determine and organize their own affairs. As is shown in the next chapter of this book, these different perspectives are supported by various arguments for and against the involvement of the state in social welfare, which have enjoyed popularity at different times.

The Nature of State Welfare

Largely because of the rapid expansion of government welfare in the middle decades of the twentieth century, the literature on international social welfare has focused primarily on statutory provision. As mentioned earlier in this book, the academic study of government welfare was pioneered by Richard Titmuss and his colleagues at the London School of Economics in the 1950s when they began to analyze state welfare programs, laying the foundations for the emergence of the interdisciplinary field of social policy. Titmuss (1968, 1971, 1974) believed that governments, and particularly social democratic governments, are best able to promote the wellbeing of their citizens by mobilizing resources and ensuring that everyone contributes to and benefits from the welfare system. State welfare, he claimed, gives expression to people's collective altruism, and in addition to meeting needs, it promotes equality and social solidarity. Titmuss's arguments augmented T. H. Marshall's (1950) contention that access to state welfare programs is a social right that should be guaranteed by governments. Midgley (2009) points out that both scholars made a huge contribution to popularizing the statist perspective in social policy. Their ideas were endorsed by social policy scholars in other European countries and in the United States where leading proponents of state welfare included Wilbur Cohen of the University of Michigan and Harry Specht and Harold Wilensky at Berkeley. These scholars are often regarded as leading members of the institutional school of social policy, or as proponents of what is known as "welfare statism" or simply as "welfarism."

When discussing state welfare, social policy writers usually focus on what are called the "big five" social services. These are social protection (including social insurance and social assistance), health and medical services, educational programs, housing, and the social work services. This latter group is also known as the personal social services or family welfare services. Although the correctional system, nutritional programs, and family planning among others also contribute to social welfare, they are seldom studied by social policy writers. In fact, research into the major social services has become increasingly specialized so that scholarly inquiry into health, education, and housing have become separate academic fields with the result that social policy is now largely focused on social protection and family welfare.

Social policy scholars point out that in addition to providing social services, governments affect people's welfare through the tax system, subsidies, incentives, mandates, and regulations. Titmuss (1958) was one of the first to demonstrate that the British government provided extensive tax breaks (fiscal welfare) and incentives to private firms (occupational welfare) that contributed positively to the welfare of middle-class people. In the United States, Howard (1997, 2007) showed that the tax system is widely used to enhance people's wellbeing creating what he calls a "hidden welfare state." Literally hundreds of billions of dollars are spent through tax incentives each year to promote homeownership, facilitate the purchase of health insurance and retirement pensions, and subsidize the wages of low-income workers. Governments also implement social policies through regulations and mandates, which for example require employers to pay their workers a prescribed minimum wage, or provide sickness and maternity leave. These mandates are now very common and complement the social services provided by government agencies. The courts also play a significant role by interpreting legislation in ways that affect social wellbeing. For example in the United States, the courts have adopted an activist approach that transcends the narrow interpretation of statutes and results in rulings that are tantamount to making law.

Social policy scholars often employ the concept of the "welfare state" when studying the welfare policies and programs of different countries. Kaufman (2012) observes that the term was introduced in Europe in the mid-twentieth century when government welfare programs were growing rapidly. Despite its popularity, Greve (2014) points out that there is no consensus about its meaning. As noted in the introduction to this book, many definitions are vague and many social policy scholars use the term without defining it at all. Greve also notes that some scholars view the welfare state as a particular type of country while others suggest that it is a particular type of government. In addition, the term is also used to refer to social policy in general so that the nexus of government social welfare provision, including the social services, laws, regulations, and subsidies that enhance wellbeing is described as comprising a country's welfare state. In this sense, countries are said to "have" a welfare state rather than "being" a welfare state. To complicate matters further, Clark (2004a) argues that the term also has a symbolic meaning serving to mobilize popular support for government intervention. He also points out that despite its imprecise use, the term is widely understood. Another problem is that many other epithets, such as "authoritarian state," "liberal-democratic state," "corporatist state," "failed state," and "developmental state" among others are now commonly used to characterize countries, and it is not clear how these terms comport with the welfare state idea.

Of these different usages, the view that the welfare state is a type of country is probably the most popular. This is reflected in one of the earliest definitions of the term by Briggs (1961) who argued that a welfare state is a country where the government intervenes to modify market forces. Many subsequent definitions have adopted a similar approach linking the notion of the welfare state to countries with interventionist governments, high levels of social spending, a strong commitment to social rights, and a good standard of living. Using these criteria, the countries of Western Europe and especially Scandinavia are usually classified as welfare states. The term has also been applied to the United States, but scholars, such as Wilensky and Lebeaux (1965), and Jansson (2005) believe that the country should be designated as a "welfare laggard" or a "reluctant welfare state." On the other hand, Japan is often classed as a welfare state even though its social spending has until recently been comparatively low.

To further complicate matters, the term is now loosely applied to many other countries, including low-income countries in Africa, Asia, and Latin America that were not previously regarded as "welfare states." This has severed its original association with countries with high levels of social spending, resulting in much confusion. Another problem is that the welfare state is a static construct that fails to accommodate the way social policies change over time. For example, the rapid expansion of government social welfare programs in New Zealand in the early decades of the twentieth century was followed by retrenchment and privatization, sullying the country's earlier reputation as a pioneering welfare state. The former communist countries of Eastern Europe, which provided extensive health care, pensions, and subsidized housing have also changed significantly over the last two decades, and today it is unclear whether they should be classified as welfare states. As noted in the last chapter of this book, even the Nordic countries have introduced a significant degree of marketization into their social policies, prompting questions about their emblematic welfare state designation.

Another problem is the Eurocentric nature of the welfare state concept which is rooted in a Western cultural approach that privileges state intervention and pays little attention to other welfare institutions. Questioning the relevance of the concept to other cultures, Walker and Wong (2013) claim that it not only reveals a Eurocentric, but ethnocentric bias reflecting the idea that Western governments that allocate substantial resources to social programs are superior to those that do not. Although these and other issues call the usefulness of the welfare state concept into question, it continues to be widely used, and is linked to attempts by social policy scholars to construct typologies of state welfare provision. These are referred to again later in the chapter, but first it may be helpful to provide a brief historical account of the evolution of state welfare.

The Historical Evolution of State Welfare

Although governments today are involved in social welfare on an unprecedented scale, some previously intervened to promote the wellbeing of their citizens by enacting mandates, or subsidizing religious charities, or providing their own social services. Among the earliest mandates with direct implications for social welfare was a set of laws promulgated by the Babylonian ruler Hammurabi in 1754 BCE. Known eponymously as the Code of Hammurabi, it contains regulations that protected widows and orphans, prohibited exploitation by merchants and landowners, regulated the employment of workers, and even the treatment of slaves (Chambliss, 1954). The Code is one of the first attempts to promulgate legal and social rights. Similarly, Hallen (1967) reports that the Indian Emperor Chandragupta Maurya, who reigned from 322 to 298 BCE, enacted several statutes to protect vulnerable and needy people. Another example is given by Mesa-Lago (1978) who reveals that the Aztec and Inca civilizations required local communities to cultivate a communal plot of land to support widows, orphans, and the infirm. Midgley (1984) observes that in the seventh-century Islamic world, the Caliph Omar formalized Islamic welfare practice by establishing public treasuries or *beit-al-mal* into which *zakat* contributions were paid. Although the centralized collection of zakat was subsequently abandoned, it has recently been revised by several Islamic governments.

Despite these early examples, nonformal institutions and religious philanthropy remained the primary form of social welfare for most of human history. A major change took place in Northern Europe after the Reformation when poor relief provided by the Protestant churches was augmented by municipal programs. This development was followed by the enactment of the Elizabethan Poor Law in England in 1601, which de Schweinitz (1943) noted was Europe's first national centrally administered system of poor relief. The adoption of this statute was prompted by a rise in the incidence of destitution brought about by war, economic upheavals, and increased population mobility. Although earlier English statutes also made provisions for the poor, the Elizabethan statute was unprecedented in scope and it is often regarded as a milestone in the development of state welfare. The Poor Law was also adopted in the British colonies of North America and in other parts of the world and formed the basis for the first statutory social welfare programs in these territories (Midgley, 2011a). Conversely, religious philanthropy remained the primary means of aiding those in need in southern Europe and in the French and Iberian colonies.

Another major step in the expansion of state involvement was taken during the nineteenth century when the German government under Chancellor von Bismarck created several statutory social insurance programs for low-income workers. The first was introduced in 1883 to provide income support during times of sickness, and this was followed by an occupational injury and retirement program, and later by unemployment insurance. Coverage was gradually extended so that most workers and their families were eventually protected by these programs. In 1908, the British government introduced a means-tested retirement pension that was subsequently replaced by a social insurance program. In 1911, Britain became the first country to provide unemployment insurance, and it also established health insurance. Many other European countries emulated these developments and by the 1930s, most had introduced similar programs. Many countries in other parts of the world also adopted social insurance, particularly for workers in regular wage employment. Mesa-Lago (1978) reports that Chile and Uruguay introduced the first social insurance programs in Latin America in the 1920s. On the other hand, Australia and New Zealand relied extensively on social assistance pensions while Kaseke, Midgley, and Piachaud (2011) observe that many British colonial territories provided retirement benefits through provident funds. These programs were designed to serve the needs of a rapidly growing male industrial working class, and are often referred to as "occupationalist" or "labourist" social policies. Since they catered primarily to male workers, feminist writers like Lewis (1992) described them as representing a male "breadwinner model" of social welfare.

In 1935, the government of the United States passed the Social Security Act that created an unemployment insurance program, a universal old age retirement, survivors and invalidity scheme, and a means-tested program for low-income families with children. This statute formed a key component of what became known as the New Deal—a term President Roosevelt used at his inauguration in 1933. It not only referred to welfare programs, but to extensive government intervention in the economy, the introduction of minimum wages and regulated working hours, improved labor relations, and infrastructural development projects designed to respond to the challenges of the Great Depression. Today, the Social Security Act remains the cornerstone of state welfare in America. Its insurance funded retirement pension program now covers almost 50 million elders and it is probably the largest program of its kind in the world. President Lyndon Johnson's Great Society initiative of the 1960s augmented the New Deal by launching medical insurance for elders, a means-tested medical assistance programs for low-income families, and community-based antipoverty programs, which had a profound effect on these communities. His administration also increased the Federal government's involvement in other social programs, such as housing and urban development that further extended government welfare intervention. In addition, an important statute, the Older Americans Act that protects the rights of elders was enacted at this time.

Another important development in the history of state welfare was the publication of the Beveridge Report in Britain in 1942. The report was prepared by a committee chaired by William Beveridge, a former civil servant, author, and director of the London School of Economics. It recommended that a comprehensive range of statutory health care, social insurance, housing, social assistance, education, and social work services be introduced. Most of its recommendations were implemented at the end of the Second World War, and at the time Britain was widely regarded as the world's leading welfare state. However, Harris (1977, p. 411) points out that Beveridge did not like the term "welfare state" believing it connoted what he called a "Santa Claus" approach to social welfare when, in fact, his report envisaged a welfare system based on full employment and extensive investments in education, health care, and housing. In the Scandinavian countries, government intervention also expanded rapidly, and as social expenditures reached unprecedented levels, the term "welfare state" was frequently used to refer to these nations. However, these initiatives were also linked to full employment policies reflecting the strong influence of Keynesian thinking in these countries. In particular, opportunities for women to participate in the labor market were expanded and governments supported this policy with extensive child care and generous maternity leave programs that facilitated women's labor force participation. In several European countries and in the United States, the expansion of state welfare involved a high degree of centralization as governments assumed responsibility for a variety of programs previously administered by the municipalities, states, and provinces.

The expansion of government welfare in the Western nations was paralleled by the social programs introduced in the communist countries. When the Soviet Union was founded at the end of the First World War, the Bolshevik government gave high priority to social welfare, but Deacon (1983) points out that its social services differed significantly from those introduced in Europe and other Western countries. One difference concerns the role of large collectivized industries and agricultural enterprises that provided health care and social services for their workers. Another difference was that income maintenance programs were directly linked to work productivity so that workers with a good employment record received higher benefits. At the end of the Second World War, when Soviet influence extended into Eastern Europe, a similar approach was adopted in these countries. However, as in the Soviet Union, resource constraints meant that access to social services and benefits were comparatively low compared to the Western countries. Although China and other communist countries in the Global South emulated the Soviet approach, Dixon (1981) points out that the primary beneficiaries of government welfare were workers in the state-owned enterprises.

When the countries of the Global South gained independence from European imperial rule in the 1950s and 1960s, many of their nationalist leaders accepted the principle of state welfare responsibility and committed their governments to expanding the social services. Midgley (2011a) points out that many built on the limited social programs introduced during the colonial period, and in particular prioritized education and health. The United Nations and its different agencies played a major role by providing technical assistance and fostering the adoption of international social rights treaties. However, Hall and Midgley (2004) observe that statutory social programs were often characterized by a distinctive urban bias. Since it was believed that the developing countries would industrialize and that rural people would migrate to the cities to find regular employment, policymakers assumed that the whole population would eventually be covered by urban social services. Today, it is recognized that with few exceptions, this has not been the case. In fact, the uneven nature of the social services has been recognized and much more attention is now being paid to the needs of the rural population, and also to migrants who live in sprawling informal urban settlements. A major event that contributed to this development was the World Summit on Social Development which was held in Copenhagen in 1995. The Summit was attended by 117 heads of states and led to the adoption of the Millennium Development Goals five years later. These have now been superseded by the adoption in 2015 of the Sustainable Development Goals by the member states of the United Nations. The Goals have provided a major impetus for the expansion of social welfare in the Global South. In addition, the promotion of a social protection floor by the International Labour Organisation (ILO) (2011) has facilitated the expansion of income protection services in many developing countries.

Many social policy scholars believe that the worldwide expansion of state welfare during the twentieth century has been driven by impersonal economic, social, and political forces. As Myles and Quadagno (2002) summarize, this view has given rise to a number of competing theoretical explanations of the reasons for increased government involvement. They show that the expansion of state welfare is attributed to factors, such as industrialization, interest group politics, and class conflict among others. However, it is increasingly recognized that these theories oversimplify very complex processes and that their highly schematic analyses belie the incremental and unsystematic nature of state welfare expansion. Instead of proceeding along a historically determined trajectory culminating in the emergence of a fully developed comprehensive welfare state, the expansion of state provision has been much more haphazard.

As mentioned in the last chapter, the rapid expansion of state welfare in the years following the Second World War has leveled off since the 1980s, and in some cases been reversed as governments retrenched, privatized, or outsourced the social services; this came about as a result of a complex set of factors that had a significant impact in many parts of the world. While many Western nations continue to allocate sizable resources to social welfare, some have curtailed social spending, imposed new conditions for the receipt of benefits, and outsourced services to commercial and nonprofit providers. Although some social policy writers believe that this has created a "welfare crisis," others disagree arguing that while the expansion of government welfare has slowed, this has not radically altered the state's involvement. Indeed, recent trends suggest that population aging, continued demand for social programs, and the negative consequences of economic upheavals will continue to necessitate government involvement. In addition, the adoption of the Millennium Development Goals and the Sustainable Development Goals as well as the expansion of social protection reveals that governments around the world continue to play a major role in social welfare. Different points of view about the changes that have taken place are examined in the following chapter.

State Welfare Around the World

It is extremely difficult if not impossible to summarize the key features of government welfare around the world today. As many more studies of statutory welfare in different countries have been published, the great variety and complex differences in state welfare between the world's nations have been recognized. To complicate matters further, government welfare is not only composed of the statutory social services, but of tax subsidies, statutory mandates, and judicial rulings, all of which affect people's wellbeing. Despite the emphasis on the role of central governments in the social policy literature, welfare programs are also implemented by local governments, including provinces, states, countries, cities, and other municipalities. It is also difficult to determine what government social welfare actually involves since outsourcing and other policies for including nonprofit and commercial providers in social welfare have been widely adopted. Nevertheless, it is possible to draw some broad and tentative conclusions about state welfare in the modern world.

This process is facilitated by welfare typologies which have been widely employed to classify countries in terms of their welfare provisions. One of the earliest typologies was developed by Wilensky and Lebeaux (1965) who distinguished between residual and institutional welfare claiming that the former characterizes countries that provide meager means-tested services that cater to the neediest sections of the population, while the latter refers to countries that extend welfare to the population as a whole. They argued that the United States has a residual welfare system, while European countries such as Britain and Sweden have institutional systems. Titmuss (1974) extended Wilensky and Lebeaux's classification by adding a third type: the work-performance model, which he believed characterized the welfare systems of Germany and the Soviet Union where health care, housing, and income support were closely tied to employment so that employees with longer service and higher wages received higher benefits. Conversely, he claimed that countries such as Britain and Sweden have adopted the institutional model and that citizens in these countries receive benefits based on their needs and as of right.

Of the many other typologies developed by social policy scholars, Esping-Andersen's (1990) is arguably the best known and most widely cited. He argues that in capitalist countries, workers sell their labor on the market turning labor into a commodity. However, unemployment insurance, state retirement pensions, and other government social programs decommodify labor even though there are differences in the degree to which this goal is achieved. In some countries, such as Australia, Britain, and the United States, there is little labor decommodification and is it widely accepted that social welfare should not undermine the work ethic. For this reason, government social services are meager, means tested, and stigmatizing. These countries, he contends, should be classified as liberal welfare states. On the other hand, in Austria, Germany, and the Netherlands, which he describes as conservative-corporatist welfare states, governments accept that social welfare is a right of citizenship and there is a moderate degree of labor decommodification. Families, voluntary, and faith-based organizations also play a major role in these countries where responsibility for welfare is devolved to these groups through the process of subsidiarity. In contrast, in Sweden and other Scandinavian countries that Esping-Andersen classifies as social democratic welfare states, the government is not the last resort, but the primary means of providing welfare. There is a high degree of labor decommodification, and citizens are freed from being dependent on the labor market for their wellbeing.

Although welfare typologies are focused on the Western countries, the typological approach has also been used in other parts of the world. Some scholars have characterized East Asian countries such as Japan, Korea, Taiwan, and Singapore as "developmental welfare states" (Kwon, 2005), or as "productivist" welfare states (Gough, 2003; Holliday, 2000). This reflects the efforts of their governments to link social welfare to industrialization and full employment. Jones (1993) believes they should be classified as Confucian welfare states since they emphasize work and family responsibility. Esping-Andersen's three world's typology also inspired Gough and his colleagues (2004) to classify African, Latin American, and East Asian countries. African countries are said to have insecurity regimes while Latin American countries have informal security regimes. The countries of East Asia are believed to constitute a productivist welfare regime.

Typologies have obvious limitations in that they oversimplify complex realities. Also, they are static representations which do not accommodate the rapidly changing world of state welfare, and they focus narrowly on statutory provisions. Nevertheless, they are helpful when seeking to identify the key features of state welfare. For example, there are many developing countries in sub-Saharan Africa, Asia, and Central America with limited statutory provisions inherited from the colonial era that may legitimately be described as comprising a residual type. In these countries, government welfare programs are poorly developed and needy people still rely extensively on family and community supports augmented by faith-based and nonprofit organizations often funded by international donors. Bevan (2004) also suggests that many African countries that can be classified as insecurity regimes have weak or corrupt governments, and often they are divided by sharp ethnic or religious differences that erupt into violence. Some are very poor, but others have substantial mineral oil wealth that is often siphoned off to political elites composed of ruling families and their supporters. Burgis (2015) believes that several African countries have conspired with Western business interests to loot the region's mineral wealth. In a number of poor countries, such as Afghanistan, the Democratic Republic of the Congo, South Sudan, and Yemen, violence has seriously impeded the ability of governments to provide welfare services; violence has also devastated the statutory welfare system in wealthier countries such as Iraq, Libya, and Syria where conflict has resulted in untold suffering. The situation is aggravated by widespread ethnic and political conflict, insurgencies, and *jihadi* militancy.

Moreover, the governments of a number of developing countries have sought to promote the wellbeing of their citizens in concert with the Millennium Development Goals. Although it was noted earlier that many have benefited from international aid, they have also mobilized their own resources and developed services appropriate to their needs. Although many developing countries inherited an urban-based residual welfare system that neglected poor people in the rural areas and in the sprawling urban informal settlements, the situation is changing. More governments are establishing community-based programs targeted at these neglected groups, and in some cases, they have introduced novel cash transfer programs directed at poor families. Following the lead of Brazil, Mexico, and South Africa, some low-income countries such as Ethiopia and Lesotho have established cash transfer programs targeted at poor families. Lesotho has joined Bolivia, Botswana, and Namibia (which are higher-income developing countries) to create universal pensions for elders. Although it cannot be claimed that these countries are moving from a residual to an institutional welfare system, their governments have made a commitment to establish a social protection floor, expand social protection as well as family and community social services, and to combine welfare programs with social development interventions.

Similar trends can be observed in higher-income developing countries throughout the Global South. North African and Middle Eastern countries have comparatively well-developed statutory programs, and they have historically provided social insurance. As more people have found employment in the formal sector, coverage has increased significantly. As Midgley and Piachaud's study (2013) reveals, this is also the case in the four "BRICS" countries of the Global South, which include Brazil, India, China, and South Africa, where governments have significantly expanded statutory services in recent years. The expansion of social protection and other statutory social services in China has now been extensively documented, and it is clear that the former communist welfare system has undergone dramatic change as the government has introduced new programs to replace the workplace welfare model adopted by the state-owned enterprises and rural communes. Although the country's social assistance program is still limited and coercive, Leung and Xu (2015) point out that the retirement social insurance program has grown rapidly even though separate systems are maintained for urban and rural workers. However, they note that the Chinese welfare system is still fragmented and challenged by administrative difficulties. In addition, Zheng and Huang (2013) observe that the country's political and administrative elites enjoy special privileges when accessing welfare services.

As the governments of other very populous countries such as India, Indonesia, and Brazil expand the statutory social services, the numbers of people covered by these programs will become very sizeable. In India, the limited services established during colonial times have been steadily extended since independence, and some of these services, such as the Employees' Provident Fund that caters to workers in regular employment, now have more than forty million members (Kaseke et al., 2011). Retirement pensions for poor elderly people in what is known as the "unorganized sector" have been provided by many of the Indian states since the 1950s, but are now being extended throughout the country. India also has an extensive rural community development program which manages a great variety of village-based economic and social development projects. Recently, the government introduced a new rural public works program known as the National Rural Guaranteed Employment Scheme, which Mutatkar (2013) reports not only guarantees regular employment to poor families to supplement their incomes, but injects cash into the local economy. In addition, the state governments operate a very large community-based childcare program known as the Integrated Child Development Scheme (ICDS), which Conley (2010) observes delivers preschool education, nutrition, immunization, and basic health care to hundreds of millions of poor children around the country. Although these programs have contributed to the decline of poverty, millions of families still live in conditions of squalor and deprivation and it is recognized that much more needs to be done to raise the population's standard of living. In addition, the government is aware of administrative inefficiencies as well as corruption which limit the effectiveness of these programs. Of course, these problems are not limited to India.

Brazil attracted international attention after its government introduced a conditional cash transfer program in the 1990s known as *Bolsa Família* that provides income benefits to poor families on condition that their children attend school and that they are immunized. Hall (2012) reports that this program currently pays benefits to more than eleven million poor families, and that it has contributed to a decline in poverty. In addition, Soares (2013) contends that it has also reduced income inequality. Levy (2006) notes that a similar program was introduced in Mexico in the 1990s and that it has also had a significant impact on the incidence of poverty. These initiatives have since been emulated in other Latin American countries and in some Asian and African countries, often with support from the World Bank. Following the transition to majority rule, the South African government also expanded the country's social assistance programs that had been racially discriminatory and limited in scope. This initiative extended coverage to millions of people, and as Patel and Trieghaardt (2008) observe, it has also reduced poverty, particularly in the rural areas.

As noted earlier, many Latin American countries followed Chile's lead and privatized their social security programs—the major exception being Brazil. However, Mesa-Lago (2008) notes that the limits of this approach have now been widely recognized. Although higher-income earners have benefited from privatized savings accounts, few lower-income workers are able to accumulate sufficient funds to receive an adequate retirement pension. In particular, women have been badly affected since many exit the labor market to rear children and many are unable to meet their retirement needs. Borzutzky (2012) reports that the Chilean government has recently amended the program by guaranteeing a minimum pension to all citizens. In Argentina, on the other hand, the government renationalized the privatized system. Huber and Stephens (2012) observe that social protection and social services are expanding rapidly in a number of Latin American countries and that this trend is largely due to the democratization of countries that were previously under military rule. Draibe and Riesco (2007) believe that several governments are attempting to link social welfare with economic development suggesting that a productivist welfare approach similar to East Asia's may be emerging. Another issue is the relative limitations of social work and community-based social services in the region, which have historically not been given as much priority as social security. This is the case in Brazil where Caetano (2014) observes that the social services are comparatively underdeveloped.

Japan and other high income Asian countries have established quite extensive state welfare programs that evolved in tandem with the rapid industrialization of the region in the decades following the Second World War. In addition, family care traditions remain strong ensuring that many elders and others in need are cared for by their relatives. Because of these factors, social expenditures in the region have been comparatively low even though living standards are high. As mentioned earlier, social policy scholars analyzing statutory welfare in the East Asian countries believe that the emphasis on work and family support is compatible with a productivist or Confucian welfare approach. In some cases like Korea, the governments initially adopted a skeptical attitude toward state welfare, but in time, health insurance, universal retirement insurance, and an unemployment insurance program were introduced. On the other hand, the government of Singapore and its First Minister, Lee Kwan Yew, were virulently opposed to European welfare statism and they extended the provident fund established during colonial times claiming that it reinforced traditional

Asian values of hard work and family obligation. However, Asher and Nandy (2008) believe that the country's welfare system is increasingly unable to meet the needs of its aging population and they urge the government to replace the provident fund with a comprehensive social insurance system. Chung (2014) observes that this issue was extensively debated in Hong Kong in the 1990s, and although it was hoped that the government would establish a social insurance program, it encountered resistance from the business community and a commercially managed savings retirement program was created instead. As noted in the last chapter, this program has serious limitations. However, Hong Kong's social assistance scheme is comparatively large, catering to sizeable numbers of low-income families, poor elders, and unemployed workers. In Singapore, Yap (2010) points out that social assistance is deliberately restricted and provided on a limited residual basis.

State welfare in the Russian Federation and the former communist nations of Eastern Europe has undergone dramatic change since communist rule ended almost a quarter of a century ago. As was mentioned earlier, welfare provisions in these countries were closely tied to the state-owned enterprises and agricultural cooperatives that operated on the socialist principle that the needs of workers would be met by these collective institutions. In addition, these provisions were augmented by government services that were quite similar to those of the Western welfare states except that faith-based and voluntary organizations played a minimal role. Most governments provided health care and education through state-operated hospitals and clinics, and schools and universities, and many had comprehensive social insurance retirement systems. In most countries, land and housing was nationalized so that the bulk of the population rented their homes from the state. However, information about the extent of coverage and the level of benefits was limited and was often shrouded in propagandistic claims that socialist welfare was far superior to that of the capitalist West. Formative studies of state welfare in these countries by Deacon (1983) and Madison (1968) showed that while most people were covered by statutory provisions, the extent and quality of coverage was lower than many governments had claimed. In addition, fiscal constraints and administrative challenges limited their effectiveness. Also, inequalities were widespread so that party members, high-ranking government officials, and military officers benefited disproportionately from state welfare programs.

With the collapse of communism, the welfare systems of most of these countries were thrown into disarray, and in some cases this resulted in widespread suffering as health care, education, and social protection programs were subjected to major budgetary cutbacks associated with the transition to a market economy. To complicate matters further, many of the new democratic governments were influenced by policy recommendations from the International Monetary Fund (IMF) and the World Bank, which were actively involved in the transition, and in some cases, pension systems were privatized and outsourcing was introduced. On the other hand, Cook (2007) reports that many administrators and politicians in these countries were reluctant to abandon the socialist model with the result that hybrid systems of provision that incorporated elements of market welfare, European welfare statism, and the former socialist approach emerged. After the situation stabilized, the government of the

Russian Federation reinstated social protection programs based on the former Soviet model. However, Cook points out that there are significant differences in coverage and the quality of services in the former communist countries. While Belarus has more or less maintained the former socialist system, other countries like Kazakhstan have embraced marketization, reducing the involvement of the central government in welfare. The welfare systems of other former Soviet states in Asia that have sizeable rural populations share many features with those of higher-income developing countries. Although a hybrid system also exists in many former communist Eastern European countries, many now have social welfare systems that are quite similar to those of the European welfare states.

The European countries have historically been regarded as welfare states because of their high social spending, preference for universal social services, reliance on social insurance for health care and retirement pensions, and the acceptance of social rights as a basis for provision. Many European nations allocate in excess of 25% of GDP to the social services. Many of these nation's citizens and politicians also believe that welfare should be provided on a collective basis since this reinforces the solidaristic cultural traditions that have historically characterized these countries. Accordingly, less emphasis has been placed on individual responsibility and the use of the market in social welfare. Although social assistance is widely used, it is not the mainstay of the social protection system. Another feature of welfare in most European countries is the payment of universal cash benefits to families with children. Known as family allowances, they comprise an important part of the statutory welfare system of the European welfare states.

However, as Esping-Andersen (1990) demonstrated there are significant differences between the welfare policies and programs of European countries. The Scandinavian countries have adopted a social democratic approach that emphasizes state responsibility and universalism while continental countries, such as Austria, Germany, and the Netherlands have strong corporatist traditions that support a more pluralist system in which faith based and voluntary organizations play a major role. In these countries, the state has major responsibility for funding, but not actually providing these services. Although Esping-Andersen did not pay much attention to southern European countries, Ferrera (1996) points out that they rely more extensively on family support than other European nations even though they also provide social insurance pensions and health care. However, a sizeable informal sector operates in many of these countries with the result that many workers are not protected by the statutory welfare system and often rely on their relatives and faith-based organizations when in need. Welfare policy in the United Kingdom also differs in many respects from other European countries. As noted previously, the country was designated by Esping-Andersen as a liberal welfare state reflecting the changes that took place since the 1980s when the Thatcher government launched a major attack on the welfare system. However, as discussed in the next chapter, the impact of the changes adopted by the Thatcher government at this time is disputed.

The policies introduced by the Thatcher government in the 1980s are no longer confined to Britain and a greater degree of marketization has also emerged in the other

European welfare states, including the Scandinavian countries where vouchers are now widely used and services are increasingly outsourced to commercial providers. In addition, there is a strong emphasis in Europe on labor activation, which involves the adoption of policies that promote employment. This approach emerged in the wake of economic stagnation and high levels of unemployment in many European countries in the 1980s and 1990s, and was also fostered by the adoption of welfare to work programs in the United States. As Moreira and Lødemel (2014) observe, labor activation is widely used throughout Europe today. Indeed, to discourage reliance on unemployment benefits, Gubring, Harsloff, and Lødemel (2014) point out that Scandinavian countries like Norway have given high priority to these programs. Many scholars believe that these developments are compatible with a wider trend toward employment focused policies that incorporate preschool childcare, maternity and family leave, and education and job training. As Bonoli (2013) observes, several European countries have also adopted what are known as labor activation or "flexicurity" policies that promote labor market liberalization while maintaining a comprehensive social protection system.

As mentioned earlier, the United States is often regarded as a "reluctant" welfare state since it conspicuously lacks family allowances and comprehensive state sponsored health insurance and relies extensively on means-tested programs. It is also claimed that the country places more emphasis on individual and family responsibility and has a weak commitment to social rights. However, this widely accepted interpretation obscures the complexity of the system that involves a variety of provisions delivered by federal, state, and municipal governments, and by nonprofits and commercial providers. Another aspect of state welfare in the United States is the widespread use of indirect measures, such as mandates, tax subsidies, and incentives. Gilbert (2010) points out that many international analyses of public expenditures fail to take into account the sizeable resources that flow through these measures; and Adema and Whiteford (2010) observe that when private expenditures on health and welfare are included, the United States has the highest social spending in the world. Private spending on housing, pensions, and health care is heavily subsidized through the tax system, and in addition direct social spending on pensions, income and nutritional subsidies, and health insurance for elders is quite substantial. The federal government's Social Security retirement insurance program, which covers almost 50 million elders, spent approximately $670 billion in pension benefits in 2013 while receiving in excess of $740 billion a year in contributions (United States, 2014). These figures are staggering and provide a glimpse into the extent of state welfare in the country, which is hardly meager. For these and other reasons, the conventional characterization of the United States as a "welfare laggard" may be questioned. On the other hand, Garfinkel, Rainwater, and Smeeding (2010) point out that while the United States was previously a leader in the fields of social insurance and education, this is no longer the case. Similarly Wilensky (2002) cautioned that social welfare in the United States remains fragmented, dependent on means testing, and that welfare outcomes are comparatively poor. There is a distinct emphasis in American social policy on programs that promote employment. Minimum wages, the earned income tax credit, health insurance subsidies, and a sizeable and generous social insurance retirement system all support what Titmuss (1974) called a work performance model. Instead of being a residual welfare state, the United States can be viewed as one of the world's leading employment focused "workfare" states where social policy is used to support and reward employment. In this respect, it shares similarities with Australia, which Castles (1996) observes has often been characterized as a "wage earners" welfare state. As Smyth (2004) points out, the country's welfare system has historically been linked to economic policies reflecting a strong Keynesian influence, but he observes that this approach has been undermined by neoliberalism. As mentioned earlier, the trend toward employment focused social welfare can also be observed in Britain, Canada, and other European countries. This issue is discussed again in the following chapter.

Suggested Additional Reading

Governments have been the main providers of social welfare since the Second World War and their activities have been extensively studied by social welfare scholars. Accordingly, the literature on state welfare is very substantial and it is difficult to identify a few key books suitable for additional reading. However, the following will be helpful for readers wishing to know more about the way governments around the world are seeking to enhance people's wellbeing.

- Castles, F. G., Leibfried, S., Lewis, J., Obinger, H., & Pierson, C. (Eds.). (2010). *The Oxford handbook of the welfare state*. New York, NY: Oxford University Press. This comprehensive publication edited by some of the leading scholars engaged in the study of government welfare is an extremely valuable resource for anyone wanting to know more about the welfare state and the way it functions in Western countries. It contains contributions that range over many different aspects of state welfare today.
- Daly, M., & Rake, K. (2003). *Gender and the welfare state: Care, work and welfare in Europe and the USA*. Malden, MA: Polity Press. The authors of this important book provide insights into the way government welfare provision in Western countries affects the lives of women. In addition to showing how women are disadvantaged and discriminated against by state welfare programs, they explain that women make a major contribution to social welfare by providing care to family members and others. The authors make a significant contribution by focusing attention on gender issues in the field.
- Kaufman, F. (2012). *European foundations of the welfare state*. New York, NY: Berghahn Books. The author is an acknowledged authority on European and particularly German social policy and in this edited collection containing some of his most important publications, he discusses the historical evolution of state welfare, the contribution of leading European thinkers in the field, and the way that government provision in Europe is changing.

- Myles, J., & Quadagno, J. (2002). Political theories of the welfare state. *Social Service Review, 76*(1), 34–57. This article provides an excellent overview of the different theories formulated by scholars to explain why governments expanded social welfare provision in the years following the Second World War. By summarizing these theories and highlighting their key features, the article will be particularly helpful to students.
- Surender, R., & Walker, R. (Eds.). (2013). *Social policy in a developing world.* Northampton, MA: Elgar. The editors of this book bring together an interesting collection of contributions dealing with different aspects of government welfare in the Global South. In addition, there are informative chapters on nonprofit organizations and international aid. The introductory chapter by Surender offers a particularly helpful account of the way scholarship into social policy in the developing countries has evolved over the years.
- Wilensky, H. (2002). *Rich democracies: Political economy, public policy and performance.* Berkeley: University of California Press. In this mammoth publication, the author, who was a pioneer in the welfare field, provides a comprehensive account of government welfare in the Western countries. Although it restates his earlier contention that the expansion of government welfare came about because of industrialization and modernization, the book covers an astonishing range of issues relating to state welfare, which demonstrates the author's mastery of the field.

Governments, Welfare, and Social Change

As noted in the last chapter, the massive expansion of state welfare in the middle decades of the twentieth century was historically unprecedented. This expansion was most pronounced in the Western countries, but government social welfare programs also grew rapidly in the communist countries and in the newly independent nations of the Global South. The growth of government welfare was also accompanied by widespread public support and the endorsement of different political parties. At the time, many social policy writers believed that the emergence of the welfare state marked the culmination of a historic process of progressive change that had significantly ameliorated the conditions of poverty and deprivation that previously characterized many Western countries. By providing adequate health care, education, income security, and decent housing, governments were addressing the problems of squalor and deprivation. As governments modified existing tax policies and expanded income transfers, many believed that the ideal of equality was being realized. It was in this context that the idealized notion of welfare state as the utopian end stage of the struggle for progress gained widespread acceptance in social policy circles. Welfare was no longer a matter of technical policymaking, but a high moral ideal.

In the 1970s, this idealized vision began to unravel as economic upheavals brought about by an exponential increase in oil prices, deindustrialization, and widespread labor disputes in the Western countries created new pressures on governments. Similar pressures affected the communist countries, and in the Global South, many governments became heavily indebted and were forced to reduce social spending. In the Western countries, academics on the political right argued that social spending was harming the economy and damaging the social fabric. Right-wing political leaders blamed government welfare for a variety of social problems and launched campaigns to persuade voters to support their anti-welfarist agendas. Although middle-class families benefited disproportionately from government welfare, many resented what they regarded as burdensome levels of taxation used to fund social services for undeserving groups of poor people. Politicians fueled this discontent by blaming single mothers, unemployed workers, and immigrants for abusing the welfare system and contributing to the economic malaise of the time. As noted in Chapter 7 of this book, the election of Prime Minister Thatcher in Britain and President Reagan in the United States marked a turning point that resulted in significant changes to the welfare system. With the adoption of market liberal policies, major changes to the economy were also introduced.

Many social policy writers believe that these events have seriously undermined state welfare. Others disagree and contend that the Western welfare states are resilient and that government provision has not been seriously affected. Still others argue that state welfare has merely been recalibrated to accommodate economic, political, and social changes. Some believe that government welfare is being renewed and they point to the adoption of the Millennium Development Goals and the European Union's Lisbon Treaty, both of which are indicative of a global recommitment to state welfare. They also observe that government welfare programs are expanding rapidly in developing countries, such as Brazil, China, India, and South Africa, and that even in poor countries governments are extending the social services to cover many more people. These different interpretations are discussed in this chapter, which pays particular attention to proposals for restructuring government welfare within a plural system of provision. But first the way that social scientists and social policy scholars have conceptualized social change should be considered.

Analyzing Social Change

Explanations of the way societies change over time and of the direction and causes of change are very old and are woven into religious texts and the writings of social thinkers since ancient times. The Greeks popularized the notion of a decline from a Golden Age, while the ancient Chinese adopted a cyclical view in which periods of progressive improvement were followed by periods of decline. In Western social thought, the idea that societies move progressively to higher states of wellbeing and prosperity was popularized during the Enlightenment. At the time, stadial interpretations that conceptualize change as progressing through discreet sequential stages were widely adopted. This approach was subsequently reinforced by Darwin's theory of evolution that had a powerful impact on nineteenth-century social thought when some sociologists drew an analogy between biological and social change, positing that societies progress through successive stages of development from primitive agriculture to urban civilization and ultimately to industrial society. By the 1950s, it was widely accepted that Western societies represented the culmination of the evolutionary process.

The view that Western societies had achieved the endpoint of development was accompanied by the belief that they are highly integrated systems able to maintain cohesion and stability. It found expression in Western economics where the neoclassical view that markets function efficiently in a state of equilibrium to balance production and consumption and promote growth and prosperity was widely accepted. Economic cycles, it was claimed, are sporadic events that are corrected through the market's self-regulating mechanisms. American structural functionalists drew on the writings of Durkheim and other nineteenth-century sociologists to emphasize the predominance of social integration rather than conflict in social life. For these sociologists, American society exemplified an ideal-typical, cohesive social system. In political science, pluralists writers like Dahl (1956, 1961) adopted an equally idealized conception of Western liberal democracies as open and stable societies that facilitate fair competition among different interest groups. These interpretations paid little attention to social change, and when they did, change was regarded as gradual and orderly.

Very few social scientists at the time viewed social change as continuous, pervasive, and inevitable. The ancient idea that societies are inherently unstable and constantly in flux, as articulated by the Greek philosopher Heraclitus, only gained popularity toward the end of the twentieth century with the writings of post-modernist scholars such as Lyotard (1984) and Bauman (1992). They rejected the static view of Western societies arguing that social, political, and economic life is fluid and contingent. Becker's (1992) theory of risk society also interpreted current realities in terms of uncertainty and volatility as did the notion of disorganized capitalism articulated by Lash and Urry (1987) and Offe and Keane (1985). These scholars challenged the neoclassic economic model and argued that with deindustrialization and globalization, the world economy had become chaotic. However, these interpretations have not exerted much influence on social policy, which retains a preference for static explanations and for a limited view of change that recapitulates the ancient idea of a decline from a Golden Age, or otherwise views change in a simplistic stadial way.

The popularity of the welfare state construct in social policy also reveals the subject's embrace of a static view of society which has extensive statutory provisions and high standards of living. It is also believed to represent the fulfilment of the struggle for social rights and the achievement of social solidarity through collective altruism. As Hemerijck (2014) suggests, Western societies are often conceptualized as "frozen welfare states." Typologies of welfare states are also static, although some, such as Wilensky and Lebeaux's (1965), imply that a gradual transition from a residual to an institutional stage is possible. On the other hand, Titmuss's (1974) typology comprises three static types—the residual, institutional, and work performance models. This is also the case with Esping-Andersen's (1990) three world's typology. Although his three types are the product of different trajectories, they describe the end state of these trajectories and do not accommodate current or future change. Certainly, these typologies do not incorporate recent interpretations of social change as ubiquitous, persistent, and volatile by post-modernists and theorists of disorganized capitalism.

However, some writers have offered stadial interpretations of change that are frequently referenced in the social policy literature. One of the most widely cited is Jessop's (1994, 2000) view of the evolution of government welfare as involving a transition from the Keynesian welfare state, which emphasized the provision of services and redistributive transfers, to the Schumpeterian workfare state, which emphasizes employment and productivity. Others like van Kersbergen and Hemerijck (2012) identify three stages in which the original welfare state of the immediate postwar years was replaced by a neoliberal phase, and more recently by a social investment phase in which governments prioritize spending on education, job training, childcare, and family services. Another periodization comes from Kananen (2014) who characterizes the changes in state welfare that have taken place in the Nordic countries as moving through three distinct periods, namely a developmental phase that led up to the creation of the welfare state after the Second World War, a period of emancipatory welfare institutions which lasted until the 1980s, and the current phase, which is marked by restructuring, contractualism, and work requirements.

While these stadial interpretations are helpful in understanding welfare change, they oversimplify complex processes and patterns of services. Their highly schematic analyses also belie the incremental and unsystematic nature of state welfare expansion. Instead of proceeding along a clear historical trajectory culminating in the emergence of fully developed welfare states, the expansion of government social services has been much more haphazard. Different welfare programs were introduced by different governments for different reasons and these programs often overlap and function in an unplanned and even contradictory way. This does not mean that different periods in the history of government welfare cannot be characterized in terms of dominant themes or policy emphases. It is clear that the concerted attack on state welfare by the political right in the 1980s was qualitatively different from social policy in the immediate post-Second World War years. Nevertheless, a more nuanced interpretation of welfare change is needed. Its complexity and ubiquity should also be kept in mind when formulating normative principles on which government provision should be based.

Changing State Welfare: From Golden Age to Crisis and Beyond

The expansion of state welfare in the Western countries in the middle decades of the twentieth century was accompanied by steady rates of economic growth and widespread prosperity as wage employment opportunities increased and disposable incomes rose. At this time, many ordinary families enjoyed rising standards of living, and unlike their parents and grandparents who struggled to make ends meet, many were able to purchase a home and motor car, enroll their children in good schools, and enjoy high standards of health and nutrition. In addition to increasing access to the social services, many governments adopted Keynesian economic policies to promote full employment and rising incomes. Although many remembered the Great Depression and the ravages of the Second World War, many were optimistic about the future. Accordingly, government welfare enjoyed widespread public support and the endorsement of political parties of different ideological persuasions. Many scholars believe that the political left and right, which had previously held very different views about state welfare, now agreed that government had a responsibility to guarantee social rights and meet the needs of their citizens. Wilensky and Lebeaux (1965) claimed that this new "welfare consensus" was the inevitable result of industrialization and that all countries experiencing industrial development would converge and eventually be transformed into welfare states with similar statutory provisions. Although some scholars like Barnett (1995) challenged the notion of a postwar welfare consensus arguing that welfare expansion in Britain was actually accompanied by bitter political struggles; most scholars believe that there was an ideological convergence around the issue of government involvement in social welfare. Indeed, Pierson (1991) observed that the notion of a "Golden Age" of state welfare was widely accepted in social policy circles at that time.

Although welfare expansion was most dramatic in the Western countries, it was explained in the last chapter that there were similar developments in the communist nations and in the newly independent countries of the Global South. Although state welfare services were hardly comprehensive or adequately funded, the governments of many developing countries increased funding for the social services, and particularly health and education. Many faced growing demands from their citizens for greater access to these services, and many were inspired by nationalist ideals to improve the wellbeing of their populations. In addition, as Hall and Midgley (2004) note, economic planning was widely adopted and many developing countries experienced steady rates of economic growth. However, a major challenge was the inappropriateness of the social services and inequities in access between urban and rural areas. Nevertheless, reviewing public expenditure data from the United Nations, Midgley (1997) concluded that social expenditure in the developing countries rose significantly in the decades following the Second World War. Although many developing countries were extremely poor and some experienced ethnic violence, political oppression, and civil wars, this period was characterized by rapidly expanding welfare services with significant improvements in people's wellbeing. These developments were accompanied by the adoption of numerous international treaties which committed governments to embrace social rights. The United Nations Declaration of Human Rights of 1948 was adopted by the great majority of the world's nation states, and subsequently most acceded to international social rights treaties, such as the *International Covenant on Economic, Social, and Cultural Rights* of 1966.

The Decline From the Golden Age and the Welfare Crisis

As mentioned earlier, the idealized notion of a Golden Age of state welfare crumbled in the 1970s as economic, social, demographic, and political events undermined the welfare consensus and as writers and politicians on the political right systematically attacked government welfare. A major factor was slowing economic growth in many countries, but particularly in the Western nations where industrial production and productivity declined. Many industries had failed to modernize and others faced competition from new manufacturing centers in Asia and South America with the result that many factories in the Western countries went out of business. At this time, a number of these countries experienced serious labor disputes as workers demanded higher salaries and benefits. Another factor was the new phenomenon of *stagflation* characterized by high inflation and stagnant economic growth which appeared to be impervious to conventional Keynesian remedies.

These problems were exacerbated in 1973 when the Organization of Petroleum Exporting Countries (OPEC) dramatically increased the price of crude oil creating a global energy crisis that seriously damaged the economies of many countries. The first oil shock was followed by a second in 1979 aggravating the situation. In many Western countries, unemployment soared and factory closures increased, contributing further to the process of deindustrialization. As traditional manufacturing and extractive industries folded, many previously cohesive blue-collar communities fell into decay. Many European countries were unable to use Keynesian policies to stimulate growth or reduce persistent high levels of unemployment, and many were said to be mired in "Eurosclerosis." At the time, many more women entered the labor force creating a dual wage earner system that persists to this day. However, many worked in relatively poorly paid service occupations, and as Warren and Tyagi (2003) observe rising divorce rates created difficult challenges for many women-headed families that struggled to meet their social needs and provide for their children.

Economic change was accompanied by new demographic realities. Arguably, aging was the most significant, particularly in the Western countries where the proportion of the population over 65 years reached unprecedented levels. In many of these countries, population aging was accompanied by declining fertility, which critics observed meant that there were fewer workers paying insurance contributions to support those in retirement. Another factor was immigration, and although most migrants to Western countries found employment or launched their own businesses, it was widely alleged that they were exploiting the welfare system and even that they had migrated primarily to obtain benefits. Although there was little evidence to support this contention, it fueled the growing anti-welfarist sentiments that accompanied economic decline in these countries. Also relevant were the cultural changes accompanying immigration that affected the sense of solidarity that characterized Western welfare states, particularly in Europe.

Because of these developments, state welfare came under increasing pressure and many governments in the Western world were unable to sustain the continued expansion of their social services. Although few actually reduced social spending in absolute terms, the steady growth of social expenditure that characterized the postwar years leveled off. This development aggravated the economic problems accompanying deindustrialization. The communist countries also experienced economic difficulties at this time, and as the United Nations (1979) revealed, social spending fell. At the same time, the Cold War and rising military expenditures in the Soviet Union placed greater pressure on social budgets. Many developing countries also experienced serious economic difficulties as energy costs increased, harming their industrial development efforts. Many had borrowed on international financial markets to fund their economic investments, but following the escalation of interest rates after the oil shocks, many could not meet their debt obligations. As many governments in the Global South turned to the International Monetary Fund and the World Bank for aid, structural adjustment programs were imposed as a condition for aid. These required major budget cuts, civil service layoffs, and the privatization of state-owned enterprises. Midgley (1997) reported that social spending in many developing countries fell significantly during the 1980s. In many African and Latin American countries, average social spending dropped by as much as 70%.

Ideological and Academic Challenges to State Welfare

It was in this context that ideological challenges to state welfare proliferated. As discussed in the last chapter, significant changes to the welfare system in the United States were introduced following President Reagan's election. A major target was the Aid to Families with Dependent Children (AFDC) program that had grown rapidly since the 1960s and which was believed by the political right to epitomize all that was wrong with government welfare. Several dramatic examples of fraud and abuse were highlighted in the media and these invariably featured women of color who were now regularly demonized. There were similar although less dramatic developments in Britain and some other European countries where state welfare was said to be the prime cause of economic stagnation. As in the United States, Prime Minister Thatcher's government replaced Keynesianism with monetarism, embarked on a vigorous campaign of privatization, and successfully attacked the unions, severely undermining their influence and historic support for government welfare programs.

These events were accompanied by systematic attacks on state welfare by academic writers on the political right. In Britain, Bacon and Eltis (1976) claimed that the country's economic malaise was due to the massive expansion of government welfare that transferred resources out of the productive economic sector to the unproductive welfare sector. In the United States, Feldstein (1974) argued that the country's social security system was impeding investment and harming economic growth. Baumol (1967) pointed out that the decline in manufacturing had serious implications for productivity, which not only affected economic development, but the revenues on which governments depended. Even progressive economists like Okun (1975) agreed that there was a trade-off between economic prosperity and egalitarian welfare and that it was extremely difficult if not impossible for governments to find a balance between the two. In addition, Buchanan and Wagner (1977) argued that expensive welfare programs had created expectations which governments could not fulfill, but in order to secure electoral support, politicians foolishly promised to further expand these programs creating a condition of "political overload" that was undermining the Western democratic system.

Focusing on the social effects of state welfare in the United States, Murray (1984) famously argued that government social programs had not only failed to raise living standards, but were responsible for rising levels of crime, teen pregnancy, poverty, and inner city decay. As he put it, the country had "lost ground" since the expansion of government welfare. Mead (1986) challenged the widely accepted notion of social rights pointing out that the narrow emphasis on rights obscured the concomitant requirement that people have responsibilities to themselves, their families, and society as a whole. The profligate payment of entitlement benefits, he claimed, had eroded traditional values. The novelist Ayn Rand (1964) also weighed in arguing that statism challenged the very basis of American democracy. She even opposed charitable giving, arguing that it destroyed self-resolve and resilience. These arguments have been frequently reiterated over the years, most recently by Eberstadt (2012) and Solomon (2014) who claim that government entitlements continue to undermine economic growth, freedom, and prosperity. In a recent account, Bartholomew (2015) argues that most countries would have been far better off if they had not created a welfare state.

Criticisms of government welfare in the 1980s were not only leveled by market liberals, but by Marxist, feminists, traditionalists, and populists. Marxists argued that extensive state welfare had beguiled the working class, and by easing their discontent with generous welfare benefits, their historic mission to confront the owners of capital and bring about an authentic socialist society had been undermined. Welfare had served as an opiate, but it did not address the fundamental problems of class exploitation that characterizes capitalist society. Marxist writers, such as O'Connor (1973) and Gough (1979) also pointed out that governments were increasingly unable to balance their commitment to maintain the capitalist system and ensure its legitimacy with the result that the system will ultimately collapse. Some Marxists and critical theorists augmented this critique by arguing that governments use welfare to control poor people. This criticism was first articulated by Piven and Cloward (1971), but it has since been reiterated by scholars such as Alexander (2010) and Wacquant (2009), particularly with regard to the way the correctional system is used to control poor people of color. Many feminist writers also focus on exploitation pointing out that government welfare is designed to serve a male industrial proletariat paying scant attention to the needs of women. In fact, these programs generally discriminate against women. What Lewis (1991, 1992) calls the male breadwinner welfare model, affirms women's traditional role as housekeeper and carer and fails to recognize that the onerous work they undertake is essential for social wellbeing.

Religious traditionalists claim that state welfare undermines nonprofits and faith-based organizations that historically catered to those in need. This argument was forcefully expressed by Olasky (1992) who contends that state welfare usurped the church's charitable mission and significantly reduced voluntary giving. Populists criticize government welfare that they allege imposes centrally administered bureaucratic provisions on local communities, weakening social support networks and people's ability to organize their own affairs. This critique is particularly apposite to the developing world where extensive community development programs give expression to the ideals of self-determination and participation. As Scott (1998) argues, much development policy in the Global South reflects the naïve statist assumption that governments will act in the best interests of their citizens, when in fact many are corrupt, inefficient, and indifferent to the needs of ordinary people.

The Welfare Crisis: Myths and Realities

Many social policy writers have interpreted events since the 1970s as a crisis that seriously retrenched government welfare causing significant harm to the population. The Golden Age of government welfare, they argue, has come to an end. Reviewing trends in different Western countries, Mishra (1984) offered one of the most compelling interpretations of the welfare crisis, claiming that everywhere welfare states were in disarray. His analysis was augmented by studies of different Western countries, including Britain (Baldock, 1989), Germany (Brauns & Kramer, 1989), Canada (Lightman, 1991; Rice & Prince, 2000), and the United States (Abramovitz, 1992; Stoesz, 1981, 1991) among others. The crisis interpretation was augmented by accounts that drew attention to deindustrialization, stagnating wages, and persistent unemployment. In particular, many social policy writers lamented the negative impact of trade and economic liberalization on state welfare. For example, Mishra (1999) argues that globalization creates new pressures as governments seek to compete internationally and are compelled to cut spending and retrench their welfare programs. Others emphasize the negative effects of population aging on state welfare. In the United States, Peterson (1996, 1999) is only one of many critics who claim that the growing demand for health care and pensions from an increasing number of elders is creating unsustainable pressures on the welfare system. The World Bank (1994) also weighed in, arguing that urgent steps are needed to avert the coming "old age crisis."

Much of the crisis literature focused on the Western welfare states, but many scholars reached similar conclusions about developments in the Global South. As mentioned earlier, the debt crisis and economic stagnation resulted in major retrenchments in government welfare. Reviewing these developments, Kaseke (1991) found that structural adjustment programs imposed on African countries had slashed social spending, seriously limited access to health and educational services, and in addition unemployment increased. There were similar developments in Latin American countries where economic stagnation accompanied by cuts in social spending and the privatization of social security in Chile and other countries were deplored by scholars like Borzutzky (1991). Although few Asian countries were believed to be experiencing similar challenges, the 1997 Asian Financial Crisis had a major impact and was often viewed as seriously undermining government provision (Tang, 2000).

Although the crisis interpretation of welfare change was very popular, some social policy scholars questioned whether major retrenchments in government social spending and social service provisions have indeed taken place. Reviewing the international evidence, Alber (1988, p. 200) concludes that "the concept of a welfare state crisis is neither necessary nor fruitful." Glennerster (1991) agrees, showing that while almost all the member states of the Organisation for Economic Co-operation and Development (OECD) reduced social spending, this did not result in the dismantling of government welfare, but rather in a leveling-off of the rapidly expanding welfare budgets of the 1950s and 1960s. Examining the impact of the Reagan and Thatcher governments on state welfare, Pierson (1994, 1996) contends that there is little basis for claiming that they significantly retrenched state welfare. Indeed, he asserts that social welfare programs became so deeply institutionalized in both countries that they remain resistant to change; together with electoral support, extensive use by both middle class and low-income families, and the endorsement of major political parties and trades unions, state welfare has become "path dependent." Although it is likely that government welfare will operate within a wider climate of economic austerity in coming years, what he calls the "new politics of welfare" will ensure its resilience and longevity. Subsequently, in an analysis of 21 OECD countries, Castles (2004) casts further doubt on the crisis interpretation pointing out that accounts of the destructive effects of globalization, population aging, and migration on government welfare are overblown. Swank (2002) focuses on the effects of globalization on state welfare in Western countries and also challenges the argument that these countries have been seriously affected by international trade and financial flows. Although globalization has undoubtedly had an impact, he contends that it has not undermined the welfare state.

On the other hand, some scholars recognize that there were significant changes in state welfare which amount to what is sometimes called a "recalibration" of the statutory welfare system. As Gilbert (2002) summarized, statutory programs in the Western countries are now more frequently outsourced to nonprofits and commercial providers and there is a far greater emphasis on individual responsibility which often entails the provision of subsidies and vouchers to needy people. Labor market policies have been modified to promote employment flexibility, and increasing use is being made of means testing. Another development is the devolution of the social services from central to local governments. These changes are characterized by social policy scholars in different ways. While Surender (2004) associates them with the "Third Way" reforms introduced by Prime Minister Blair in Britain and President Clinton in the United States, Bonoli (2012, 2013) believes they reflect a new emphasis on "active welfare." Taylor-Gooby, Gumy, and Otto (2014) describe these changes as "New Welfare," while Hemerijck (2013) links them to a new emphasis on "social investment."

While challenging the "myths" of a welfare state crisis, Castles (2004) cautions that the negative effects of change on government provision should not be overlooked. Contemplating the future of state welfare, he believes that unless checked, economic stagnation will indeed impede government's ability to meet the needs of their citizens in the future. Increasing military expenditures are also likely to depress future welfare allocations. Another issue is declining fertility, which is affecting age dependency ratios and cannot be offset by immigration. Similarly, Wilensky (2002) pointed out that many Western governments are retrenching social programs that serve low-income families and using cost control measures to limit expenditure growth. Goldberg and Rosenthal's (2002) collection of country case studies reached a similar conclusion, revealing that sizeable cuts to means-tested programs have been imposed and that many governments have adopted policies that promote responsibility and choice. They also report that these changes have been accompanied by rising poverty rates among lower-income groups, and particularly among poor women with children.

Sweeping generalizations about the welfare crisis and its negative effects have also been countered by more nuanced analyses of welfare state change that recognize its complexity and unexpected effects. For example, in his discussion of the impact of the Asian Financial Crisis on social security in Hong Kong, Ngan (2007) observes that the government made extensive use of the notion of crisis in an attempt to retrench spending, but that there were in fact adequate resources to fund the social services. In his account of the impact of the Asian Financial Crisis in Korea, Kwon (2001) notes that instead of retrenching the welfare system, the government expanded social programs to deal with rising rates of unemployment. This, he contends, actually strengthened the role of the state. Prasad and Gerecke (2010) make a similar observation showing that several European governments responded to the Great Recession by extending rather than retrenching their social protection programs. Examining trends in Latin America and the Caribbean, Mesa-Lago (2010) reports that while some governments reduced social security spending, others expanded social provisions. Generally, he concludes, the region coped well with the economic downturn.

Although the notion of crisis eventually fell into disuse following the Great Recession, it has recently been revived. Tracing events in the United States, Gorton (2010) shows that unemployment soared, social spending was cut, and many families lost their homes. Kuttner (2013) reaches a similar conclusion about developments in Europe and believes that there has been a significant reversal in the social democratic commitment to state welfare. The imposition of austerity has aggravated the situation, particularly in heavily indebted countries like Greece, where public spending cuts and high unemployment resulted in widespread misery. One of the most pessimistic interpretations of recent developments comes from Wahl (2011) who believes that poverty and inequality in the Nordic welfare states have reached unprecedented levels and that the situation will only get worse as governments acquiesce to the pressures of globalization and marketization. Another pessimistic view comes from Laqueur (2012) who argues that economic stagnation in Europe coupled with large scale migration and rising youth unemployment marks the end of the European dream; without robust economic growth, standards of living will continue to fall.

While it is true that significant changes have taken place in state welfare in many countries resulting in greater outsourcing, individual responsibility, means testing, and budgetary retrenchments to programs that serve low-income families, government welfare has expanded in other parts of the world. As mentioned earlier, the Millennium Development Goals prompted a renewal of government intervention in many developing countries, and this involvement will continue following the adoption of the new Sustainable Development Goals. Many governments have adopted the International Labour Organisation's (ILO) (2011) social protection floor initiative and have introduced conditional cash transfer programs, most noticeably in Mexico and Brazil, which have extended government welfare to many millions of people. Other developing countries are currently introducing similar programs usually with aid from the World Bank. The South African government has massively expanded its means-tested cash transfer programs to cover more families with the result that the poverty rate has declined. In China and India, statutory welfare provisions have also been significantly expanded. Of particular interest is the introduction of universal, tax-funded retirement pensions in Bolivia and in low-income African countries, including Botswana, Lesotho, and Namibia.

These developments reveal the volatile and complex nature of welfare change in the modern world and suggest that the vogue for static concepts, typologies, and stadial interpretations are of limited value in analyzing the changes that are taking place. As discussed earlier in this chapter, many social welfare scholars have embraced simplistic interpretations that bear little resemblance to the haphazard and contingent nature of welfare change. For this reason, a far more dynamic understanding of change is needed. The notion of frozen welfare states needs to be replaced by an interpretation that views government provision as continuously subject to change and the effects of different forces. Of course, this does not mean that general patterns cannot be discerned, but rather that broad generalizations should be cautiously interpreted. This observation is particularly relevant to normative interpretations about the future of state welfare. Although many scholars believe that the state's role will be recalibrated and that many countries will be characterized by a greater degree of welfare pluralism, the welfare mix will still require extensive government involvement. In the new pluralism, the state does not withdraw from the welfare system, but purposefully manages it. In addition, in the fluid and complex policy mix that comprises state welfare around the world today, governments of different ideological persuasions will seek to shape the new pluralism to further their own agendas.

The Future of State Welfare: Shaping the New Pluralism

In the 1950s, a group of political scientists in the United States popularized the view that in Western societies multiple interest groups compete in the political arena to shape decision making. Instead of dominating politics, the government serves as a neutral umpire creating an even playing field on which these groups can pursue their goals. Dahl (1956, 1961), a leading member of this group, claimed that the pluralist system can be contrasted favorably with the highly centralized political systems that characterize many other countries. He and his colleagues also argued that pluralism is highly conducive to democratic participation. Although competition among interest groups often involves a struggle, Dahl was optimistic that "any active and legitimate group will make itself heard effectively at some stage in the process of decision-making" (1956, p. 150). It is in this spirit that advocates of welfare pluralism seek to promote the involvement of multiple agents in the welfare system.

As criticisms of state welfare became more common in the 1980s, the contribution of non-statutory providers attracted growing attention. In addition to market liberals, advocates of community involvement and nonprofits also attacked government welfare. In a searing critique, Hadley and Hatch (1981) lamented the way they had been sidelined by the statutory welfare system in Britain, and Gilbert (2009) observed that the Wolfenden Commission, which was appointed by the British government following lobbying by nonprofit advocates, also contributed to an appreciation of the evolving pluralist system. In the United States, Kammerman (1983) was one of the first social policy writers to recognize what she described as the "mixed economy of welfare." Since then, advocacy of welfare pluralism has become common, and as Powell (2007) points out various terms, including the "welfare mix," "welfare pluralism," and the "mixed economy of welfare" are now in common use.

Although welfare systems around the world are increasingly characterized by pluralism, the contribution of nonprofits and commercial providers in many countries is still limited when compared to the role of state. In some countries like China the government is gradually permitting them to expand and they are also becoming more prominent in the Scandinavian countries where they previously played a limited role. Although comparatively few developing countries have a sizable nonprofit sector, the situation is changing as nonprofits funded by international donors proliferate. The result is a complex welfare mix which Johnson (1999) observes is composed of different combinations of statutory and non-statutory involvement in different countries. In addition, the balance between state, nonprofit, nonformal, and commercial providers in these countries varies between the different welfare sectors. For example, social assistance programs are largely the prerogative of the government while housing is largely supplied through the market. In turn, family welfare services often involve nonprofits. Of course, nonformal agents, including families and communities also contribute.

It is sometimes assumed that this complex system is the result of a benign compromise between different providers, but it actually involves a struggle between different interest groups with different agendas. As Hacker (2002) observes with reference to the United States, these struggles amount to "battles." It is in this regard that normative debates about shaping the welfare system have become increasingly intense. There are also variations in the extent that different interest groups, including commercial providers, advocates of nonprofit and faith-based involvement, environmentalists, traditionalists, and radical populists among others exert pressure on the state and implement their agendas. To add to this complexity, there are differences also in the ways that governments respond to these pressures. In addition, governments may themselves take the initiative and proactively mold policy agendas. Cultural traditions, institutionalized political systems, and differences in statecraft also play a role in determining the features of the pluralist welfare system.

Different views have emerged about the way the new pluralism should evolve. Many advocates of state welfare commend the corporatist and state-centered approach that characterizes welfare pluralism in Europe. Corporatist governments have institutionalized the principle of subsidiarity and incorporated faith-based and nonprofits in a wider framework of state managed provision. They have also permitted a degree of commercial involvement. Nevertheless, in countries with corporatist political systems, welfare pluralism is directed and managed by the state. This is also the case in the Scandinavian welfare states even though the role of nonprofits and commercial providers is expanding, welfare administration is being decentralized, and as Gubring, Harsloff, and Lødemel (2014) point out, labor activation programs feature more prominently. Of course, critics, such as Wahl (2011) and Kananen (2014) take a dim view of these developments, which they believe are undermining government's historic commitment to welfare.

Other scholars argue that the new pluralism should involve the principles of collective altruism and solidarity that characterized earlier welfarist values. With the demise of neoliberalism, government should reinstate the principles of social rights, which guaranteed an adequate level of living for all. Fitzpatrick (2004) argues for a new "post-productivist" welfare system that decouples people's wellbeing from work and the economy, and ensures that the needs of all families are adequately met. Van Parijs (2006) operationalizes this idea by urging governments to introduce a guaranteed basic income for all individuals that will be adequate to meet their needs. An income benefit of this kind should not be means tested, but be paid to all citizens as a right. In a recent publication, he and Vandeborght (2015) suggest that the costs of a benefit of this kind could be met through taxing natural resources, such as oil and other types of mineral wealth.

Others believe that government should shape the new pluralism by promoting greater market participation and personal responsibility. Of course, it was shown earlier in this book that neoliberals, such as Hayek and Friedman argued forcefully that nonprofit and commercial providers should be primarily responsible for meeting social needs with governments limiting their involvement to helping the poorest groups. Radical populists and advocates of community engagement also argue that the state's role should be limited so that communities and local groups can take responsibility for their own wellbeing. Others like Gilbert (2002, 2013) argue that governments should play what he describes as an enabling role which "advances a market oriented approach" (2002, p. 44). This, he claims, will foster individual responsibility, make greater use of means-tested benefits, and promote labor force participation. Although he believes that the United States is the emblematic "enabling state," he contends that this approach is being adopted in many other Western countries, including the Nordic welfare states. His views are compatible with the writings of Sen (1985, 1999) and Nussbaum (2011) who adopt an individualist approach contending that people's wellbeing is enhanced when they are able to realize their capabilities, exercise choice, and fulfill their potential. Discussing wider political trends, Levy (2006) provides evidence to support Gilbert's view that governments in the Western world are moving away from a market directing governance style in which they regulated the market, to a market supporting style in which they actively promote market activities. Marketization is less prevalent in the Global South, but the situation may change as advocates of what Rainford (2001) calls the individual enterprise approach to social development exert growing influence. In India, for example, Prime Minister Mohdi's government has indicated that it will stimulate market involvement in the welfare system. Together with the expansion of nonprofits, the greater involvement of commercial providers can also be expected in China.

Arguably the most vigorous attempt to shape the new pluralism comes from advocates of the social investment approach, which has been described as Third Way reforms, active welfare, New Welfare, and social investment. This approach recalibrates, but still requires extensive state involvement. Hemerijck (2013) believes that many European governments have adopted this approach by placing more emphasis on human capital investments to ensure that people have the knowledge and skills to secure decent employment and remunerative wages. Preschool programs, family leave, technical training, labor activation, and flexicurity employment policies are also given priority. These and other innovations are funded and directed by governments. State-centered welfare pluralism can also be found in several East Asian, Latin American, and other countries which have adopted what Midgley and Tang (2001) describe as the welfare developmentalist approach. Governments in these countries prioritize employment and economic participation and directly link welfare to wider economic and social development policies. Midgley (2014) observes that similar developments have taken place in many other parts of the Global South where social investments include community development, human capital, employment promotion, assets and social protection programs that have been given greater emphasis with the adoption of the Millennium Development Goals. Although the Goals were not primarily focused on social investments, but on meeting minimum standards, Sachs (2005) notes that the commitment by the world's nations to eradicate poverty and hunger, enhance the status of women, and promote universal primary education has a strong social investment function. These activities are likely to be given priority as the Sustainable Development Goals are implemented in the coming years.

However, the social investment approach is controversial. Some question its close integration with economic policy, and others believe that social investment is a thinly disguised form of neoliberalism that prioritizes economic participation over historic welfare values, such as social rights, solidarity, and redistribution. On the other hand, the advocates of social investment insist that governments must play an active role in shaping an investment focused pluralist welfare system. For these writers, social investment offers a neo-Keynesian alternative to market liberalism accompanied by technocratic government. They also believe that social investments should augment rather than replace traditional cash transfers, and as Midgley (1999) argued, can redistribute resources.

If social investment does become an important feature of welfare pluralism around the world, the state's central role in promoting the wellbeing of its citizens will be affirmed. A social investment approach is also compatible with the way many governments are again proactively engaging in economic development and challenging the neoliberal orthodoxy. This trend finds expression in the creation of huge sovereign wealth funds, the promotion of technological innovation, the expansion of state sponsored research and educational opportunities, and the adoption of novel welfare programs, such as conditional cash transfers. Micklethwait and Wooldridge (2014) suggest that the current process of reinventing the state is being led by Asian governments that may result in a revolution in statecraft with far-reaching consequences for other countries. Mussacchio and Lazzarini (2014) observe that government's role in planning and managing their economies is also expanding in other parts of the world. Arguably, a state-centered pluralist welfare system in which governments proactively use social investments as well as conventional welfare interventions to promote the wellbeing of their citizens, offers the best way forward.

Suggested Additional Reading

Since the popularization of neoliberal ideas in the 1980s, many social welfare scholars have concluded that attacks on government welfare provision coupled with economic difficulties, cuts to social service budgets, and the increasing use of outsourcing have resulted in a crisis with dire consequences for social wellbeing around the world. A large number of books dealing with this issue have been published in recent years and although the idea of a crisis in welfare is not as prominent as before, many scholars recognize that significant changes to state welfare have taken place. The following are just some of the books that deal with the issue. They reach very different conclusions about welfare change.

- Castles, F. G. (2004). *The future of the welfare state: Crisis myths and crisis realities.* New York, NY: Oxford University Press. This interesting book critically examines the idea that government welfare has experienced a crisis that has negatively affected people's wellbeing in the Western countries. Drawing on the literature and a substantial body of social science research, the author questions the view that Western welfare states are being dismantled. On the other hand, he recognizes that changes have taken place and that government provision is challenged by demographic, political, and economic realities.
- Gilbert, N. (2002). *The transformation of the welfare state: The silent surrender of public responsibility.* New York, NY: Oxford University Press. The author discusses the way that government welfare has changed in Western countries, showing that the social democratic belief that the government should not only fund, but deliver social services has been significantly altered by the widespread use of outsourcing, increased means testing, and an emphasis on welfare to work programs. Although these changes began in the United States, they now characterize the social policies of many European countries as well.
- Hemerijck, A. (2013). *Changing welfare states.* New York, NY: Oxford University Press. In this impressive book, the author discusses changes in government welfare provision in European countries over the last two decades. Rejecting the idea that these changes amount to a crisis, he shows how many European governments in concert with the European Union have sought to adapt to new economic, demographic, and political realities. Drawing on statistical data and official reports, he contends that a new social investment approach is emerging. This approach, he argues, offers the best rationale for government welfare in the future.
- Kananen, J. (2014). *The Nordic welfare state in three eras: From emancipation to discipline.* Brookfield, VT: Ashgate. This book traces the historical evolution of government welfare in the Nordic countries showing that welfare change can be viewed as passing through three stages: namely, the developmental phase that preceded the creation of the welfare state after the Second World War; the second phase of the fully blown welfare state that provided comprehensive benefits and enhanced people's wellbeing; and finally the current phase in which governments are restructuring and outsourcing their programs and placing more emphasis on welfare to work programs. Although the book deals only with the Nordic countries, it is an interesting example of how social policy scholars have used stadial models to characterize welfare change.
- Midgley, J., & Piachaud, D. (Eds.). (2013). *Social protection, economic growth and social change: Goals, issues and trajectories in China, India, Brazil and South Africa.* Cheltenham, UK: Edward Elgar. This edited collection summarizes research studies undertaken in China, India, Brazil, and South Africa by the contributors who examine the historical evolution and current features of state welfare provision in each of these four "BRICS" countries. They also speculate on the future directions of government welfare in these countries, demonstrating the close relationship between economic development and state welfare in societies undergoing rapid change.

10

Social Welfare and International Social Development

❖

S ocial development is a distinctive approach to social welfare that emerged in the Global South in the years after the Second World War. Although not generally recognized as a welfare institution in the way that the family, philanthropy, and state provision are regarded as culturally institutionalized approaches to welfare, social development's unique perspective is widely acknowledged, and today social development interventions are implemented all over the world by nonprofits, faith-based, and government agencies. International organizations such as the United Nations and the World Bank are also involved, and in fact have actively promoted social development over the years. Since the first World Summit on Social Development in 1995, and the adoption of the Millennium Development Goals and subsequently the Sustainable Development Goals by the member states of the United Nations, social development's contribution to enhancing the wellbeing of the peoples of the Global South has been widely recognized.

While social development shares a commitment to promoting wellbeing with the other institutionalized approaches discussed earlier, it has distinctive features. It is primarily known for linking economic development with social welfare. The idea of development was given high priority in the years following the Second World War when the governments of many newly independent countries sought to transform their agrarian economies and raise standards of living by promoting economic growth. Although many countries recorded respectable rates of growth, poverty and deprivation remained widespread, resulting in what may be called "distorted development." As it became clear that growth does not automatically result in higher standards of living for the whole population, social development advocates urged the adoption of policies and programs that ensure everyone's wellbeing. Since then, social development has sought to achieve this goal by requiring that economic growth promote social wellbeing, and conversely that social programs contribute to economic development.

Social development originated in the developing countries of the Global South and may be viewed as a unique "Third Worldist" approach to social welfare, but it is also attracting attention in the Western countries. Although policies and programs designed to promote social wellbeing were previously regarded as separate from the economy, the need to link economic and social policies is increasingly recognized and social programs that invest in people's capabilities are now being prioritized. In addition, there is greater support for inclusive egalitarian policies that address the problem of distorted development and equitably distribute the benefits of growth. For these reasons, social development is now playing a more important role in international social welfare thinking.

This chapter provides an overview of social development by outlining its key features, tracing its history, and discussing key social development interventions. Although the literature on social development has grown rapidly in recent years, the term is still poorly defined. Social development also lacks a sound theoretical base. Indeed, social development is often viewed as an eclectic set of practice interventions that are haphazardly linked to economic development. However, this chapter shows that there is greater clarity today about theoretical ideas, and that a more coherent conceptual basis for social development has emerged. The practice strategies used by social development practitioners have also been more extensively documented. The chapter reviews these practice strategies and concludes by examining some of the controversies that have arisen about social development and its role in international social welfare.

Features of Social Development

Although the term "social development" has been used since the 1950s, it means different things to different people. In the academic world, it is widely used in the interdisciplinary field of development studies, but also finds expression in sociology, economics, social work, and social policy. Among practitioners, the term is often identified with community projects, such as microenterprises, women's groups, cooperatives, maternal and child welfare programs, the provision of safe drinking water, and the construction of schools and clinics. However, it also refers to national planning and government policies concerned with the 'social aspect' of development, such as reducing poverty, increasing literacy, combating malnutrition, and improving access to health and education. Recently, some writers have employed the term to refer to the efforts of individuals and families to enhance their capabilities and to function independently in the market. In contrast to this practical approach, Midgley (1995) observes that the term is also used to connote the achievement of lofty ideals such as progress, social integration, peace, and social justice.

These different uses reflect social development's eclectic nature and its lack of theoretical sophistication. Nevertheless, progress has been made in identifying social development's key features and the theoretical ideas that inform practice. In addition, several useful definitions have been formulated by social development writers. One of the earliest by Paiva (1977, p. 332) defined social development as the "capacity of people to work continuously for their own and society's welfare." In a pioneering book on the subject, Pandey (1981, p. 33) suggested that social development is a process that fosters the "improvement of the quality of life of people . . . a more equitable distribution of resources . . . and special measures that will enable marginal groups and communities to move into the mainstream." On the other hand, Omer's (1979, p. 15) definition is more ambitious viewing social development as a process that "gives expression to the values of human dignity, equality and social justice." Aspalter and Singh (2008, p. 12) adopt a similarly expansive view by defining social development as a process that "enables people to achieve greater happiness, satisfaction and a peaceful life." Focusing on the field's practical aspects, Midgley (2014, p. 13) defines social development as "a process of planned social change designed to promote the wellbeing of the population as a whole within the context of a dynamic, multifaceted development process."

These definitions share common features. They draw on an interdisciplinary political economy approach to emphasize social development's role in bringing about social change and wellbeing. They also reflect the numerous practice innovations that have been implemented over the years to address the problem of distorted development that has accompanied economic growth. The notion of intervention is also a common feature of these definitions positing that social development does not occur naturally, but is the result of purposeful planning and policymaking, and the implementation of a large number of programs and community-based projects. Most definitions also stress social development's commitment to participation and inclusiveness. Social development promotes an egalitarian approach that raises standards of living and enhances everyone's wellbeing. This requires that the benefits of economic growth are equitably distributed. It also requires that people participate actively in development. Ensuring that poor and vulnerable communities, women, minorities, and other marginalized groups are included in the development process is given high priority. Although social development practice is largely focused on poverty alleviation, many scholars believe that its concern for poor people and oppressed groups takes place within a wider universalistic context of interventions that promote the welfare of all. Finally, some writers contend that social development prioritizes social welfare interventions that are "productivist" and stress the role of social investments. Common to these definitions is the idea that social welfare should contribute to economic development and that everyone should benefit from economic growth.

These different definitions embody values, beliefs, and ideologies, and as will be shown the field has been shaped by normative perspectives associated with different practice strategies. For example, social development's historic engagement with communities owes much to populist thinking. On the other hand, its use of national planning and state intervention is rooted in social democratic and socialist values.

More recently, the promotion of microenterprise, social business, and other market-based innovations reflect the growing influence of individualism and market liberalism in social development. As will become apparent in the following discussion of the field's historical evolution, these competing normative approaches affect social development practice in different ways.

The History of Social Development

The term social development was only popularized in the 1950s and 1960s, but it has far older roots reflecting the way that many cultures have been preoccupied with change and progress. Nisbet (1980) reveals that social thinkers have offered different explanations of how societies experience change. The ancient Chinese favored cyclical interpretations in which periods of growth and prosperity are followed by decline. The ancient Greeks popularized the idea of a decline from a Golden Age, while in Europe after the Renaissance progressive theories involving a linear process of steady improvements became popular. These progressive theories reflected the growing material prosperity and intellectual progress of the time. Some scholars attributed the causes of change to natural forces, but others emphasized the role of ideas and human agency, believing that social progress is the result of the purposeful actions of social reformers, activists, and progressive politicians. In the nineteenth century, some argued that governments needed to direct the process of change. Social liberals and social democrats, including Hobhouse in Britain and Veblen in the United States claimed that the widespread conditions of poverty and deprivation associated with rapid industrialization and urbanization could best be addressed through state intervention. It was in this context that the term "social development" was coined by Hobhouse in 1924 to connote the need for statutory programs that promote progressive social improvements.

Although state intervention increased steadily in the early decades of the twentieth century, government involvement in economic and social affairs increased rapidly during the Great Depression of the 1930s as many Western governments adopted policies to revitalize the economy and create jobs. In the United States, President Roosevelt's administration launched a massive recovery program designed to stimulate growth and generate employment. Public works programs, which resulted in the construction of hospitals, parks, museums, schools, roads, bridges, airports, and other facilities were created to provide jobs for unemployed workers. Leighninger (2007) points out that these projects also had long-term social and economic benefits. The writings of the British economist John Maynard Keynes played a major role in shaping these policies and his work also informed economic policy after the Second World War. Interventionist ideas also found expression in economic planning, and particularly in Soviet centralized planning. In fact, Soviet planning inspired the governments of many developing countries to produce five-year development plans to guide the process of development. It was in this context that social development ideas began to take shape.

At the time, the governments of many developing countries prioritized economic growth believing that growth resulting from rapid industrialization would increase wage employment and raise standards of living. Because growth was given high priority,

Livingston (1969) reports that the limited welfare services introduced during the colonial era were often criticized for impeding economic development. Colonial welfare officials in West Africa responded to this criticism by introducing mass literacy campaigns as well as a variety of community-based projects that promoted people's wellbeing through their participation in local economic projects. Community-based projects introduced by Gandhi and Tagore in India before this time also sought to promote improvements in people's wellbeing at the local level through innovations in agriculture and village industry, and they also emphasized the need for education and health care. These interventions exemplified the idea that social welfare should contribute positively to development. In the 1950s, the term community development was adopted to describe these activities. Community development programs subsequently spread throughout the Global South largely through the efforts of the United Nations, which became a major proponent of social development. Today, Pawar (2014b) points out that community development projects and programs continue to feature prominently in social development. The adoption of community development by many governments in the Global South and its advocacy by the United Nations and other international organizations made a major contribution to the formulation of the social development approach.

By the 1960s, it became apparent that the economic policies adopted by many governments had not created wage employment on a scale that significantly reduced poverty. In addition, it was recognized that economic development had disproportionately benefited political, business, and military elites as well as those who found employment in the modern sector and in the expanding civil service, while the vast majority of the population continued to suffer widespread deprivation. In addition, many rural people flocked to the cities in search of work resulting in rapid urban growth and the proliferation of informal settlements where large numbers of migrants lived in conditions of appalling poverty. As Midgley (1995) argued, the process of development had become distorted, benefiting a few but excluding the majority from the achievements of growth.

To address the problem, United Nations officials consulted with leading development economists, including Gunnar Myrdal and Hans Singer who recommended that economic planning be augmented by a greater focus on the social aspects of development. Hall and Midgley (2004) observed that this required increased budgetary allocations to health, education, shelter, and nutrition and a new focus on poverty alleviation. Myrdal was especially committed to an egalitarian approach that ensures that the benefits of growth reach poor people and raise their standards of living. He argued that planning agencies should refocus their conventional economic activities that focused on industrial development and concentrate on promoting social welfare instead. Although Myrdal used the cumbersome phrase "unified socio-economic development planning" to connote this new emphasis, the term "social development" was soon adopted to characterize the new statist approach in the field. The term now referred both to community-level projects and programs and to national-level interventions.

The spread of social development was fostered by several United Nations resolutions and the involvement of other international organizations. They included the

United Nations Children's Emergency Fund (UNICEF), the World Health Organization (WHO), and the International Labour Organisation (ILO), which urged its member states to deal with the root causes of poverty by meeting people's basic needs (ILO, 1976). Under the leadership of Robert McNamara, the World Bank also refocused its lending policies, which had previously been concerned with large scale development projects, to allocate more resources for education, health, and housing. In a major publication, the World Bank (1975) argued for greater spending on key social sectors, such as education, health care, housing, and community development, pointing out that spending of this kind amounted to social investments that would foster economic development. In addition, UNICEF and WHO actively promoted the spread of community-based projects that addressed the health and social needs of poor communities in both the rural and urban areas.

By the 1960s, many governments had adopted social development ideas and many embraced the term social development. Many central planning agencies began to employ social planners and national development plans gave increasing recognition to social programs and objectives. Following an important meeting of ministers of social welfare in New York in 1968 (United Nations, 1969) many welfare ministries were renamed ministries of social development and charged with promoting a developmental focus in their programs. Many also became responsible for national community development programs.

The idea that development involves the implementation of social as well as economic policies was subsequently broadened by a growing emphasis on gender equality and environmental sustainability. Feminist scholars like Boserup (1970) and Rogers (1980) campaigned for a greater focus on the gender dimensions of development, and soon social development projects serving women proliferated. These campaigns were also fostered by the adoption of the United Nations Convention on the Elimination of all Forms of Discrimination against Women (CEDAW) in 1979 as well as increased international aid for women's programs managed by nonprofit organizations and grassroots women's groups. Growing concern about the environmental impact of economic growth also resulted in the adoption of the sustainable development approach advocated by the Brundtland Commission (1983). These events fostered a broader, holistic conception of development that transcended the narrow economic focus of conventional development policy and gave greater emphasis to social, environmental, gender, and other interventions in the field.

However, as has been discussed previously, the state's role in development was increasingly questioned by market liberals and populist critics in the 1970s. Market liberals challenged the role of the state claiming that excessive taxation, bureaucratic regulation, and national planning had stifled economic growth. Many community activists also criticized the role of the state in social development viewing governments as authoritarian, corrupt, and incompetent. They claimed that poverty would only be eradicated by ensuring that people participated democratically in the development process. Similarly, feminists argued that women's associations, particularly at the grassroots level, would make a more significant contribution to social development than government agencies. As a result of these events, social development programs and projects sponsored by governments were curtailed and a more pluralistic approach emerged in which nonprofit organizations, women's groups, and grassroots community associations played a significantly more important role. Increasingly, as Lewis and Kanji (2009) report, international aid donors bypassed governments and directed resources toward these nongovernmental organizations creating a more complex system of provision.

Although it seemed by the 1990s that the statist approach to social development had been seriously undermined, the United Nations countered by convening the World Summit on Social Development in Copenhagen in 1995. The Summit was attended by many international leaders who agreed on a set of social development targets that were enshrined in the Copenhagen Declaration (United Nations, 1996). Five years later, at a special session of the United Nations General Assembly, the organization's member states passed the Millennium Declaration which launched the Millennium Development Goals. This document proposed to halve the incidence of global poverty and achieve other key social targets by 2015 (United Nations, 2005). Despite uneven progress, a meeting of the United Nations in September 2010 to assess the situation concluded that the incidence of absolute poverty had declined in many parts of the world and that progress had also been made in meeting other goals, such as increased school enrollments, and reductions in child mortality (United Nations, 2010). On the other hand, progress is decidedly mixed with regard to nutrition, shelter, and improvements in the status of women. Nevertheless, the Millennium initiative has been characterized by an unusually high degree of international support and a renewed commitment to social development resulting in tangible gains in many parts of the world. In 2015, the United Nations General Assembly replaced the Millennium Development Goals with the Sustainable Development Goals, which have set even more ambitious targets that will undoubtedly have a major effect on social development around the world in the coming years.

Social Development: Theory and Practice

As discussed earlier, social development is primarily a practical affair consisting of multiple projects, programs, and policies implemented by many different agents at the community, national, and international levels. Although theory has not been given priority, attempts have been made to identify the theoretical ideas that inform practice. Scholars and practitioners working in the field have examined the goals of social development, the values on which practice are based, and the different ways that social development ideas have been implemented. Several thoughtful definitions of social development that identify its key features have also been formulated, and in addition, the different practice strategies associated with social development have been documented and critically assessed. As the academic literature on social development expands, a more coherent approach will hopefully emerge to strengthen social development's contribution to social welfare.

Social development encompasses philosophical ideas, such as social progress and intervention, which Midgley (2003) suggests reflect social development's rich intellectual heritage. Although they provide the foundations for social development practice, these philosophical ideas reveal that very different values and beliefs about how social progress can be achieved influence social development scholars and practitioners. These find expression in a variety of normative approaches, including populism, communitarianism, statism, and market liberalism; all of which inform social development practice. Despite these different perspectives, Midgley (1995, 2014) believes that social development has a set of core principles and values. Drawing on a political economy approach and the insights of different normative perspectives, he has sought to formulate a comprehensive conceptual interpretation of social development that reveals the field's egalitarianism and commitment to redistributive policies that address the problem of distorted development.

Midgley (2014) believes that social development is a distinctive approach to social welfare because it integrates social policies in a multifaceted development process comprising economic, social, gender, and environmental interventions. This idea finds expression in three axioms: the first requires that the different components of the development process are harmonized, and that organizational arrangements for achieving this goal are created at the community and national levels. Social development practice is by definition interventionist in that projects, programs, policies, and plans are used to mobilize multiple agents, including households, community groups, nonprofits, faith-based organizations, government agencies, and even the international organizations for social welfare purposes. Social planning provides an opportunity to coordinate the respective contributions of these agents within a comprehensive development framework.

A second axiom is that economic development policies should be "people-centered," sustainable, and promote the wellbeing of the population as a whole by addressing the distortions that have characterized economic development for many years. This has been a recurrent theme in social development writing and requires that development policies and programs actively promote economic participation through creating remunerative employment, raising incomes, investing in education and skills, ensuring that economic growth is people-centered, and by improving the living standards of the whole population.

A third axiom is that social policies, programs, and projects should be "productivist" in that they use social investments to enhance participation in development. Social investments play a key role in social development practice and give expression to the idea that social welfare interventions should enhance people's capabilities and contribute positively to development. Social investments enhance participation in development giving expression to social development's commitment to inclusiveness and universalism. Social investments also have a redistributive function since they involve progressive resource transfers by the state (Midgley, 1999). Finally, by investing in people, families, communities, and those with special needs, social investments are better able to cope with and respond to adverse events, both individually and collectively. It is in this sense that social investment has a preventive and promotive function that transcends the conventional remedial and maintenance approach characteristic of professional social work and conventional welfare services.

Social Development Practice Strategies

Numerous policies, programs, and projects that reflect social development ideas and normative preferences have been implemented over the years. As is discussed below, these interventions can be grouped into a number of practice strategies that are associated with the social development approach. All are based on the principles of progressive change, intervention, and participation, and to varying degrees reflect the normative perspectives outlined earlier. All link economic and social interventions within a multifaceted development process, and all are productivist in that they have an explicit social investment function. Since these interventions have been well documented by social development writers, such as Midgley and Sherraden (2009) and Pawar and Cox (2010), the following provides a brief overview of these strategies and the way they give expression to social development principles.

Human capital investments provide the knowledge, skills, and capabilities people need to participate effectively in the productive economy. The need for knowledge and skills is being emphasized all over the world today, and many governments are committed to improving educational opportunities. Emphasis is also being placed on child care, preschool education, literacy training, job skilling and re-skilling, and lifelong learning. Most people, including poor people, recognize the importance of education and many make major sacrifices to send their children to school. Social development requires that governments support their efforts and provide universal and free access to education. It is in this regard that human capital investments can effectively mobilize the contributions of individual households, communities, and the state to enhance economic participation and to improve living standards. Although educational interventions are regarded as a primary means of mobilizing human capital, policies that promote nutrition and health care are also included. Pioneering research undertaken by Schultz (1981) found that antimalarial campaigns in India were directly responsible for increased agricultural production, and subsequently, studies undertaken by the World Bank (1975) demonstrated that investments in nutrition, health, and housing contribute positively to economic growth. These programs not only have intrinsic value, but have positive consequences for development and people's wellbeing.

Social capital refers to investments that strengthen social networks and enhance participation in civil society and the life of the community. The creation of social capital fosters cooperation and solidarity, and as Putnam, Leonardi, and Nanetti (1993) demonstrated in their pioneering research in Italy, it also promotes economic development and raises standards of living. Accordingly, as Dasgupta and Serageldin (2000) point out, community development projects that integrate social and economic activities are emphasized in social development today. These ideas also find expression in the conventional community development programs established in many developing countries in the 1950s. Pawar (2014b) points out that they have a major social investment function, mobilize local people and foster their participation in development. Participation in democratic decision making and civic affairs is also given high priority. The concepts of empowerment and activism have played a major role in community social development, and through participation, people are encouraged to take control of their own affairs and resist exploitation and oppression. Although the mobilization of social capital gives expression to a "bottom up" populist strategy, it also requires investments provided by the state and international donors.

The promotion of wage employment has been a primary goal of economic development policy since the 1950s, and it is equally important in social development where poor people and those with special needs are the focus of many job creation projects. However, social development also stresses the need for broader universal interventions that promote remunerative incomes and decent work for all. Policies that prevent discrimination and exploitation are also prioritized. While social development advocates believe that governments should play a major role in promoting decent work, business enterprises and unions are also involved, and through the efforts of the ILO and several governments, positive partnerships between workers, commercial firms, and the state have been forged. Nevertheless, as the recent Great Recession revealed, unemployment is a serious problem and the prospect of finding long-term regular employment is challenging, particularly for youth and people with special needs. Although many governments have established special workshops for people with special needs, it is difficult to integrate them into the work force in countries with abundant labor. For this reason, self-employment and particularly cooperative enterprises comprising workers with special needs have been established. Some governments have also provided incentives to commercial enterprises and cooperatives to employ casual and low-skilled workers, unemployed youth, and people with special needs. In addition, state-funded community works projects that have been used for many years to alleviate poverty, are again being used to create jobs and raise incomes. One important innovation is the Indian government's National Employment Guarantee Scheme that was established in 2005 to provide short term work for poor people in the rural areas (Mutatkar, 2013). However, the importance of comprehensive macroeconomic policies that create wage employment and ensure that everyone has access to decent work and remunerative and satisfying employment are given high priority in social development.

The role of self-employment has been recognized by many social development writers and practitioners who believe that microenterprises funded through small loans make a contribution to social development. Spurred by the success of the Grameen Bank and similar programs, microenterprise initiatives have proliferated. Although the claims of microenterprise advocates are often overly optimistic and should be tempered by the recognition that this approach is only likely to benefit some families who have the knowledge and skills to launch small businesses, microenterprise and microfinance are an integral part of social development practice, and as Remenyi and Quinones (2000) show, they have reduced poverty in many countries. On the other hand, a number of critical accounts of the expansions of microfinance programs in the developing world have been published by scholars such as Roy (2010) and Bateman (2010). Unfortunately, some microfinance organizations that were previously committed to funding small business development have now become commercial lenders that provide credit for a variety of purposes, which often fostered indebtedness. This has resulted in scandals in India and elsewhere that have sullied the role of microenterprise as a social development strategy. As Midgley (2008) argues, microenterprises have a role to play in social development provided they are properly regulated and integrated with other social investments.

Asset development programs have also become popular in recent years. Asset building involves the accumulation of financial assets by individuals and households as well as the creation of community-owned assets, such as schools, clinics, clean water supplies, and feeder roads. The accumulation of financial assets has been promoted through the creation of child savings accounts in some countries and through matched savings accounts, known as Individual Development Accounts or IDAs. Invented by Sherraden (1991), these accounts have been introduced in the United States and some other countries. Matches are provided by nonprofit organizations, foundations, and governments to create incentives for poor families to save. Although studies have shown that the amounts saved are not large, Schreiner and Sherraden (2007) observe that they increase the credit worthiness of poor families, provide access to banks, and have positive psychological and social effects.

Many communities also own assets collectively, but as Kretzman and McKnight (1993) point out, this has not always been recognized and for this reason greater emphasis is placed on community asset building today. The community-based asset approach shares many similarities with conventional community development programs, although as Mathie and Cunningham's (2008) case studies reveal, there are significant variations in the extent to which local people access external resources for this purpose. Assets, such as the air and sea, rivers and lakes, and other natural resources have also received some attention in social development circles. They comprise what is known as the Commons and should be safeguarded for the benefit of all humankind. Although oil and other mineral resources also form a part of the Commons, many governments have leased or sold rights to exploit these resources to commercial firms. Similarly, state-owned forests, land, and water supplies have been transferred to private owners on the grounds that they are better stewards of these resources. Despite Ostrom's (1990) careful research that challenged this belief, many governments remain committed to the privatization agenda. On the other hand, Midgley (2014) points out that some governments have retained collective ownership of natural resources and created sovereign wealth funds that provide funding for social development. Mussacchio and Lazzarini (2014) point out that these funds now augment state-sponsored social development initiatives in a growing number of countries.

Social protection programs have not been a major part of social development in the past, but as the investment implications of income transfers are being recognized, social protection has become an important social development practice strategy. The conditional cash transfer programs established in Mexico and Brazil in the 1990s reveal that income transfers are investments that contribute to development. Fiszbein and Schady (2009) observe that they also appeal to governments and international donors because they promote human capital while reducing poverty. However, conventional "unconditional" transfer programs, such as means-tested child allowances and pensions for elders have also been introduced or expanded by some governments in the Global South, largely because they have a significant impact on poverty. The

South African government made a major commitment to programs of this kind, and in addition to alleviating poverty and raising the health and nutritional status of poor families, Patel and Trieghaardt (2008) report that the country's social protection initiatives have a strong social investment function. By injecting cash into the budgets of poor families, their demand for goods and services increases, in turn stimulating the economy. These transfers also provide start-up capital for household enterprises. Few other African countries have expanded social protection on the same scale, but Ellis, Devereux, and White (2009) observe that many community-based organizations and nonprofits in these countries now operate local social protection projects that are often funded by international donors. This is also the case in other parts of the Global South.

Although social planning is usually associated with national economic development planning, the term is more broadly defined in social development to include community level planning and the coordination of social programs and projects. As noted earlier in this chapter, social planning played a major role in social development's history promoting the statist approach and mobilizing and coordinating a large number of social development initiatives at the national level. With the spread of market liberal ideas, social planning was undermined, but as many governments have recognized the need for planning to implement the Millennium Development Goals, it has recently been reinvigorated. Of course, some countries such as China, India, Korea, and Malaysia have used social planning to good effect for many years; today, social planners work in central planning ministries and in sectoral agencies where they help formulate and implement plans for health, education, community development, housing, and other social development initiatives. Social planning plays a particularly important role in identifying and prioritizing social needs and directing resources toward the most disadvantaged groups. In addition to promoting universalism in social development, Midgley (2014) notes that social planning is also an effective means of implementing a rights-based social development agenda.

Recognizing that there are many barriers that prevent the participation of poor people in development, policies that facilitate participation are an important social development strategy. These barriers include discriminatory practices against women, minorities, people with disabilities, and the elderly among others. Removing barriers of this kind requires an active role for the state in enacting and enforcing nondiscriminatory legislation and affirmative action programs. It also requires that governments address institutionalized inequalities and strengthen opportunities for people to recognize their potential. In addition, participation in the economy requires that issues of peace and justice be addressed. Social development goals are unlikely to be realized in societies where violence is commonplace and where entrenched elites perpetuate their privileges and impede the efforts of the majority to improve their standards of living. In these cases, activism can contribute to the election of governments that serve the interests of their citizens.

Social Development: Limitations and Prospects

Although social development is now widely recognized around the world, it has limitations that should be addressed. As noted earlier, social development comprises an eclectic collection of different programs and projects that have been implemented in an incremental way. Also, while the field is rich in rhetoric, social development is still theoretically underdeveloped. Nevertheless, progress has been made in articulating its conceptual basis and identifying the major practice strategies that characterize social development's unique approach. By recognizing the field's limitations and responding to its critics, social development theory and practice can be refined and strengthened.

A major critique comes from scholars who reject social development's optimism and commitment to progress that they allege naïvely underestimates the challenges facing humanity today. They contend that problems of violence, oppression, poverty, and deprivation are so severe that attempts to deal with them through an ad hoc collection of interventions are unlikely to make much difference. Indeed, some despair that current conditions are so bad that meaningful change is unlikely, if not impossible. Nisbet (1980) pointed out that many respected scholars and literary figures reject the Western belief in progress arguing instead that conflict, oppression, totalitarianism, poverty, hunger, inequality, and alienation characterize the human condition. In the 1930s, the critical theorists of the Frankfurt School took a very pessimistic view of social conditions, and more recently, postmodernists have ridiculed the idea of progress. The grand narratives of change, they believe, cloak the oppressive impact of modernist social science that has legitimated oppression. Similar ideas have been expressed by post-development scholars like Sachs who believe that development "stands like a ruin . . . delusion and disappointment, failures and crimes have been the steady companion of development" (2010, p. 1).

Other critics question social development's belief that social progress can be achieved through combining economic and social policies within a comprehensive development process. Environmental critics challenge the view that economic growth is an effective way of achieving improvements in standards of living and claim instead that it has fostered consumerism causing environmental damage. They contend that social development's faith in economic growth is misplaced, and instead propose the creation of a steady-state economy and small scale sustainable productive activities (Daly, 1996; Jackson, 2009). Others are critical of the way economic development has undermined traditional values and community solidarity. They too advocate for a return to traditional community-based economic activities that provide the means by which families can earn their livelihoods. Others like Titmuss (1974) are skeptical of the idea that social policy should serve economic interests. He criticized the "handmaiden" approach to social policy that links social welfare to work performance and argued instead that welfare services should be provided solely on the basis of need. Similarly, Morel, Pallier and Palme (2012) question social development's productivism for being instrumentalist and utilitarian. Titmuss's criticism has been echoed by others who are concerned that the emphasis placed on social investments in social development may ignore the needs of those who are unable to participate in the economy. They are particularly concerned that social development's emphasis on labor participation may result in the withdrawal of aid to needy groups on the grounds that employment is a viable and available alternative.

Other critics are more troubled about social development's commitment to intervention, particularly by the state. Their concerns, which range from a dogmatic rejection of government intervention of any kind, to unease about bureaucratic inefficiency, are hardly new. Indeed, in the nineteenth century, the philosopher Herbert Spencer vigorously attacked the charities as well as government "interference," which he claimed impedes society's natural evolution toward higher levels of civilization. As was noted in Chapter 7 of this book, scholars such as von Hayek and Friedman also criticized state intervention, claiming that it not only harms the natural functioning of the economy, but leads to increasing government control over people's lives. Critiques of state intervention have also been made by radical populists who believe that governments are invariably corrupt, inefficient, and engaged in a bureaucratically managed "top down" style of development that oppresses local people. Together with Marxist inspired activists, they reject the idea that social development's incrementalist approach can bring about progressive change. Instead, they believe that radical resistance and even revolutionary violence is needed. Some also contend that the field's commitment to economic development amounts to little more than a thinly disguised embrace of capitalist ideas. As will be apparent, these criticisms reflect competing normative preferences that have created tensions as advocates of different perspectives insist on the validity of their own approaches and dismiss or ignore others.

Although attempts have been made to respond to these critiques, and even to reconcile the field's competing normative preferences and practice strategies, it is clear that many challenges remain. More work is needed to refine the social development approach and enhance its theoretical standing. Also, the formidable obstacles to achieving social development goals need to be realistically assessed and addressed. Nevertheless, social development scholars and practitioners believe that the strategies and interventions discussed in this chapter can bring about significant improvements in social welfare. They are also persuaded that much has been achieved. They contend that the Millennium Development Goals, which exemplify the social development approach, has for the first time in history brought the world's nations together in a common commitment to eradicate poverty and deprivation. They also applaud the adoption of the new Sustainable Development Goals. Despite ongoing challenges, including wars and conflicts, global recession, hatred and discrimination, climate adversity, and entrenched power structures that deny human rights to many of the world's peoples, the adoption of the Goals as well as other progressive developments suggest that social development has a vitally important role to play in promoting social wellbeing today.

❖

Suggested Additional Reading

For many years, the literature on social development consisted of reports published by international agencies, such as the United Nations and the World Bank; but since the 1980s, academic publications in the field have appeared with increasing frequency. Although the literature on social development is still limited, more books and articles on the subject are being published and more information about social development practice in different countries is now available. In addition, a number of scholars have examined the theoretical foundations of social development and formulated conceptual models on which social development practice can be based.

- Beneria, L. (2003). *Gender, development and globalization: Economics as if all people mattered.* New York, NY: Routledge. Drawing on a well-established literature showing that women's contribution has been neglected in mainstream economics and development studies, the author makes the case for an approach to development that incorporates a gendered perspective and is wholly inclusive.
- Hall, A., & Midgley, J. (2004). *Social policy for development.* Thousand Oaks, CA: SAGE. This comprehensive book specifically links social development to the interdisciplinary subject of social policy and provides a broad overview of the different fields comprising social development. These include poverty and inequality, rural development, basic education, health services, social security, social work, and human services.
- Jones, J., & Pandey, R. (Eds.). (1981). *Social development: Conceptual, methodological and policy issues.* New York, NY: St. Martin's Press. This edited collection was the first to define social development as a distinctive academic and practice field. Although much of the book's contents are now out of date, the definitions by Pandey and Pavia and their discussion of social development's features remain relevant and useful.
- Midgley, J. (2014). *Social development: Theory and practice.* London, UK: SAGE. Building on his earlier book *Social Development: The Developmental Perspective in Social Welfare.* London, UK: SAGE, 1995, the author provides an account of the history, theoretical dimensions, and practice strategies that are used to promote social development. These include human capital, employment policies and programs, social capital, microenterprise, asset development, social protection, and social planning. The book concludes with the author's own normative interpretation of the best way that the social development agenda can be achieved.
- Pawar, M. S., & Cox, D. (Eds.). (2010). *Social development: Critical themes and perspectives.* New York, NY: Routledge. This book reviews key themes and issues in social development. It focuses largely on community-based activities, such as participation, self-reliance, and capacity building. However, it also discusses conceptual approaches to social development and considers ethical issues in the field.
- United Nations. (2000). *The Millennium Declaration.* New York, NY: Author. The Millennium Declaration adopted at a special session of the United Nations General Assembly has played an important role in social development over the last decade. It provides useful insights into the way governments and international bodies like the United Nations define social development.

Part III

Social Welfare for a Global Era

11

International Collaboration in Social Welfare

Although the world's governments have entered into diplomatic compacts and trade agreements for centuries, international collaboration in social welfare is of more recent origin. Many scholars believe that the first purposeful attempts to foster international social welfare collaboration were made in the nineteenth century when a number of nonprofits in Europe and North America established links with their counterparts in other countries. Concerned with the abolition of slavery, the promotion of peace, securing votes and other rights for women, and advocating for temperance, these efforts resulted in the creation of the first international social welfare organizations. Their activities were augmented when governments established the first international organizations to deal with problems that reached beyond their own borders. The first of these emerged in the years following the Napoleonic wars to promote collaboration in fields such as water rights and public health.

Today, international cooperation is commonplace as many governments establish exchange programs with other nations, and a great variety of nonprofit and faith-based organizations provide services in multiple countries. A number of nonprofits such as Save the Children Fund, OXFAM, as well as faith-based organizations like CARITAS now operate on a truly global scale. Arguably, the most important form of international collaboration takes place through the official international organizations like the United Nations and its affiliate agencies. They have actively promoted international collaboration through conferences, consultation, and a sizeable number of treaties signed by their member states. These treaties set standards and promote collaboration in a number of fields. Of considerable importance are the Millennium Development Goals which committed the member states of the United Nations to improve social welfare by achieving a set of measurable social targets. They also require extensive collaboration between different governments and the involvement of nonprofits and international organizations. Collaboration will continue as the new Sustainable Development Goals are implemented. As will be apparent, these diverse activities have fostered a complex mix of international cooperative activities that enhance social wellbeing at the global level. It is likely that international collaboration in social welfare will intensify in the future.

Although this chapter is largely concerned with the work of the official international organizations, such as the United Nations, World Bank, International Labour Organisation (ILO) and similar bodies, it also examines the role of international nonprofits, faith-based organizations, and foundations as well as the contribution of ordinary people who give donations or send remittances and gifts abroad. The chapter begins with a historical overview of international social welfare collaboration and then discusses the different ways international organizations, nonprofits, and governments work together. Some of the challenges of international social welfare collaboration are also discussed. It concludes that many of these challenges can be met and that international collaboration is making a major contribution to enhancing social welfare in the global era.

History of International Social Welfare Collaboration

As mentioned earlier, international cooperation in social welfare began on an organized basis in the nineteenth century when European governments began to collaborate and the first international nonprofit organizations were established. Before the nineteenth century, cooperation in the field was largely limited to religious charities, which accompanied the spread of the world religions as monasteries, temples, mosques, and churches dispensed aid to the needy in different societies. Although political alliances have been forged throughout history, Mazower (2012) observes that it was only in the nineteenth century that the precursors of modern international organizations were created. He believes that the Concert of Europe (mentioned in the book's introduction), was a major step, but that the primary impetus for international cooperation actually came from social reformers. Among the earliest was the Anti-Corn League which campaigned in the 1830s against the British government's restrictions on the importation of grains that unfairly protected wealthy landowners. American temperance campaigners who hosted the first World Temperance Convention in 1846, and the international peace movement which convened its first Peace Conference in Brussels in 1848 also made pioneering contributions. The founding of the International Workingmen's Association in 1864 to organize industrial workers and support the nascent trade union movement was another important development; its work was inspired by the writings of Karl Marx and Friedrich Engels, both of whom were active members of the organization. Women were also extensively involved in social reform playing a leading role in the antislavery, temperance, and peace movements and campaigning tirelessly for voting rights. This period was also marked by important international events. The first world trade fair was held in London in 1851, the first transatlantic telegraph cable was laid in 1858, and the first modern Olympic Games were held in 1896.

These developments were accompanied by increased cooperation between governments. Iriye (2002) believes that the first intergovernmental organization in modern times was the Central Commission for the Navigation of the Rhine that was created by the Concert of Europe at the end of the Napoleonic wars. Another early example was the Superior Council of Health, which was established by a group of European governments together with the Ottoman Turkish imperial authorities in 1838 to combat the spread of communicable diseases. Intergovernmental organizations of this kind proliferated during the nineteenth century to manage international mail, telegraphic communications, and coastal navigation among others. Treaties were formulated and acceded to by member governments to ensure that these international organizations had sufficient funds and support. Increased governmental cooperation in social welfare also fostered policy learning as politicians and administrators traveled to other countries to study welfare innovations. One example is the Japanese government's decision in the late nineteenth century to send senior civil servants to several European countries and to the United States to collect information that could inform its own social welfare initiatives. Goodman (1998) reports that Japan under the Meiji government was one of the first countries to base local policy innovations on studies of welfare practices elsewhere.

International nonprofits proliferated in the latter half of the nineteenth century. Although some nonprofits campaigned for social reform, others provided social services, and yet others represented the emerging professions of medicine, law, and engineering. Some emerged to provide humanitarian assistance and some were international federations of national nonprofit organizations. These activities were augmented by a growing number of international welfare conferences. Friedlander (1975) notes that these meetings spawned many new international nonprofit organizations and that dozens emerged by the end of the nineteenth century. Iriye (2002) reports that many were funded by their members, but that some secured support from wealthy donors. Others like the Red Cross were sponsored by governments. Still others garnered support from the churches and religious donors. One example is the Young Men's Christian Association (YMCA) that was established in London in 1844 to provide accommodation for young men seeking work in the city, but it soon spread to many other countries.

In 1910, the leaders of the expanding international nonprofit movement founded a coordinating organization known as the *Office Central des Associations Internationales* with its headquarters in Brussels. The Office served as a clearinghouse, published a journal, and actively supported the expansion of new organizations. In addition to coordinating the activities of its member organizations, Iriye (2002) points out that it was committed to promoting wider cosmopolitan ideals. The International Council on Social Welfare (ICSW), which was founded in 1928, is one of the organization's successors. Today, ICSW is composed of representatives of national nonprofit organizations from around the world. Leaders at the ICSW also fostered the international spread of social work and supported the creation of the International Association of Schools of Social Work (IASSW) in 1929. This organization represents professional social work schools in many countries. Another international social work organization is the

International Federation of Social Workers (IFSW) which was established in 1956 to represent the interests of social work practitioners. Healy (2008) reports that both organizations actively promote social work education and practice around the world today.

The creation of the League of Nations at the end of the First World War was a major development in the history of international social welfare collaboration. Like its successor, the United Nations it was primarily committed to promoting peace, but it also sponsored several international social welfare initiatives. Although the League failed in its peace mission, Mazower (2012) observes that it successfully fostered international cooperation in education, health, and social welfare. The League created a separate public health agency and initiated relief activities for refugees fleeing persecution from the civil war in the new Soviet Union. The World Health Organization and the United Nations High Commission for Refugees are successors of these early initiatives. The League also encouraged its member states to deal with social issues, such as opium addiction and the trafficking of women. Another major development was the creation of the ILO in 1919, which has promoted international collaboration in labor relations, employment, and social security.

The League also inspired the European imperial powers to expand education, health, and social services in their colonies. In the British Empire, local colonial administrations were required to use their own resources to fund social services, but Midgley (2011a) reports that additional resources were allocated in terms of the *Colonial Welfare and Development Acts* to expand education, health care, and social work programs. This development resulted in the creation of new social service programs and the training of professional staff. Initially, staff were sent to universities in the metropolitan countries to obtain professional qualifications, but subsequently local training schools were established. A number of important international conferences which brought welfare officials from different colonial territories to England were also convened. In addition to expanding the social services, Jones Finer (2004) observes that these activities laid the foundation for subsequent international collaboration between the independent British Commonwealth countries.

During the imperial era, a number of nonprofit organizations that had been established in the European countries extended their work to the colonial territories. Missionary organizations had been active in these territories for many years, but now several secular organizations followed, creating branches in the colonies. One example is the British charity Barnardo's Children's Homes which established programs in several African and Asian countries. Nonprofits also began to undertake international humanitarian work. One of the first was Save the Children Fund that was established in London to meet the needs of children affected by the First World War. Another is OXFAM which was founded in 1942 to provide assistance to civilians affected by the Second World War—it was originally known as the Oxford Committee for Famine Relief. In addition to its humanitarian activities, it has since engaged in advocacy and development work. Although the United Nations International Children's Emergency Fund (UNICEF), now known simply as the United Nations Children's Fund, is an international governmental agency, it also came into being at the end of the Second World War to provide humanitarian assistance to refugees and needy families with children.

Following the creation of the United Nations in 1945, international social welfare cooperation increased rapidly. In addition to its many other mandates, Article 55 of United Nations Charter directs the organization to promote social progress among its member states. As Deacon (2007) points out, the United Nations and its specialized agencies have exerted a profound international influence on social welfare since then. The international spread of social work, global reductions in infant mortality, world-wide improvements in public health, the promotion of human rights, the protection of refugees, and many other achievements can be attributed to the organization's diverse programs. In addition, the United Nations and its affiliate agencies have promoted the adoption of many international treaties ranging over issues such as discrimination against women, slavery and human trafficking, and children's rights—all of which are linked to its landmark Universal Declaration of Human Rights of 1948.

Another important international organization is the World Bank, which like its twin the International Monetary Fund (IMF) has been primarily concerned with ensuring global economic stability, but it has also funded social projects on a significant scale. During the presidency of Robert McNamara, it led a major initiative to reduce world poverty and it actively supported the expansion of health, education, and rural community development in the Global South. However, after the 1980s it changed course, and as Hall and Midgley (2004) point out, its structural adjustment programs resulted in serious retrenchments in the social services as well as falling living standards in developing world. At this time, it also encouraged the privatization of social security in Latin America and elsewhere. As noted earlier in this book, these policies reflected its vigorous advocacy of a market liberal approach, which in collaboration with the IMF and the United States government was dubbed the Washington Consensus (Williamson, 1990). However, more recently, it has supported the implementation of the United Nations Millennium Development Goals and prioritized poverty reduction by requiring recipient nations to develop Poverty Reduction Strategy Papers which formulate proposals for achieving this goal. Despite this apparent change in direction, Woods (2006) and others believe that the Bank remains committed to a market-based globalization agenda, and that it only provides tacit support for the Millennium Development Goals.

Regional and other specialized organizations have also proliferated over the last half century to promote international economic, military, and political collaboration. Although they are not primarily engaged in social welfare, they have affected the social policies and programs of their member states. They include regional development banks, such as the Asian and African Development Banks; the United Nations regional social and economic commissions; the Arab League; the African Union; and the European Union which, as Pochet and Degryse (2010) point out, has been very active in social policy since its founding in 1993. The Union's Lisbon Treaty that came into force in 2009 is currently promoting the social investment approach to social welfare. The Organisation for Economic Co-operation and Development (OECD), which was established in 1961 by the high-income countries, has also influenced the social policies of its member states. In the 1980s, it urged its members to reduce social spending on the grounds that welfare was harming economic growth. However, it has since changed its position and recognized that human capital investments and employment generating programs make a positive contribution to economic development. Recently, it published a major report advocating policies that promote greater income equality (OECD, 2015).

Since the Second World War, national governments have become more active in international social welfare. As members of international organizations, they participate in international initiatives and many have signed treaties dealing with social issues; international aid also plays an important role. Although governments previously gave limited aid, primarily to provide disaster relief and other forms of humanitarian assistance, it is now widely used as an instrument of political and economic policy. One of the first and probably most remarkable aid initiatives of modern times was the Marshall Plan adopted by the United States government in 1948. Named after the American Secretary of State and former Army Chief of Staff General George C. Marshall, it allocated approximately $100 billion in today's money to reconstruct the war ravaged European economies (Berhman, 2007). Recognizing its political and diplomatic potential, President Truman expanded the government's aid program, and at his inaugural address in 1949, he enunciated his famous "four points," which laid the foundation for American aid to the developing world. It combined the goals of economic assistance and the provision of technical expertise with political motives that prevented the spread of communism. Since then, literally hundreds of billions of dollars have been transferred to the Global South by the United States, other Western countries, and the former Soviet Union.

International nonprofits and faith-based organizations have also expanded rapidly in recent years. Although it was mentioned earlier that missionaries have been active in international social welfare in the Global South for many years, large international faith-based organizations have become increasingly prominent. The international trade union movement and international associations of cooperatives have also encouraged international collaboration among their member organizations, and there has been an increase in activist organizations concerned with the promotion of civil and political rights, environmental protection, poverty eradication, and women's rights, to name just a few. These developments have been accompanied by the growth of international social movements that mobilize millions of people for social reform. As mentioned in Chapter 3, anti-globalization protesters have taken to the streets of many cities to advocate for policies that regulate trade and financial flows.

Promoting International Social Welfare Cooperation

As the preceding historical overview reveals, international cooperation in social welfare is promoted by many different agents, including governments, international organizations, international nonprofits, faith-based organizations, international federations of trade unions, large business firms, and activist social movements. Individual citizens, professionals, and academics are also involved, and large business corporations also contribute through their social responsibility programs. Although international collaboration comprises a complex nexus of provision that is difficult to summarize, the following provides a brief overview of the role of the organizations and agents involved in international social welfare collaboration today.

International organizations such as the United Nations, the ILO, and the World Bank are also known as "supranational organizations," "intergovernmental organizations," and "official international organizations." They provide funds, technical assistance, and promote international collaboration through a number of instruments, including treaties, conferences, and publications. The United Nations and its specialized agencies are arguably the most prominent, but the World Bank has also made a major contribution, as has the OECD, the European Union, and other regional organizations. Although primarily concerned with economic and political collaboration, these bodies have exerted a major influence on social welfare among their member states. They are also contributing to a new system of global governance by which the international organizations exert increasing political power.

The contribution of the United Nations and its specialized agencies has been immense. As noted earlier, the organization's Charter specifically directs it to promote the social wellbeing of the people of its member states. Its Secretariat in New York, together with the Economic and Social Council (ECOSOC) and various committees and commissions collaborates closely with its specialized agencies concerned with social welfare. These include a veritable alphabet soup of agencies, such as the Food and Agricultural Organization (FAO); the United Nations Development Program (UNDP); the World Health Organization (WHO); the United Nations Fund for Population Activities (UNFPA); and the United Nations Fund for Women (UNIFEM), now known as UN Women as well as those agencies mentioned earlier, such as UNICEF and the ILO. Some agencies like UNICEF have a direct social welfare mission while others such as the United Nations Educational, Cultural, and Scientific Organization (UNESCO) affect welfare indirectly. As Kennedy (2006) notes, the United Nations' wider diplomatic and peacekeeping mission also contributes indirectly to social wellbeing around the world by seeking to mediate between conflicting parties and to foster peace.

International organizations promote collaboration in various ways. They encourage their member states to adopt social welfare innovations, send advisers and expert missions to support program development, conduct research, and produce numerous publications that provide information about best practices. Leading publications include the United Nations *Report on the World Social Situation,* which has appeared regularly ever since the organization was founded, and the *World Development Reports* published annually by the World Bank. Another is the *Human Development Report* published regularly by UNDP. The United Nations also designates particular days, years, and decades to increase public awareness of social issues. For example, the Decade of Women (1975–1985) was designed to draw attention to international efforts to promote the rights of women while the Development Decades (1960–1980) were intended to create greater awareness of its efforts in the fields of economic and social development.

Treaties have been used for centuries to secure legally binding collaborative agreements between governments that are known as State Parties. Treaties are also known as conventions, covenants, compacts, agreements, or accords. In the United Nations system, many international treaties are specifically designed to promote social welfare, but many others that have an indirect effect have also been adopted. Treaties are often based on declarations arising from international meetings. Although declarations are not legally binding, they are usually forwarded to the organization's member states for signature and ratification followed by the adoption of the treaty. The United Nations *Declaration on Human Rights* of 1948 formed the basis for many international treaties, notably the *International Covenant on Civil and Political Rights,* and the *International Covenant on Economic, Social, and Cultural Rights,* both of which were adopted by the General Assembly in 1966. The latter treaty covers issues such as the right to self-determination, an adequate standard of living, and freedom from discrimination as well as more immediate social welfare concerns such as the right to social security, parental leave, and access to primary education. An important treaty in the social welfare field is the *Convention on the Rights of the Child,* which was adopted by the General Assembly in 1989—thirty years after it was first proposed as the *Declaration on the Rights of the Child.*

Other international organizations, such as the ILO and WHO, also make use of declarations and treaties. An important ILO treaty is the *Social Security Minimum Standards Convention* of 1952 that outlined the obligations of State Parties to promote social protection. It has since been succeeded by a large number of instruments dealing with different aspects of social protection. Important international human rights treaties that have a direct bearing on social welfare include the *European Convention on Human Rights and Fundamental Rights* of 1950 adopted by the Council of Europe; the *American Convention on Human Rights,* also known as the *Pact of San Jose* adopted in 1969 by the member states of the Organization of American States; and the *African Charter on Human and People's Rights* of 1981, adopted by the Organization of African Unity, which is now known as the African Union. In some cases, declarations and compacts that are not adopted as treaties nevertheless play an important role in promoting social welfare goals. One example is the *Declaration of Alma-Ata* that was adopted at an international WHO conference in Kazakhstan in 1978, and which inspired a significant shift in health policy around the world. Another is the *Global Compact* initiated by the United Nations and adopted by the World Economic Forum to encourage businesses to engage in social and environmental activities.

International meetings and conferences are another important way of promoting international collaboration in social welfare. They provide opportunities for government officials, academics, and the leaders of nonprofit organizations to meet and discuss welfare concerns. A large number of conferences in the social welfare field have been convened over the years, and some have been particularly important in setting international policy agendas. One of these was the First World Conference on Women held in Mexico City in 1975, which prompted the United Nations to announce the 1975–1985 Decade of Women. It also set into motion procedures for the adoption of the *Convention on the Elimination of all Forms of Discrimination against Women* (CEDAW) by the General Assembly in 1979. The World Social Summit for Social Development held in Copenhagen in 1995 was very important since it led to the adoption of the Millennium Development Goals at a meeting of the General Assembly in 2000. Both meetings were unusual in that they were attended by the majority of the world's heads of state. They also mobilized governments as well as international organizations like the World Bank to participate in an unprecedented collaborative effort to reduce the incidence of world poverty and address other social concerns. The Millennium Summit was the first time in history that the world's nations jointly agreed to a plan of action of this kind. The adoption of the new Sustainable Development Goals in 2015 is evidence of an ongoing commitment among the world's governments to promote social progress at both the national and global levels.

National Governments, Nonprofits, and Other Agents

Today, national governments, nonprofit and faith-based organizations, as well as individuals make a significant contribution to international social welfare collaboration. The governments of many nation states enter into agreements with other governments to share information and expertise and fund social programs. Moreover, a good deal of informal collaboration like visits to study social welfare innovations in other countries takes place. Also, as members of international organizations such as the United Nations and the ILO, national governments pay dues which are used to fund international programs. However, many are international donors in their own right and provide what is known as *bilateral aid* or Official Development Assistance (ODA) to governments and nonprofits in other countries. Aid involves the transfer of resources from donors to recipients, but third parties that contract with donors to provide services or manage social programs are also involved. Today, nonprofits are often contracted to implement social programs and projects funded through international aid. Although aid is mostly provided by Western countries, South to South cooperation as it is known has become common. Surender and Urbina-Ferretjans (2013) report that many developing countries, and especially rapidly growing countries such as Brazil, China, and India, now provide international aid to low-income countries.

Although international aid has been primarily concerned with economic development and particularly large-scale infrastructural projects, military aid and especially the supply of weapons and technologies also feature prominently in the aid budgets of Western countries. In the social welfare field, aid usually funds the construction of schools, clinics, and community centers as well as a variety of social programs and community development projects. This usually involves the provision of technical assistance in the form of advisers and experts. However, Hall and Midgley (2004) point out that social welfare aid comprises only a small part of international aid allocations. International volunteers provided by national governments are also an important form of social welfare aid. Although the American government's Peace Corps that usually assigns its volunteers to work on community-based social projects is probably the best known, many other countries also have programs of this kind. It should be remembered that most aid is given in the form of low interest concessionary loans and must be repaid. Grant aid is also given, but it is usually targeted at low-income developing countries, and is often restricted to humanitarian programs catering to refugees or for disaster relief.

Among the best known international nonprofit organizations concerned with international social welfare today are large humanitarian organizations such as Oxfam, Save the Children, ActionAid, and the Red Cross. Because of their size, these organizations are sometimes known as BINGOs—Big International Nongovernmental Organizations. They are organizationally complex, mobilize considerable resources, and have a global reach working through branches in different countries. They also make effective use of the media to publicize their activities, especially their humanitarian programs in famine or war-ravaged countries. In addition to fundraising among the general public, they also access resources from national governments and large foundations, particularly in Western countries. Foundations are also active at the international level, and as Lewis and Kanji (2009) point out, they are major sponsors of social development programs in the Global South.

Less well-known, but equally important, are faith-based and missionary organizations that augment their evangelical role with educational, health, and social services. They include organizations such as Christian Aid, CARITAS, and World Vision as well as international Islamic, Buddhist, and similar organizations. In addition to well-established Muslim organizations such as the Red Crescent Society and the Aga Khan foundation, Harrigan and El-Said (2009) point out that Islamist political organizations such as the Muslim Brotherhood and Hamas sponsor a variety of social programs in Middle Eastern countries. Also, Jawad (2009) notes that many Islamic congregations raise funds to establish social services to meet the needs of Muslim communities in poor countries. Christian congregations are also engaged in fundraising of this kind; in addition, Wuthnow (2009) reports that many support international activism by lobbying for human rights, poverty eradication, and peace. Marshall and Van Saanen (2007) observe that faith-based organizations now make a major contribution to social development by providing community development, child and maternal health, safe drinking water, and similar programs in the Global South. Their contribution is increasingly recognized by international organizations like the World Bank.

Federations of national organizations comprise another type of international non-profit organization. The International Council on Social Welfare (ICSW) mentioned earlier is an example of this type of organization. Usually, international professional associations consist of federations of national organizations. One example is the International Federation of Social Workers (IFSW), which represents national organizations of professional social workers. A sizable number of international academic organizations have also been established to represent the interests of scholars working in different fields. Some international organizations represent groups of people with special needs who organize on their own behalf. These self-help groups generally operate at the domestic level, but they have also formed international bodies to advocate at the global level. Also, trade unions in many countries are affiliated with international bodies like the International Confederation of Free Trade Unions (ICFTU) that not only represent workers' interests globally, but advocate for social causes.

A related form of international social welfare collaboration comes from the cooperative movement. Although neglected in the international social welfare literature, cooperatives have played a major role in social welfare around the world, and as Williams (2007) points out, are increasingly influencing international thinking in the field. They feature prominently in the Millennium Development Goals agenda, and are the core of the fair trade movement that has garnered popular support in Western countries. Nicholls and Opal (2005) believe that the fair trade movement has not only helped small producers in the Global South to improve their livelihoods, but has fostered greater understanding of the challenges facing developing countries. It has also mobilized support for international development programs.

Some international nonprofit organizations are engaged in activism. Many make extensive use of the media to garner support for their causes, and some like Greenpeace use provocative tactics to draw public attention to their activities. Others such as Amnesty International and Human Rights Watch, are less confrontational, but nevertheless are resolute in their determination to expose human rights abuses and to protect political prisoners. These organizations are often linked to wider social movements that emerge spontaneously around particular issues. Many give voice to millions of people who are concerned about the oppression of women, environmental degradation, climate change, the eradication of AIDS, world poverty, the effects of economic globalization, and the violation of human rights; but often they emerge without a coherent organizational base and are seldom represented by a single and easily recognized organization, as is the case with Greenpeace and Amnesty International. However, they often garner support from better established organizations. They also influence public opinion and the policies of national governments and international organizations. As Ahmed and Potter (2006) point out, their campaigns have often fostered the adoption of international social welfare treaties.

A seldom recognized feature of international social welfare collaboration is the involvement of millions of ordinary people who support programs in other countries by giving donations or volunteering their time. Many migrants send remittances to family members and friends abroad, and many people provide financial support to international nonprofits and social movement organizations that campaign for social change. As mentioned earlier in this book, some people also participate through the Internet by making direct donations to nonprofits in low-income countries, or to individuals in need. Others use the Internet to promote small business development in the Global South through organizations like the microfinancing nonprofit KIVA, which is based in San Francisco. These initiatives build on child sponsorship programs which are popular among Western donors. Another form of individual giving comes from wealthy celebrities who have established charities in other countries or adopted children from abroad. In many cases, their activities have been accompanied by extensive media coverage and are sometimes referred to as "glamour" or "celebrity" aid. Popular concerts that raise money for humanitarian relief have also attracted large numbers of supporters and media attention.

The role of the business community in international social welfare should also be recognized. Although commercial firms are primarily engaged in economic production and providing services for profit, many have social responsibility programs that support social welfare activities around the world. Although these programs are often dismissed as amounting to little more than a public relations exercise, some do make a positive contribution. In addition, large multinationals are sensitive to media campaigns that affect their brands. Campaigns against labor exploitation in developing countries and particularly the exploitation of women and children have been quite effective, and some firms have responded positively. Also, as was noted earlier, commercial firms provide health, education, and social services in many countries on a contract for-profit basis with governments and international organizations. Although still limited largely to the Western countries, contracting by commercial firms is likely to increase internationally. However, the role of commercial enterprises in international social welfare remains controversial.

Issues and Challenges of International Social Welfare Cooperation

While the positive impact of international cooperation in social welfare is universally recognized, the collaborative activities discussed earlier face numerous challenges. International organizations and nonprofits experience ongoing difficulties in mobilizing sufficient resources to promote international cooperation, and they are also faced with implementation challenges, such as a lack of proper coordination, poor planning, and inadequate staff training. In addition to these practical problems, international collaboration raises a number of contentious issues. These concern the contribution of international aid, the effectiveness of international organizations, the appropriateness of policy transfers, and the role of power and ideology in international social welfare collaboration.

Although it is widely accepted that aid is an indispensable means of promoting social welfare in the Global South, it has been a topic of intense debate for many years. It has been claimed that international social welfare aid, like other forms of aid, is primarily designed to promote the commercial and political interests of donor countries, and that the people of the low-income countries for whom the aid is intended derive few benefits. Governments receiving aid are usually required to purchase goods and services from donor countries, and since aid is given in the form of credit, recipient governments actually pay for these goods and services. In addition, many donors use aid to promote diplomatic goals and to secure the loyalty of recipient governments. Aid programs have also been widely criticized for poor management and wastage. A significant proportion of aid is spent on administration and salaries, and many managers, government officials, and expatriate advisors receive disproportionately high remuneration. Aid is sometimes siphoned off by political and administrative elites, and staff are often hired because of their political or family connections. Corruption has recently become a major issue in international aid, and in a best-selling book, Moyo (2009) contends that because of corruption and mismanagement, aid to Africa is a primary cause of the continent's stagnation.

Humanitarian aid is generally viewed positively by the public, but it has also been criticized. Hall and Midgley (2004) contend that contrary to popular media images, the poorest countries have not been the primary recipients of humanitarian aid that has actually gone to countries such as Iraq, Israel, and the states of the former Yugo-slavia primarily to promote political goals. In a scathing critique, Polman (2010) links humanitarian aid to political and military motives pointing out that it actually sustains violence by providing resources to those who are responsible for the conflict in the first place. For example, by providing humanitarian aid to the refugee Hutu militias that fled Rwanda after the genocide, aid organizations perpetuated the conflict. She alleges that both governments and nonprofits are involved in these "war games," as she calls them.

However, not all humanitarian aid works in this way, and international emer-gency relief has undoubtedly alleviated suffering and saved millions of lives. Certainly, many people are motivated by a genuine sense of compassion when viewing distress-ing media images of the victims of floods, earthquakes, famines, and other disasters, and many give generously. Nevertheless, humanitarian aid organizations have been criticized for exploiting these images to fund their own organizations and opera-tions. Coordination between different organizations that deploy rapidly to disaster stricken areas has also been a major problem, and in many cases, duplication, wastage, and even competition between aid agencies has impeded relief efforts. In addition, humanitarian agencies have been criticized for being more concerned with short-term relief than long-term reconstruction. For example, despite allocating many millions of dollars to help those affected by the disastrous 2010 earthquake in Haiti, many people remain homeless and still live in poverty and squalor.

Another concern relates to the work of the international organizations, such as the United Nations and World Bank. In addition to criticisms about managerial efficiency, bureaucratization, and the cost of operations, both organizations have been subject to ideological attacks. During the 1990s, with the rise of neoconservative factions in the United States, the United Nations was vilified by Americans on the political right for pandering to the wishes of its members from the Global South and for failing to take a stand on human rights and democratic governance. They were also incensed by the organization's position on the environment and reproductive rights, and its opposi-tion to the settlement policies of the Israeli government. They were in particular infu-riated by the organization's failure to approve the American invasion of Iraq. During President George Bush's administration, the United States representative at the United Nations, Mr. John Bolton, retaliated by seeking to block collaboration on social issues, such as the Millennium Development Goals.

On the other hand, the World Bank has been criticized by those on the political left for promoting capitalist interests and failing to address the needs of the world's poor. Stiglitz's (2002) critique attracted considerable media attention since he had served as the Bank's chief economist, but similar criticisms have been published. One of these by Berkman (2008), who also served on the Bank's staff, takes a particularly jaundiced view attacking the organization for mismanagement, wastage, and poor oversight over its projects. Despite the Bank's claims to have contributed significantly to improved living standards in the Global South, he contends that its impact on poverty has been negligible. Other international organizations, such as the OECD and even the European Union have also been criticized by the left for promoting market liberalism. Criticisms have also been leveled at the United Nations' Millennium

Development Goals for failing to address the needs of women and ignoring the issue of inequality. Pogge (2010) even believes that this international initiative amounts to little more than a public relations exercise. However, these critiques have been countered by more positive assessments of the work of the international organizations like Rodgers' (2009) account of the ILO, which he argues has been a leading champion of international social justice.

Nevertheless, as Goldin (2013) points out, there are genuine concerns about the effectiveness of the international organizations and the extent to which they actually promote collaboration. A major problem is their size, bureaucratization, and lack of coordination not only between different organizations, but within the same organization. One example of this problem is the use of the term "social development" by the United Nations Secretariat in New York, and the term "human development" by UNDP. This does not mean that the work of these organizations should be dismissed as ineffectual, but rather that reforms are needed. In her assessment of the World Bank's policies and programs, Woods (2006) calls for a recommitment to its original mission of stabilizing the international economy and protecting the livelihoods of hundreds of millions of hard-working people. Similarly, several writers, including Kennedy (2006) and Mazower (2012) make recommendations for improving the United Nations system, and Deacon (2007) offers a comprehensive set of proposals for enhancing global governance.

Despite their positive contribution, international nonprofit and faith-based organizations also face challenges relating to funding, managerial efficiency, and the coordination of services. They have also been criticized on wider policy grounds. A major concern, which was raised in Chapter 5 of this book, is the extent to which nonprofit organizations are truly independent and able to pursue their mission without being co-opted by governments, foundations, and the business community. As Ahmed and Potter (2006) point out, the relationship between nonprofits and donors is delicate since donor governments and foundations usually expect their funds to be used to further their own agendas rather than those of recipient nonprofits. Many nonprofits have also been criticized for drifting into cozy relationships with governments and international agencies with the result that their advocacy mission has been diluted. In addition, Choudry and Kapoor (2013) observe that they often promote the careers of their staff rather than the interests of the people they serve. Foundations have also been criticized for using their considerable resources to control nonprofits. Partnerships with the business community have also been denounced because nonprofits contracted by multinational firms to ensure decent working conditions in their factories abroad have failed to achieve this goal. The disastrous factory fires in Bangladesh in 2012 and 2013 are dramatic examples of this problem. Equally problematic are the partnerships being forged between multinational firms and nonprofit organizations in the developing countries that market commercial products. Faith-based organizations have also been criticized for lacking independence, and even for promoting sectarianism. Despite contributing to social development, they remain committed to a particular religious view, and as Flanigan (2010) argues, many exacerbate existing religious tensions by focusing resources on their own congregants.

There has been a good deal of debate around the issue of policy transfer, which plays a major role in international social welfare collaboration today. In the 1950s and 1960s, it was widely assumed that the social welfare policies and practices of the former colonial powers represented a modern and efficient way of meeting social needs and should be emulated by the newly independent developing countries. Accordingly, many copied Western educational, health, housing, and social service models. Since then, this approach has been widely criticized for being expensive, urban based, and exclusionary. For example, hospital-based medical care consumes the greater part of the national health care budget of many developing countries diverting resources from primary care that better serves the needs of the majority of the population. Similarly, disproportionate government spending on universities and elite secondary schools limits access to primary education. Housing estates designed ostensibly for the poor have instead accommodated civil servants and military officers, and welfare services that focus on the urban destitute ignore the needs of the deprived majority who live in the rural areas.

There is far more awareness of the need for reciprocal policy learning and for the adaptation of international innovations to fit local conditions. As explained in Chapter 1 of this book, this has become a major concern of scholars working in the field. Nevertheless, inappropriate policy exchanges still take place on a significant scale and often involve the transfer of innovations that serve wider ideological agendas. For example, Easterly (2006) challenges the use of international aid, particularly by the IMF and World Bank to promote market liberalism in the developing world, contending that this has wreaked havoc on local economic development. Similarly, Orenstein (2008) criticizes the Bank's role in advocating pension privatization that he claims has fostered highly inappropriate policy transfers. One particularly dramatic example of this problem is given by Casey and Dostal (2008) who show that the replication of the Chilean pension privatization by the government of Nigeria has been little short of disastrous. On the other hand, advocates of market liberal development, such as Polak and Warwick (2013) insist that the developing countries will only prosper when they adopt wide-ranging market reforms. Instead of relying on aid, which they contend amounts to little more than a pernicious form of charity, governments should borrow on commercial markets to invest in productive enterprises that foster economic growth and development.

As these examples reveal, international collaboration in social welfare is not always based on mutual understanding and the pursuit of common goals, and as noted earlier, many problems need to be resolved. Although this does not mean that international social welfare cooperation has been ineffectual, it does require a realistic and pragmatic approach that recognizes the role of values, ideologies, and power differences in international exchanges. In addition, the criticisms of international social welfare collaboration discussed earlier are useful for exposing underlying challenges and pointing the way toward more productive and mutually supportive exchanges based on trust, reciprocal learning, sound research, and the documentation of best practices. They also suggest that a wider commitment to cosmopolitan values that promote a one world perspective is needed. This issue is taken up in the following Epilogue.

Suggested Additional Reading

International collaboration in social welfare has increased rapidly in recent years as governments, international agencies, and nonprofit organizations have cooperated to address pressing social problems around the world. The business community, activist social movements, and committed individuals have also contributed. The following books provide useful insights into international social welfare collaboration today and the way it is contributing to people's wellbeing in the global era.

- Ahmed, S., & Potter, D. M. (2006). *NGOs in international politics.* Bloomfield, CT: Kumarian Press. Nongovernmental organizations have played an increasingly important role in international social welfare collaboration since the 1980s. Discussing their activities and their relationships with governments and international organizations, the authors provide an insightful analysis of their contribution. They also discuss the way nonprofits exert political influence at the global level.
- Deacon, B. (2007). *Global social policy and governance.* London, UK: SAGE. The author, who is an acknowledged leader in the international social welfare field, provides a comprehensive overview of the many organizations involved in international social welfare collaboration today. In addition to documenting the work of the United Nations, the World Bank, and other intergovernmental organizations, he discusses the role of nonprofit organizations, trade unions, and the business community. He concludes with an analysis of how social policy will evolve at the global level in the future.
- Easterly, W. (2006). *The White man's burden: Why the West's efforts to aid the rest has done so much ill and so little good.* New York, NY: Penguin Books. In this racy and provocative book, the author criticizes international aid programs for failing to achieve their goals. He is particularly critical of aid that is tied to ideological agendas, which he claims are inimical to grassroots development efforts in the Global South. The book contains a number of recommendations for addressing these problems.
- Hokenstad, M. C., & Midgley, J. (Eds.). (2004). *Lessons from abroad: Adapting international social welfare innovations.* Washington, DC: NASW Press. This was one of the first books to discuss international collaboration among professional social workers with reference to the way they and social policymakers in the United States can learn from colleagues in other nations, including the developing countries of the Global South.
- Kennedy, P. (2006). *The parliament of man: The past, present and future of the United Nations.* New York, NY: Random House. The United Nations, which currently has more than 190 member states, has played a major role in the construction of the modern world order. In this useful book, Kennedy traces the history of the ideas on which the organization was founded and discusses the events and activities that led to its creation in 1945. The book concludes with an interesting discussion of the organization's likely future.
- Mazower, M. (2012). *Governing the world: The history of an idea.* New York, NY: Penguin Press. This very readable book traces the evolution of international collaboration in its various forms since the nineteenth century. It shows how the governments of nation states through diplomacy, international law, peace efforts,

and collaboration in a number of fields, including social welfare have sought to enhance cooperation between the world's nations.

- Woods, N. (2006). *The globalizers: The IMF, the World Bank and their borrowers.* Ithaca, NY: Cornell University Press. Tracing the history of the IMF and World Bank, the author critically examines their policies and programs in the light of their original mission to stabilize the global economy, assist governments experiencing financial difficulties, and promote development. Arguing that these goals have been increasingly subsumed under a globalizing mission that is concerned with promoting neoliberalism, she calls for wide-ranging policy reforms.

12

Epilogue: Toward a One World Perspective in Social Welfare

This book has shown that a very complex system of provision comprising different welfare institutions, agents, and interventions has evolved over the years to enhance the wellbeing of the world's peoples. It has focused on the welfare institutions that provide a cultural context for the different policies and practices that meet social needs, solve problems, and maximize opportunities. It has also shown that despite making significant progress, many challenges still need to be addressed. These range from administrative and funding problems to more profound concerns, such as the pervasiveness of violence and the perpetuation of cultural, religious, economic, and political divisions that continue to afflict the global community. Addressing these divisions by fostering inclusiveness and a shared identity among the world's people is arguably the most pressing of these challenges. Although the promotion of a one world perspective that can foster this goal seems unlikely in the face of persistent violence, poverty, exploitation, oppression, and hatred, advocates of international social welfare should aspire to achieve this goal.

This Epilogue examines the prospect of adopting a one world perspective that can provide a framework for international social welfare policy and practice as well as scholarly inquiry. Although a great deal has already been achieved, particularly through the work of the international organizations, more effort is needed to ensure that international social welfare promotes social wellbeing everywhere. Scholarly inquiry into international social welfare has expanded greatly in recent years, but there is a need for a single conceptual framework that incorporates the insights of different disciplines and provides a comprehensive foundation for practice. In particular, the tendency to see the world as a divided place in which nations are separated into simple categories—such as the North South typology—needs to be replaced with a one world perspective that views the world as a single human community. Similarly, the practice of imposing Western conceptual frameworks on other countries to analyze their welfare policies and practices should be ended.

To promote a one world perspective in social welfare, the Epilogue draws liberally on the theory of cosmopolitanism that has inspired proposals for uniting the world's people over the years. It discusses the concept and its history and reviews different proposals for creating a single global community. Although some of these are of little relevance to the approach adopted here, they can be contrasted with the cosmopolitan position advocated in this chapter that is rooted in social democratic thinking. This approach, it is argued, can form the basis for a one world perspective in social welfare. Because of its liberal pluralistic commitments, it promotes democratic participation and accommodates diversity within a wider global order. It also requires the creation of institutions, guaranteed by states, which enhance wellbeing and foster inclusion and equality. However, it should be recognized that this approach will be vigorously contested. Because it involves deeply held values, identities, and issues of power and privilege, there are many who will oppose efforts to achieve global unity, promote international social welfare, and redistribute resources.

Roots of the One World Perspective

The term one world is taken from the title of a best-selling book published in 1943 by the American politician Wendell Wilkie who unsuccessfully campaigned against President Roosevelt in the 1940 presidential election. After the election, Roosevelt asked Wilkie to undertake an international fact-finding mission that could inform the administration's foreign policy at a time when war seemed imminent. During 1941 and 1942, Wilkie visited more than a dozen countries and met with various world leaders, public figures, military officers, soldiers, and citizens. Although often construed as a travelogue, the book addressed many international policy issues. Wilkie strongly supported the President's proposals for the creation of the United Nations, argued for greater American engagement in the world, and advocated for improvements in international trade and greater efforts to prevent future wars. He called for an end to European imperialism, and unusual for the time, devoted a whole chapter to what he called "imperialism at home," namely the oppression of people of color in the United States. Anticipating Giddens's (1998) concepts of space and time compression, he argued that the world has not only become "smaller on the map, but in people's minds," and in the future, he suggested that "our thinking must be worldwide" (1943, p. 2). Although his book was vigorously attacked by critics on the political right, it reflected the spirit of internationalism of the time and its title captured the essence of the approach adopted in this book. This approach is based on the idea that despite their cultural, religious, and linguistic differences, the world's people are members of one community, and that as members of this community their wellbeing deserves the highest priority.

This idea reflects the centuries-old tradition of cosmopolitanism that today inspires efforts to promote global governance and international cooperation. It also provides a normative framework for international social welfare. The term cosmopolitanism is derived from the Greek word *cosmopolis*, which is variously translated as world state, world government, and world citizen. It is said to have originated with the peripatetic Cynic philosopher Diogenes, who when asked about his citizenship replied that he was a citizen of the world. This idea was taken up by Zeno and the Stoic philosophers who linked the notion of world citizenship to universal government and universal law. Although the Stoics recognized that the citizens of the *polis* are subject to the laws of their legislative assemblies, they pointed out that people everywhere are also subject to a higher natural law. By virtue of reason and conscience, people of different languages, religions, and cultures are able to discern and comply with the natural law. This idea was subsequently augmented by the theory of natural rights that posits that the natural law entitles and protects. However, to safeguard against violations of the natural law, an international authority that guarantees rights is needed. Indeed, it is the idea of establishing some form of world government that has dominated cosmopolitan thought over the centuries.

Although based on shared principles, the cosmopolitan ideal has been interpreted in different ways. One of the oldest interpretations is *hegemonic or imperial cosmopolitanism,* which is based on the idea that a single political authority should govern culturally diverse people to bring unity, peace, and prosperity. This idea has legitimated imperial rule over the centuries, and although no truly global empire has ever emerged, imperial rulers often claimed authority over the world's nations. This was dramatically illustrated in 1795 when Lord Macartney, the British envoy to the Chinese imperial court, was informed that the Celestial Emperor ruled the whole world and that the British monarch, like the rulers of other countries, was subject to his authority. Of course, the British saw things differently, and within a century they had not only eroded Chinese rule, but controlled vast territories and a large proportion of the world's population. Although European imperialism collapsed in the twentieth century, imperialist beliefs have persisted. Indeed, they were resurrected in the 1990s by American neoconservative advocates of unipolarism who argued that following the collapse of the Soviet Union, the United States had become the world's only superpower, its *de facto* government, and the guarantor of international peace (Frum & Perle, 2003; Mandelbaum, 2005). Just as the Romans and the British brought order, stability, and the "benefits" of civilization to diverse nations, Ferguson (2004) argues that the United States is now charged with exercising benevolent authority over the world's people.

Another interpretation, known as *sectarian or theological cosmopolitanism* is based on the claim that a single theocratic authority should have jurisdiction over the world's nations by virtue of its superior religious conviction. Advocates of this position claim that because there is one omnipotent God, the world's people are subject to his authority and those who are able to discern his will, such as priests and religious scholars, are best able to prescribe the beliefs and rituals that everyone should adopt. This idea was taken up by the Christian church, and during the European imperial era, forced conversions of native people in the subjugated colonial territories were commonplace. Similar ideas were expressed in Islam, and have recently been resurrected by the Islamic State and other jihadis committed to the creation of a global *caliphate*.

Another example comes from some evangelical Christians in the United States who believe that with the Messiah's return, a world government will be established to bring peace and prosperity to the world's people. They are highly critical of international organizations like the United Nations, which they contend are heretical institutions in conflict with God's purpose. The Bible, they believe, provides universal precepts for governing the world's nation, and as McDowell (2004) argues, it is only when God's laws are obeyed that peace and justice will be achieved. On the other hand, it should be recognized that many religious people do not seek to impose their beliefs on others, and indeed some religious scholars like Hans Küng have argued for accepting diverse values and beliefs. Similar ideas can be found among the followers of the Baha'i faith and in Buddhism. Indeed, the Dalai Lama's tireless commitment to world peace reflects this wider approach.

Various *secular* interpretations of cosmopolitanism have also been formulated. Of these, liberal cosmopolitanism is probably the most influential. Derived from Kant and Bentham's writings and the campaigns of nineteenth-century middle-class reformers, it inspired President Woodrow Wilson's famous "Fourteen Points" speech, the creation of the League of Nations, and the subsequent emergence of the United Nations and other international organizations. However, there are several variants of this approach. As was noted earlier in this book, market liberal advocates of globalization, such as Lal (2006) and Norberg (2003) argue that international prosperity, democracy, and peace can best be achieved by the creation of a global capitalist order. Fukuyama (1992) agrees, claiming that the spread of markets and liberal democracy is unifying the world's nations, fostering a universal ideology, and marking the "end of history." Marxists take a different view, arguing that cosmopolitan ideals can only be achieved through international socialism. These ideas were articulated by Marx and Engels and inspired Lenin's commitment to establish a "world party" and "world government" under communist leadership. Another variant is social democratic cosmopolitanism that has much in common with liberal cosmopolitanism except that it places greater emphasis on state intervention by proactive and democratic governments that act in the interests of their citizens. Shaped by the values of cooperation, collectivism, participation, and equality, social democratic cosmopolitanism has extensively influenced government welfare around the world. The social democratic approach also informs the one world approach adopted in this book.

Although seldom acknowledged, liberal and social democratic cosmopolitanism already provides a normative basis for international social welfare. The programs for the international organizations reflect these values and most international social welfare scholars also owe a debt to cosmopolitanism. Although these ideas have not been fully developed, the writings of Deacon (2007), Deacon and Stubbs (2013), Yeates (2001, 2008), and others associated with the journal *Global Social Policy* are promoting a cosmopolitan perspective in the field. This research is supported by Midgley's (2013b) contention that to understand international social welfare, the perspectives of diverse disciplinary and interdisciplinary discourses should be integrated and used to inform policy and practice.

Elements of a One World Perspective

Although social democratic cosmopolitanism already influences international social welfare thinking and practice, a more ambitious agenda that transcends current efforts to enhance international collaboration is needed. Similarly, greater effort to integrate different scholarly discourses in international social welfare inquiry is required. The following are some elements of a one world perspective that can promote a more holistic approach and foster the unity as well as the welfare of the world's peoples.

First, a one world perspective requires that changes should be made to the way the world is currently perceived and interpreted. The idea that the world has become a single place is not reflected in current classifications of the world's nations and the perpetuation of political divisions between people. The insights of world systems and world cultures theorists (Lechner & Boli, 2005; Wallerstein, 1980) suggest that the current international architecture based on a two world North-South typology, or on the older Three Worlds idea, should be revised in the light of changing events. Many countries are experiencing such rapid economic and social development so that these classifications are no longer valid. In addition to Korea and Singapore, which have become high-income countries in a relatively short period of time, China has been transformed from a poor rural society into a global economic and political power. The high level of economic modernization already achieved in many Latin American countries, as well as rapid economic growth and social improvements in many African countries, further challenges conventional classifications of the world's nation states. Also, as the United Nations Development Programme (UNDP) (2013) points out, established views about the modern world are changing as the growing interconnectedness of the nations of the Global North and South are recognized. Indeed, the realities of globalization and efforts to promote economic and political integration in Europe and elsewhere suggest that nation states themselves may not serve as the constituent units of the global era in the future. Although nation states are still the building blocks of the global era, these changing realities should be recognized.

Second, achieving a one world perspective is dependent on the reform of global governance. The enormous progress made over the last century should be augmented by a renewed commitment to strengthening international institutions, promoting social welfare and economic collaboration, and renewing a commitment to end violence, militarism, and unipolarism. It is unlikely that the current system of sovereign nation states that comprises the global era will be replaced by some form of world government, but a renewed commitment is needed to political institutions that achieve the ideals that Kant, Bentham, and others articulated many years ago. Despite its impressive achievement in responding to poverty and others social needs, few would claim that the United Nations and other international organizations have fulfilled the cosmopolitan vision. Similarly, the United Nations and other international organizations have not been able to restrain superpower ambitions and factional struggles between their member states that impede its efforts to unify the world's nations. The large, and some would claim, unwieldy bureaucracies of these organizations exacerbate these problems.

Numerous proposals for strengthening global governance and reforming the United Nations and other international organizations have been made. One of the most thoughtful is Held's (2005) Global Covenant proposal mentioned earlier in this book, which outlines a global governance framework that devolves decision making to appropriate subsidiary levels within a unitary political system. In addition, steps should be taken to expand democratic decision making on a worldwide scale. Several writers have argued for an elected world assembly and for regional legislatures that coordinate the activities of national governments. Unlike the current United Nations, an assembly of this kind would represent the population strength of different countries and have authority to implement a global agenda. It has also been argued that the Internet could be used for global electoral purposes to give voice to the world's diverse peoples. Similarly, as noted in Chapter 3 of this book, scholars like Bello (2002) and Monbiot (2003) have formulated proposals for the restructuring of the global economic system. New political and economic institutions that foster this goal should be accompanied by renewed efforts to promote peace and end exploitative and oppressive practices that are currently legitimated under the guise of globalization. Unipolar tendencies as exemplified by the imperial adventures of powerful nation states should be more vigorously resisted. By adopting these and other proposals, the world's people may enjoy full membership in a global community.

Third, international social welfare practice should be restructured. This requires improved coordination and efficient service provision within an effective system of global governance. Despite many achievements, international social welfare collaboration still faces challenges such as inadequate funding, fragmentation of services, duplication, and even interagency rivalries. A major problem is that different organizations pursue their own agenda without accommodating or even considering the priorities of other agencies. A lack of coordination is particularly evident when the programs of nonprofits, donor governments, and international organizations are compared. Despite enormous obstacles, a unitary governance structure for international social welfare can be established. The implementation of the Millennium Development Goals is a step in the right direction, but even here, improved coordination between government agencies must be augmented by greater efforts to harmonize the contributions of nonprofits, faith-based organizations, and grassroots organizations with those of other providers.

Fourth, a one world perspective requires significant changes to international social welfare scholarship, which is fragmented, based on incompatible disciplinary perspectives, and limited in explanatory power. It is also of limited value to practice. Scholars working in one disciplinary field are often ignorant of the contributions of others, impeding the development of effective practice models. A major problem is the imposition of *etic* Eurocentric concepts and theories on other societies, which Midgley (2013a) contends has been extremely unhelpful and needs to be replaced with *emic* interpretations that give expression to the voices, cultures, and lived experiences of the world's diverse people. He believes that the different discourses that pervade international social welfare inquiry should also be synthesized to generate a coherent and unitary approach that incorporates multiple institutions functioning at different levels. By drawing on the insights of world system, world society, and world cultures theory, it may be possible to situate international social welfare scholarship within a truly global conceptual framework that has ontological reality over and above that of local and national welfare activities. However, as awareness of these challenges among international social welfare scholars increases, there is scope for optimism. Indeed, scholars like Deacon and Stubbs (2013) believe that the need for a unitary methodology is more widely accepted today. Their own proposals make an important contribution toward achieving this goal.

Finally, the adoption of a one world perspective involves values and issues of power that have not been adequately addressed by international social welfare practitioners and scholars. Values are often assumed to be self-evident and the notions of social rights, social justice, and other desirable sentiments that pervade the international social welfare literature are poorly defined and seldom translated into specific agendas. It is in this regard that the values of social democratic cosmopolitanism can provide a normative framework for practice. These values include cooperation, collectivism, participation, and equality. Although rooted in the Western tradition, they have diffused internationally, and if adopted by international social welfare practitioners and scholars could provide the value basis for a one world approach.

Cooperation and collectivism are key social democratic values which posit that collective effort is needed to promote social wellbeing. Collectives, ranging from community-based cooperatives to trade unions to large associations and ultimately to the state are the best institutions for achieving this goal. Collectivism is already evident in the programs of the international organizations and also found in the statutory social services that characterize welfare provision around the world. However, as social democrats themselves recognize, state collectivism has limitations and it is for this reason that welfare pluralism is more widely accepted today, even though most social democrats insist on extensive state regulation and oversight of different providers. Other forms of collective provision like cooperatives should also be strengthened. Although they have played a historical role in social welfare, their contribution has not always been recognized. It is encouraging that the United Nations declared 2012 the Year of Cooperatives and that they are now attracting considerably more attention in social development circles. In fact, Kelly (2012) argues that cooperatives are enjoying a resurgence and contributing to a new "ownership revolution." Because they promote collectivism and foster the value of participation, cooperatives should feature more prominently in international social welfare policy and practice.

The value of equality is perhaps the most pertinent to international social welfare policy and practice. Although interpreted in different ways, egalitarianism draws on notions of social rights, social justice, and redistribution to inform a range of interventions designed to promote social inclusion and enhance social wellbeing. In recent times, egalitarian ideals have been assailed by market liberals who claim that redistribution amounts to a confiscatory Robin Hood strategy that undermines economic development and fosters dependency. Recently, however, equality is again on the agenda and social democrats are now more inclined to advocate for redistribution through progressive taxation and the provision of universal social services. Recently, the redistributive effects of cash transfers has been recognized, and it has been shown that these programs not only contribute to poverty alleviation, but foster greater income equality. As Soares (2013) reveals, this is the case with Brazil's *Bolsa Família* program that was introduced in the 1990s by President Cardoso, a social democrat, and expanded under his successor, President Lula da Silva who is equally committed to egalitarian ideals.

In addition to national programs of this kind, egalitarian policies should be adopted at the global level. International aid should not only be increased, but reformed so that resources flowing from the West to developing countries promote social rather than political, economic, or diplomatic goals. Levies on international financial transactions and on governments should also be imposed. Deacon (2005) notes that various proposals for a Tobin type tax to fund social initiatives have been made, and he argues that this approach could be used to support the ILO's (2011) proposal for a universal social protection floor. As Cichon and Hagemejer (2007) point out, it would not pose a heavy fiscal burden on the Western countries to fund an initiative of this kind. Similarly, it is entirely feasible that Townsend and Gordon's (2002) proposal for a universal child benefit to be paid (in cash) to all the world's children can be funded by the high income nations.

The principle of equality also requires the implementation of a social rights agenda that challenges oppressive and discriminatory practices against women, children, ethnic minorities, people with disabilities, elders, immigrants, and indigenous people, among others. The perpetuation of these oppressive structures is directly associated with high levels of income and wealth inequality, which, in turn, reflect entrenched inequalities in power and privilege. Because social wellbeing is best achieved in egalitarian societies in which human beings can realize opportunities, high priority must be given to ensuring the implementation of social rights and egalitarian policies. As suggested in the introduction to this book, this also requires a commitment to peace, social solidarity, and democratic participation. Although promoting these ideals at the international level presents a formidable challenge, a rights-based approach is already enshrined in the constitutions of many countries, and since the majority of the world's nations have acceded to the 1966 *International Covenant on Economic, Social, and Cultural Rights,* the foundations of this approach have already been laid. The adoption of the basic needs approach (ILO, 1976; Streeten, Burki, Ul Haq, Hicks, & Stewart, 1981) and more recently the Sustainable Development Goals agenda also suggests that implementing social rights internationally is achievable.

Challenges to a One World Perspective: Values and Power

As noted earlier, the values and prescriptions of the one world approach are controversial and will be contested. While there are honest differences of opinion about values, they reflect deeply held beliefs, and because of their powerful emotional appeal are often vigorously defended. Indeed, it is not surprising that people sometimes resort to violence to protect the values they hold dear. In addition, it is likely that the values articulated earlier will be opposed because they challenge the power and privilege of established interest groups. Also, there are many practical and technical challenges to implementing a one world perspective in social welfare. If this perspective is to be adopted, these challenges should be anticipated and addressed.

Reference has already been made to the formidable funding, administrative, and implementation challenges of adopting a one world perspective. In addition, many will view the proposals made here with incredulity simply because of the sheer scale of the problems facing the world today. In addition to widespread poverty, hunger, ill-health, and other social problems, hatred and violence remain endemic. At the time of this writing, the tragedy of Syria, ethnic and religious hatred in different parts of the world, widespread political conflict, the suffering of refugees, and the rise of extremist *jihadi* fundamentalism as well as superpower rivalries, and a resurgence of nationalism suggest that adopting a one world perspective is naïve—to say the least. Its cosmopolitan ideal of viewing the world's people as members of a single community bound by common values and interests seems to be hopelessly out of touch with these realities and will be challenged and even ridiculed.

A similar criticism comes from scholars of the realist school of international relations who also dismiss cosmopolitanism as idealistic and utopian. For example, Kristol and Kagan (2000) contend that the real world is a dangerous place composed of aggressive nation states that use all means at their disposal to secure advantage. They point out that governments manipulate the international organizations for their own purposes, and although paying lip service to the ideals of cooperation, peace, and human rights, they actually pursue their own agendas. A recent and trenchant argument of this kind comes from Hopgood (2013) who takes a dismal view of international human rights claiming that they are invariably subjugated to the interests of powerful nations. It is no accident, he suggests, that the International Criminal Court failed to indict Western leaders who violated international law, but aggressively pursued African politicians with little international influence. In addition, realists argue that it is only through understanding international power relations and pragmatically promoting a balance of power between the world's strongest nation states that their influence can be held in check.

Many will reject the one world perspective on ideological and value grounds and for seeking to homogenize the world's cultures and create a powerful dictatorial world government. Although it is true that some cosmopolitans like H. G. Wells, made no secret of his desire for a world government, most subscribe to the political pluralism inherent in liberal and social democratic cosmopolitanism. This is also the case with cultural pluralism. Indeed, as mentioned in Chapter 3 of this book, greater cultural exchanges are taking place today, and some writers like Cowen (2002) believe that cultural diffusion is already contributing to the emergence of a syncretic, global culture based on greater diversity and respect for different beliefs.

However, this idea is repugnant to those who oppose cosmopolitanism like nationalists who claim that it dilutes identity, abrogates sovereignty, and undermines people's rights to self-determination. Similarly, religious fundamentalists challenge cosmopolitanism on the grounds that there can only be one set of beliefs to which all people must subscribe, while traditionalists argue that cosmopolitanism undermines cherished national values and weakens family and community bonds. Even communitarians are skeptical claiming that human beings are embedded in their communities and societies and that the relationships they forge with others gives meaning to their lives. It is simply not possible to experience solidarity with people of so many different cultures, languages, and religions. Although they do not reject international cooperation, they agree with liberal internationalists that this is best achieved through civil society institutions rather than the consolidation of state power at the global level.

Although these are trenchant criticisms, most cosmopolitans believe that it is possible for the world's people to belong to a single human community without subjecting them to some remote and powerful global political authority. They also believe that it is possible for people to share a common commitment to cosmopolitan ideals while retaining their religious, cultural, and ethnic identity. In his efforts to promote ecumenical understanding, the Catholic theologian Hans Küng (1998) insists that there is more that unites than divides the world's religions, and that all religions share a common "global ethic." Similarly, Appiah (2006) argues that cultural diversity can be accommodated in a cosmopolitan order based on shared values and universal rights. Although it can be claimed that these ideals reflect a particularly Western liberal view of cosmopolitanism, many examples can be given of how religious and cultural diversity have been respected in the past, and how people of different religions, ethnicities, and languages today live together in peace and harmony. Nevertheless, the difficulties of transcending cultural and religious differences among the world's people must be recognized.

The values articulated earlier will also be contested because they challenge powerful interests. The value of collectivism that provides a basis for state intervention is particularly contentious since it provides an alternative to market liberalism and the idea that prosperity can be achieved solely through the pursuit of profits. Market liberal ideas now enjoy a good deal of support, and as Haring and Douglas (2012) point out, are endorsed by some influential academics whose opposition to state intervention has legitimated privatization and deregulation initiatives that favor those with wealth and power. Their arguments have also been used to persuade electorates to legitimate budgetary retrenchments to the social services. Egalitarian ideals are regularly assailed for harming economic growth and causing other ills when in fact they counter the entrenched power and privilege of business and political elites. Although the recent global financial crisis and popular movements against capitalism have exposed these interests, they continue to influence policymaking in many countries and present daunting challenges to implementing a one world perspective.

Scholars and practitioners advocating the adoption of a one world perspective need to recognize that these criticisms pose a formidable challenge. They also need to accept that there are no simple solutions to the problems facing the human community in today's global era, but that an ongoing process of struggle will be needed to bring about meaningful change. Closer cooperation between practitioners and different organizations engaged in international social welfare must be strengthened, and scholars must foster academic interpretations that capture the complexities of the global era, and at the same time provide a sound basis for practice. If practitioners and academics engaged in international social welfare collaborate more closely and commit themselves to the struggle ahead, there are grounds for optimism and Wendell Wilkie's prophetic commitment to the one world ideal may well be realized. As has been suggested already, much has been achieved and much more is possible.

References

Aaron, H. (1967). Social security: International comparisons. In O. Eckstein (Ed.), *Studies in the economics of income maintenance* (pp. 13–48). Washington, DC: Brookings Institution.

Abramovitz, M. (1992). The Reagan legacy: Undoing class, race and gender accords. *Journal of Sociology and Social Welfare, 19*(1), 91–110.

Adema, W., & Whiteford, P. (2010). Public and private social welfare. In F. G. Castles, S. Leibfried, J. Lewis, H. Obinger, & C. Pierson (Eds.), *The Oxford handbook of the welfare state* (pp. 121–138). New York, NY: Oxford University Press.

Aguero, F. (2005). The promotion of corporate social responsibility in Latin America. In C. Sanborn & F. Portocarrero (Eds.), *Philanthropy and social change in Latin America* (pp. 103–134). Cambridge, MA: Harvard University Press.

Ahmed, S., & Potter, D. M. (2006). *NGOs in international politics.* Bloomfield, CT: Kumarian Press.

Alber, J. (1988). Is there a crisis of the welfare state? Cross national evidence from Europe, North America and Japan. *European Sociological Review, 4*(2), 181–207.

Alexander, M. (2010). *The new Jim Crow: Mass incarceration in the age of colorblindness.* New York, NY: New Press.

Alinsky, S. (1946). *Reveille for radicals.* Chicago, IL: University of Chicago Press.

Alip, J. A., & Amenomori, T. (2011). Formalizing grassroots social security: The experience of CARD in the Philippines. In J. Midgley & M. Hosaka (Eds.), *Grassroots social security in Asia: Mutual aid, microinsurance and social welfare* (pp. 64–78). New York, NY: Routledge.

Almanzor, A. C. (1967). The profession of social work in the Philippines. In Council on Social Work Education (Ed.), *An intercultural exploration: Universals and differentials in social work values, functions and practice* (pp. 123–137). New York: New York Council on Social Work Education.

Amenomori, T. (1997). Japan. In L. M. Salamon & H. K. Anheier (Eds.), *Defining the nonprofit sector: A cross national analysis* (188–214). Manchester, England: Manchester University Press.

Amenomori, T. (2010). From microcredit to microinsurance: Creating social security where there is none. In J. Midgley & K. L. Tang (Eds.), *Social policy and poverty in East Asia: The role of social security* (pp. 142–154). New York, NY: Routledge.

Amin, S. (1974). *Accumulation on a world scale.* New York, NY: Monthly Review Press.

Anderson, P. (2009). *The new old world.* New York, NY: Verso.

Anderson, S. (2014). *New strategies for social innovation: Market-based approaches for assisting the poor.* New York, NY: Columbia University Press.

Anheier, H. K. (2005). *Nonprofit organizations: Theory, management, policy.* New York, NY: Routledge.

Appiah, K. A. (2006). *Cosmopolitanism: Ethics in a world of strangers.* New York, NY: Norton.

Appleby, R. S. (2005). Global civil society and the Catholic social tradition. In J. A. Coleman (Ed.), *Globalization and Catholic social thought: Present crisis, future hope.* Ottawa, Canada: Novalis.

Apt, N. A. (2002). Aging and the changing role of the family and the community: An African perspective. *International Social Security Review, 55*(1), 39–47.

Ardener, S., & Burman, S. (Eds.). (1995). *Money-go-rounds: The importance of rotating savings and credit associations for women.* Herndon, VA: Berg.

Armstrong, B. N. (1932). *Insuring the essentials: Minimum wage plus social insurance—a living wage program.* New York, NY: Macmillan.

Aronowitz, S. (2005). *Just around the corner: The paradox of the jobless recovery.* Philadelphia, PA: Temple University Press.

Asher, M., & Nandy, A. (2008). Singapore's policy responses to aging, inequality and poverty: An assessment. *International Social Security Review, 61*(1), 41–60.

Aspalter, C., & Singh, S. (2008). Debating social development: An introduction. In S. Singh & C. Aspalter (Eds.), *Debating social development* (pp. 1–10). Manchester, UK: Casa Verde.

Atlas, J. (2010). *The seeds of change: The story of ACORN, America's most controversial antipoverty community organizing group.* Nashville, TN: Vanderbilt University Press.

Azaiza, F. (2007). The perception and utilization of social support in times of cultural change: The case of Arabs in Israel. *International Journal of Social Welfare, 17*(3), 198–203.

Bacon, R., & Eltis, W. (1976). *Britain's economic problems: Too few producers.* London, UK: Macmillan.

Bailey, G. (2014). The global agenda … steps and beyond. *International Social Work, 57*(4), pp. 411–412.

Baldock, J. (1989). United Kingdom: A perpetual crisis of marginality. In B. Munday (Ed.), *The crisis in welfare: An international perspective on social services and social work* (pp. 23–50). New York, NY: St. Martin's Press.

Banarjee, A. V., & Duflo, E. (2011). *Poor economics: A radical rethinking of the way to fight global poverty.* New York, NY: Public Affairs Press.

Barker, R. (Ed.). (2003). *The social work dictionary* (5th ed.). Washington, DC: NASW Press.

Barker, R. (Ed.). (2013). *The social work dictionary* (6th ed.). Washington, DC: NASW Press.

Barnett, C. (1995). *The lost victory: British dreams, British realities 1945–1950.* New York, NY: Macmillan.

Barretta-Herman, A. (2012). Comparative cross-national research (world census). In L. M. Healy & J. R. Link (Eds.), *The handbook of international social work: Human rights, development and the global profession* (pp. 356–364). New York, NY: Oxford University Press.

Barrientos, A. (2013). *Social assistance in developing countries.* New York, NY: Cambridge University Press.

Bartholomew, J. (2015). *The welfare of nations.* London, UK: Biteback.

Bartkowski, J. P., & Regis, H. A. (2003). *Charitable choices: Religion, race, and poverty in the post welfare era.* New York, NY: New York University Press.

Bass, M. (2013). *The politics and civics of national service.* Washington, DC: Brookings Institution Press.

Bateman, M. (2010). *Why doesn't microfinance work?: The destructive rise of local neoliberalism.* New York, NY: Zed Books.

Bauman, Z. (1992). *Imitations of post-modernity.* New York, NY: Routledge.

Bauman, Z. (1998). *Globalization: The human consequences.* New York, NY: Columbia University Press.

Baumol, W. J. (1967). The macroeconomics of unbalanced growth. *American Economic Review, 57*(4), 415–426.

Bebbington, A. J., Hicky, S., & Mitlin, D. C. (Eds.). (2008). *Can NGOs make a difference?: The challenge of development alternatives.* New York, NY: Palgrave Macmillan.

Becker, U. (1992). *Risk society: Towards a new modernity.* Newbury Park, CA: SAGE.

Bello, W. (2002). *Deglobalization: Ideas for a new world economy.* London, UK: Zed Books.

Benda-Beckmann, F. von, & Benda-Beckmann, K. von. (1994). Coping with insecurity. *Focaal, 22/23,* 7–31.

Benda-Beckmann, F. von, Benda-Beckmann, K. von, Casino, E., Hirtz, F., Woodman, G. R., & Zacher, H. F. (Eds.). (1988). *Between kinship and the state: Social security and law in developing countries.* Dordrecht, Netherlands: Foris.

Benda-Beckmann, F. von, & Kirsch, R. (1999). Informal security systems in Southern Africa and approaches to strengthen them through policy measures. *Journal of Social Development in Africa, 14*(2), 21–38.

Beneria, L. (2003). *Gender, development and globalization: Economics as if all people mattered.* New York, NY: Routledge.

Berhman, G. (2007). *The most noble adventure: The Marshall Plan and the time when America helped save Europe.* New York, NY: Free Press.

Berkman, S. (2008). *The World Bank and the gods of lending.* Bloomfield, CT: Kumarian Press.

Bernstein, W. J. (2008). *A splendid exchange. How trade shaped the world from prehistory to today.* New York, NY: Atlantic Monthly Press.

Bettman, J. E., Jacques, G., & Frost, C. J. (2013). *International social work practice: Case studies from a global context.* New York, NY: Routledge.

Bevan, P. (2004). The dynamics of Africa's insecurity regimes. In I. Gough & G. Woods (Eds.), *Insecurity and welfare regimes in Asia, Africa and Latin America* (pp. 202–254). New York, NY: Cambridge University Press.

Beveridge, W. (1948). *Voluntary action: A report on methods of social advance.* London, UK: Allen & Unwin.

Bhagwati, J. N. (2004). *In defense of globalization.* New York, NY: Oxford University Press.

Bhagwati, J. N., Binder, A., & Friedman, B. M. (2009). *Outsourcing of American jobs: What response from U.S. economic policy.* Cambridge, MA: MIT Press.

Bhagwati, J. N., & Panagariya, A. (2013). *Why growth matters: How economic growth in India reduced poverty and the lessons for other developing countries.* New York, NY: Public Affairs.

Bishop, M., & Green, M. (2008). *Philanthrocapitalism: How giving can save the world.* New York, NY: Bloomsbury.

Bonoli, G. (2012). Active labour market policy and social investment: A changing relationship. In N. Morel, B. Pallier, & J. Palme (Eds.), *Towards a social investment welfare state? Ideas, policies and challenges* (pp. 181–204). Bristol, UK: Policy Press.

Bonoli, G. (2013). *The origins of active social policy: Labour market and childcare policies in comparative perspective.* New York, NY: Oxford University Press.

Bortie-Doku, E., & Aryeetey, E. (1995). Mobilizing cash for business: Women in rotating Susu clubs in Ghana. In S. Ardener & S. Burman (Eds.), *Money-go-rounds: The importance of rotating savings and credit associations for women* (pp. 77–94). Herndon, VA: Berg.

Borzutzky, S. (1991). The Chicago boys, social security and welfare in Chile. In H. Glennerster & J. Midgley (Eds.), *The radical right and the welfare of state: An international assessment* (pp. 79–99). Savage, MD: Barnes and Noble.

Borzutzky, S. (2002). *Vital connections: Politics, social security and inequality in Chile.* Notre Dame, IN: Notre Dame University Press.

Borzutzky, S. (2008). Chile: Social security, privatization and economic growth. In J. Midgley & K. L. Tang (Eds.), *Social security, the economy and development* (pp. 110–136). New York, NY: Palgrave.

Borzutzky, S. (2012). Reforming the reform: Attempting social solidarity and equity in Chile's privatized social security system. *Journal of Policy Practice, 11*(1/2), 77–91.

Boserup, E. (1970). *Women's role in economic development.* London, UK: Allen and Unwin.

Bradshaw, J. (1972). The concept of social need. *New Society, 20*(496), 640–643.

Brandt, W. (1980). *North-South: A programme for survival.* London, UK: Pan Books.

Brauns, H., & Kramer, D. (1989). West Germany: The breakup of consensus and the demographic threat. In B. Munday (Ed.), *The crisis in welfare: An international perspective on social services and social work* (pp. 124–154). New York, NY: St. Martin's Press.

Brecher, J., Costello, T., & Smith, B. (2000). *Globalization from below: The power of solidarity.* Cambridge, MA: South End Press.

Briggs, A. (1961). The welfare state in historical perspective. *European Journal of Sociology, 2*(2), 221–258.

Bromley, R., & Gerry, C. (Eds.). (1979). *Casual work and poverty in third world cities.* Chichester, UK: Wiley.

Brundtland Commission. (1983). *Our common future, from one earth to one world: An overview by the World Commission on Environment and Development.* Geneva, Switzerland: United Nations.

Buchanan, J., & Wagner, R. E. (1977). *Democracy in deficit.* New York, NY: Academic Press.

Burgis, T. (2015). *The looting machine: Warlords, tycoons, smugglers and the systematic theft of Africa's wealth.* New York, NY: Public Affairs Press.

Caetano, M. A. (2014). Recent history, perspectives and challenges to pension policy: The Brazilian case. In K. Hujo (Ed.), *Reforming pensions in developing and transition countries.* New York, NY: Palgrave Macmillan.

Calbezas, A., Reese, E., & Waller, M. (2007). *The wages of empire: Neoliberal policies, repression and women's poverty.* New York, NY: Paradigm.

Calderisi, R. (2013). *Earthly mission: The Catholic church and world development.* New Haven, CT: Yale University Press.

Campanini, A. (2012). Social work in Europe. In L. M. Healy & R. J. Link (Eds.), *The handboook of international social work: Human rights, development and the global profession* (pp. 388–392). New York, NY: Oxford University Press.

Casey, B. H., & Dostal, J. M. (2008). Pension reform in Nigeria: How not to 'learn from others.' *Global Social Policy, 8*(2), 238–266.

Cassidy, J. (2009). *How markets fail: The logic of economic calamities.* New York, NY: Farrar, Straus and Giroux.

Castells, M. (1996). *The rise of the network society.* Oxford, UK: Blackwell.

Castells, M. (2001). *The Internet galaxy: Reflections on the Internet, business and society.* New York, NY: Oxford University Press.

Castells, M. (Ed.). (2004). *The network society: A cross-cultural perspective.* Malden, MA: Elgar.

Castles, F. G. (1996). Needs-based strategies of social protection in Australia and New Zealand. In G. Esping-Andersen (Ed.), *Welfare states in transition: National adaptations in global economies* (pp. 88–115). London, UK: SAGE.

Castles, F. G. (2004). *The future of the welfare state: Crisis myths and crisis realities.* New York, NY: Oxford University Press.

Castles, F. G., Leibfried, S., Lewis, J., Obinger, H., & Pierson, C. (Eds.). (2010). *The Oxford handbook of the welfare state.* New York, NY: Oxford University Press.

Chambliss, R. (1954). *Social thought from Hammurabi to Comte.* New York, NY: Holt, Rinehart, and Winston.

Chang, H. J. (2008). *Bad samaritans: The myth of free trade and the secret history of capitalism.* New York, NY: Bloomsbury.

Chappell, M. (2010). *The war on welfare: Family, poverty, and politics in modern America.* Philadelphia: University of Pennsylvania Press.

Chen, M. (2008). A spreading Banyan tree: The employed women's association, India. In A. Mathie & G. Cunningham (Eds.), *From clients to citizens: Communities changing the course of their own development* (pp. 181–206). Rugby, England: Intermediate Technology Publications.

Cheung, M., & Delavega, E. (2011). Child savings accounts: Learning from poverty reduction policies in the world. *International Social Work, 55*(1), 71–94.

Choudry, A., & Kapoor, D. (2013). Introduction. In A. Choudry & D. Kapoor (Eds.), *NGOization: Complicity, contradictions and prospects* (p. 1023). London, UK: Zed Books.

Chua, A. (2003). *World on fire.* New York, NY: Anchor Books.

Chung, K. (2014). The legitimacy crisis of the mandatory provident fund scheme in Hong Kong. In J. Lee, J. Midgley, & Y. Zhu (Eds.), *Social policy and change in East Asia* (pp. 141–160). Lanham, MD: Lexington Books.

Churchill, C. (Ed.). (2006). *Protecting the poor: A microinsurance compendium.* Geneva, Switzerland: International Labour Organization.

Cichon, M., & Hagemejer, K. (2007). Changing the development policy paradigm: Investing in a social security floor for all. *International Social Security Review, 60*(2/3), 169–196.

Clark, J. (2004a). *Changing welfare, changing states: New directions in social policy.* London, UK: SAGE.

Clark, J. (2004b). *Islam, charity and activism: Middle-class networks and social welfare in Egypt, Jordan and Yemen.* Bloomington, IN: Indiana University Press.

Cobbs Hoffman, E. (2000). *All you need is love: The Peace Corps and the spirit of the 1960s.* Cambridge, MA: Harvard University Press.

Cohen, D. (2006). *Globalization and its enemies.* Cambridge, MA: MIT Press.

Collins, D., Morduch, J., Rutherford, S., & Ruthven, O. (2009). *Portfolios of the poor: How the world's poor live on $2 a day.* Princeton, NJ: Princeton University Press.

Conley, A. (2010). Childcare: Welfare or investment? *International Journal of Social Welfare, 19*(2), 173–181.

Cook, L. J. (2007). *Postcommunist welfare states: Reform politics in Russia and Eastern Europe.* Ithaca, NY: Cornell University Press.

Cowen, T. (2002). *Creative destruction: How globalization is changing the world's cultures.* Princeton, NJ: Princeton University Press.

Cowen, T. (2011). *The great stagnation.* New York, NY: Dutton.

Cox, D., & Pawar, M. (2006). *International social work: Issues, strategies and programs.* Thousand Oaks, CA: SAGE.

Crouch, C. (2011). *The strange non-death of neoliberalism.* Malden, MA: Polity Press.

Dahl, R. A. (1956). *A preface to democratic theory.* Chicago, IL: University of Chicago Press.

Dahl, R. A. (1961). *Who governs? Democracy and power in an American city.* New Haven, CT: Yale University Press.

Dallal, A. (2004). The Islamic institution of *Waqf:* A historical overview. In S. P. Heyneman (Ed.), *Islam and social policy* (pp. 13–43). Nashville, TN: Vanderbilt University Press.

Daly, H. (1996). *Beyond growth: The economics of sustainable development.* Boston, MA: Beacon Press.

Daly, L. (2006). *God and the welfare state.* Cambridge, MA: MIT Press.

Daly, M., & Rake, K. (2003). *Gender and the welfare state: Care, work and welfare in Europe and the USA.* Malden, MA: Polity Press.

Dasgupta, P., & Serageldin, I. (2000). *Social capital: A multifaceted perspective.* Washington, DC: World Bank.

de Bruijn, M. (1994). Coping with crisis in Sahelian Africa: Fulbe agro-pastoralists and Islam. *Focaal, 22/23*(1), 47–65.

de Schweinitz, K. (1943). *England's road to social security.* Philadelphia: University of Pennsylvania Press.

de Waal, F. (2009). *The age of empathy: Nature's lessons for a kinder society.* New York, NY: Harmony Books.

Deacon, B. (1983). *Social policy and socialism: The struggle for socialist relations of welfare.* London, UK: Pluto Press.

Deacon, B. (2005). Allocating a global levy. In Fabian Society (Ed.), *Just world: A Fabian manifesto* (pp. 46–51). London, UK: Fabian Society.

Deacon, B. (2007). *Global social policy and governance.* London, UK: SAGE.

Deacon, B., & Stubbs, P. (2013). Global social policy studies: Conceptual and analytical reflections. *Global Social Policy, 13*(1), 5–23.

Dean, H. (2009). Critiquing capabilities: The distractions of a beguiling concept. *Critical Social Policy, 29*(2), 261–278.

Dean, H. (2010). *Understanding human needs: Social issues, policy and practice.* Bristol, UK: Policy Press.

Dean, H. (2015). *Social rights and social welfare.* New York, NY: Routledge.

Dixon, J. (1981). *The Chinese welfare system, 1949-1979.* New York, NY: Praegar.

Dominelli, L. (2002). *Anti-oppressive social work theory and practice.* New York, NY: Palgrave.

Dominelli, L. (2006). *Women and community action.* Bristol, UK: Policy Press.

Draibe, S. M., & Riesco, M. (2007). Introduction. In M. Riesco (Ed.), *Latin America: A new developmental welfare state model in the making?* (pp. 1–17). New York, NY: Palgrave Macmillan.

Drakeford, M. (2000). *Privatisation and social policy.* New York, NY: Longman.

Easterly, W. (2006). *The White man's burden: Why the West's efforts to aid the rest has done so much ill and so little good.* New York, NY: Penguin Books.

Eberstadt, N. (2012). *A nation of takers: America's entitlement epidemic.* West Conshohocken, PA: Templeton Press.

Eckl, J. (2014). The power of private foundations: Rockefeller and Gates in the struggle against malaria. *Global Social Policy, 14*(1), 91–116.

Elliott, D. (2012). Social development and social work. In L. M. Healy & R. J. Link (Eds.), *The handboook of international social work: Human rights, development and the global profession* (pp. 102–108). New York, NY: Oxford University Press.

Elliott, K. A., Kar, D., & Richardson, J. D. (2004). Assessing globalization's critics: "Talkers are no good doers." In R. E. Baldwin & L. A. Winters (Eds.), *Challenges to globalization: Analyzing the economics* (pp. 17–64). Chicago, IL: University of Chicago Press.

Ellis, F., Devereux, S., & White, P. (2009). *Social protection in Africa.* Northampton, MA: Edward Elgar.

Esping-Andersen, G. (1990). *The three worlds of welfare capitalism.* Cambridge, UK: Polity Press.

Estes, R. (1984). *The social progress of nations.* New York, NY: Praegar.

Etzioni, A. (1993). *The spirit of community: Rights, responsibilities, and the communitarian agenda.* New York, NY: Crown.

Fabian Society. (2005). *Just world: a Fabian manifesto.* London, UK: Author.

Fairbourne, J., Gibson, S. W., & Dyer, W. G. (2007). *Microfranchising: Creating wealth at the bottom of the pyramid.* Northampton, MA: Elgar.

Feldstein, M. B. (1974). *Social security and private savings.* Cambridge, MA: Harvard University Institute of Economic Research.

Ferguson, I. (2008). *Reclaiming social work: Challenging neo-liberalism and promoting social justice.* Los Angeles: SAGE.

Ferguson, N. (2003). *Empire: The rise and demise of the British world order and the lessons for global power.* New York, NY: Basic Books.

Ferguson, N. (2004). *Colossus: The price of America's empire.* New York, NY: Penguin.

Ferrera, M. (1996). The southern model of welfare in social Europe. *Journal of European Social Policy, 6*(1), 17–37.

Fiszbein, R., & Schady, N. (2009). *Conditional cash transfers: Reducing present and future poverty.* Washington, DC: World Bank.

Fitzpatrick, T. (2004). A post-productivist future for social democracy? *Social Policy & Society, 3*(3), 213–224.

Fitzpatrick, T., Kwong, H. J., Manning, N., Midgley, J., & Pascall, G. (Eds). (2005). *International encyclopedia of social policy.* London, UK: Routledge.

Flanigan, S. (2010). *For the love of God: NGOs and religious identity in a violent world.* Sterling, VA: Kumarian Press.

Frank, A. G. (1967). *Capitalism and underdevelopment in Latin America.* New York, NY: Monthly Review Press.

Frank, A. G. (1975). *On capitalist underdevelopment.* New York, NY: Oxford University Review Press.

Freire, P. (1972). *Pedagogy of the oppressed.* Harmondsworth, England: Penguin Books.

Friedlander, W. (1955). *Introduction to social welfare.* New York, NY: Prentice Hall.

Friedlander, W. (1975). *International social welfare.* Englewood Cliffs, NJ: Prentice Hall.

Friedman, M. (1962). *Capitalism and freedom.* Chicago, IL: University of Chicago Press.

Friedman, M., & Friedman, R. (1980). *Free to choose.* London, UK: Secker & Warburg.

Frum, D., & Perle, R. (2003). *An end to evil: How to end the war on terror.* New York, NY: Random House.

Fukuyama, F. (1992). *The end of history and the last man.* New York, NY: Free Press.

Fukuyama, F. (2011). *The origins of political order: From prehuman times to the French revolution.* New York, NY: Farrar, Straus and Giroux.

Furukawa, K. (2008). *Social welfare in Japan: Principles and applications.* Melbourne, Australia: Trans Pacific Press.

Furuto, S. B. C. L. (Ed.). (2013). *Social welfare in East Asia and the Pacific.* New York, NY: Columbia University Press.

Garfinkel, I., Rainwater, L., & Smeeding, T. (2010). *Wealth and welfare states: Is America a laggard or leader?* New York, NY: Oxford University Press.

Geertz, C. (1962). The rotating credit association: A 'middle rung' in development. *Economic Development and Cultural Change, 10*(3), 241–263.

Gellner, E. (1983). *Nations and nationalism.* Oxford, UK: Basil Blackwell.

George, M., & Krishnakumar, J. (2014). Revisiting the landscape of professional social work in India. *Social Development Issues, 36*(2), 53–64.

George, V., & Wilding, P. (1976). *Ideology and social welfare.* London, UK: Routledge & Kegan Paul.

George, V., & Wilding, P. (1994). *Welfare and ideology.* New York, NY: Harvester-Wheatsheaf.

Georgeou, N. (2012). *Neoliberalism, development, and aid volunteering.* New York, NY: Routledge.

Gerbaudo, P. (2012). *Tweets and the streets: Social media and contemporary activism.* London, UK: Pluto.

Ghemawat, P. (2011). *World 3.0: Global prosperity and how to achieve it.* Boston, MA: Harvard Business Review Press.

Gibelman, M. (1998). Theory, practice, and experience in the purchase of services. In M. Gibelman & H. Demone (Eds.), *The privatization of human services: Policy and practice issues* (pp. 1–52). New York, NY: Springer.

Giddens, A. (1998). *The third way: The renewal of social democracy.* Cambridge, UK: Polity Press.

Giddens, A. (1999). *Runaway world: How globalization is reshaping our lives.* London, UK: Profile Books.

Gilbert, N. (1976). Alternative forms of social protection for developing countries. *Social Security Review, 50*(4), 363–387.

Gilbert, N. (2002). *The transformation of the welfare state: The silent surrender of public responsibility.* New York, NY: Oxford University Press.

Gilbert, N. (2009). Welfare pluralism and social policy. In J. Midgley & M. Livermore (Eds.), *Handbook of social policy* (pp. 236–245). Thousand Oaks, CA: SAGE.

Gilbert, N. (2010). Comparative analyses of stateness and state action: What can we learn from patterns of expenditure? In J. Alber & N. Gilbert (Eds.), *United in diversity: Comparing social models in Europe and America* (pp. 133–150). New York, NY: Oxford University Press.

Gilbert, N. (2013). Citizenship in the enabling state: The changing balance of rights and obligations. In A. Evers & A. Guillemard (Eds.), *Social policy and citizenship: The changing landscape* (pp. 80–96). New York, NY: Oxford University Press.

Gingrich, N. (1995). *To renew America.* New York, NY: Harper.

Glennerster, H. (1991). The radical right and the future of the welfare state. In H. Glennerster & J. Midgley (Eds.), *The radical right and the welfare state: An international assessment* (pp. 163–174). Savage, MD: Barnes and Noble.

Goldberg, G. S., & Rosenthal, M. G. (Eds.). (2002). *Diminishing welfare: A cross-national study of social provision.* Westport, CT: Auburn House.

Goldin, I. (2013). *Divided nations: Why global governance is failing and what we can do about it.* New York, NY: Oxford University Press.

Goode, W. J. (1963). *World revolution and family patterns.* New York, NY: Free Press.

Goodman, R. (1998). The Japanese-style welfare state and the delivery of personal social services. In R. Goodman, G. White, & H. J. Kwon (Eds.), *The East Asian welfare model: Welfare orientalism and the state* (pp. 119–138). New York, NY: Routledge.

Gorton, G. B. (2010). *Slapped by the invisible hand: The panic of 2007.* New York, NY: Oxford University Press.

Gough, I. (1979). *The political economy of the welfare state.* London, UK: Macmillan.

Gough, I. (2003). Welfare regimes in East Asia and Europe compared. In K. Marshall & O. Butzbach (Eds.), *New social policy agendas for Europe and Asia* (pp. 27–44).Washington, DC: World Bank.

Gough, I., & Wood, G. (2004). Introduction. In I. Gough, G. Wood, A. Barrientos, P. Bevan, P. Davis, & G. Room (Eds.), *Insecurity and welfare regimes in Asia, Africa and Latin America* (pp. 1–11). New York, NY: Cambridge University Press.

Grannovetter, M. S. (1973). The strength of weak ties. *American Journal of Sociology, 78*(6), 1360–1380.

Gray, J. (1998). *False dawn: The delusions of global capitalism.* London, UK: Granta Books.

Gray, M., & Coates, J. (2010). Indigenization in a globalizing world: A response to Huang and Zhang. *International Social Work, 53*(1), 115–127.

Gray, M., Coates, J., & Yellow Bird, M. (Eds.). (2008). *Indigenous social work around the world: Towards culturally relevant practice.* Burlington, VT: Ashgate.

Gray, M., & Fook, J. (2004). The quest for universal social work: Some issues and implications. *Social Work Education, 23*(5), 625–644.

Greve, B. (2014). *Historical dictionary of the welfare state* (3rd ed.). Lanham, MD: Rowan & Littlefield.

Grupp, J. (2008). *Corporatism: The secret government of the new world order.* Joshua Tree, CA: Progressive Press.

The Guardian. (2013, June 14). India's NGOs Hit Funding Roadblock.

Gubring, E., Harsloff, I., & Lødemel, I. (2014). Norwegian activation reform on a wave of wider welfare state change: A critical assessment. In I. Lødemel & A. Moreira (Eds.), *Activation or workfare? Governance and the neo-liberal convergence* (pp 19–46). New York, NY: Oxford University Press.

Hacker, J. S. (2002). *The divided welfare state: The battle over public and private social benefits in the United States.* New York, NY: Cambridge University Press.

Hadley, R., & Hatch, S. (1981). *Social welfare and the failure of the state.* London, UK: Allen and Unwin.

Hagen, E. (1962). *On the theory of social change.* Homewood, IL: Dorsey Press.

Haggard, S., & Kaufman, R. R. (2008). *Development, democracy, and welfare states: Latin America, East Asia and Eastern Europe.* Princeton, NJ: Princeton University Press.

Hall, A. (2012). The last shall be first: Political dimensions of conditional cash transfers in Brazil. *Journal of Policy Practice, 11*(1/2), 25–41.

Hall, A., & Midgley, J. (2004). *Social policy for development.* Thousand Oaks, CA: SAGE.

Hallen, G. C. (1967). *Social security in India.* Meerut, India: Rastogi.

Hammack, D. C., & Anheier, H. K. (2013). *A versatile American institution: The changing ideals and realities of philanthropic foundations.* Washington, DC: Brookings Institution Press.

Harding, S. (2004). The sound of silence: Social work, the academy and Iraq. *Journal of Sociology and Social Welfare, 31*(2), 179–196.

Haring, N., & Douglas, N. (2012). *Economists and the powerful, convenient theories, distorted facts, ample rewards.* New York, NY: Anthem Press.

Harrigan, J., & El-Said, H. (2009). *Economic liberalisation, social capital and Islamic welfare provision.* New York, NY: Palgrave Macmillan.

Harris, J. (1977). *William Beveridge: A biography.* Oxford, UK: Clarendon Press.

Harrison, A. (2007). Globalization and poverty: An introduction. In A. Harrison (Ed.), *Globalization and poverty* (pp. 1–30). Chicago, IL: University of Chicago Press.

Hart, K. (1973). Informal income opportunities and urban employment in Ghana. *Journal of Modern African Studies, 11*(1), 61–89.

Harvey, D. (2005). *A brief history of neoliberalism.* New York, NY: Oxford University Press.

Hasenfeld, Y., & Garrow, E. E. (2012). Nonprofits, human-service organizations, social rights, and advocacy in a neoliberal welfare state. *Social Service Review, 86*(2), 295–322.

Hayek, F. von. (1948). *Individualism and economic order.* London, UK: Routledge & Kegan Paul.

Hayek, F. von. (1960). *The constitution of liberty.* Chicago, IL: University of Chicago Press.

Healy, L. M. (1995). Comparative and international overview. In T. D. Watts, D. Elliott, & N. Mayadas (Eds.), *International handbook on social work education* (pp. 421–440). Westport, CT: Greenwood Press.

Healy, L. M. (2008). *International social work: Professional action in an interdependent world.* New York, NY: Oxford University Press.

Held, D. (Ed.). (2000). *A globalizing world?: Culture, economics, politics.* London, UK: Routledge.

Held, D. (2004). *Global covenant: The social democratic alternative to the Washington consensus.* Cambridge, UK: Polity Press.

Held, D. (Ed.). (2005). *Debating globalization.* Cambridge, UK: Polity Press.

Held, D., & McGrew, A. (2002). *Globalization/anti-globalization.* Cambridge, UK: Polity Press.

Hemerijck, A. (2013). *Changing welfare states.* New York, NY: Oxford University Press.

Hemerijck, A. (2014). The reform capacities of European welfare states. In B. Cantillon & F. Vandenbroucke (Eds.), *Reconciling work and poverty reduction: How successful are European welfare states* (pp. 238–259). New York, NY: Oxford University Press.

Hertz, N. (2001). *The silent takeover: Global capitalism and the death of democracy.* London, UK: Heinemann.

Hines, C. (2000). *Localization: A global manifesto.* London, UK: Earthscan.

Hirst, P., & Thompson, G. (1996). *Globalization in question.* Cambridge, MA: Polity Press.

Hobhouse, L. T. (1924). *Social development: Its nature and conditions.* London, UK: Allen and Unwin.

Hoefer, R., & Curry, C. (2012). Food security and social protection in the United States. *Journal of Policy Practice, 11*(1/2), 59–76.

Hokenstad, M. C., & Midgley, J. (Eds.). (2004a). *Lessons from abroad: Adapting international social welfare innovations.* Washington, DC: NASW Press.

Hokenstad, M. C., & Midgley, J. (2004b). Lessons from other countries: Current benefits and future opportunities. In M. C. Hokenstad & J. Midgley (Eds.), *Lessons from abroad: Adapting international social welfare innovations* (pp. 1–12). Washington, DC: NASW Press.

Holliday, I. (2000). Productivist welfare capitalism: Social policy in East Asia. *Political Studies, 48*(4), 706–723.

Hooyman, N. R., & Kiyak, H. A. (2008). *Social gerontology: A multidisciplinary perspective.* Boston, MA: Allyn and Bacon.

Hopgood, S. (2013). *The endtimes of human rights.* Ithaca, NY: Cornell University Press.

Howard, C. (1997). *The hidden welfare state: Tax expenditures and social policy in the United States.* Princeton, NJ: Princeton University Press.

Howard, C. (2007). *The welfare state nobody knows: Debunking myths about U.S. social policy.* Princeton, NJ: Princeton University Press.

Hozelitz, B. F. (1960). *Sociological factors in economic development.* New York, NY: Free Press.

Huang, C., Deng, G., Wang, Z., & Edwards, R. L. (2013). *China's nonprofit sector: Progress and challenges.* New Brunswick, NJ: Transaction.

Huang, Y., & Zhang, X. (2008). A reflection on the indigenization discourse in social work. *International Social Work, 51*(5), 611–622.

Huang, Y., & Zhang, X. (2011). Further discussion of indigenization in social work: A response to Gray and Coats. *International Social Work, 55*(1), 40–52.

Huber, E., & Stephens, J. D. (2012). *Democracy and the left: Social policy and inequality in Latin America.* Chicago, IL: University of Chicago Press.

Hugman, R. (2010). *Understanding international social work: A critical analysis.* New York, NY: Palgrave Macmillan.

Hujo, K., & Rulli, M. (2014). Towards more inclusive protection: A comparative analysis of the political process and socio-economic impact of pension reforms in Argentina and Chile. In K. Hujo (Ed.). *Reforming pensions in developing and transition countries* (pp 278–310). New York, NY: Palgrave Macmillan.

Hulme, D., & Edwards, M. (Eds.). (1997). *NGOs, states and donors: Too close for comfort.* New York, NY: Macmillan.

Huntington, S. P. (1996). *The clash of civilizations and the remaking of the world order.* New York, NY: Simon & Schuster.

Hytrek, G., & Zentgraf, K. M. (2007). *America transformed: Globalization, inequality and power.* New York, NY: Oxford University Press.

ILO: See International Labour Organisation

Imhoff, D. (1996). Community supported agriculture: Farming with a face on it. In J. Mander & D. Goldsmith (Eds.), *The case against the global economy and for a turn towards the local* (pp. 425–433). San Francisco, CA: Sierra Club Books.

International Federation of Social Workers and International Association of Schools of Social Work (2014). *Definition of social work.* Retrieved from http://ifsw.org/policies/definition-of-social-work

International Labour Organisation. (1976). *Employment, growth and basic needs: A one world problem.* Geneva, Switzerland: Author.

International Labour Organisation. (2004). World commission on the social dimensions of globalization. *A fair globalization: Creating opportunities for all.* Geneva, Switzerland: Author.

International Labour Organization. (2011). *Social protection floor for a fair and inclusive globalization* (Report of the Advisory Group chaired by Michelle Bachelet). Geneva, Switzerland: Author.

Iriye, A. (2002). *Global community: The role of international organizations in the making of the contemporary world.* Berkeley: University of California Press.

Jackson, T. (2009). *Prosperity without growth: Economics for a finite planet.* London, UK: Earthscan.

Jansson, B. S. (2005). *The reluctant welfare state: A history of American social welfare policies.* Pacific Grove, CA: Brooks/Cole.

Jawad, R. (2009). *Social welfare and religion in the Middle East: A Lebanese perspective.* Bristol, England: Policy Press.

Jenkins, S. (Ed.). (1969). *Social security in international perspective*. New York, NY: Columbia University Press.

Jessop, B. (1994). The transition to post-Fordism and the Schumpeterian workfare state. In R. Burrows & B. Loader (Eds.), *Towards a Post-Fordist welfare state* (pp. 13–37). New York, NY: Routledge.

Jessop. B. (2000). From the KWNS to the SWPR. In G. Lewis, S. Gerwitz & J. Clarke (Eds.), *Rethinking social policy* (pp. 171–184). London, UK: SAGE.

Jessop, B. (2013). Hollowing out the 'nation-state' and multilevel governance. In P. Kennett (Ed.), *Handbook of comparative social policy* (pp. 11–26). Northhampton, MA: Edward Elgar.

Johnson, N. (1999). *Mixed economies of welfare: A comparative perspective*. London, UK: Prentice Hall.

Johnston, D. C. (2007). *Free lunch: How the wealthiest Americans enrich themselves at government expense (and stick you with the bill)*. New York, NY: Portfolio.

Jones, C. (1985). *Patterns of social policy*. London, UK: Tavistock.

Jones, C. (1993). The Pacific challenge: Confucian welfare states. In C. Jones (Ed.), *Perspectives on the welfare state in Europe* (pp. 198–217). London, UK: Routledge.

Jones Finer, C. (2004). British social policy tradition in relation to empire and commonwealth. In C. Jones Finer & P. Smyth (Eds.), *Social policy and the commonwealth* (pp. 11–28). New York, NY: Palgrave.

Jones, J., & Pandey, R. (Eds.). (1981). *Social development: Conceptual, methodological and policy issues*. New York, NY: St. Martin's Press.

Kammerman, S. (1983). The new mixed economy of welfare: Public and private. *Social Work, 28*(1), 5–11.

Kananen, J. (2014). *The Nordic welfare state in three eras: From emancipation to discipline*. Brookfield, VT: Ashgate.

Kaseke, E. (1991). The social impact of economic structural adjustment programs in Africa and implications for social work programs. In N. Hall (Ed.), *The social implications of structural adjustment in Africa*. Harare, Zimbabwe: School of Social Work.

Kaseke, E., Midgley, J., & Piachaud, D. (2011). The British influence on social security policy: Provident funds in Asia and Africa. In J. Midgley & D. Piachaud (Eds.), *Colonialism and welfare: Social policy and the British imperial legacy* (pp. 144–158). Cheltenham, UK: Edward Elgar.

Kasente, D., Asingwire, N., Banugire, F., & Kyomuhenda, S. (2002). *Social Security in Uganda: Journal of Social Development in Africa, 17*(2), 159–184.

Kaufman, F. (2012). *European foundations of the welfare state*. New York, NY: Berghahn Books.

Keane, J. (2003). *Global civil society?* Cambridge, UK: Cambridge University Press.

Kelly, M. (2012). *Owning our future: The emerging ownership revolution*. San Francisco, CA: Berrett-Koehler.

Kendall, K. (2000). *Social work education: Its origins in Europe*. Alexandria, VA: Council on Social Work Education.

Kennedy, P. (2006). *The parliament of man: The past, present and future of the United Nations*. New York, NY: Random House.

Kennett, P. (Ed.). (2013). *Handbook of comparative social policy* (2nd ed.). Northhampton, MA: Edward Elgar.

Kenny, C. (2011). *Getting better: Why global development is succeeding and how we can improve the world even more*. New York, NY: Basic Books.

Khinduka, S. K. (1971). Social work in the third world. *Social Service Review, 45*(2), 62–73.

Kidd, A. (1999). *State, society and the poor in nineteenth century England*. New York, NY: St. Martin's Press.

Knuttila, M., & Kubik, W. (2000). *State theories: Classical, global and feminist perspectives*. London, UK: Zed Books.

Korten, D. C. (1995). *When corporations rule the world*. Bloomfield, CT: Kumarian Press.

Kreitzer, L. (2012). *Social work in Africa: Exploring culturally relevant education and practice in Ghana*. Calgary, Canada: University of Calgary Press.

Kretzman, J., & McKnight, J. (1993). *Building communities from the inside out: A path toward finding and mobilizing community's assets*. Evanston, IL: Institute for Policy Research, Northwestern University.

Kristol, I. (1978). *Two cheers for capitalism*. New York, NY: Basic Books.

Kristol, W., & Kagan, R. (2000). Introduction: National interest and global responsibility. In R. Kagan and W. Kristol (Eds.), *Present dangers: Crisis and opportunity in American foreign and defense policy* (pp. 3–24). San Francisco, CA: Encounter Books.

Kropotkin, P. (1902). *Mutual aid: A factor of evolution*. London, UK: Heinemann.

Krugman, P. (1996). *Pop internationalism*. Cambridge, MA: MIT Press.

Ku, H. B., Yueng, S. C., & Sung-Chan, P. (2005). Searching for a capacity building model in social work education in China. *Social Work Education, 24*(2), 213–233.

Küng, H. (1998). *A global ethic for global politics and economics*. New York, NY: Oxford University Press.

Kuti, E. (2001). Different European countries at different crossroads. In H. K. Anheier & J. Kendall (Eds.), *Third sector policy at the crossroads: An international nonprofit analysis* (pp. 193–202). New York, NY: Routledge.

Kuttner, R. (1997). *Everything for sale: The virtues and limits of markets.* New York, NY: Knopf.

Kuttner, R. (2013). *Debtor's prison: The politics of austerity versus possibility.* New York, NY: Knopf.

Kuznetsova, I., & Round, J. (2014). Communities and social care in Russia: The role of Muslim welfare provision in everyday life in Russia's Tatarstan region. *International Social Work, 57*(5), 486–496.

Kwon, H. (2001). Globalization, unemployment and policy responses in Korea: Repositioning the state. *Global Social Policy, 1*(2), 213–234.

Kwon, H. (Ed.). (2005). *Transforming the developmental welfare state in East Asia.* New York, NY: Palgrave Macmillan.

Lal, D. (2000). *The poverty of development economics.* Cambridge, MA: MIT Press.

Lal, D. (2006). *Reviving the invisible hand: The case for classical liberalism in the twenty-first century.* Princeton, NJ: Princeton University Press.

Lang, S. (2013). *NGOs, civil society and the public sphere.* New York, NY: Cambridge University Press.

Laqueur, W. (2012). *After the fall: The end of the European dream and the decline of a continent.* London, UK: Dunne.

Lash, S., & Urry, J. (1987). *The end of organized capitalism.* Cambridge, UK: Polity Press.

Layard, R. (2005). *Happiness: Lessons from a new science.* New York, NY: Penguin.

Le Grand, J. (2007). *The other invisible hand: Delivering public services through choice and competition.* Princeton, NJ: Princeton University Press.

Lechner, F. J., & Boli, J. (2005). *World culture: Origins and consequences.* Malden, MA: Blackwell.

Leece, J., & Bornat, J. (Eds.). (2006). *Developments in direct payments.* Bristol, UK: Policy Press.

Leighninger, L. (1987). *Social work: Search for identity.* New York, NY: Greenwood Press.

Leighninger, R. (2007). *Long range public investment: The forgotten legacy of the New Deal.* Columbia: University of South Carolina Press.

Lerner, D. (1958). *The passing of traditional society.* New York, NY: Free Press.

Leung, J. C. B., & Xu, Y. (2015). *China's social welfare: The third turning point.* Cambridge, UK: Polity Press.

Levitsky, S. (2014). *Caring for our own: Why there is no political demand for new American social welfare rights.* New York, NY: Oxford University Press.

Levy, J. D. (2006). The state also rises: The roots of contemporary state activism. In J. D. Levy (Ed.), *The state after statism: New state activities in the age of liberalization.* Cambridge, MA: Harvard University Press.

Levy, S. (2006). *Progress against poverty: Sustaining Mexico's Progresa-Oportunidades Program.* Washington, DC: Brookings Institution Press.

Lewis, D., & Kanji, N. (2009). *Non-governmental organizations and development.* New York, NY: Routledge.

Lewis, J. (1991). *Women, family, work and the state since 1945.* Oxford, UK: Blackwell.

Lewis, J. (1992). Gender and the development of welfare regimes. *Journal of European Social Policy, 2*(3), 159–173.

Lightman, E. (1991). Caught in the middle: The radical right and the Canadian welfare state. In H. Glennerster & J. Midgley (Eds.), *The radical right and the welfare state: An international assessment* (pp. 141–160). Savage, MD: Barnes and Noble.

Little, K. (1965). *West African urbanization: A study of voluntary associations in social change.* Cambridge, UK: Cambridge University Press.

Livingston, A. (1969). *Social policy in developing countries.* London, UK: Routledge and Kegan Paul.

Lødemel, I., & Moreira, A. (2014). Introduction. In I. Lødemel and A. Moreira (Eds.), *Activation or workfare? Governance and the neo-liberal convergence* (pp. 1–18). New York, NY: Oxford University Press.

Loewe, M. (2006). Downscaling, upgrading, or linking?: Ways to realize micro-insurance. *International Social Security Review, 59*(2), 37–59.

Lombard, A., & Twikirize, M. (2014). Promoting social and economic equality: Social workers' contribution to social justice and social development in South Africa and Uganda. *International Social Work, 57*(4), 313–325.

Lubove, R. (1965). *The professional altruist: The emergence of social work as a career.* Cambridge, MA: Harvard University Press.

Lukhele, A. K. (1990). *Stokvels in South Africa.* Johannesburg, South Africa: Amagi Books.

Lynch, F. R. (2011). *One nation under AARP: The fight over Medicare, social security, and America's future.* Berkeley: University of California Press.

Lyotard, J. (1984). *The postmodern condition: A report on knowledge.* Minneapolis: University of Minnesota Press.

MacPherson, S. (1982). *Social policy in the Third World: The dilemmas of underdevelopment.* Brighton, England: Harvester.

MacPherson, S., & Midgley, J. (1987). *Comparative social policy and the Third World.* Brighton, England: Wheatsheaf.

Madison, B. Q. (1968). *Social welfare in the Soviet Union.* Stanford, CA: Stanford University Press.

Mair, L. (1944). *Welfare in the British colonies.* London, UK: Royal Institute for International Affairs.

Mandelbaum, M. (2005). *The case for Goliath: How America acts as the world's government in the 21st century.* New York, NY: Public Affairs.

Mander, J., & Tauli-Corpuz, V. (2006). *Paradigm wars: Indigenous peoples' resistance to globalization.* San Francisco, CA: Sierra Club Books.

Mapp, S. C. (2008). *Human rights and social justice in a global perspective: An introduction to international social work.* New York, NY: Oxford University Press.

Margolin, L. (1997). *Under the cover of kindness: The invention of social work.* Charlottesville: Virginia University Press.

Marshall, K., & Van Saanen, M. (2007). *Development and faith: Where mind, heart and soul work together.* Washington, DC: World Bank.

Marshall, T. H. (1950). *Citizenship and other essays.* Cambridge, UK: Cambridge University Press.

Maslow, A. H. (1943). A theory of motivation. *Psychological Review, 50*(4), 370–398.

Mathie, A., & Cunningham, G. (2008). *From clients to citizens: Communities changing the course of their own development.* Rugby, England: Intermediate Technology Publications.

Mazower, M. (2012). *Governing the world: The history of an idea.* New York, NY: Penguin Press.

McDowell, S. K. (2004). *Building Godly nations: Lessons from the Bible and America's Christian history.* Charlottesville, VA: Providence Foundation.

McLuhan, M. (1962). *The Gutenberg galaxy: The making of typographic man.* Toronto, Canada: University of Toronto Press.

McLuhan, M., & Powers, R. (1989). *The global village: Transformations in world life and media in the 21st century.* New York, NY: Oxford University Press.

Mead, L. M. (1986). *Beyond entitlement: The social obligations of citizenship.* New York, NY: Free Press.

Mecker-Lowry, S. (1996). Community money: The potential of local currency. In J. Mander & D. Goldsmith (Eds.), *The case against the global economy and for a turn towards the local* (pp 446–459). San Francisco, CA: Sierra Club Books.

Mesa-Lago, C. (1978). *Social security in Latin America.* Pittsburgh, PA: University of Pittsburgh Press.

Mesa-Lago, C. (2008). *Reassembling social security: A survey of pensions and healthcare reforms in Latin America.* New York, NY: Oxford University Press.

Mesa-Lago, C. (2010). *World crisis effects on social security in Latin America and the Caribbean: Lessons and policies.* London, UK: Institute for the Study of the Americas.

Micklethwait, J., & Wooldridge, A. (2014). *The fourth revolution: The global race to reinvent the state.* New York, NY: Penguin Press.

Midgley, J. (1981). *Professional imperialism: Social work in the Third World.* London, UK: Heinemann.

Midgley, J. (1984). *Social security, inequality and the Third World.* New York, NY: Wiley.

Midgley, J. (1991). The radical right, politics and society. In H. Glennerster & J. Midgley (Eds.), *The radical right and the welfare state: An international assessment* (pp. 3–23). Hemel Hempstead, UK: Harvester Wheatsheaf.

Midgley, J. (1995). *Social development: The developmental perspective in social welfare.* Thousand Oaks, CA: SAGE.

Midgley, J. (1997). *Social welfare in global context.* London, UK: SAGE.

Midgley, J. (1999). Growth, redistribution and welfare: Towards social investment. *Social Service Review, 77*(1), 3–21.

Midgley, J. (2003). Social development: The intellectual heritage. *Journal of International Development, 15*(7), 831–844.

Midgley, J. (2004). Welfare, poverty and social services: International experiences. In M. C. Hokenstad & J. Midgley (Eds.), *Lessons from abroad: Adapting international social welfare innovations* (pp. 93–116). Washington, DC: NASW Press.

Midgley, J. (2008). Microenterprise, global poverty and social development. *International Social Work, 51*(4), 467–479.

Midgley, J. (2009). The institutional approach to social policy. In J. Midgley & M. Livermore (Eds.), *Handbook of social policy* (2nd ed., pp. 181–194). Thousand Oaks, CA: SAGE.

Midgley, J. (2010). The theory and practice of developmental social work. In J. Midgley & A. Conley (Eds.), *Social work and social development: Theories and skills for developmental social work* (pp. 3–28). New York, NY: Oxford University Press.

Midgley, J. (2011a). Imperialism, colonialism and social welfare. In J. Midgley & D. Piachaud (Eds.), *Colonialism and welfare: Social policy and the British imperial legacy* (pp. 36–54). Cheltenham, UK: Edward Elgar.

Midgley, J. (2011b). Challenges to mutual aid: The microinsurance response. In J. Midgley and M. Hosaka (Eds.), *Grassroots social security in Asia: Mutual aid, microinsurance and social welfare* (pp. 29–43). New York, NY: Routledge.

Midgley, J. (2012). Social protection and the elderly in the developing world: Mutual aid, microinsurance and the state. *Journal of Comparative Social Welfare, 28*(2), 153–163.

Midgley, J. (2013a). Social development and social protection: New opportunities and challenges. In L. Patel, J. Midgley, & M. Ulriksen (Eds.), *Social protection in Southern Africa: New opportunities for social development* (pp. 2–12). New York, NY: Routledge.

Midgley, J. (2013b). Social development and social welfare: Implications for comparative social policy. In P. Kennett (Ed.), *A handbook of comparative social policy* (pp. 182–204). Cheltenham, UK: Edward Elgar.

Midgley (2014). *Social development: Theory and practice.* Thousand Oaks, CA: SAGE.

Midgley, J., & Hosaka, M. (Eds.). (2011). *Grassroots social security in Asia: Mutual aid, microinsurance, and social welfare.* New York, NY: Routledge.

Midgley, J., & Piachaud, D. (Eds.). (2013). *Social protection, economic growth and social change: Goals, issues and trajectories in China, India, Brazil and South Africa.* Cheltenham, UK: Edward Elgar.

Midgley, J., & Sherraden, M. (2009). The social development perspective in social policy. In J. Midgley & M. Livermore (Eds.), *Handbook of social policy* (2nd ed., pp. 263–278). Thousand Oaks, CA: SAGE.

Midgley, J., & Tang, K. L. (2001). Social policy, economic growth and developmental welfare. *International Journal of Social Welfare, 10*(4), 242–250.

Mishra, R. (1984). *The welfare state in crisis.* Brighton, UK: Wheatsheaf.

Mishra, R. (1999). *Globalization and the welfare state.* Northampton, MA: Edward Elgar.

Mokomane, Z. (2012). Social protection as a mechanism for family protection in sub-Saharan Africa. *International Journal of Social Welfare, 22*(3), 248–259.

Monbiot, G. (2003). *Manifesto for a new world order.* New York, NY: New Press.

Morel, N., Pallier, B., & Palme, J. (Eds.) (2012). *Towards a social investment welfare state? Ideas, policies and challenges.* Bristol, UK: Policy Press.

Morris, A. J. F. (2010). *The limits to voluntarism: Charity and welfare from the New Deal through the Great Society.* New York, NY: Cambridge University Press.

Morris, D. M. (1979). *Measuring the condition of the world's poor.* New York, NY: Pergamon.

Moyo, D. (2009). *Dead aid: Why aid is not working and how there is a better way for Africa.* New York, NY: Penguin Books.

Mupedzisa, R., & Ntseane, D. (2014). The contribution of non-formal social protection to social development in Botswana. In J. Midgley, L. Patel, & M. Ulriksen (Eds.), *Social protection in Southern Africa: New opportunities for social development* (pp. 84–97). New York, NY: Routledge.

Murray, C. (1984). *Losing ground: American social policy, 1950-1980.* New York, NY: Basic Books.

Murray, C. (2006). *In our hands: A plan to replace the welfare State.* Washington, DC: AEI Press.

Murray, C. (2012). *Coming apart: The state of White America 1960-2010.* New York, NY: Crown Forum.

Mussacchio, A., & Lazzarini, S. G. (2014). *Reinventing state capitalism: Leviathan in business, Brazil and beyond.* Cambridge, MA: Harvard University Press.

Mutatkar, R. (2013). Social protection in India: Current approaches and issues. In J. Midgley & D. Piachaud (Eds.), *Social protection, economic growth and social change: Goals, issues and trajectories in China, India, Brazil and Africa* (pp. 102–116). Cheltenham, UK: Edward Elgar.

Mwansa, L. (2012). Social work in Africa. In L. M. Healy & R. J. Link (Eds.), *The handboook of international social work: Human rights, development and the global profession* (pp. 365–371). New York, NY: Oxford University Press.

Mwansa, L. (2013). Non-governmental organisations and poverty reduction in Africa: The need for a paradigms shift. *Journal of Social Development in Africa, 22*(1), 53–70.

Mwansa, L. J., & Kreitzer, L. (2012). Social work in Africa. In K. Lyons, T. Hokenstad, M. Pawar, N. Heugler, & N. Hall (Eds.), *The Sage handbook of international social work* (pp. 393–406). Los Angeles, CA: SAGE.

Myles, J., & Quadagno, J. (2002). Political theories of the welfare state. *Social Service Review, 76*(1), 34–57.

Nadkarni, V. V. (2014). News and views from IASSW. *International Social Work, 57*(3), 181–184.

New Internationalist. (2013, September). *Deported without your kids.* Issue 646.

Ngan, R. (2007). The crisis of social security funding in Hong Kong. In J. Lee & K. Chan (Eds.), *The crisis of welfare in East Asia* (pp. 125–146). Lanham, MD: Lexington Books.

Ngwenya, B. N. (2003). Redefining kin and family social relations: Burial societies and emergency relief in Botswana. *Journal of Social Development in Africa, 18*(1), 85–111.

Nicholls, A. (2008). *Social entrepreneurship: New models of sustainable social change.* New York, NY: Oxford University Press.

Nicholls, A. (2014). Filling the capital gap institutionalizing social finance. In S. Denny & F. Seddon (Eds.), *Social enterprise: Accountability and evaluation around the world* (pp. 161–195). New York, NY: Routledge.

Nicholls, A., & Opal, C. (2005). *Fair trade: Market-driven ethical consumption.* Thousand Oaks, CA: SAGE.

Nisbet, R. (1980). *History of the idea of progress.* New York, NY: Basic Books.

Noah, T. (2007). *The great divergence: America's growing inequality crisis and what can be done about it.* New York, NY: Bloomsbury.

Noble, C., & Nash, M. (2012). Social work in Australia and New Zealand. In L. M. Healy & R. J. Link (Eds.), *The handboook of international social work: Human rights, development and the global profession* (pp. 377–382). New York, NY: Oxford University Press.

Norberg, J. (2003). *In defense of global capitalism.* Washington, DC: Cato Institute.

Nussbaum, M. C. (2011). *Creating capabilities: The human development approach.* Cambridge, MA: Belknap Press.

O'Connor, J. (1973). *The fiscal crisis of the state.* New York, NY: St. Martin's Press.

OECD: See Organisation for Economic Co-operation and Development

Offe, C., & Keane, J. (1985). *Disorganized capitalism: Contemporary transformations of work and politics.* Cambridge, MA: MIT Press.

Okamoto, M. (2011). Safety net measures for Mongolian herders: Coping with risks in a transition economy. In J. Midgley & M. Hosaka (Eds.), *Grassroots social security in Asia: Mutual aid, microinsurance and social welfare* (pp. 95–109). New York, NY: Routledge.

Okun, A. (1975). *Equality and efficiency: The big tradeoff.* Washington, DC: Brookings.

Olasky, M. (1992). *The tragedy of American compassion.* Washington, DC: Regnery.

Omer, S. (1979). Social development. *International Social Work, 22*(3), 11–26.

Omhae, K. (1991). *The borderless world: Power and strategy in the interlinked economy.* New York, NY: Harper.

Omhae, K. (1996). *The end of the nation state: The rise of regional economies.* New York, NY: Free Press.

Omhae, K. (2005). *The next global stage: Challenges and opportunities in our borderless world.* Philadelphia, PA: Wharton School.

Onokerhoraye, A. G. (1984). *Social services in Nigeria.* London, UK: Routledge and Kegan Paul.

Opych, N. J., & Yu, J. L. H. (2014). A historical analysis of evidence-based practice in social work: The unfinished journey toward an empirically grounded profession. *Social Service Review, 88*(1), 3–58.

Orenstein, M. A. (2008). *Privatizing pensions: The transnational campaign for social security reform.* Princeton, NJ: Princeton University Press.

Organisation for Economic Co-operation and Development (OECD). (2015). *In it together: Why less inequality benefits all* [Remarks by A. Gurría]. Paris, France: Author.

Osborne, D., & Gaebler, T. (1992). *Reinventing government: How the entrepreneurial spirit is transforming government.* Reading, MA: Addison-Wesley.

Osei-Hwedie, K., Ntseane, D., & Jacques, G. (2006). Searching for appropriateness in social work education in Botswana. *Social Work Education, 25*(6), 569–590.

Ostrom, E. (1990). *Governing the commons: The evolution of institutions for collective action.* New York, NY: Cambridge University Press.

Paiva, F. J. X. (1977). A conception of social development. *Social Service Review, 51*(2), 327–336.

Pallotta, D. (2008). *Uncharitable: How restraints on nonprofits undermine their potential.* Medford, MA: Tufts University Press.

Pallotta, D. (2012). *Charity case: How the nonprofit community can stand up for itself and really change the world.* San Francisco, CA: Jossey-Bass.

Pandey, R. (1981). Strategies for social development: An analytical approach. In J. Jones & R. Pandey (Eds.), *Social development: Conceptual, methodological and policy issues* (pp. 33–49). New York, NY: St. Martin's Press.

Patel, L., (2005). *Social welfare and social development in South Africa.* Johannesburg, South Africa: Oxford University Press.

Patel, L., & Hochfelt, T. (2012). Developmental social work in South Africa: Translating policy into practice. *International Social Work, 56*(5), 690–704.

Patel, L., & Trieghaardt, J. (2008). South Africa: Social security, poverty and development. In J. Midgley & K. L. Tang (Eds.), *Social security, the economy and development* (pp. 85–109). New York, NY: Palgrave Macmillan.

Pawar, M. (2014a). *Water and social policy.* New York, NY: Palgrave Macmillan.

Pawar, M. S. (2014b). *Social and community development practice.* New Delhi, India: SAGE.

Pawar, M. S., & Cox, D. (Eds.). (2010). *Social development: Critical themes and perspectives.* New York, NY: Routledge.

Pawar, M., & Tsui, M. (2012). Social work in Southern and Eastern Asia. In K. Lyons, T. Hokenstad, M. Pawar, N. Heugler, & N. Hall (Eds.), *The Sage handboook of international social work* (pp. 407–420). Los Angeles, CA: SAGE.

Peillon, M. (2001). *Welfare in Ireland: Actors, resources and strategies.* Westport, CT: Praegar.

Peterson, P. (1996). *Will America grow up before it grows old?* New York, NY: Random House.

Peterson, P. (1999). *Gray dawn: How the coming age wave will transform America and the world.* New York, NY: Times Books.

Petras, J., & Veltmeyer, H. (2001). *Globalization unmasked: Imperialism in the 21st century.* London, UK: Zed Books.

Pierson, C. (1991). *Beyond the welfare state: The new political economy of welfare.* Cambridge, UK: Polity Press.

Pierson, P. (1994). *Dismantling the welfare state: Reagan, Thatcher and the politics of retrenchment.* New York, NY: Cambridge University Press.

Pierson, P. (1996). The new politics of the welfare state. *World Politics, 48*(2), 143–179.

Piketty, T. (2014). *Capital in the twenty-first century.* Cambridge, MA: Belknap Press.

Pinker, R. (1979). *The idea of welfare.* London, UK: Heinemann.

Pinker, S. (2011). *The better angels of our nature: Why violence has declined.* New York, NY: Viking.

Piven, F. F., & Cloward, R. (1971). *Regulating the poor: The functions of public welfare.* New York, NY: Pantheon.

Pochet, P., & Degryse, C. (2010). Social policies of the European union. *Global Social Policy, 10*(2), 248–257.

Pogge, T. (2010). *Politics as usual: What lies behind the pro-poor rhetoric.* Malden, MA: Polity Press.

Polak, P., & Warwick, M. (2013). *The business solution to poverty: Designing products and services for three billion new customers.* San Francisco, CA: Berrett-Koehler.

Polanyi, K. (1944). *The great transformation: The political and economic origins of our time.* New York, NY: Farrar and Rinehart.

Polman, L. (2010). *War games: The story of aid and war in modern times.* New York, NY: Penguin.

Powell, M. (Ed.). (2007). *Understanding the mixed economy of welfare.* Bristol, UK: Policy Press.

Prahalad, C. K. (2005). *The fortune at the bottom of the pyramid: Eradicating poverty through profits.* Upper Saddle River, NJ: Wharton School.

Prasad, N., & Gerecke, M. (2010). Social security spending in times of crisis. *Global Social Policy, 10*(2), 218–247.

Prins, N. (2014). *All the President's bankers: The hidden alliances that drive American power.* New York, NY: Nation Books.

Prokosch, M., & Raymond, L. (2002). *The global activist's manual: Local ways to change the world.* New York, NY: Nation Books.

Putnam, R. D., Leonardi, R., & Nanetti, R. Y. (1993). *Making democracy work: Civic traditions in modern Italy.* Princeton, NJ: Princeton University Press.

Queiro-Tajali, I. (2012). Social work in Latin America. In L. M. Healy & R. J. Link (Eds.), *The handbook of international social work: Human rights, development and the global profession* (pp. 393–399). New York, NY: Oxford University Press.

Rainford, W. (2001). Promoting welfare by enhancing opportunity: The individual enterprise approach to social development. *Social Development Issues, 23*(1), 51–57.

Rand, A. (1964). *The virtue of selfishness: A new concept of egoism.* New York, NY: Signet.

Ransom, D. (2001). *The no-nonsense guide to fair trade.* London, UK: Verso.

Reich, R. (1991). *The work of nations: Preparing ourselves for 21st century capitalism.* New York, NY: Knopf.

Remenyi, J., & Quinones, B. (Eds.). (2000). *Microfinance and poverty alleviation: Case studies from Asia and the Pacific.* New York, NY: Pinter.

Rice, J. R., & Prince, M. J. (2000). *Changing politics of Canadian social policy.* Toronto, Canada: University of Toronto Press.

Richmond, M. (1917). *Social diagnosis.* New York, NY: Russell Sage.

Rimlinger, G. (1971). *Welfare policy and industrialization in Europe, North America and Russia.* New York, NY: Wiley.

Robertson, R. (1992). *Globalization: Social theory and global culture.* Thousand Oaks, CA: SAGE.

Rodgers, B. N., Greve, J., & Morgan, J. S. (1968). *Comparative social administration.* London, UK: Allen and Unwin.

Rodgers, D. (1998). *Atlantic crossings: Social politics in a progressive age.* Cambridge, MA: Harvard University Press.

Rodgers, G. (2009). *The International Labour Organization and the quest for social justice, 1919-2009.* Ithaca, NY: Cornell University Press.

Rodney, W. (1972). *How Europe underdeveloped Africa.* Dar es Salaam: Tanzania Publishing.

Rodrik, D. (2011). *The globalization paradox: Democracy and the future of the world economy.* New York, NY: Norton.

Rogers, B. (1980). *The domestication of women: Discrimination in developing countries.* London, UK: Tavistock.

Roy, A. (2010). *Poverty capital: Microfinance and the making of development.* New York, NY: Routledge.

Rozario, P. A., & Kay, R. (2014). Contested representations of a family responsibility law: The case of Singapore's Maintenance of Parents Act of 1995. *Journal of Policy Practice, 13*(2), 118–132.

Ruthven, M. (2004). *Fundamentalism: The search for meaning.* New York, NY: Oxford University Press.

Sachs, J. (2005). *The end of poverty: Economic possibilities for our time.* New York, NY: Penguin Books.

Sachs, W. (2010). Introduction. In W. Sachs (Ed.), *The development dictionary: A guide to knowledge and power* (2nd ed., pp. xv–xx). London, UK: Zed Books.

Sadhak, H. (2013). *Pension reform in India.* New Delhi, India: SAGE.

Salamon, L. M. (2001). The nonprofit sector at the crossroads: The case of America. In H. K. Anheier & J. Kendall (Eds.), *Third sector policy at the crossroads: An international nonprofit analysis* (pp. 17–35). New York, NY: Routledge.

Salamon, L. M. (Ed.). (2014). *New frontiers of philanthropy: A guide to the new tools and actors reshaping global philanthropy and social investment* (pp. 3–88). New York, NY: Oxford University Press.

Salamon, L. M. (2014). The revolution on the frontiers of philanthropy: An introduction. In L. M. Salamon (Ed.), *New frontiers of philanthropy: A guide to the new tools and actors reshaping global philanthropy and social investment* (pp. 3–88). New York, NY: Oxford University Press.

Salamon, L. M., & Anheier, H. K. (1997). Towards a common definition. In L. M. Salamon & H. K. Anheier (Eds.), *Defining the nonprofit sector: A cross national analysis* (pp. 29–50). Manchester, England: Manchester University Press.

Samuelson, P. A. (1954). The pure theory of public expenditure. *Review of Economics and Statistics, 36*(4), 387–389.

Sanborn, C. (2005). Philanthropy in Latin America: Historical traditions and current trends. In C. Sanborn & F. Portocarrero (Eds.), *Philanthropy and social change in Latin America* (pp. 3–30). Cambridge, MA: Harvard University Press.

Sandel, M. J. (2012). *What money can't buy: The moral limits of markets.* New York, NY: Farrar, Straus and Giroux.

Sanger, M. B. (2003). *The welfare marketplace: Privatization and welfare reform.* Washington, DC: Brookings Institution Press.

Saracostti, M., Reininger, T., & Parada, H. (2012). Social work in Latin America. In K. Lyons, T. Hokenstad, H. N. Pawar, & N. Hall (Eds.), *The Sage handboook of international social work* (pp. 466–479). Los Angeles, CA: SAGE.

Saul, J. R. (2005). *The collapse of globalism and the reinvention of the world.* London, UK: Atlantic Books.

Scholte, J. A. (2000). *Globalization: A critical introduction.* New York, NY: Palgrave.

Schreiner, M., & Sherraden, M. (2007). *Can the poor save? Saving and asset building in individual development accounts.* New Brunswick, NJ: Transaction.

Schultz, T. W. (1981). *Investing in people.* Berkeley: University of California Press.

Schumpeter, J. A. (1939). *Business cycles: A theoretical, historical and statistical analysis of the capitalist process.* New York, NY: McGraw Hill.

Scott, D. W., & Russell, L. (2001). Contracting: The experience of service delivery agencies. In M. Harris & C. Rochester, (Eds.), *Voluntary organizations and social policy in Britain: Perspectives on change and choice* (pp. 49–64). New York, NY: Palgrave.

Scott, J. C. (1998). *Seeing like a state: How certain schemes to improve the human condition have failed.* New Haven, CT: Yale University Press.

Seldon, A. (1996). Pensions without the state. In A. Seldon (Ed.), *Privatising welfare after the lost century* (pp. 63–80). London, UK: Institute of Economic Affairs.

Sen, A. (1985). *Commodities and capabilities.* Amsterdam, Netherlands: Elsevier.

Sen, A. (1999). *Development as freedom.* New York, NY: Knopp.

Sewpaul, V., & Jones, D. (2004). Global standards for social work education and training. *Social Work Education, 23*(5), 493–513.

Shang, X. (2008). The role of extended families in childcare and protection: The case of rural China. *International Journal of Social Welfare, 17*(3), 204–215.

Shawky, A. (1972). Social work education in Africa. *International Social Work, 15*(3), 3–16.

Sherraden, M. (1991). *Assets and the poor: A new American welfare policy.* Armonk, NY: M. E. Sharpe.

Shigetomi, S., & Okamoto, I. (2014). *Local societies and rural development: Self-organization and participatory development in Asia.* Cheltenham, UK: Elgar.

Sirojudin & Midgley, J. (2012). Microinsurance and social protection: The social welfare insurance program for informal sector workers in Indonesia. *Journal of Policy Practice, 11*(1/2), 121–136.

Slater, D., & Tonkiss, F. (2001). *Market society.* Malden, MA: Polity Press.

Smillie, I. (2009). *Freedom from want: The remarkable success story of BRAC, the global grassroots organization that's winning the fight against poverty.* Sterling, VA: Kumarian Press.

Smith, J. H. (2009). *The art of doing good: Charity in late Ming China.* Berkeley: University of California Press.

Smyth, P. (2004). The British social policy legacy and the 'Australian Way.' In C. J. Finer & P. Smyth (Eds.), *Social policy and the Commonwealth* (pp. 167–180). New York, NY: Palgrave.

Soares, S. (2013). The efficiency and effectiveness of social protection against poverty and inequality in Brazil. In J. Midgley & D. Piachaud (Eds.), *Social protection, economic growth and social change: Goals, issues and trajectories in China, India, Brazil and Africa* (pp. 153–165). Cheltenham, UK: Edward Elgar.

Soliman, H. H. (Ed.). (2013). *Social work in the Middle East.* New York, NY: Routledge.

Solomon, L. D. (2014). *Building an opportunity society: A realistic alternative to an entitlement state.* New Brunswick, NJ: Transaction Books.

Sooryamoorty, R., & Gangrade, K. D. (2001). *NGOs in India: A cross-sectional study.* Westport, CT: Greenwood Press.

Soros, G. (2002). *On globalization.* New York, NY: Public Affairs Press.

Specht, H., & Courtney, M. (1994). *Unfaithful angels: How social work has abandoned its mission.* New York, NY: Free Press.

Spencer, P., & Wollman, H. (2002). *Nationalism: A critical introduction.* Thousand Oaks: CA: SAGE.

Speth, J. G. (Ed.). (2009a). *Worlds apart: Globalization and the environment.* Washington, DC: Island Press.

Speth, J. G. (2009b). *The bridge at the edge of the world: Capitalism, the environment and crossing from crisis to sustainability.* New Haven, CT: Yale University Press.

Spitzer, H., Twikirize, J. M., & Wairire, G. G. (Eds.). (2014). *Professional social work in East Africa: Towards social development, poverty reduction and gender equality.* Kampala, Uganda: Fountain.

Steurle, C. E. (2000). Common issues for voucher programs. In C. E. Steurle, V. D. Ooms, G. Peterson, & R. D. Reschauer (Eds.), *Vouchers and the provision of public services* (pp. 3–39). Washington, DC: Brookings Institution Press.

Stiglitz, J. E. (2002). *Globalization and its discontents.* New York, NY: Norton.

Stiglitz, J. E. (2007). *Making globalization work.* New York, NY: Norton.

Stoesz, D. (1981). A wake for the welfare state: Social welfare and neoconservative challenge. *Social Service Review, 55*(4), 398–410.

Stoesz, D. (1991). The American welfare state at twilight. *Journal of Social Policy, 31*(3), 487–503.

Stoesz, D. (2013). Paradigms of anti-poverty policy. In J. Berkenmaier, M. Sherraden, & J. Curley (Eds.), *Financial capability and asset development: Research, education, policy and practice* (pp. 62–82). New York, NY: Oxford University Press.

Stoesz, D., Karger, H., & Carrillio, T. E. (2010). *A dream deferred: How social work education lost its way and what can be done.* New Brunswick, NJ: Transaction.

Streeten, P., Burki, S. J., Ul Haq, M., Hicks, N., & Stewart, F. (1981). *First things first: Meeting basic needs in developing countries.* New York, NY: Oxford University Press.

Surender, R. (2004). Modern challenges to the welfare state and the antecedents of the third way. In J. Lewis & R. Surender (Eds.), *Welfare state change: Towards a third way* (pp. 3–24)? New York, NY: Oxford University Press.

Surender, R. (2013). The role of historical contexts in shaping social policy in the Global South. In R. Surender & R. Walker (Eds.), *Social policy in a developing world* (pp. 2–13). Northampton, MA: Elgar.

Surender, R., & Urbina-Ferretjans, M. (2013). South-South cooperation: A new paradigm for global social policy. In R. Surender & R. Walker (Eds.), *Social policy in a developing world* (pp. 237–257). Northampton, MA: Elgar.

Surender, R., & Walker, R. (Eds.). (2013). *Social policy in a developing world.* Northampton, MA: Elgar.

Swank, D. (2002). *Global capital, political institutions and policy change in developed welfare states.* New York, NY: Cambridge University Press.

Tan, N. T. (2012). Social work in Asia. In L. M. Healy & R. J. Link (Eds.), *The handboook of international social work: Human rights, development and the global profession* (pp. 372–376). New York, NY: Oxford University Press.

Tanaka, Y. (2002). Singapore: Subtle NGO control by a developmentalist welfare state. In S. Shigetomi (Ed.), *The state and NGOs: Perspectives from Asia* (pp. 200–221). Tokyo, Japan: Sasakawa Peace Foundation.

Tang, K. L. (2000). Asian crisis, social welfare and policy responses: Hong Kong and Korea compared. *International Journal of Sociology and Social Policy, 20*(5/6), 49–71.

Taylor, J. B. (2009). *Getting off track: How government actions and interventions caused, prolonged and worsened the financial crisis.* Stanford, CA: Hoover Institution Press.

Taylor, J. B. (2012). *First principles: Five keys to restoring America's prosperity.* New York, NY: Norton.

Taylor-Gooby, P., Gumy, J. M., & Otto, A. (2014). Can 'New Welfare' address poverty through more and better jobs? *Journal of Social Policy, 44*(1), 83–105.

Terao, T. (2002). Taiwan: From subjects of oppression to the instruments of "Taiwanization." In S. Shigetomi (Ed.), *The state and NGOs: Perspectives from Asia* (pp. 263–287). Tokyo, Japan: Sasakawa Peace Foundation.

Thompson, J., & Scott, J. M. (2014). Social enterprise or social entrepreneurship: Which matters and why. In S. Denny & F. Seddon (Eds.), *Social enterprise: Accountability and evaluation around the world* (pp. 13–27). New York, NY: Routledge.

Ting, G., & Woo, J. (2009). Elder care: Is legislation or family responsibility the solution? *Asian Journal of Geriatrics, 4*(2), 72–75.

Titmuss, R. M. (1958). The social divisions of welfare. In R. M. Titmuss (Ed.), *Essays on the welfare state* (pp. 34–55). London, UK: Allen and Unwin.

Titmuss, R. M. (1968). *Commitment to welfare.* London, UK: Allen and Unwin.

Titmuss, R. M. (1971). *The gift relationship: From human blood to social policy.* London, UK: Allen and Unwin.

Titmuss, R. M. (1974). *Social policy: An introduction.* London, UK: Allen and Unwin.

Titmuss, R. M., & Abel-Smith, B. (1961). *Social policies and population growth in Mauritius.* London, UK: Methuen.

Townsend, P., & Gordon, D. (2002). Conclusion: Constructing an anti-poverty strategy. In P. Townsend & D. Gordon (Eds.), *World poverty: New policies to defeat an old enemy* (pp. 413–432). Bristol, UK: Policy Press.

Townsend, R. (1994). Risk and insurance in village India. *Econometrica, 62*(4), 539–592.

Uchitelle, L. (2006). *The disposable American: Layoffs and their consequences.* New York, NY: Knopf.

United Nations. (1969). *Proceedings of the international conference of ministers responsible for social welfare.* New York, NY: Author.

United Nations. (1979). *Patterns of government expenditure on social services.* New York, NY: Author.

United Nations. (1996). *Report of the world summit for social development* [Copenhagen, Denmark, 6–12 March 1995]. New York, NY: Author.

United Nations. (2000). *The United Nations Millennium Declaration* (Resolution 55/2). New York, NY: Author.

United Nations. (2005). *Investing in development: A practical plan to achieve the millennium development goals.* New York, NY: Author.

United Nations. (2010). *Keeping the promise: A forward-looking review to promote an agreed action agenda to achieve the millennium development goals by 2015.* New York, NY: Author.

UNDP: See United Nations Development Programme

United Nations Development Programme. (1990). *Human development report 1990.* New York, NY: Oxford University Press.

United Nations Development Programme. (2013). *Human development report 2013: The rise of the south: Human progress in a diverse world.* New York, NY: Author.

United States, Social Security and Medicare Boards of Trustees. (2014). *Summary of the 2014 Annual Reports.* Washington, DC: Government Printing Office.

van Ginneken, W. (Ed.). (1999). *Social security for the excluded majority.* Geneva, Switzerland: International Labour Office.

van Ginneken, W. (2007). Extending social security coverage: Concepts, global trends and policy issues. *International Social Security Review, 60*(2/3), 39–59.

van Ginnekin, W. (2010). Social security coverage extension: A review of recent evidence. *International Social Security Review, 63*(1), 57–76.

van Kersbergen, K., & Hemerijck, A. (2012). Two decades of change in Europe: The emergence of the social investment state. *Journal of Social Policy, 41*(3), 475–492.

Van Leeuwen, I. (2005). *Gender and microinsurance.* The Hague, Netherlands: Institute of Social Studies.

Van Parijs, P. (2006). Basic income: A simple and powerful idea for the twenty first century. In B. Ackerman, A. Alstott, & P. Van Parijs (Eds.), *Redesigning distribution: Basic income and stakeholder grants as cornerstones for an egalitarian capitalism,* (pp. 3–42). New York, NY: Verso.

Van Parijs, P., & Vanderborght, Y. (2015). Basic income in a globalized economy. In R. Hasmath (Ed.), *Inclusive growth, development and welfare policy: A critical assessment* (pp. 229–247). New York, NY: Routledge.

Wacquant, L. (2009). *Punishing the poor: The neoliberal government of social insecurity.* Durham, NC: Duke University Press.

Wahl, A. (2011). *The rise and fall of the welfare state.* London, UK: Pluto.

Walker, A., & Wong, C. K. (2013). The ethnocentric construction of the welfare state. In P. Kennett (Ed.), *Handbook of comparative social policy* (pp. 98–114). Northhampton, MA: Edward Elgar.

Wallerstein, I. (1980). *The capitalist world economy.* New York, NY: Cambridge University Press.

Walton, R. G., & El Nassr, M. M. (1988). The indigenization and authentication of social work in Egypt. *Community Development Journal, 23*(3), 148–155.

Warren, E., & Tyagi, A. W. (2003). *The two-income trap: Why middle-class mothers and fathers are going broke.* New York, NY: Basic Books.

Weber, O. (2014). Social banking: Concept, definition and practice. *Global Social Policy, 14*(2), 265–266.

Weismiller, T., & Whitaker, T. (2008). Social work profession: Workforce. In T. Mizrahi & L. E. Davis (Eds.), *Encyclopedia of social work* (pp. 164–168). New York, NY: Oxford University Press.

Wenger, C. (1984). *The supportive network: Coping with old age.* London, UK: Allen and Unwin.

Whittaker, J. K., & Garbarino, J. (1983). *Social support networks: Informal helping in the human services.* New York, NY: Aldine.

Whitworth, A., & Wilkinson, K. (2014). Tackling child poverty in South Africa: Implications of ubuntu for this system of social grants. In J. Midgley, L. Patel, & M. Ulriksen (Eds.), *Social protection in Southern Africa: New opportunities for social development* (pp. 121–134). New York, NY: Routledge.

Wilensky, H. (1975). *The welfare state and equality.* Berkeley: University of California Press.

Wilensky, H. (2002). *Rich democracies: Political economy, public policy and performance.* Berkeley: University of California Press.

Wilensky, H., & Lebeaux, C. (1965). *Industrial society and social welfare.* New York, NY: Free Press.

Wilkie, W. L. (1943). *One world.* New York, NY: Simon & Schuster.

Wilkinson-Maposa, S. (2008). Jansenville development forum: Linking community and government in the rural landscape of the Eastern Cape Province, South Africa. In A. Mathie and G. Cunningham (Eds.), *From clients to citizens: Communities changing the course of their own development* (pp. 237–260). Rugby, England: Intermediate Technology Publications.

Williams, R. C. (2007). *The cooperative movement: Globalization from below.* Burlington, VT: Ashgate.

Williamson, J. (1990). What Washington means by policy reform. In J. Williamson (Ed.), *Latin American adjustment: How much has happened?* Washington, DC: Institute for International Economics.

Wilson, P. H. (2009). *The thirty years war: Europe's tragedy.* Cambridge, MA: Harvard University Press.

Wolf, M. (2004). *Why globalization works.* New Haven, CT: Yale University Press.

Woods, N. (2006). *The globalizers: The IMF, the World Bank and their borrowers.* Ithaca, NY: Cornell University Press.

World Bank. (1975). *The assault on world poverty.* Baltimore, MD: Johns Hopkins University Press.

World Bank. (1991). *World Development Report, 1991: The challenge of development.* Washington, DC: Author.

World Bank. (1994). *Averting the old age crisis: Policies to protect the old and promote growth.* Washington, DC: Author.

Wuthnow, R. (2009). *Boundless faith: The global outreach of American churches.* Princeton, NJ: Princeton University Press.

Yap, M. T. (2010). Social assistance programmes in Singapore. In J. Midgley & K. L. Tang (Eds.), *Social policy and poverty in East Asia. The role of social security* (pp. 66–80). New York, NY: Routledge.

Yeates, N. (2001). *Globalization and social policy.* Thousand Oaks, CA: SAGE.

Yeates, N. (2008). The idea of global social policy. In N. Yeates (Ed.), *Understanding global social policy* (pp. 1–24). Bristol, UK: Policy Press.

Yip, D. (2004). A Chinese cultural critique of the global qualifying standards for social work education. *Social Work Education, 23*(5), 597–612.

Yu, N. G. (2006). Interrogating social work: Philippine social work and human rights under martial law. *International Journal of Social Welfare, 15*(3), 257–263.

Zheng, Y., & Huang, Y. (2013). Political dynamics of social policy reform in China. In L. Zhao (Ed.). *China's social development and policy: Into the next stage.* New York, NY: Routledge.

Zimmer, A. (2001). Corporatism revisited: The legacy of history and the German nonprofit sector. In H. K. Anheier & J. Kendall (Eds.), *Third sector policy at the crossroads: An international nonprofit analysis* (pp. 114–125). New York, NY: Routledge.

Zuberi, D. (2006). *Differences that matter: Social policy and the working poor in the United States and Canada.* Ithaca, NY: Cornell University Press.

Index

Aaron, H., 11
AARP, 81–82
Abed, Fazle Hassan, 83
Abel-Smith, B., 9
Addams, Jane, 95, 104–105
Adema, W., 142
Advocacy
 nonprofit and faith-based organizations and, 75, 81–82
 social work and, 105
Africa. *See* Middle East and North Africa; Sub-Saharan Africa
Agents (welfare agents), definition and types of, 5
Aguero, F., 84
Ahmed, S., 189, 192
Aid, international and humanitarian, 187, 190–191, 193
Aid to Families with Dependent Children (ADFC), U.S., 151
Alber, J., 153
Alexander, M., 152
Alinsky, Saul, 82
Alip, M. A., 68
Alliances, 26
Almanzor, A. C., 104
Altruism, 61
Amenomori, T., 68, 69, 77
Amin, S., 40
Amnesty International, 189
Analytic research, 12
Anderson, P., 44
Anderson, S., 84
Anheier, H. K., 75, 80, 84
Anti-Corn League, 180
Appiah, K. A., 206
Appleby, R. S., 51
Applied research, 13
Apt, N. A., 64
Aristotle, xiii
Armstrong, B. N., 9, 13
Aronowitz, S., 47
Asher, M., 140
Asia. *See* East Asia; South Asia; South East Asia, social conditions in
Asian Financial Crisis (1997), 153, 154
Aspalter, C., 163
Asset development programs, 171
Association of Community Organizations for Reform Now (ACORN), 82

Asymmetrial information, 121–122
Atlas, J., 82
Attlee, Clement, 78–79
Australasia, 30
Azaiza, F., 64

Bacon, R., 151
Banarjee, A. V., 12
Bangladesh, 83
Banks and credit unions, community-based, 118
Barker, R., 92
Barnett, C., 149
Barretta-Herman, A., 101
Barrientos, A., 69
Bartkowski, J. P., 81
Bass, M., 85
Bateman, M., 170
Bauman, Z., 41, 47, 147
Baumol, W. J., 151
Bebbington, A. J., 87
Becker, U., 147
Beit-ul-mal, 67, 132
Bello, W., 52, 202
Benda-Beckmann, F. von, 62, 70
Benda-Beckmann, K. von, 62
Benevolent societies, 76
Bentham, Jeremy, xii, xiii, xiv, 8, 40, 200, 201
Berkman, S., 191
Bernstein, W. J., 46
Bettman, J. E., 98
Bevan, P., 137
Beveridge, William, 79, 133
Beveridge Report, 133
Bhagwati, J. N., 46, 47
Big Society Capital (Britain), 84
Bilateral aid, 187
Binder, A., 47
BINGOs (Big International Nongovernmental Organizations), 188
Bishop, M., 84
Bismarck, Otto von, 132
Blair, Tony, 113
Blumberg, Michael, 14
Boko Haram, 66
Boli, J., xii, 41, 43

Bolsa Familia program, Brazil, 138–139, 203–204
Bolton, John, 191
Bonoli, G., 142, 154
Bornat, J., 119
Borzutsky, S., 113, 115, 122, 139, 153
Boserup, E., 166
Bottom of the pyramid (BoP) approach, 118
BRAC, 83
Bradshaw, J., xiv
Brandt Commission, 28
Brazil
    Bolsa Familia program, 138–139, 203–204
    corporate social responsibility in, 84
Brecher, J., 51
BRICS countries, state welfare in, 138
Briggs, , A., 131
Brundtland Commission, 166
Buchanan, J., 151
Burgis, T., 137
Burial societies, 64, 67, 68
Businesses. *See* Commercial enterprises; Markets and
    commercial provision

Caetano, M. A., 139
Calbezas, A., 47
Calderisi, R., 86
Caliph Umar, 67
Campanini, A., 98, 99
Cardoso, Fernando Henrique, 204
Caregiving, 61, 67
Carrillio, T. E., 102–103
Case study approach, 10–11
Casework, 93, 94–95
Casey, B. H., 193
Castells, M., 41, 42
Castles, F. G., 143, 153–154
Center for Agriculture and Rural Development (CARD),
    Philippines, 68
Central America, social conditions in, 30
Central Asia, 30–31, 33–34
Central Commission for the Navigation of the Rhine, 181
Chalmers, Thomas, 76
Chandragupta Maurya, 132
Chang, H. J., 48, 49, 50, 122, 123
Chappell, M., 66
Charity Organization Society, London, 78, 94, 95
Chen, M., 68
Cheung, M., 119–120
Child care, 61, 67
Child Trust Fund, Britain, 120
Chilean social insurance retirement system, 115, 122
China, 76, 82, 138
Choudry, A., 87, 192
Christianity, 22, 199–200. *See also* Faith-based organizations
Chua, A., 48–49

Chung, K., 115, 123
Church missions, 77–78
Church Taxes, 80
Cichon, M., 204
Citizenship, 21, 24
Civil society, 75
Clark, J. A., 16, 82, 130–131
Clinton, Bill, 113, 154
Cloward, R., 152
Coates, J., 104
Code of Hammurabi, 132
Cohen, D., 45
Cohen, William, 129
Cold War and social conditions, 32
Collaboration and cooperation
    collectivism and social democratic cosmopolitanism, 203
    globalization and, 40
    governments, nonprofits, and other agents, 187–190
    history of, 179, 180–184
    issues and challenges, 190–193
    before nation states, 20
    nonformal welfare institutions and, 59, 61
    promotion of, 184–187
Collectivism, 203, 206
Collins, D., 69
Colonialism, 22, 23
Colonial Welfare and Development Acts, UK, 182
Commercial enterprises
    as formal social welfare institutions, 8
    nonprofit sector and, 79
    social responsibility programs, 84, 189–190
    See also Markets and commercial provision
Commons, 59
Commonwealth, notion of, xiii
Communist Manifesto (Marx and Engels), 40, 120
Community activism, 82
Community-based assets, 171
Community development programs in India, 165
Community welfare practices, 6, 20
Community work in social work, 93
Comparative analysis, 14
Comparative Nonprofit Sector Project, Center for Civil
    Society Studies, John Hopkins University, 75
Concert of Europe, 22, 26, 180, 181
Confraternia, 76
Confucius (Kung Fu Tsu), xiii
Conley, A., 138
Conservative-corporatist welfare states, 136
Contracting. *See* Outsourcing (contracting)
Convention on the Elimination of all forms of
    Discrimination against Women (CEDAW),
    UN, 166, 186
Convention on the Rights of the Child (1989), 186
Cook, L. J., 140–141
Cooperation. *See* Collaboration and cooperation

Cooperative movement, 188–189
Cooperatives, 81, 83
Copenhagen Declaration, 167
Coram, Captain, 76
Corporate social responsibility, 84, 189–190
Corporate welfare provision. *See* Markets and commercial provision
Cosmopolitanism, 198–200, 203, 205–206
Costello, T., 51
Courtney, M., 103
Cowen, T., 47, 49, 205
Cox, D., 99, 169
Cross-cultural welfare, xi
Cross-national welfare, xi
Cultural classification of nation states, 25–26
Cultural diffusion, 48–49
Cultures, traditional, 35, 64–65, 67, 109, 120
Cunningham, G., 171
Curry, C., 119

Dahl, R. A., 147, 156
Dalai Lama, 200
Dallal, A., 76
Daly, L., 77
Daly, M., 61
Darwin, Charles, 146
Dasgupta, P., 169
Deacon, B., xii, 10, 17, 42–43, 134, 140, 183, 192, 200, 203, 204
Dean, H., xiv, 113
de Bruijn, M., 65
Declaration of Alma-Ata (1978), 186
Degryse, C., 183
Delavega, E., 119–120
Demand side marketization policies, 114, 117–120
Democratic socialists, xiii–xiv
Dependency theory, 40–41, 49–50
de Schweinitz, K., 67, 132
Descriptive research, 10–12
"Developed" vs. "underdeveloped" countries, 27–28
Development
    classification of nation states by, 27–28
    "market friendly" development policies, 113
    NGOs and, 83
    See also Social development
Developmental welfare states, 136–137
Development studies, 40
Devereux, S., 172
de Waal, F., 61
Dickens, Charles, 123
Diestenweg, Adolph, 96
Diogenes, 199
Direct payments, 119
Dixon, J., 10, 134
Dominelli, L., 82

Donations by citizens, 84, 189
Dostal, J. M., 193
Douglas, N., 111, 206
Draibe, S. M., 139
Drakeford, M., 122
Duflo, E., 12
Durkheim, Émile, 147
Dyer, W. G., 118

East Asia
    social conditions in, 31
    social progress in, 33
    state welfare in, 136–137, 139–140
Easterly, W., 193
Eastern Europe
    post-Soviet restructuring and social conditions in, 32
    social progress in, 33–34
    social work, emergence of, 97
    state welfare in, 140–141
    See also Soviet Union
Eberstadt, N., 152
Eckl, J., 86
Economic alliances, 26–27
Economic development classification of nation states, 27–28
Economic Security Council (proposed), 52
Edwards, M., 86
Egalitarianism, 203–204
Elder care, 61, 67
Elizabethan Charitable Uses statute (1601, England), 76
Elizabethan Poor Law (1601, England), 132
Elliott, D., 99
Elliott, K. A., 51
Elliott, Larry, 42
Ellis, F., 172
El-Nassr, M. M., 104
El-Said, H., 188
Eltis, W., 151
Employees Provident Fund, India, 138
Endogenous development, 39
Engels, Friedrich, xii, 22, 40, 111, 120, 180, 200
Esping-Andersen, G., 12, 17, 136–137, 141, 147
Ethnicity concept, roots of, 21
Ethnos, 21
Etzioni, A., 120
Eudaimonia, xiii
Europe
    faith-based organizations and Church Taxes, 80–81
    integration and, 44
    social conditions in, 30
    social progress in, 34
    social work, evolution of, 96
    welfare statism and, 141–142
European Union as alliance, 27
Evaluation studies, 12
Explanatory research, 12

Fabian Society, 52, 95
Fairbourne, J., 118
Fair trade, 51
Faith-based organizations
    challenges and role of, 85–88
    Church Taxes in Europe, 80–81
    collaboration and, 185, 188, 192
    definitions, 74–75
    as formal social welfare institution, 7
    historical perspectives, 76–79
    in international context, 80–85
    social workers and, 99–100
Family, 6, 63–64
Family studies, 13
Federations and collaboration, 188
Feldstein, M. B., 151
Ferguson, N., 103, 199
Ferrera, M., 141
First World, 27
Fiszbein, R., 171
Fitzpatrick, T., 157
Flanigan, S., 192
Fook. J., 104
Formal welfare institutions, types and role of, 7–8. *See also* State welfare
For-profit services. *See* Commercial enterprises; Markets and commercial provision
Foundations, philanthropic, 84, 192
Founding Hospital, London, 76
Frank, A. G., 40
Free trade, 48, 49–50
Freire, Paulo, 82, 98
Friedlander, W., 9, 181
Friedman, B. M., 47
Friedman, M., 112, 114, 118, 158, 174
Friedman, R., 114
Friendly societies, 59, 62, 77, 81
Frost, C. J., 98
Fukuyama, F., 128, 200
Funding of nonprofit organizations, 85–86
Furukawa, K., 10
Furuto, S. B. C. L., 15, 17, 98

Gaebler, T., 113
Gandhi, Mohandas, 120, 165
Gangrade, K. D., 83
Garbarino, J., 60
Garfinkel, I., 142
Garrow, E. E., 87
Geertz, C., 61
Gellner, E., 21
Geographic classification of nation states, 25
George, M., 104, 105
George, V., 12
Georgeou, N., 87

Gerbaudo, P., 82
Gereke, M., 154–155
Germany, 86–87, 132
Ghemawat, P., 45
Gibelman, M., 115
Gibson, S. W., 118
Giddens, A., 41, 42, 198
Gilbert, N., 60, 112–113, 115, 142, 154, 156, 158
Gingrich, Newt, 114
Glennerster, H., 153
Global Compact, 186
Global Covenant proposal, 202
"Global," defined, xii
Global era, 20–24
Globalization
    ancient, 38–39
    definitions of, xii, 37–38, 42, 43–45
    dimensions of, 41–43
    first, 39
    historical and academic perspectives, 38–41
    impact of, 46–49
    interaction, interdependence, integration, and internationalization, 43–45
    nation states and, 20
    responses to, 49–52
    second, 39
    as shaper of global era, 24
    third, 42
    welfare crisis and, 153, 154
Global North, 28, 201
Global social policy, defined, xi
Global South
    as classification, 28
    nonprofit and faith-based organizations in, 81, 82–83
    one world perspective and, 201
    research on social welfare and, 10, 16
    social work, evolution of, 97
    state welfare programs, 134–135
Goldberg, G. S., 154
Goldin, I., 192
Goode, W. J., 63
Goodman, R., 181
Gordon, D., 204
Gorton, G. B., 155
Gough, I., 12, 137, 152
Government policies
    definition and purpose of, 4
    demand side marketization policies, 114, 117–120
    outsourcing, 80, 86
    redistributive, 121
    traditional welfare system, impacts on, 66, 67
    See also Market liberalism (neoliberalism)
Government welfare. *See* State welfare
Grameen Bank, 83, 118
Gray, J., 47, 49

Gray, M., 104
Great Recession
　globalization and, 48
　Keynesian principles and, 120
　market liberalism and, 32
　nonprofit sector and, 86
　state protection of markets and, 122
　unemployment and, 34, 170
　welfare crisis and, 154–155
Great Society Initiative, U.S., 133
Green, M., 84
Greve, B., 130
Greve, J., 9
Gronnovetter, M. S., 61
Group work in social work, 93
Gubring, E., 142, 157
Guilds, 59, 76
Gumy, J. M., 154

Hacker, J. S., 157
Hadley, R., 156
Hagemejer, K., 204
Haggard, S., 16
Hall, A., 28, 98, 134, 139, 149, 165, 183, 187, 190–191
Hallen, G. C., 132
Hammack, D. C., 84
Hammurabi, 132
Harding, S., 105
Haring, N., 111, 206
Harrigan, J., 188
Harris, J., 133
Harrison, A., 49
Harsloff, I., 142, 157
Harvey, D., 111
Hasenfeld, Y., 87
Hatch, S., 156
Hayek, F. von, 111, 114, 122, 158, 174
Healy, L. M., xi, 96, 102, 182
Hegemonic cosmopolitanism, 199
Held, D., 42, 52, 202
Hemerijck, A., 147, 148, 154, 158
Heraclitus, 147
Herder, J. G., 21
Herodotus, 39
Hertz, N., 47, 49
Hicky, S., 87
Hines, C., 50
Hirst, P., 45
Hobhouse, L. T., 164
Hochfelt, T., 99
Hoefer, R., 119
Hokenstad, M. C., 9
Hong Kong, 115, 123, 140
Hooyman, N. R., 61
Hopgood, S., 205

Hopkins, Harry, 78–79
Howard, C., 130
Huang, Y., 104, 138
Huber, E., 139
Hugman, R., 97, 100, 101, 103–104
Hujo, K., 115
Hull House, Chicago, 95
Hulme, D., 86
Human capital investments, 169
Human Development Index (HDI), 27, 29
Humanitarian aid, 190–191
Human Rights Watch, 189
Huntington, S. P., 26
Hytrek, G., 47

Imhoff, D., 50
Imperial cosmopolitanism, 199
Imperialism, 22, 77, 198
Income transfers, 171–172
Independent Living Movement, 81
India, 68, 138, 165
Indigenous activism, 68
Individual Development Accounts (IDAs), 119, 171
Industrialization, 59
Institute of Economic Affairs, London, 112
Institutional vs. residual welfare, 136
Institutions, nonformal vs. formal, 5–8. *See also* Nonformal
　welfare institutions
Insurance firms, 68–69
Integrated Child Development Scheme (ICDS), India, 138
International Association of Schools of Social Work
　(IASSW), 101, 181
International Convention on Economic, Social, and Cultural
　Rights (1966), 204
International Council on Social Welfare (ICSW), 181, 188
International Criminal Court, 205
"International," defined, xii
International Federation of Social Workers (IFSW),
　98, 182, 188
Internationalism, 22
Internationalization and globalization, 45
International Labour Association (ILO)
　Basic Needs approach, xiv
　creation of, 182
　globalized interaction and, 44
　social protection floor initiative, 135, 155, 204
　Social Security Minimum Standards Convention
　　(1952), 186
　on traditional welfare, 60, 70
International Monetary Fund (IMF), 113, 140, 184
International social policy, defined, xi
International social welfare, defined, xi–xii
International social welfare, field of
　academic aspects, 8–13
　benefits of, 13–14

challenges to, 14–17
practical aspects, 4–8
International social work, defined, xi
International Workingmen's Association (First
    International), 40, 180
Interventions, xi–xii, 4–5
Investment funds, commercial, 84, 117
Iriye, A., 42, 181
Islam
    cosmopolitanism and, 199
    sharia law, 62, 76
    zakat and *sadaqah* giving, 58, 59, 62, 67, 70, 76, 132
    See also Faith-based organizations
Islamic State extremists, 66

Jacques, G., 98, 104
Jannson, B. S., 131
Jansenville Development Forum, South Africa, 68
Jarrett, Mary, 96
Jawad, R., 188
Jenkins, S., 9
Jessop, B., 24, 48, 147–148
Johnson, Lyndon, 133
Johnson, N., 157
Johnston, D. C., 122
Jones, C., 11, 137
Jones Finer, C., 182
Judaism, 59

Kagan, R., 205
Kammerman, S., 156
Kananen, J., 148, 157
Kanji, N., 68, 167, 188
Kant, Immanuel, xii, 8, 22, 40, 200, 201
Kapoor, D., 87, 192
Kar, D., 51
Karger, H., 102–103
Kaseke, E., 133, 153
Kaufman, F., 130
Kaufman, R. R., 16
Kay, R., 67
Keane, J., 41, 42, 147
Kelley, Florence, 104–105
Kelly, M., 81, 203
Kendall, K., 95
Kennedy, John F., 84
Kennedy, P., 185, 192
Kenny, C., 35
Keynes, John Maynard, 164
Keynesian principles, 120, 134, 143, 148, 150
Khinduka, S. K., 104
Kidd, A., 59
Kirsch, R., 70
Kiyak, H. A., 61
Knuttila, M., 128

Korten, D. C., 47
Kossuth, Lajos, 21
Kreitzer, L., 99, 100, 101
Kretzman, J., 171
Krishnakumar, J., 104, 105
Kristol, I., 120
Kristol, W., 205
Kropotkin, P., 61
Krugman, P., 45
Kubic, W., 128
Küng, Hans, 200, 206
Kung Fu Tsu (Confucius), xiii
Kuti, E., 88
Kuttner, R., 121, 155
Kuyper, Abraham, 77
Kuznetsova, I., 62
Kwon, H., 48, 154

Labor decommodification, 136
Ladies of Charity, 76
Lal, D., 46, 200
Lang, S., 87
Laozi, xiii
Laqueur, W., 155
Lash, S., 41, 47, 147
Latin America. *See* Central America, social conditions in;
    South America
Layard, R., xiii
Lay societies, 76
Lazzarini, S. G., 159, 171
League of Nations, 182
Lebeaux, C., 9, 11, 59, 131, 136, 147, 148–149
Lechner, F. J., xii, 41, 43
Leece, J., 119
Lee Kwan Yew, 139
Le Grand, J., 113, 119
Leighninger, L., 78
Leighninger, R., 164
Leonardi, R., 169
Leo XIII, Pope, 77
Leung, J. C. B., 138
Levitsky, S., 61, 65
Levy, Santiago, 139, 158
Lewis, D., 68, 167, 188
Lewis, J., 152
Liberal cosmopolitanism, 200, 205
Liberal welfare states, 136
Lisbon Treaty, 146, 184
Little, K., 61–62
Livingston, A., 165
Lobbyists, 122–123
Localization and globalization, 50
Lodemel, I., 118, 142, 157
Loewe, M., 64
Lubove, R., 95

Lula da Silva, Luiz Inácio, 204
Lynch, F. R., 81
Lyotard, J., 41, 147

Macartney, George, 199
MacPherson, S., 10, 15
Madison, B. Q., 9, 140
Maintenance of Parents Act (Singapore, 1995), 67
Mair, L., 9
Managerialism, 87, 103
Mandatory Provident Fund Scheme, Hong Kong, 115, 123
Mander, V., 68
Mao Zedong, 27
Mapp, S. C., 100
Marco Polo, 39–40
Margolin, L., 103
Market-based welfare. *See* Markets and commercial provision
Market economy, defined, 111
Market liberalism (neoliberalism)
    on commercial provision of services, 111–113
    definition of, 111
    globalization and, 42, 46–47
    government role, disagreement on, 114–115
    history of, 112–113
    managerialism and neoliberalism, 87
    nonprofit organizations and, 79
    social conditions, effects on, 32
    social enterprise approach to nonprofits, 83–84
    traditional welfare system and, 66
    wellbeing, view of, xiv
Markets and commercial provision
    demand side policies, 114, 117–120
    government involvement, disagreement over, 114–115
    history of, 110–111
    institutional approach and the market, 8
    limitations of, 120–123
    mutual aid, marketization of, 68–69
    neoliberalism, markets, and marketization, 111–113
    supply side (privatization and contracting), 114, 115–117
    terminology, 111
Marshall, George C., 184
Marshall, K., 83, 188
Marshall, T. H., 129
Marshall Plan, 185
Marx, Karl, xii, 22, 40, 111, 120, 121, 180, 200
Marxism, xiv, 152, 200
Maslow, A. H., xiv
Mathie, A., 171
Mazower, M., xii, 22, 180, 182, 192
Mazzini, Giuseppe, 21, 22
McDowell, S. K., 200
McGrew, A., 42
McKnight, J., 171
McLuhan, M., 41

McNamara, Robert, 166, 183
Mead, L. M., 151
Mecker-Lowry, S., 50
Membership associations, 77, 78, 81
Mesa-Lago, C., 132, 133, 139, 155
Micklethwait, J., 159
Microenterprise programs, 118, 170–171
Middle East and North Africa
    nonprofit organizations in, 82
    social conditions in, 30–31
    social progress in, 34
    state welfare in, 138
Midgley, J., 9, 10, 15, 16, 28, 60, 63, 68, 69, 77, 83, 97, 98, 99, 100, 104, 119, 129, 133, 134, 138, 149, 150–151, 158–159, 162, 163, 165, 167–168, 169, 171, 172, 182, 183, 187, 190–191, 200, 202
Military alliances, 27
Millennium Development Goals
    adoption of, 134
    collaboration and, 179–180, 184, 189
    criticisms of, 191–192
    one world perspective and, 202
    social development and, 161, 167, 174
    social investment approach and, 159
    social progress and, 33
    state welfare and, 137, 146
    statistical data issues, 16
    welfare crisis and, 155
Mishra, R., 48, 152–153
Missionaries, 77
Mitlin, D. C., 87
Modernization theory, 40
Modern world
    classifications and groupings of nation states, 25–28
    nation states and emergence of global era, 20–24
    social change and progress, 31–35
    social conditions, current, 29–31
    social conditions and social wellbeing, 28–29
    UN membership and, 24–25
Mohdi, Narendra, 158
Mokomane, Z., 65, 66
Monbiot, George, 42, 52, 202
Morduch, J., 69
Moreira, A., 118, 142
Morel, N., 173
Morgan, J. S., 9
Morris, A. J. F., 79
Moyo, D., 190
Mupedzisa, R., 62
Murray, C., 119, 121, 151
Mussacchio, A., 159, 171
Mutatkar, R., 138
Mutual aid associations, 57, 62, 64, 68–69
Mwansa, L., 87, 101
Mwansa, L. J., 99

Myles, J., 135
Myrdal, Gunnar, 165

Nandy, A., 140
Nanetti, R. Y., 169
Napoleon, 21
Nash, M., 98
Natio, 21
National Association of Social Workers (NASW), 98
Nationalism, 21–23, 43
Nationality concept, roots of, 21
National Rural Guaranteed Employment Scheme, India, 138
Nation states
  citizenship and, 24
  classifications and groupings of, 25–28
  decline, debate over, 24
  emergence of, 20–24
  globalization and, 20
  internationalism and, 22
  invention of, 19–20
  nationalism and, 21–22
  power differentials among, 23–24
  UN membership, 24–25
  variation among, 25
  See also State welfare
Neoliberalism. *See* Market liberalism (neoliberalism)
Networks for social support, 60–61. *See also* Collaboration and cooperation
Ngan, R., 154
Ngwenya, B. N., 64, 67
Nicholls, A., 51, 83, 117, 189
Nisbet, R., 164, 173
Nixon, Richard, 41
Noah, T., 47
Noble, C., 98
Non-aligned Movement, 27
Nonformal welfare institutions
  academic analyses of, 60–62
  challenges to, 63–66
  definitions of, 62–63
  formal institutions vs., 6
  formalization of, 67–69
  historical role of, 58–59
  integration of, 69–70
  policy implications of, 57–58
  types of, 6, 57, 62
Nongovernmental organizations (NGOs), 74, 83, 188
Nonprofit organizations
  challenges and role of, 85–88
  collaboration and, 181, 185, 188–189, 192
  as formal social welfare institutions, 7
  globalization activism and, 50–51
  governments and, 78–79, 80, 82, 86
  historical perspectives, 76–79

  in international context, 80–85
  social workers and, 99–100
  terminology and definitions, 74–75
Norberg, J., 46, 200
Normative analysis, 12
North Africa. *See* Middle East and North Africa
North America
  social conditions in, 30
  social progress in, 34
Ntseane, D., 62, 104
Nussbaum, M. C., 113, 158

O'Connor, J., 152
Offe, C., 41, 147
Office Central des Associations Internationales, 181
Office of Faith-Based Community Initiatives, the White House (U.S.), 81
Official Development Assistance (ODA), 187
Oil crisis (1970s), 150
Okamoto, I., 62, 66
Okun, A., 151
Olasky, M., 152
Omar, Caliph, 132
Omer, S., 163
Omhae, K., 24, 42, 46
One world perspective
  challenges to, 204–207
  cosmopolitanism and, 198–200, 203, 205–206
  elements of, 201–204
  origins of term, 198
Onokerhoraye, A. G., 10
Opal, C., 51, 189
Opportunities and social wellbeing, xv
Opych, N. J., 103
Orenstein, M. A., 193
Organization for Economic Cooperation and Development (OECD), 184–185
Osborne, D., 113
Osei-Hwedie, K., 104
Ostrom, E., 171
Otto, A., 154
Outsourcing (contracting)
  disadvantages of, 123
  manipulation of, 122
  as market-based welfare, 114, 115–117
  nonprofit organizations and, 80, 86
  social work and, 99
OXFAM, 182

Paiva, F. J. X., 163
Pallier, B., 173
Pallotta, D., 87
Palme, J., 173
Panagariya, A., 46
Pandey, R., 163

Parada, H., 98
Patel, L., 80, 99, 139, 172
Pawar, M. S., 99, 102, 122, 165, 169
Peace Corps, 84, 187
Peillon, M., 80
Personal care budgets, 119
Peterson, P., 153
Petras, J., 45
Piachaud, D., 133, 138
Pierson, C., 149
Pierson, P., 153
Piketty, T., 121
Pinker, R., 11
Pinker, S., 33
Piven, F. F., 152
Planning, social, 172
Plans, definition and purpose of, 4
Pochet, P., 183
Pogge, T., 16, 192
Polak, P., 193
Polanyi, K., 122
Poles, 26
Policies. *See* Government policies
Policy learning, 13–14, 193
Policy transfer, 193
Political classification of nation states, 26
Polman, L., 191
Postmodern theory, 41
Potter, D. M., 189, 192
Poverty Reduction Strategy Papers, 184
Powell, M., 156
Power blocs, 26
Power differentials, nation states and, 23–24
Powers, R., 41
Prahalad, C. K., 118
Prasad, N., 154–155
Prins, N., 122
Private vs. public goods, theory of, 112
Privatization, 114, 115
Productivist welfare states, 136–137
Professional development, 14
"Professional imperialism," 97
Professions and the institutional approach, 7
Programs, definition and purpose of, 5
Projects, definition and purpose of, 5
Prokosch, M., 50–51
Protectionism, 49–50
Psychoanalysis, 96
Public vs. private goods, theory of, 112
Putnam, R. D., 169

Quadagno, J., 135
Quakers, 77
Queiro-Tajali, I., 97–98, 100, 101, 102
Quinones, B., 170

Radlinska, Helene, 96
Rainford, W., 158
Rainwater, L., 142
Rake, K., 61
Rand, Ayn, 151
Ransom, D., 51
Raymond, L., 50–51
Reagan, Ronald, 112, 146, 151
Redistributive policies, 121
Reese, E., 47
Regis, H. A., 81
Reich, R., 45
Reininger, T., 98
Remenyi, J., 170
Rerum Novarum Encyclical (Leo XIII), 77
Residual vs. institutional welfare, 136
Ricardo, David, xii, 40
Richardson, J. D., 51
Richmond, Mary, 95–96
Riesco, M., 139
Rimlinger, G., 9
Robertson, R., 43
Rodgers, B. N., 9
Rodgers, D., 9
Rodgers, G., 192
Rodney, W., 40
Rodrik, D., 49
Rogers, B., 166
Roosevelt, Franklin D., 133, 164, 198
Rosenthal, M. G., 154
Rotating savings and credit associations (ROSCAs), 57, 67
Round, J., 62
Roy, A., 170
Rozario, P. A., 67
Rulli, M., 115
Russell, L., 86
Rutherford, S., 69
Ruthven, M., 48
Ruthven, O., 69

Sachs, J., 159
Sachs, W., 173
Sadaqah, 59, 62, 76
Sadhak, H., 69
Salamon, L. M., 75, 84, 86
Salomon, Alice, 96
Samuelson, P. A., 112, 114, 121
Sanborn, C., 80–81
Sandel, M. J., 121
Sanger, M. B., 79, 80, 113, 115, 123
Saracostti, M., 98
Saul, J. R., 50
Schady, N., 171
Scholte, J. A., 42
Schreiner, M., 171

Schultz, T. W., 169
Schumpeter, J. A., 47
Scott, D. W., 86
Scott, J. C., 152
Scott, J. M., 83
Secessionist movements, 23
Second World, 27
Sectarian cosmopolitanism, 199–200
Secular charities, 76
Secular philanthropy, 7
Seldon, A., 112
Selective comparisons method, 11
Self-Employed Women's Association (SEWA), India, 68
Self-employment, 170
Sen, A., xv, 79, 113, 118, 158
Serageldin, I., 169
Services, social, 4–5, 130
Settlement houses, 78, 95
Shang, X., 65
Sharia law, 62, 76
Shawky, A., 104
Sherraden, M., 119, 169, 171
Shigetomi, S., 62
Singapore, 67, 139–140
Singer, Hans, 165
Singh, S., 163
Sirojudin, J., 69
Slater, D., 111
Smeeding, T., 142
Smillie, I., 83
Smith, Adam, xii, 112
Smith, B., 51
Smith, J. H., 76
Smyth, P., 143
Soares, S., 139, 204
Social capital, 75, 169–170
Social change
    analyses of state welfare and, 146–148
    progress and reversals, 31–33
    by region, 33–35
    traditional welfare institutions and, 63
Social conditions
    current status by regional grouping, 29–31
    data for, 29
    defined, 28
    social progress and, 31–35
    social wellbeing, social illfare, and, 28
    study of, 11
Social Darwinism, 61
Social democratic cosmopolitanism, 200, 203, 205
Social democratic welfare states, 136
Social development
    as approach, 161–162
    definitions and features of, 162–164
    history of, 164–167

institutional approach and, 8
    limitations and prospects, 172–174
    practice strategies, 169–172
    theory, 167–168
Social Diagnosis (Richmond), 96
Social economy, 75
Social enterprise approach to nonprofits, 83–84
Social illfare, x–xi, xv, 28
Social impact bonds, 117
Social investment approach, 158–159. *See also* Social
    venture funds
Social justice, 105
Social planning, 172
Social policy, field of, 129–130
Social problems, perspectives on, xiv–xv
Social protection, as term, 16
Social protection floor initiative (ILO), 135, 155, 204
Social protection programs as social development,
    171–172
Social rights agenda, 204
Social security, as term, 16
Social Security Minimum Standards Convention (1952)
    (ILO), 186
Social Security program, U.S., 142, 151
Social services, 4–5, 130
Social support networks, 60–61
Social venture funds, 84, 117
Social welfare, concept and definition of, xii, xiii, xv
Social welfare aid, 187, 190
Social wellbeing
    concept and perspectives, xiii–xv
    levels of, 29
    measurement of, xv–xvi
    social conditions in the modern world, 28–35
Social work and social workers
    around the world, 98–102
    challenges and issues, international, 102–106
    cooperation through organizations for, 181–182
    definitions of, 92–94, 103–104
    functions of, 94
    historical evolution and professionalization of,
        94–98
    institutional approach and, 7
    practice methods and fields of practice, 93
    on social welfare and social problems, xiv–xv
Socrates, xiii
Soliman, H. H., 98
Solomon, L. D., 152
Sooryamoorty, R., 83
Soros, G., 51
South America
    social conditions in, 30–31
    social progress in, 34–35
    social work, emergence of, 96–97
    state welfare in, 139

South Asia
 social conditions in, 30
 social progress in, 33
South East Asia, social conditions in, 31
Soviet Union
 collapse and restructuring of, 32, 79, 113
 social programs, 134
Specht, Harry, 103, 129
Spencer, Herbert, 174
Spencer, P., 22
Speth, J. G., 47
Sphere sovereignty theory, 77
Spitzer, H., 99
State, concept of, 128–129
State as formal social welfare institution, 7
State welfare
 around the world, 135–143
 collaboration and, 187
 Golden Age and decline, 148–151
 historical evolution of, 132–135
 ideological and academic challenges to, 151–152
 importance of, 127
 nature of, 129–130
 neoliberal attacks on, 112
 new pluralism and future of, 156–159
 nonprofit sector and, 78–79
 scholarship on, 127–128
 social change and, 146–148
 social workers and, 99–100
 state, concept of, 128–129
 tax systems, subsidies, incentives, mandages, and
  regulations, 130
 typologies of, 136–137, 147
 welfare crisis, 135, 152–156
 welfare state concept and, 130–131
 See also Government policies; Welfare states and welfare
  statism
Statistical data issues, 16
Stephens, J. D., 139
Steurle, C. E., 119
Stiglitz, J. E., 48, 51, 191
Stoesz, D., 102–103, 118
Stokvels, 67, 68
Streeten, P., xiv
Structural adjustment programs
 international collaboration and, 183
 "market friendly" development policies and, 113
 market liberalism and, 32, 42
 nonprofits and, 79
 social workers and, 100
 state welfare and, 150
 welfare crisis and, 153
Stubbs, P., 17, 203
Sub-Saharan Africa
 social conditions in, 30

 social progress in, 33
 state welfare in, 137
Superior Council of Health, 181
Supplemental Nutrition Assistance Program (SNAP),
 U.S., 119
Supply side market-based welfare, 114, 115–117
Surender, R., 16, 154, 187
Sustainable Development Goals
 adoption of, 135
 collaboration and, 180, 187
 social development and, 161, 167, 174
 social investment approach and, 159
 social progress and, 33
 welfare crisis and, 155
Swank, D., 48, 154
Sweden, marketization in, 112–113
Systematic comparisons approach, 11

Tagore, Rabindranath, 165
Taiwan (Republic of China), 25
Tan, N. T., 97, 101
Tanaka, Y., 82
Tang, K. L., 158
Tauli-Corpuz, V., 68
Tax advantaged savings accounts, 119–120
Taxes credits and negative income tax, 118
Tax exempt status, 80
Taylor, J. B., 114, 120
Taylor-Gooby, P., 154
Temperance movement, 78
Terao, T., 81
Thatcher, Margaret, xiv, 112, 141, 146, 151
Theological cosmopolitanism, 199–200
Third World, as classification, 27–28
Thompson, G., 45
Thompson, J., 83
Ting, G., 67
Titmuss, Richard M., x, 9, 11, 12, 61, 112, 121, 129, 130, 136,
 143, 147, 173
Tonkiss, F., 111
Townsend, P., 204
Townsend, R., 62
Toynbee Hall, London, 95
Trades unions, 78
Traditional welfare institutions. *See* Nonformal welfare
 institutions
Treaties as collaboration, 185–186
Treaty of Westphalia (1648), 21
Trieghaardt, J., 139, 172
Truman, Harry, 185
Tsui, M., 102
Twikiriswe, J. M., 99
Tyagi, A. W., 150
Typologies, 11–12
Tzedakah, 59

Uchitelle, L., 47
Unconditional transfer programs, 171–172
UN Declaration on Human Rights (1948), 149, 186
UN Development Programme, 27, 29
UN High Commission for Refugees, 182
UN International Children's Emergency Fund (UNICEF),
        166, 182
United Nations (UN)
    collaboration and, 184, 185
    criticisms of, 191
    globalized interaction and, 44
    membership of nation states in, 24–25
    reform of, 202
    social development and, 165–166
    See also specific initiatives
United States as reluctant welfare state, 142. *See also specific
        persons, topics, and initiatives*
United Way, 78
UN Millennium Development Goals. *See* Millennium
        Development Goals
UN Year of Cooperatives, 203
Urbanization, 59
Urbina-Ferretjans, M., 187
Urry, J., 41, 47, 147

Vandeborght, Y., 157–158
van Ginneken, W., 60, 69
van Keesberg, K., 147–148
Van Leeuwen, I., 64
Van Parijs, P., 157–158
Van Saanen, M., 83, 188
Veblen, T., 164
Veltmeyer, H., 45
Voluntary organizations, 74. *See also* Faith-based
        organizations; Nonprofit organizations
Voluntary sector, 75, 85–88. *See also* Faith-based
        organizations; Nonprofit organizations
Volunteering, 84–85, 189
Vouchers, 118–119

Wacquant, L., 152
Wagner, R. E., 151
Wahl, A., 155, 157
Wairire, G. G., 99
Walker, A., 17, 131
Walker, R., 16
Waller, M., 47
Wallerstein, I., xii, 41, 43
Walton, R. G., 104
Warren, E., 150
Warwick, M., 193
Webb, Beatrice, 105
Weber, Max, 128
Weber, O., 118
Weismiller, T., 94, 98

Welfare consumerist approach, 117–118
Welfare effort, as term, 11
Welfare states and welfare statism
    concept of, 130–131
    developmental, 136–137
    market liberalism, effects of, 32
    perspectives on, xiii–xiv
    social policy scholars and, 129
    term, use of, 16, 17
    typologies, 136–137, 147
    See also State welfare
Welfare-to-work programs, 66, 116, 118, 142, 160
Wellbeing, concept of, xiii–xvi
Wells, H. G., 205
Wenger, C., 60
Western Europe. *See* Europe
Whitaker, T., 94, 98
White, P., 172
Whiteford, P., 142
Whittaker, J. K., 60
Whitworth, A., 70
Wilding, P., 12
Wilensky, Harold, 9, 11, 59, 129, 131, 136, 142, 147,
        148–149, 154
Wilkie, Wendell, 198, 207
Wilkinson, K., 70
Wilkinson-Maposa, S., 68
Williams, R. C., 82, 189
Williamson, J., 42
Wilson, P. H., 21
Wilson, Woodrow, 200
Wolf, M., 46
Wolfenden Commission, 156
Wollman, H., 22
Wong, C. K., 17, 131
Woo, J., 67
Woods, N., 48, 183, 192
Wooldridge, A., 159
Working men's clubs, 78
Work-performance model, 136, 143
World Bank
    collaboration and, 184
    criticisms of, 191, 192
    Eastern Europe and, 140
    globalized interaction and, 44
    "market friendly" development policies, 113
    social development and, 166
    welfare crisis and, 153
World Conference on Women, First (Mexico City,
        1975), 186
World Development Report (World Bank), 27, 29
World Fair Trade Organization (proposed), 52
World Health Organization (WHO), 13, 166, 182
World Summit on Social Development (Copenhagen, 1995),
        33, 134, 167, 186–187

World Trade Organization (WTO), 50
World War II, 31
Wuthnow, R., 188

Xu. Y., 138

Yap, M. T., 140
Yeates, N., xii, 200
Yellow Bird, M., 104
Yip, D., 104

Young Men's Christian Association (YMCA), 181
Yu, J. L.-H., 103
Yunus, Muhammad, 83, 118

Zakat payments, 58, 59, 62, 67, 70, 76, 132
Zeno, 199
Zentgraf, K. M., 47
Zhang, X., 104
Zheng, Y., 138
Zimmer, A., 86–87

About the Author

James Midgley is the Harry and Riva Specht Professor of Public Social Services and Dean Emeritus at the University of California, Berkeley. Originally from South Africa, he studied at the University of Cape Town and the London School of Economics and held academic appointments at both universities before moving to the United States in 1985 where he served as Dean of the School of Social Work and Associate Vice Chancellor for Research at Louisiana State University. He accepted the appointment as Specht Professor and Dean of the School of Social Welfare at Berkeley in 1997.

He has published widely on issues of social development, social policy, social work, and international social welfare. His major books include: *Professional Imperialism: Social Work in the Third World*, Heinemann, 1981; *Social Security, Inequality and the Third World*, Wiley, 1984; *Comparative Social Policy and the Third World*, Harvester, 1987 (with Stewart MacPherson); *The Social Dimensions of Development: Social Policy and Planning in the Third World*, Gower, 1989 (with Margaret Hardiman); *Social Development: The Developmental Perspective in Social Welfare*, Sage, 1995; *Social Welfare in Global Context*, Sage, 1997; *Social Policy for Development*, Sage, 2004 (with Anthony Hall) and *Social Development: Theory and Practice*, Sage, 2014.

In addition, he has edited or coedited many books on international social welfare and social development. Among the most recent are *Social Work and Social Development: Theories and Skills for Developmental Social Work*, Oxford University Press, 2010 (with Amy Conley); *Social Policy and Poverty in East Asia: The Role of Social Security*, Routledge, 2010 (with K. L. Tang); *Grassroots Social Security in Asia*, Routledge, 2011 (with Mitsuhiko Hosaka); *Colonialism and Welfare: Social Policy and the British Imperial Legacy*, Edward Elgar, 2011 (with David Piachaud); *Planning and Community Development: Case Studies*, Technical University of Madrid, 2012 (with Adolfo Carzola); *Social Protection, Economic Growth and Social Change: Goals, Issues and Trajectories in China, India, Brazil and Africa*, Edward Elgar, 2013 (with David Piachaud); *Social Protection in Southern Africa: New Opportunities for Social Development*, Routledge, 2014 (with Leila Patel and Marian Ulricksen); and *Social Policy and Social Change in East Asia*, Lexington Books, 2014 (with James Lee and Yapeng Zhu).

He is a Fellow of the American Academy of Social Work and Social Welfare and has Honorary Professorial appointments at the University of Johannesburg in South Africa, Nihon Fukushi University in Japan, Sun Yat-sen University in China, and the Hong Kong Polytechnic University. He holds honorary doctoral degrees from the University of Johannesburg in South Africa and the Polytechnic University of Madrid in Spain.

SAGE was founded in 1965 by Sara Miller McCune to support the dissemination of usable knowledge by publishing innovative and high-quality research and teaching content. Today, we publish over 900 journals, including those of more than 400 learned societies, more than 800 new books per year, and a growing range of library products including archives, data, case studies, reports, and video. SAGE remains majority-owned by our founder, and after Sara's lifetime will become owned by a charitable trust that secures our continued independence.

Los Angeles | London | New Delhi | Singapore | Washington DC | Melbourne